The Essential
Adam Smith

The Essential Adam Smith

Edited and with

Introductory Readings by

Robert L. Heilbroner

with the Assistance of

Laurence J. Malone

W · W · NORTON & COMPANY · *New York* · *London*

Printed in the United States of America.

The text of this book is composed in Electra, with display type set in Bernhard Modern. Composition and Manufacturing by the Maple-Vail Book Manufacturing group.

First published in Norton paperback 1987

Library of Congress Cataloging-in-Publication Data

Smith, Adam, 1723-1790.
  The essential Adam Smith.
  Includes index.
  1. Smith, Adam, 1723–1790—Addresses, essays, lectures. 2. Economics—Addresses, essays, lectures. I. Heilbroner, Robert L. II. Malone, Laurence J. III. Title.
HB103.S6A48 1986   330.15'3   85–21394

ISBN 0-393-95530-3

W. W. Norton & Company, Inc., 500 Fifth Avenue, New York, N.Y. 10110
www.wwnorton.com

W. W. Norton & Company Ltd., Castle House, 75/76 Wells Street, London W1T 3QT

2 3 4 5 6 7 8 9 0

Contents

The Essential
Adam Smith

The Man and His Times

No economist's name is more frequently invoked than that of Adam Smith, and no economist's works are less frequently read. An aura surrounds Smith, endowing his name with an authority not enjoyed by any other worldly philosopher except Marx. Needless to say, Smith and Marx were embarked on projects of entirely different and generally diametrically opposed kinds, but the ability to bestow a near-religious blessing by the mere invocation of their names is a privilege they share in common, to a degree enjoyed by very few writers in any field.

It is this aura of venerable respectability that is likely to attract a reader to a book on the writings of Adam Smith in the first place. We come to Smith expecting to find a great monument of classical economic thought, and we will not be disappointed—Smith is indeed the greatest of all classical economists, and many would claim the greatest economist of any kind. But we will not be properly prepared to appreciate Smith's depth and breadth if we approach him in too reverential a frame of mind or with too narrowly defined a field of expectations. Smith is deep, complex, and historical—characteristics that we do not always discover in the writings of those who call on his conservative shade. He is a writer in political economy (the term "economics" had not yet been invented) whose object of scrutiny was the social world in its widest dimensions and furthest reaches. Human nature, history, social psychology are the bedrocks on which his architecture of ideas was raised; and although his conclusions about mankind appear profoundly conservative to contemporary readers (which was assuredly not the case with Smith's contemporaries), we soon discover that his enormous authority resides, in the end, in the same property that we discover in Marx: not in any ideology, but in an effort to see to the bottom of things. In both cases, their greatness rests on an unflinching confrontation with the human condition as they could best make it out.

This suggests that we would do well to locate Smith in his times before we move to a consideration of his works. That is what I intend to provide in this introduction to his writings. We shall start by reviewing quickly the ambition of the Age of Enlightenment in which Smith lived and of which he was a central figure. Then we shall take a moment to sketch in the man himself. That will prepare the way for an overview of his work as a whole, the vast undertaking that Smith set out to achieve. Finally I will speak about the organization of this book and the manner in which I have tried to reduce Smith's writings to their "essential" core.

THE ENLIGHTENMENT

The Enlightenment is a term we use to designate a period of intellectual history that begins roughly after the Glorious Revolution in England in 1688 and ends with the French Revolution a century later. It is a period better defined in some respects by names than by dates. In France it embraces the work of Montesquieu (not so much a member as a precursor of the movement), Voltaire, Diderot, Rousseau, and a number of less well-known *philosophes*, to use the name that history has accorded these figures; in Germany it centers on the illustrious Kant; in Italy it claims the astonishing historian-philosopher Giambattista Vico and the jurist-sociologist Beccaria; in England it boasts of Locke and Gibbon and Burke; in America it has Benjamin Franklin; and in remote Scotland it bursts forth with a dazzling assortment that includes David Hume, the greatest of all British philosophers, as well as our hero, Adam Smith.

These names give us some feeling of the stature and diversity of interests of the figures of the Englightenment, but do not yet convey a sense of what the movement as a whole hoped to accomplish. Peter Gay, its most distinguished contemporary historian, has described it thus:

> In 1784, when the Enlightenment had done most of its work, Kant defined it as man's emergence from his self-imposed tutelage, and offered as its motto *Sapere aude*—"Dare to know." Like the other philosophers . . . , Kant saw the Enlightenment as man's claim to be recognized as an adult, responsible being.[1]

The immediate object of this bold effort at the emancipation of mankind was its liberation from the tyranny of clericalism, the archenemy of the Enlightenment movement. Anti-clericalism is not to be confused with atheism. With few exceptions, the *philosophes* were deists—believers in an all-powerful and benign God. His mode of operation was, however, far removed from the preachings of dogmatic religion. Science was, in fact, far closer to the *philosophes'* conception of the workings of the divine intent than theology. The aim of the Enlightenment writers was accordingly to instruct mankind that its destiny on earth could be investigated and understood, not merely accepted in the dumb suffering of "religious" passivity. Education, clarification, demystification—these were the watchwords of the intellectual leaders of the age, and they were aimed, first and foremost, at the heavy hand of an intellectually oppressive church.

The very belief in emancipation through enlightenment implied, of course, a view about the men and women to whom the *philosophes* addressed their message. A conception of "human nature" lies at the heart of the Enlightenment's efforts, a conception that placed a vast confidence in the educability of humankind. Yet the Enlightenment did not repose that confidence because of a blind commitment to the power of reason. On the contrary, all its leading thinkers—certainly Adam Smith—placed the "passions" (feelings and emotions), not reason, at the center of human nature. Moreover they placed them there not as a regrettable but as a necessary fact. As we shall later see, Smith's critically important conception of an Invisible Hand—an indirect intervention of the Divinity into the mechanisms of social life—is based on the *inability* of human reason to achieve social harmony by itself. Reason has its role to play, but the passions are both the bedrock and the driving force of human society.

The Enlightenment view of human nature, stressing its powerful passions

1. Peter Gay, *The Enlightenment* (New York, Knopf, 1966), p. 3.

Switch Day → sign up for all this classes and go.

and its frail capacities for reasoned foresight, would seem to put into question its unbounded faith in education and the growth of understanding. But the two are reconciled because the aim of the Enlightenment was never to remake society entire. Revolutionary or millennial visions were not in the repertoire of the *philosophes* who, on the contrary, regularly inveighed against "enthusiasm"—the zeal they associated with proselytizing clericalism. The education they advocated was directed more at reforming than reconstituting society, more at removing its more egregious excrescences than at redesigning its interior structure. Adam Smith, like all his contemporaries, believed firmly in the need for a well-defined social hierarchy and a firm adherence to the principle of property. "The peace and order of society," he wrote, "is of more importance than even the relief of the miserable."[2] Education was thus a means for achieving a better-functioning society that embodied very ancient values, not a means for tearing down the existing order to build a new one.

In this essentially conserving vision of social continuity and order, the Enlightenment thinkers found the basis for their distinctive brand of philosophical and historical conservatism. Convinced of the need for—indeed, the inescapable necessity of—a stratified, property-based social system, they were free to look on their surroundings with critical distance and emotional detachment. We come to Smith correctly expecting to find a great social thinker in what we today call the conservative tradition, but we are not likely to anticipate finding in him that "Laws and government may be considered . . . as a combination of the rich to oppress the poor," or to read that merchants and manufacturers are "an order of men, whose interest is never exactly the same with that of the public, who generally have an interest to deceive and even to oppress the public, and who accordingly have, upon many occasions, both deceived and oppressed it."[3]

Smith could speak in these seemingly radical, and certainly critical terms because neither he nor any of his contemporaries imagined a society in which exploitation and oppression would not be present, although their excesses might be much reduced. So it is that he can write, in a manner half resigned and half approving, that the admiration of the lower orders for the rich and powerful teaches them "to acquiesce with less reluctance under that government which an irresistible force imposes on them, and from which no reluctance can deliver them."[4]

Yet, to turn the coin over, it would be as mistaken to call the Enlightenment writers reactionary as to imagine them as radical. Smith's sympathies for the laboring poor and his revulsion from the behavior of their masters are explicit, as we shall have frequent occasion to see. What we find, however, is that all the *philosophes*, including Smith, share one limit to their social imaginations. This is an inability to imagine that the lower orders might some day exercise sovereignty over society. Democracy, with all its implicit threats to property and hierarchy, was not yet on the political agenda and would not be put there until the French Revolution ushered in a new

2. Adam Smith, *The Theory of Moral Sentiments* (Oxford, Clarendon Press, 1976), p. 226.
3. Adam Smith, *Lectures on Jurisprudence* (Oxford, Clarendon Press, 1978), p. 208, and *The Wealth of Nations* (Oxford, Clarendon Press, 1976), p. 267.
4. Smith, *The Theory of Moral Sentiments*, p. 253.

age. But I think we can see that the very boundedness of the political imagination of the Enlightenment provided the basis for its outspoken critical
stance. It is far easier to pass unflinching judgment on a social order that is
regarded as being unchangeable in its essentials, than to offer criticisms that
might be used as the grounds for dangerous political adventures. That is why
the Enlightenment writers, with Smith as a foremost example, depart so far
from the tone of so much modern conservative thought. The *philosophes*
were neither defensive nor aggressive in their social philosophy. They could
espouse liberty and education and the perfectibility of man with the secure
conviction that they were helping to create an orderly society of emancipated
individuals and enlightened classes, not a disorderly society of anarchistic
individuals and contending classes.

ADAM SMITH'S LIFE

I begin with these words about the political complexion of the Enlightenment because they help us to locate Adam Smith in the intellectual milieu
of his age. Now we must try to catch a glimpse of the person himself. This
is not so easy as to describe his "times," for Smith was a poor correspondent,
a jealous husbander of his writings (a number of which he ordered to be
burned from his deathbed), and a man whose quiet and secluded life has
not left a rich trail for his biographers.

Smith was born in 1723 (we do not even know his date of birth) in the
small but thriving fishing village of Kirkcaldy, Scotland; the son of Adam
Smith, controller of customs of the town, who died before his birth, and of
Margaret Douglas, daughter of a substantial landowner. We know next to
nothing of his childhood, except for one curious incident. When Adam was
four, he was abducted by a passing band of gypsies. The alarm was mounted
and Adam was soon recovered: "He would have made, I fear, a poor gypsy,"
comments John Rae, his first full-scale biographer.[5]

In 1737, at the then normal entering age of fourteen, Smith became a
student at the University of Glasgow, already remarkable as one of the centers of the Scottish Enlightenment. There he came under the tutelage of
Francis Hutcheson—the "never to be forgotten Dr Hutcheson," as Smith
was to refer to him in a letter written fifty years later[6]—whose force of character we can perhaps sense when we learn that he was the first to break with
precedent by lecturing to his students in English, not Latin.

Three years later, having won a scholarship, Smith matriculated at Balliol
College, Oxford. There he stayed for six years in a virtual intellectual isola-
tion chamber, Oxford paying no attention to the education of its students
except to protect them from pernicious influences: Smith was nearly expelled
when a copy of David Hume's "heretical" *Treatise of Human Nature* was
discovered in his rooms. The years were therefore largely devoted to self-
instruction. But they were far from wasted. Smith returned from Oxford
with a comprehensive knowledge of classical learning—Greek and Roman
authors were cited as familiarly by the writers of his time as Marx and Freud
by the writers of ours—a wide acquaintance with the works of his contemporaries, and with the framework of a large intellectual project already in
mind.

5. John Rae, *Life of Adam Smith* (Macmillan and
Co., London, 1895), p. 5.

6. Adam Smith, *Correspondence* (Oxford, Clarendon Press, 1977), p. 309.

Back in Glasgow in his early twenties Smith looked about for suitable employment, and with the aid of his mother and of Lord Henry Kames, a jurist and philosopher of some account, arranged to give a series of public lectures in Edinburgh. The lectures, which covered a wide range of subjects from rhetoric to political economy, were well received, *Gentleman's Magazine* commenting many years later in an obituary on Smith that "His pronunciation and his style were much superior to what could, at that time, be acquired in Scotland only."[7]

There was evidently much more than style and pronunciation to be gained from Smith's performance because in 1751, at the age of twenty-seven, he was offered the chair in logic at Glasgow University. A year later he transferred to the professorship of moral philosophy, Francis Hutcheson's former domain, a subject that embraced the subjects of natural theology, ethics, jurisprudence, and political economy.

As professor at Glasgow Smith entered on a period of his life that he afterward described as "by far the most useful, and, therefore, as by far the happiest and most honourable period of my life."[8] Arising early in the morning, he lectured for an hour to his young students five times a week at seven-thirty, examining them again at noon; and gave a "private" class as well at eleven o'clock three days a week.[9] Afternoons were taken up with university affairs as Smith rose to a position of preeminence within the faculty, becoming its dean in 1758. Evenings were devoted to his favorite game, whist, and to the remarkably stimulating company of the city. Among his friends and acquaintances Smith included a considerable number of the aristocracy, many connected with the government, and a circle of intellectual and scientific figures—Joseph Black, a pioneer in the field of chemistry, James Watt of steam engine fame, Robert Foulis, who was to become the founder of the British Academy of Design, and David Hume, now Smith's close friend. Smith was also acquainted with Andrew Cochran, merchant, former provost of Glasgow, and founder of the Political Economy Club, from whom Smith gained a knowledge of the business world that was later to impart such vitality to *The Wealth of Nations*.

Smith's first great work, *The Theory of Moral Sentiments*, was published in 1759. Written in a highly polished, florid style, rich in anecdote, analytic and didactic by turn, the book made an immense impression. Hume wrote a long teasing letter to Smith in which various persons "interrupt" him just as he is about to tell Smith of the reception of the book, concluding finally with "melancholy News, that your Book has been very unfortunate: For the Public seem disposed to applaud it extremely. . . . The Mob of Literati are beginning already to be very loud in its Praises. Three Bishops called yesterday at Millars's shop in order to buy copies, and ask questions about its Author. . . . You may conclude what Opinion true Philosophers will entertain of it, when these Retainers to Superstition praise it so highly. . . ."[10] The letter is reprinted here on pages 325–327.

The book was a success at all levels. Smith became something of a local celebrity. Little busts of him appeared in booksellers' windows. People came

7. Adam Smith, *Lectures on Rhetoric and Belles Letters* (Oxford, Clarendon Press, 1983), p. 7.
8. Smith, *Correspondence*, p. 309.
9. W. R. Scott, *Adam Smith as Student and Professor* (Jackson, Son and Co., Glasgow, 1937), p. 69.
10. Smith, *Correspondence*, p. 35.

great distances to hear him lecture, including two students from Moscow who seem not to have been very successful in conveying the message home. Boswell made a point of hearing Smith. Perhaps of greatest importance for Smith's career was the decision of Charles Townshend, an influential statesman (whose fate was to become the chancellor of the exchequer responsible for the measures of taxation that provoked the American Revolution) to engage its author as the tutor to his stepson, the young duke of Buccleuch. Townshend's terms were difficult to refuse. Smith was to receive a salary of £500 per year plus traveling expenses and a pension of the same amount thereafter, almost double what he had earned at Glasgow, where a professor's income was derived from students' fees. It is pleasant to note that on leaving Smith offered a refund to his pupils at Glasgow, who refused it, saying they had already been sufficiently recompensed.

In 1763 Smith set off with his young charge for France. They stayed mainly in Toulouse, where Smith learned the meaning of ennui. "The Life which I led at Glasgow was a pleasureable, dissipated life in comparison to that which I lead at present," he wrote to Hume, who had become secretary to the British Embassy in Paris. "I have begun to write a book to while away the time".[11] The book was to become *The Wealth of Nations*. After eighteen months of Toulouse, Smith enjoyed a two-month respite in Geneva where he met Voltaire, after which he journeyed with his charge to Paris and the company of his beloved Hume. In the Parisian salons he met for the first time the physician François Quesnay, leader of the interesting movement called *les économistes*, a movement that sought to modernize French agriculture through a reform of the tax system. Known to posterity as Physiocracy, because of its emphasis on the "order of nature" (which is what the word meant), Quesnay's theoretical analysis was sophisticated and deep—probing, above all in its ambitious attempt to combine an analysis of how expenditure circulated throughout the economy, with the way in which production generated wealth and economic growth.

Smith did not agree with all of Quesnay's diagnosis, especially with the French doctor's belief that only agricultural workers, working directly with nature (the land), actually produced more wealth than they consumed during their labors, but he was sufficiently impressed by the French economist to have intended to dedicate the *Wealth* to him, had not Quesnay died before its publication.

Meanwhile, however, Smith's tour came to an unexpected and tragic end. The young duke's brother visited them in Paris, and both young men contracted a serious fever. Smith called on the aging Quesnay for guidance, but in vain. The young duke survived, but his brother did not. Smith and his charge returned to London, where Smith worked with Lord Townshend until the spring of 1767. It was during this period that Smith was elected to the Royal Society and that he made the acquaintance of Edmund Burke, Samuel Johnson, Edward Gibbon, and perhaps Benjamin Franklin. Late that year he returned to Kirkaldy where he mainly remained, dictating and refining his great work.

The Wealth of Nations was published in 1776, an instant critical success.

11. Smith, *Correspondence*, p. 102. See below, p. 327.

"Euge! Belle! Dear Mr. Smith: I am much pleas'd with your Performance," wrote Hume. "It was a work of so much Expectation, by yourself, by your Friends, and by the Public, that I trembled for its Appearance; but am now much relieved" (*Correspondence*, 186). Hume's expectations were quickly realized. Smith received praise from all sides. When he was appointed to the post of Commissioner of Customs for Scotland—a sinecure paying £600 a year—he received from Gibbon the following letter:

> Dear Sir
> Among the strange reports, which are every day circulating in this wide town, I heard one to-day so very extraordinary, that I do not know how to give credit to it. I was informed that a place of Commissioner of the Customs of Scotland had been given to a Philosopher who for his own glory and for the benefit of mankind had enlightened the world by the most profound and systematic treatise on the great objects of trade and revenue which had ever been published in any age or in any Country. But as I was told that this Philosopher was my particular friend, I found myself forcible [sic] inclined to believe, what I most sincerely wished and desired. [12]

There is not a great deal to add. On receiving his commissionership, Smith offered to decline his pension, but the duke of Buccleuch declared that his honor would never permit him to stop paying it. Smith was therefore affluent in his older age. He lived quietly in Edinburgh, with occasional trips to London and Glasgow, where he was now rector of the University. Extensive revisions were made in the *Moral Sentiments*, small ones in the *Wealth*. There were no further publications, and as I have mentioned, some existing manuscripts were consigned to the flames at Smith's direction. He died in 1790, at the age of sixty-seven. Full of honors and recognition, he was buried in the churchyard at Canongate under a simple tombstone saying that the author of *The Wealth of Nations* lay buried there.

I am afraid that next to nothing is available of the private detail that is the biographer's delight. Smith never married and little is known about his personal life. Devoted to his mother, he lived with her in Kirkaldy until her death in 1784; thereafter with his cousin. There is only one portrait of the man, the medallion profile reproduced as the frontispiece of this book. It shows us a heavy-lidded face, with a protruding lower lip. "I am a beau in nothing but my books," Smith once remarked to a friend. From various accounts he was a man of somewhat peculiar traits, including a "vermicular" gait and a propensity for impenetrable absent-mindedness. Yet contemporaries also wrote of the expression of "inexpressible benignity" on his face, and the attitudes of men like Hume and Gibbon testify to his capacity to win deep and abiding affection.

THE WORK AS A WHOLE

Like Karl Marx, to whom he offers such sharp contrasts and such surprising resemblances, Adam Smith had a "project"—a vision apparent, although

12. Smith, *Correspondence*, p. 228.

never explicitly articulated, in the larger pattern of his work. Moreover, like Marx's, Smith's project was concerned with the question of human emancipation. From very different points of view and embodying very different ideas of the word, freedom lay at the center of their intellectual concerns.

It will help us understand Smith's large-scale undertaking if we look initially at Marx's. For Marx, freedom is an immense possibility within history—a possibility that sometimes appears as an inevitable outcome of social evolution, sometimes as an outcome that hinges on the conscious action of humankind. Whatever the means, the possibility of freedom appears because a gradual but cumulative change carries society from what Marx calls "primitive communism"—what we would call primitive society—toward the eventual attainment of socialism, and then full communism. Under the conditions of primitive communism, life is intellectually and materially impoverished, but it is also "free" in that society has not yet moved under the domination of a ruling class of any kind. In socialism and finally in full communism, as Marx saw it, freedom from domination would again be possible, but under the entirely different, and much more favorable conditions of widespread material abundance and intellectual fulfillment.

In this immense journey, the period of history occupied by capitalist society played a strategic role. For the workings of the capitalist system, to Marx, provided two critical ingredients for the attainment of freedom. First, it created the condition of material abundance without which Marx thought human self-determination was impossible. And second, it polarized society into a large class of exploited workers and a small class of exploiting capitalists, thereby immensely simplifying the demise of its system of domination by reducing it to the most evident form.

This is not the place to comment on that utopian vision, in whose name some of the most extreme departures from freedom have taken place. I invoke it, rather, to offer us a comparison with Smith's vision. It is not surprising, given the Enlightenment's commitment to emancipation, that self-determination is a grand theme within Smith's work. But it is freedom of a different kind from that envisaged by Marx—not so much the fullest possible unshackling of the individual from the thrall of class-ruled societies, as his partial delivery from the specific hobbles that Smith viewed as "superstitions" or as outmoded and unnecessary encumbrances. Therefore Smith's freedom eagerly embraced an end to the social impediments of feudal life, but stopped short of any jettisoning of social rank based on wealth and power. In a word, freedom for Smith is more narrowly defined than it is for Marx—more concentrated on the specific gains, such as the freedom of contract, indispensable for the operation of a commercial society, and not so concerned with the freedom of social or political action that might be necessary for a socialist, not to say ideal communist one.

However differently freedom is conceived by Smith and Marx, capitalism is indispensable for its attainment. As we would imagine, however, it is indispensable for different reasons. We have already seen that capitalism is strategic for Marx because it is the staging ground for the society of socialism, when true freedom could first appear. For Smith capitalism is essential because it *was* the period of history in which freedom appeared. Smith sees commercial society, as he designates the early capitalism of his day, as a time in which "natural liberty" finally emerges as the organizing principle of society, in place of feudal or mercantilist restrictions. As Smith puts it, "all systems either of preference or of restraint, being taken away, the obvious and simple system of natural liberty establishes itself of its own accord."[13]

The conception of capitalism as the period in history when freedom is finally established sets an intellectual agenda for Smith, just as the conception of capitalism as a way station toward freedom sets a different one for Marx. For Marx, the question is: What are the dynamics that make capitalism a crucial period for the attainment of true freedom to come? For Smith the question is: What are the dynamics of a society that has finally incorporated economic freedom as its central institution? Again, for Marx, the conception of freedom as a goal still to be attained raises questions about the limitations of "bourgeois freedom," whereas for Smith the achievement of a society of "perfect liberty" raises questions about the kinds of *social norms* that will emerge within such a society.

Let me repeat that the theme of human freedom lies in the background rather than in the forefront of Smith's work, as it does in the work of Marx. I bring the theme forward, nonetheless, because it serves very well to indicate the span of Smith's concerns, and because it once more raises the crucial issue of the nature of his social vision. As we go along, the themes of social order and economic movement will come to the fore, especially when we examine Smith's views about the socialization of behavior in his *Theory of Moral Sentiments* and when we turn to his discussion of the trajectory of a society of natural liberty in *The Wealth of Nations*. But it is useful to have these large ideas with us at the outset, so that we can look for them in the background of his writings.

SMITH'S WORKS

Adam Smith is the author of only two books, just mentioned. There exist as well two sets of lecture notes, probably taken down by students, the first called *Lectures on Rhetoric and Belles Lettres*, the second *Lectures on Jurisprudence*. Both are taken from lectures to his classes at Glasgow in the early 1760s. Of the famous series in Edinburgh that won him his appointment to Glasgow, no trace remains, although perhaps they will some day turn up— the notes on his rhetoric lectures were unearthed only in 1958!

To these four works—two of them second-hand versions of Smith's thought—we can only add a handful of other written material. There are a half dozen essays, some of them minor critical reviews printed in Smith's lifetime; others, of greater substance, preserved by their dying author's express desire as he was consigning his unpublished manuscripts to the flames. Of these preserved essays the most famous is "The History of Astronomy," first published in 1795. In addition, there is a collection of Smith's correspondence, of which only a few letters are of general interest.

I have sorted these writings into three main categories for the purpose of this book. The first covers the early writings, in which I also include the lecture reports on rhetoric and jurisprudence. The second is entirely devoted to the remarkable treatise on *The Moral Sentiments*. The third covers the

13. Smith, *Wealth*, p. 687.

celebrated *Wealth*. I have also added a very brief selection from Smith's letters.

In their full bulk these three categories, plus the correspondence, fill seven volumes in the definitive Glasgow edition, totaling almost three thousand pages. I have cut them severely, but with a conscious purpose in mind. Rather than presenting bits and pieces of Smith's work—excerpts from this and that essay along with fragments of his famous masterworks—I have eliminated the minor writings entirely, reserving a few choice or illustrative bits for the brief introductions that I have written for each section of the book. That enables me to present the writings in large, almost unexcerpted parts, with extended ellisions where I felt that these were most easily borne by the text. Wherever useful, Laurence Malone or I have also indicated briefly the nature of the excluded matter. Scholars will no doubt wince at many excisions, but I hope they will discern our intention to retain the central core of argument, and to leave aside matters that are essentially supportive in detail or of interest mainly to scholars.

A final word must be added about the Glasgow edition from which this text is prepared. These books, beautifully edited by well-known scholars, and issued by the Oxford Clarendon Press (with an accompanying volume of essays by various contributors) constitute the only complete and annotated text of Smith's writings and lectures. That is why I have used this edition in preference to the very convenient and excellent Modern Library version of the *Wealth*, and a number of good versions of the *Moral Sentiments*. All footnotes refer to this edition, the full citation of which follows.*

In addition to the texts themselves, there is an enormous literature of commentary on Smith, some of it of very high quality. Before this near-library of books and articles, I have hesitated a long while before deciding not to append a bibliography that could only be incomplete. In its place I have included, in the citation of the Glasgow edition below, a volume commissioned by the editors—*Essays on Adam Smith*—which includes references to a wide range of the secondary literature, and can thereby serve as a rich source of materials for anyone wishing to pursue further some of the issues in Smith. No popular or up-to-date biography of Smith exists. I have omitted any listing of biographical sources, in anticipation of the announced biography by I. S. Ross to be published as part of the Glasgow undertaking.

BIBLIOGRAPHY

The Glasgow Edition of the Works and Correspondence of Adam Smith, published by the Clarendon Press, Oxford, England.

The Theory of Moral Sentiments, edited by D. D. Raphael and A. L. Macfie (1976)

An Inquiry into the Nature and Causes of the Wealth of Nations, edited by R. H. Campbell and A. S. Skinner; textual editor W. B. Todd (1976)

Essays on Philosophical Subjects (and Miscellaneous Pieces), edited by W. P. D. Wightman, (1980) comprising:

---

*In the interests of clarity and ease of reading, a few departures have been made from the Glasgow text. Paragraphing has been added where it was deemed helpful to the reader. Excised material has been indicated by dots (. . .). All footnotes, keyed by asterisks, are invariably our own, not those of Smith or the Glasgow editors, and spelling has been conformed with modern usage.

"The History of the Ancient Logics and Metaphysics"
"The History of the Ancient Physics"
"The History of Astronomy"
"Of the Affinity between certain English and Italian Verses"
"Of the External Senses"
"Of the Nature of that Imitation which takes place in what are called
    the Imitative Arts"
"Considerations Concerning the First Formation of Languages"
Lectures on Rhetoric and Belles Lettres (including "Considerations concern-
    ing the First Formation of Languages"), edited by J. C. Bryce (1983)
Lectures on Jurisprudence (including the "Early Draft" of part of *The Wealth
    of Nations*), edited by R. L. Meek, D. D. Raphael, and P. G. Stein (1978)
Correspondence of Adam Smith, edited by E. C. Mossner and I. S. Ross
    (1977)
Associated volumes:
Essays on Adam Smith, edited by A. S. Skinner and T. Wilson (1975)
Life of Adam Smith by I. S. Ross (in preparation)

Early Writings

Adam Smith's "early" writings comprise his essays and the lectures of which we have some record, dating before 1759, when *The Theory of Moral Sentiments* appeared. Only three of these efforts were published in his lifetime—a laudatory but critical review of Samuel Johnson's famous dictionary, an admiring account of the great encyclopedia of Diderot and d'Alembert, and a third essay, "Considerations Concerning the First Formation of Languages." Other works never saw the light of day—an essay on the characteristics of touch and sight and the other senses ("Of the External Senses") and two other manuscripts covering the history of "Ancient Logics and Metaphysics" and of "Ancient Physics." I think it fair to say that Smith's reputation would not be diminished if all these essays disappeared without a trace. In a volume devoted to the essential Adam Smith they can be safely omitted.

THE RHETORIC

This is not the case with three other works: *Lectures on Rhetoric and Belles Lettres*, the essay on "The History of Astronomy," and the *Lectures on Jurisprudence*. These are writings that add to Smith's stature and that enable us better to understand the scope and reach of his lifetime intellectual project.

Rhetoric, as we know, was one of the topics that Smith covered in his initial Edinburgh lectures. It is a subject we are inclined to associate with histrionics and elocution. This is a mistake. Rhetoric is the art of cogent argument and convincing demonstration in fields, or on occasions, when resort to the certainties of formal logic is not available. As such, rhetoric is much more than embellishment; it is the very basis of persuasion. And as we shall see, persuasion is an important part of the basis on which Smith's own work stands.

It should be pointed out that the *Lectures on Rhetoric and Belles Lettres* are not Smith's own words. They are a transcription of lectures delivered to his class at Glasgow, written down afterwards by two (unidentified) students who wracked their brains and consulted their notes to reconstruct what the professor had said. "Not a word more can I remember," we read at one point.[1] There is no doubt, however, that the transcription accurately covers Smith's discourse—a discourse that ranges from Thucidides and Polybius to Swift and Pope, providing us with a running commentary on the merits and dangers of styles of prose; on modes of exposition; on oratorical strategies; and on related elements of style and effectiveness.

The lectures make abundantly clear the range of Smith's reading and the general perspicuity of his critical judgment. It was, after all, on the basis of

---

1. Smith, *Rhetoric*, p. 103.

similar lectures that he originally came to be chosen for his Glasgow appointment. All that said, however, there is not much here to interest the modern reader. The subject of rhetoric has gone out of fashion, and Smith's discursions on style do not make gripping reading. There is, nevertheless, one aspect of these lectures that helps us distill the "essential" Smith. Let me illustrate it from Lecture 24, a presentation on the art of didactic writing. Here the question is how an orator or writer can best go about presenting his case. Smith begins by differentiating between two situations, one in which the writer is sure of the sympathy of his audience, and one in which he is not. In the former instance says Smith, the writer should set out the central propositions of his argument at once, later buttressing them with subsidiary considerations. On the other hand, when the writer knows from the start that the audience is unsympathetic, "we are not to shock them by rudely affirming what we are satisfied is disagreeable, but are to conceal our design, and beginning at a distance, bring them slowly on to the main point and having gained the more remote ones we get the nearer ones of consequence."[2]

What is of importance here is Smith's own intellectual style and strategy. His argument is not based on logic but on a shrewd grasp of our ways of thinking, and more deeply yet, on patterns that are manifested in the unconscious determination of our thoughts. That capacity for intuition and insight is further revealed as Smith goes on to advise us how best to group and present our subsidiary arguments:

> We are to observe that . . . subordinate propositions should not be above five in number. When they exceed this number the mind cannot easily comprehend them at one view; and the whole runs into confusion. Three or thereabout is a very proper number; and it is observed that this number is much more easily comprehended than two or four. In the number three there is, as it were, a middle and two extremes; but in two or four there is no middle on which attention can be fixed. . . . The rule is in this matter the same as in architecture; the mind cannot there comprehend a number at sight and without counting above nine or ten. . . . In architecture we may comprehend this number with tolerable readiness (but) we cannot in writing reach so far. Columns and windows are things exactly similar and are for that reason more easily comprehended, as when we know one or two we know the whole. But the propositions which are brought as secondary to the primary one are often no ways connected . . . ; and we have not only the number but the nature of each proposition to remember.
>
> It may often happen that it will be necessary to prove fourteen or fifteen subordinate propositions in order to confirm the principal one. In that case it is much better to form three or five propositions on which the truth of the principal one evidently depends; and under each of these propositions to arrange five or three of those which are necessary to confirm the primary one.[3]

The striking aspect of this passage is its feeling for *psychological* truth. There was, it should be remembered, no systematic psychology in Smith's day, other than these kinds of ad hoc appreciations and aperçus. The *Rhetoric* is thus an early testimonial to a capacity for psychological penetration that is one of the least appreciated sources of Smith's greatness. As we shall later see, the *Moral Sentiments* and the *Wealth of Nations* will derive much of their own powers of persuasion because they will be built on Smith's remarkable understanding of the workings of the human psyche.

THE ESSAY ON ASTRONOMY

"The History of Astronomy" is a bold sally that continues Smith's explorations of human nature. In a letter to Hume, Smith refers to it as one of his "juvenile" productions—it was probably written in 1758, a year before the publication of the *Moral Sentiments*—but as we have seen, he thought well enough of it to rescue it from oblivion by entrusting it to his executors for posthumous publication.

The main body of the essay recounts in considerable detail the changing conceptions of the heavenly order, from Ptolemy's hypothesis of concentric spheres, through the struggles of Kepler and Copernicus to explain the vagaries of planetary motion, to the summative achievement of Newton. As such, it is an excellent review of the historical development of a science, reminiscent, in its emphasis on the succession of one temporarily successful account by another, of Thomas Kuhn's well-known modern treatment of science as a succession of vulnerable "paradigms" or conceptual frameworks.[4]

This is not the reason, however, that I have included a reading from the astronomy essay. It is because the review of astronomical theory is prefaced by another remarkable demonstration of Smith's psychological penetration. Before he settles down to his historical account of astronomical theory, Smith asks a disconcerting question: why do men theorize in the first place, whether about astronomy or anything else? Smith's answer, like his discussion of the superiority of the number three over the number four in the architecture of argument, draws on his sense of deep-seated psychological drives and resting points. Men theorize, he says, because they are impelled to set at rest the "tumult" they feel in the face of new observations. It is not an abstract drive for truth that impels the search for theory, but the concrete promptings of anxiety.

When we first encounter anything that is not familiar or expected, Smith argues, we are struck by the feelings we call Surprise and Wonder. These are not welcome feelings. Humankind needs to classify and categorize its knowledge: we may not know any more about something when we can place it into a general class of like things, but we feel vastly relieved at being able to do so. Comets are less frightening when we can describe them as "astronomical bodies"; bird watchers are relieved when they can say that a barely glimpsed bird was some kind of warbler. Hence Surprise and Wonder are unwelcome because they arouse the acute distress we experience when we have no category into which to put a thing. "The imagination and memory exert themselves to no purpose, and in vain look around all their classes of ideas in order to find one under which [the new and singular thing] may be arranged. . . . It is this fluctuation and vain recollection, together with the

---

4. Thomas Kuhn, *The Structure of Scientific Revolutions* (University of Chicago Press, Chicago, 1964).

emotion or movement of the spirits that they excite, which constitute the sentiment properly called *Wonder*, and which occasion that staring, and sometimes that rolling of the eyes, that suspension of the breath, and that swelling of the heart, which we may all observe, both in ourselves and in others, when wondering at some new object. . . ."[5]

Hence we theorize, or invoke the powers of philosophy, to restore our peace of mind. "[T]he repose and tranquillity of the imagination is the ultimate end of philosophy," he writes. "Philosophy, by representing the invisible chains which bind together all these disjointed objects, endeavours to introduce order into this chaos of jarring and discordant appearances, to allay this tumult of the imagination."[6] This does not mean that we necessarily understand what we "explain" by philosophy or science, but by categorizing things we come to be at peace with them. The touchstone for science and philosophy thereby becomes disconcertingly like that of daily life. We draw the venom from Wonder by applying the poultice of familiarity, now including the scientific familiarity provided by philosophical "systems."

Smith's view does not mean that scientific inquiry cannot lead toward truth. It means, rather, that criteria quite different from truth have an important, often overlooked, part to play in guiding the course of scientific (Smith would say "philosophical") argument. As Smith shows, much of the work of philosophers in the historical evolution of astronomy has been an effort to lessen the anxiety of Wonder by placing observations within a reassuring "system" of ideas. Thus the real aim of science goes beyond the attempt to penetrate the recesses of nature. Science seeks to help us to live in a universe where Surprise and Wonder threaten to undo our necessary equilibrium, our essential peace of mind.

Smith's achievement, then, is to allow us to appreciate the rhetorical (persuasive) and esthetic (humanly scaled) attributes of science—to see science not merely as an awesome encounter with the Universe, but as a much less exalted undertaking whose purpose is simply to place the universe within the ambit of human understanding. This is very much in the modern temper. Although couched in a language that bespeaks his age, Smith's account of science is in many ways as contemporary as his descriptions of our patterns of conscious thought and unconscious feeling.

JURISPRUDENCE

The subject that formed the focal point of Smith's teaching endeavors at Glasgow was entitled Moral Philosophy. From John Millar, one of Smith's pupils and later himself a distinguished writer on social structure, we know that Smith lectured on four basic subjects. One was natural theology, in all likelihood a review of forms of religious belief, culminating in the Deism that was the natural religion of the *philosophes*. We would dearly love to turn up the lecture notes of some diligent student who attended these classes, for they would undoubtedly clarify for us the elusive idea of the Invisible Hand. For the moment, however, the content of these lectures is unknown.

A second subject was ethics, broadly construed, from which Smith was to build the brilliant text of *The Theory of Moral Sentiments*, to which we will

5. Smith, "The History of Astronomy," in *Essays on Philosophical Subjects* (Oxford, Clarendon Press, 1980), p. 39.
6. Ibid., pp. 61; 45–46.

turn in our next section. The third and fourth parts of the course are the
ones that interest us now. These spanned problems that began with the
subject of jurisprudence—"the theory of the general principles of law and
government"⁷—and that extended into what Smith (following his teacher)
called Police, Revenue, and Arms. Here we find in embryo the subject
matter that would become the text of *The Wealth of Nations.* *

As with the *Rhetoric* and the essay on Astronomy there is a great deal in
the *Jurisprudence* that can be omitted from the essential Smith. With one
short but important exception, I shall make no effort to review Smith's treatment of the development of jurisprudence itself—i.e., the general principles
of law and government. Together with the discussion concerning Arms, the
matters covered are not germane to the embryonic political economy that
finds its expression in these lectures. Instead I shall concentrate on two themes
that tie this work into the unwritten major opus to come.

The first of these themes concerns that short but important exception
mentioned above. Early in the lectures on the evolution of law and government—even before we look at the Greek city-states—we come upon a theme
of continuing importance for all of Smith's political economy. This is his
evolutionary conception of history, in which society passes through a succession of "stages," each distinguished by changes in the organization of its
material life. Smith distinguishes four such stages: "hunters" (later, in the
Wealth to be called "early and rude society"); a stage of agricultural nomads,
driving their herds; a stage of settled agriculture, or pastoral society; and a
final stage of commercial society, the material setting for the arrival of the
institutions of natural liberty.

What is crucial here is that Smith does not attribute this evolutionary
trend in the institutions of justice or government to the development of ideas
and ideals. The moving force is the evolution of the material, socioeconomic needs of each stage of collective human life. "Among hunters," he
writes, "there is no regular government; they live according to the laws of
nature. The appropriation of herds and flocks, which introduced an inequality of fortune, was that which first gave rise to regular government. Till there
be property there can be no government, the very end of which is to secure
the wealth, and to defend the rich from the poor."⁸

We recognize again that blunt admission of the need for the defense of
property that we have met early on in this book. But the matter at stake now
is not Smith's unembarrassed conservatism, but what we would call his
"materialist" interpretation of history. Along with most of his Scottish intellectual contemporaries, Smith believed that socioeconomic needs largely
preceded and determined the structure of intellectual or juridical ideas, rather
than the other way around. This view of history would later find its more
developed expression in the *Wealth*, and—as many readers will have antic-
ipated—in the historical materialism of Marx.

We will return to the "stadial," or stagelike, theory of history when we

*We possess two transcriptions of these lectures, the first taken down in the year 1762–63, the second
probably in the following year. The two sets of notes are sufficiently alike so that we know with fair
certainty the subject matter that Smith covered, but the second set has been edited and smoothed, perhaps
for sale by its amanuensis. I have used the second set as the basis for the readings to follow.

7. Smith, *Jurisprudence*, p. 398.   8. Smith, *Jurisprudence*, p. 404.

come to the *Wealth*, but we must first take up the second of those two main themes that tie the lectures into the greater works to follow. This brings us to the section entitled "Police," a word that covered quite different matters: cleanliness and security on the one hand; cheapness and plenty on the other. The first two are considered by Smith as "too mean" to be discussed in a general discourse on jurisprudence, but the latter two constitute nothing less than the foundation of the study of political economy itself.

We gain some idea of the thread of this second subdivision of "Police" when we note some of the titles of the lectures: "Of the Natural Wants of Mankind"; "How the Division of Labour Multiplies the Product"; "What Circumstances Regulate the Price of Commodities"; "Of Money as the Measure of Value and Medium of Exchange"; and finally "Of the Slow Progress of Opulence."* This is only a partial listing of the *Jurisprudence* lectures in this section, but it is enough to allow us to see that in very rough form this is a first sketch of *The Wealth of Nations*.

Three aspects of this rough sketch are very much notable as part of the essential Smith. The first is simply how much of the *Wealth* was already present in his mind, fifteen years before he published his great opus. Not only do we find such key conceptions as the crucial role of the division of labor in bringing about economic growth, and the effect of competition in pressing daily "market" prices toward long run "natural" prices (both ideas that will be featured in the *Wealth*), but many phrases that will achieve immortality in that later book are already present in Smith's lectures: "Nobody ever saw a dog, the most sagacious animal, exchange a bone with his companion for another," and "The brewer and the baker serve us not from their benevolence but from selflove."[9] We can compare their finished expression in the *Wealth*—"Nobody ever saw a dog make a fair and deliberate exchange of one bone for another with another dog," and "It is not from the benevolence of the butcher, the brewer, or the baker, that we expect our dinner, but from their regard to their own interest."[10]

Thus we can see the lectures as a kind of trying ground for the book to come—so much so, in fact, that we are moved to ask what is absent. If we ask the question only of Smith's economic vision, the important answer is that the description of the activities of a commercial society in the lectures does not yet feature the process that will constitute the very armature of its conception in his final form. This is the tendency of such a society to *accumulate capital*, the essential prerequisite by which the division of labor will be effected. In his lecture on the causes for the slow growth of opulence, Smith mentions the need to accumulate "stock" (capital) as a necessary condition for growth, but this process is far from occupying the linchpin position it will later enjoy.

There are, of course, other differences between the lectures given in the early 1760s and the book that would appear in 1776. As we would expect, a number of specific ideas had not yet taken shape, such as the distinction between "productive" and "unproductive" labor, or the complex treatment

---

*The titles were actually added to the transcript in 1896 by the eminent economist and scholar Edwin Cannan.

9. Ibid., pp. 492–93.	10. Smith, *Wealth*, pp. 26–27.

of value, or the role of government. In a word, an encompassing treatise on national wealth was present only in a formative stage.

There is, in addition, one element that may interest us because it links the *Lectures on Jurisprudence* with the psychological insights that I have emphasized in these early writings. In the lectures, Smith calls attention to two psychological characteristics of considerable economic consequence. These are the human propensity for dissatisfaction and the human need for variety. "Such is the delicacy of man alone," he writes, "that no object is produced to his liking. He finds in every thing there is need for improvement . . . ," and "Man is the only animal possessed of such a nicety that the very color of an object hurts him. . . . Nothing without variety pleases us: a long uniform wall is a disagreeable object."[11] This is a promising beginning for a theory of economic demand—an explanation of why humankind seeks wealth. Such a theory constitutes an important part of the foundation on which Smith builds his political economy, but unaccountably Smith never used these perceptive observations in his discussion of demand in the *Wealth*.

We leave the *Jurisprudence* at this point. That it is unfinished is evident. It is work in progress. We read it because it gives us the rare chance to see a first draft of a monumental work to come, in that respect akin to Marx's Rough Draft (the *Grundrisse*) that served as a work book for *Capital*.

THE "EARLY DRAFT"

One last manuscript must be mentioned—the so-called early draft of the *Wealth of Nations* discovered by Professor W. R. Scott in 1935. The early draft is a first attempt, probably undertaken in 1763, to cast the material of the lectures on Jurisprudence into book form. The chapter-length manuscript was never published and interests us primarily because we can see so many of Smith's phrases and images assuming the form they would take in the *Wealth*. The pin factory that exemplifies the division of labor, the "propensity to truck, barter, and exchange one thing for another," the seeming resemblance between human cooperation and that of two dogs chasing a hare, the comparison of the philosopher to a porter ("not half so different as a mastiff is from a greyhound")—these and other word pictures that are famous in the *Wealth* are found in finished, or nearly finished, form in the Draft.

The Draft is not, however, a completed piece of work—much less so than the Lectures—nor is it significant save as an exercise for the great work to come. It deserves attention in an overview of Smith's early writings, but I will not pursue further a manuscript mainly of interest to scholars.

THE READINGS*

As we will have occasion to remark again, Smith's prose, like that of all eighteenth-century writers, must be read at the measured pace for which its cadenced periods are intended. This—and alas! most of these readings—

*In all these readings, we repeat, spellings have been modernized, paragraphing has been added, and dots (. . .) indicate where sections have been excluded. Footnotes marked by asterisks are invariably ours.

11. Ibid., pp. 487, 488.

cannot be profitably or even enjoyably "skimmed." They must be read leisurely, preferably in small bites. They can be put down and taken up—the argument will not fade easily. They are a cultivated taste, like lobster and champagne.

There are three readings in this section. From the essay on astronomy we have reproduced, almost in its entirety, the preface that contains Smith's theory of Surprise and Wonder and the exposition of the role of philosophy in calming the "tumult" of the distrubed mind, plus some concluding paragraphs on Newton.

From the *Jurisprudence* we have included the sections that deal with the the stagelike theory of history, and enough of the lectures on "Police" to enable the reader to grasp the overarching structure of the lectures as a whole. In this portion we have used the titles of the lectures of the earlier Cannan edition which greatly simplifies a grasp of the argument,[12] and we have put paragraph breaks in the manuscript where appropriate.

12. Adam Smith, *Lectures on Justice, Police, Revenue and Arms* (Oxford, Clarendon Press, 1896).

THE

PRINCIPLES

WHICH LEAD AND DIRECT

PHILOSOPHICAL ENQUIRIES;

ILLUSTRATED BY THE

HISTORY of ASTRONOMY

The History of Astronomy

Wonder, Surprise, and Admiration are words which, though often confounded, denote, in our language, sentiments that are indeed allied, but that are in some respects different also, and distinct from one another. What is new and singular, excites that sentiment which, in strict propriety, is called Wonder; what is unexpected, Surprise; and what is great or beautiful, Admiration.

We wonder at all extraordinary and uncommon objects, at all the rarer phenomena of nature, at meteors, comets, eclipses, at singular plants and animals, and at every thing, in short, with which we have before been either little or not at all acquainted; and we still wonder, though forewarned of what we are to see.

We are surprised at those things which we have seen often, but which we least of all expected to meet with in the place where we find them; we are surprised at the sudden appearance of a friend, whom we have seen a thousand times, but whom we did not imagine we were to see then.

We admire the beauty of a plain or the greatness of a mountain, though we have seen both often before, and though nothing appears to us in either, but what we had expected with certainty to see. . . .

SECTION I

Of the Effect of Unexpectedness, or of Surprise

When an object of any kind, which has been for some time expected and foreseen, presents itself, whatever be the emotion which it is by nature fitted to excite, the mind must have been prepared for it, and must even in some measure have conceived it before-hand; because the idea of the object having been so long present to it, must have before-hand excited some degree of the same emotion which the object itself would excite: the change, therefore, which its presence produces comes thus to be less considerable, and the emotion or passion which it excites glides gradually and easily into the heart, without violence, pain, or difficulty.

But the contrary of all this happens when the object is unexpected; the passion is then poured in all at once upon the heart, which is thrown, if it is a strong passion, into the most violent and convulsive emotions, such as sometimes cause immediate death; sometimes, by the suddenness of the ecstasy, so entirely disjoint the whole frame of the imagination, that it never after returns to its former tone and composure, but falls either into a frenzy or habitual lunacy; and such as almost always occasion a momentary loss of reason, or of that attention to other things which our situation or our duty requires.

How much we dread the effects of the more violent passions, when they come suddenly upon the mind, appears from those preparations which all men think necessary when going to inform any one of what is capable of exciting them. Who would choose all at once to inform his friend of an extraordinary calamity that had befallen him, without taking care beforehand, by alarming him with an uncertain fear, to announce, if one may say so, his misfortune, and thereby prepare and dispose him for receiving the tidings?

Those panic terrors which sometimes seize armies in the field, or great cities, when an enemy is in the neighbourhood, and which deprive for a time the most determined of all deliberate judgments, are never excited but by the sudden apprehension of unexpected danger. Such violent consternations, which at once confound whole multitudes, benumb their understandings, and agitate their hearts, with all the agony of extravagant fear, can never be produced by any foreseen danger, how great soever. Fear, though naturally a very strong passion, never rises to such excesses, unless exasperated both by Wonder, from the uncertain nature of the danger, and by Surprise, from the suddenness of the apprehension.

Surprise, therefore, is not to be regarded as an original emotion of a species distinct from all others. The violent and sudden change produced upon the mind, when an emotion of any kind is brought suddenly upon it, constitutes the whole nature of Surprise.

But when not only a passion and a great passion comes all at once upon the mind, but when it comes upon it while the mind is in the mood most unfit for conceiving it, the Surprise is then the greatest. Surprises of joy when the mind is sunk into grief, or of grief when it is elated with joy, are therefore the most unsupportable. The change is in this case the greatest possible. Not only a strong passion is conceived all at once, but a strong passion the direct opposite of that which was before in possession of the soul. When a load of sorrow comes down upon the heart that is expanded and elated with gaiety and joy, it seems not only to damp and oppress it, but almost to crush and bruise it, as a real weight would crush and bruise the body. On the contrary, when from an unexpected change of fortune, a tide of gladness seems, if I may say so, to spring up all at once within it, when depressed and contracted with grief and sorrow, it feels as if suddenly extended and heaved up with violent and irresistible force, and is torn with pangs of all others most exquisite, and which almost always occasion faintings, deliriums, and sometimes instant death.

For it may be worthwhile to observe, that though grief be a more violent passion than joy, as indeed all uneasy sensations seem naturally more pungent than the opposite agreeable ones, yet of the two, Surprises of joy are still more insupportable than Surprises of grief. We are told that after the battle of Thrasimenus, while a Roman lady, who had been informed that her son was slain in the action, was sitting alone bemoaning her misfortunes, the young man who escaped came suddenly into the room to her, and that she cried out and expired instantly in a transport of joy. Let us suppose the contrary of this to have happened, and that in the midst of domestic festivity and mirth, he had suddenly fallen down dead at her feet, is it likely that the effects would have been equally violent? I imagine not. The heart springs to joy with a sort of natural elasticity, it abandons itself to so agreeable an emotion, as soon as the object is presented; it seems to pant and leap forward to meet it, and the passion in its full force takes at once entire and complete possession of the soul.

But it is otherways with grief; the heart recoils from, and resists the first approaches of that disagreeable passion, and it requires some time before the melancholy object can produce its full effect. Grief comes on slowly and gradually, nor ever rises at once to that height of agony to which it is increased after a little time. But joy comes rushing upon us all at once like a torrent. The change produced therefore by a Surprise of joy is more sudden, and upon that account more violent and apt to have more fatal effects, than that which is occasioned by a Surprise of grief; there seems too to be something in the nature of Surprise, which makes it unite more easily with the brisk and quick motion of joy, than with the slower and heavier movement of grief. Most men who can take the trouble to recollect, will find that they have heard of more people who died or became distracted with sudden joy, than with sudden grief. Yet from the nature of human affairs, the latter must be much more frequent than the former. A man may break his leg, or lose his son, though he has had no warning of either of these events, but he can hardly meet with an extraordinary piece of good fortune, without having had some foresight of what was to happen. . . .

SECTION II

Of Wonder, or of the Effects of Novelty

It is evident that the mind takes pleasure in observing the resemblances that are discoverable between different objects. It is by means of such observations that it endeavours to arrange and methodize all its ideas, and to reduce them into proper classes and assortments. Where it can observe but one single quality, that is common to a great variety of otherwise widely different objects, that single circumstance will be sufficient for it to connect them all together, to reduce them to one common class, and to call them by one general name. It is thus that all things endowed with a power of self-motion, beasts, birds, fishes, insects, are classed under the general name of Animal; and that these again, along with those which want that power, are arranged under the still more general word Substance: and this is the origin of those assortments of objects and ideas which in the schools are called Genera and Species, and of those abstract and general names, which in all languages are made use of to express them.

The further we advance in knowledge and experience, the greater number of divisions and subdivisions of those Genera and Species we are both inclined and obliged to make. We observe a greater variety of particularities amongst those things which have a gross resemblance; and having made new divisions of them, according to those newly observed particularities, we are then no longer to be satisfied with being able to refer an object to a remote genus, or very general class of things, to many of which it has but a loose and imperfect resemblance. A person, indeed, unacquainted with botany may expect to satisfy your curiosity, by telling you that such a vegetable is a weed, or, perhaps in still more general terms, that it is a plant. But a botanist will neither give nor accept of such an answer. He has broken and divided that great class of objects into a number of inferior assortments, according to those varieties which his experience has discovered among them; and he wants to refer each individual plant to some tribe of vegetables, with all of which it may have a more exact resemblance, than with many things comprehended under the extensive genus of plants. A child imagines that it gives a satisfactory answer when it tells you that an object whose name it knows not is a thing, and fancies that it informs you of something, when it thus ascertains to which of the two most obvious and comprehensive classes of objects a particular impression ought to be referred; to the class of realities or solid substances which it calls *things*, or to that of appearances which it calls *nothings*.

Whatever, in short, occurs to us we are fond of referring to some species or class of things, with all of which it has a nearly exact resemblance; and though we often know no more about them than about it, yet we are apt to fancy that by being able to do so, we show ourselves to be better acquainted with it, and to have a more thorough insight into its nature.

But when something quite new and singular is presented, we feel ourselves incapable of doing this. The memory cannot, from all its stores, cast up any image that nearly resembles this strange appearance. If by some of its qualities it seems to resemble, and to be connected with a species which we have before been acquainted with, it is by others separated and detached from that, and from all the other assortments of things we have hitherto been able to make. It stands alone and by itself in the imagination, and refuses to be grouped or confounded with any set of objects whatever. The imagination and memory exert themselves to no purpose, and in vain look around all their classes of ideas in order to find one under which it may be arranged. They fluctuate to no purpose from thought to thought, and we remain still uncertain and undetermined where to place it, or what to think of it.

It is this fluctuation and vain recollection, together with the emotion or movement of the spirits that they excite, which constitute the sentiment properly called *Wonder*, and which occasion that staring, and sometimes that rolling of the eyes, that suspension of the breath, and that swelling of the heart, which we may all observe, both in ourselves and others, when wondering at some new object, and which are the natural symptoms of uncertain and undetermined thought. What sort of a thing can that be? What is that like? are the questions which, upon such an occasion, we are all naturally disposed to ask. If we can recollect many such objects which exactly resemble this new appearance, and which present themselves to the imagination naturally, and as it were of their own accord, our Wonder is entirely at an end. If we can recollect but a few, and which it requires too some trouble to be able to call up, our Wonder is indeed diminished, but not quite destroyed. If we can recollect none, but are quite at a loss, it is the greatest possible.

With what curious attention does a naturalist examine a singular plant, or a singular fossil, that is presented to him? He is at no loss to refer it to the general genus of plants or fossils; but this does not satisfy him, and when he considers all the different tribes or species of either with which he has hitherto been acquainted, they all, he thinks, refuse to admit the new object among them. It stands alone in his imagination, and as it were detached from all the other species of that genus to which it belongs. He labours, however, to connect it with some one or other of them. Sometimes he thinks it may be placed in this, and sometimes in that other assortment; nor is he ever satisfied, till he has fallen upon one which, in most of its qualities, it resembles. When he cannot do this, rather than it should stand quite by itself, he will enlarge the precincts, if I may say so, of some species, in order to make room for it; or he will create a new species on purpose to receive it, and call it a Play of Nature, or give it some other appellation, under which he arranges all the oddities that he knows not what else to do with. But to some class or other of known objects he must refer it, and between it and them he must find out some resemblance or other, before he can get rid of that Wonder, that uncertainty and anxious curiosity excited by its singular appearance, and by its dissimilitude with all the objects he had hitherto observed.

As single and individual objects thus excite our Wonder when, by their uncommon qualities and singular appearance, they make us uncertain to what species of things we ought to refer them; so a succession of objects which follow one another in an uncommon train or order, will produce the same effect, though there be nothing particular in any one of them taken by itself.

When one accustomed object appears after another, which it does not usually follow, it first excites, by its unexpectedness, the sentiment properly called Surprise, and afterwards, by the singularity of the succession, or order of its appearance, the sentiment properly called Wonder. We start and are surprised at feeling it there, and then wonder how it came there. The motion of a small piece of iron along a plain table is in itself no extraordinary object, yet the person who first saw it begin, without any visible impulse, in consequence of the motion of a loadstone at some little distance from it, could not behold it without the most extreme Surprise; and when that momentary emotion was over, he would still wonder how it came to be conjoined to an event with which, according to the ordinary train of things, he could have so little suspected it to have any connection.

When two objects, however unlike, have often been observed to follow each other, and have constantly presented themselves to the senses in that order, they come to be so connected together in the fancy, that the idea of the one seems, of its own accord, to call up and introduce that of the other. If the objects are still observed to succeed each other as before, this connection, or, as it has been called, this association of their ideas, becomes stricter and stricter, and the habit of the imagination to pass from the conception of the one to that of the other, grows more and more rivetted and confirmed. As its ideas move more rapidly than external objects, it is continually running before them, and therefore anticipates, before it happens, every event which falls out according to this ordinary course of things. When objects succeed each other in the same train in which the ideas of the imagination have thus been accustomed to move, and in which, though not conducted by that chain of events presented to the senses, they have acquired a tendency to go on of their own accord, such objects appear all closely connected with one another, and the thought glides easily along them, without effort and without interruption. They fall in with the natural career of the imagination; and as the ideas which represented such a train of things would seem all mutually to introduce each other, every last thought to be called up by the foregoing, and to call up the succeeding; so when the objects themselves occur, every last event seems, in the same manner, to be introduced by the foregoing, and to introduce the succeeding. There is no break, no stop, no gap, no interval. The ideas excited by so coherent a chain of things seem, as it were, to float through the mind of their own accord, without obliging it to exert itself, or to make any effort in order to pass from one of them to another.

But if this customary connection be interrupted, if one or more objects appear in an order quite different from that to which the imagination has been accustomed, and for which it is prepared, the contrary of all this happens. We are at first surprised by the unexpectedness of the new appearance, and when that momentary emotion is over, we still wonder how it came to occur in that place. The imagination no longer feels the usual facility of passing from the event which goes before to that which comes after. It is an order or law of succession to which it has not been accustomed, and which it therefore finds some difficulty in following, or in attending to. The fancy is stopped and interrupted in that natural movement or career, according to which it was proceeding. Those two events seem to stand at a distance from each other; it endeavours to bring them together, but they refuse to unite; and it feels, or imagines it feels, something like a gap or interval between them. It naturally hesitates, and, as it were, pauses upon the brink of this interval; it endeavours to find out something which may fill up the gap, which, like a bridge, may so far at least unite those seemingly distant objects, as to render the passage of the thought between them smooth, and natural, and easy. The supposition of a chain of intermediate, though invisible, events, which succeed each other in a train similar to that in which the imagination has been accustomed to move, and which link together those two disjointed appearances, is the only means by which the imagination can fill up this interval, is the only bridge which, if one may say so, can smooth its passage from the one object to the other. Thus, when we observe the motion of the iron, in consequence of that of the loadstone, we gaze and hesitate, and feel a want of connexion between two events which follow one another in so unusual a train. But when, with Descartes, we imagine certain invisible effluvia to circulate round one of them, and by their repeated impulses to impel the other, both to move towards it, and to follow its motion, we fill up the interval between them, we join them together by a sort of bridge, and thus take off that hesitation and difficulty which the imagination felt in passing from the one to the other. That the iron should move after the loadstone seems, upon this hypothesis, in some measure according to the ordinary course of things. Motion after impulse is an order of succession with which of all things we are the most familiar. Two objects which are so connected seem no longer to be disjoined, and the imagination flows smoothly and easily along them.

Such is the nature of this second species of Wonder, which arises from an unusual succession of things. The stop which is thereby given to the career of the imagination, the difficulty which it finds in passing along such disjointed objects, and the feeling of something like a gap or interval between them, constitute the whole essence of this emotion. Upon the clear discovery of a connecting chain of intermediate events, it vanishes altogether. What obstructed the movement of the imagination is then removed. Who wonders at the machinery of the opera house who has once been admitted behind the scenes? In the Wonders of nature, however, it rarely happens that we can discover so clearly this connecting chain. With regard to a few even of them, indeed, we seem to have been really admitted behind the scenes, and our Wonder accordingly is entirely at an end. Thus the eclipses of the sun and moon, which once, more than all the other appearances in the heavens, excited the terror and amazement of mankind, seem now no longer to be wonderful, since the connecting chain has been found out which joins them to the ordinary course of things. Nay, in those cases in which we have been less successful, even the vague hypotheses of Descartes, and the yet more indetermined notions of Aristotle, have, with their followers, contributed to give some coherence to the appearances of nature, and might diminish, though they could not destroy, their Wonder. If they did not completely fill up the interval between the two disjointed objects, they bestowed upon them, however, some sort of loose connexion which they wanted before.

That the imagination feels a real difficulty in passing along two events which follow one another in an uncommon order, may be confirmed by many obvious observations. If it attempts to attend beyond a certain time to a long series of this kind, the continual efforts it is obliged to make, in order to pass from one object to another, and thus follow the progress of the succession, soon fatigue it, and if repeated too often, disorder and disjoint its whole frame. It is thus that too severe an application to study sometimes brings on lunacy and frenzy, in those especially who are somewhat advanced in life, but whose imaginations, from being too late in applying, have not got those habits which dispose them to follow easily the reasonings in the abstract sciences. Every step of a demonstration, which to an old practitioner is quite natural and easy, requires from them the most intense application of thought. Spurred on, however, either by ambition, or by admiration for the subject, they still continue till they become, first confused, then giddy, and at last distracted.

Could we conceive a person of the soundest judgment, who had grown up to maturity, and whose imagination had acquired those habits, and that mould, which the constitution of things in this world necessarily impress upon it, to be all at once transported alive to some other planet, where nature was governed by laws quite different from those which take place here; as he would be continually obliged to attend to events, which must to him appear in the highest degree jarring, irregular, and discordant, he would soon feel the same confusion and giddiness begin to come upon him, which would at last end in the same manner, in lunacy and distraction. Neither, to produce this effect, is it necessary that the objects should be either great or interesting, or even uncommon, in themselves. It is sufficient that they follow one another in an uncommon order. Let any one attempt to look over even a game of cards, and to attend particularly to every single stroke, and if he is unacquainted with the nature and rules of the game; that is, with the laws which regulate the succession of the cards; he will soon feel the same confusion and giddiness begin to come upon him, which, were it to be continued for days and months, would end in the same manner, in lunacy and distraction. But if the mind be thus thrown into the most violent disorder, when it attends to a long series of events which follow one another in an uncommon train, it must feel some degree of the same disorder, when it observes even a single event fall out in this unusual manner: for the violent disorder can arise from nothing but the too frequent repetition of this smaller uneasiness.

That it is the unusualness alone of the succession which occasions this stop and interruption in the progress of the imagination, as well as the notion of an interval between the two immediately succeeding objects, to be filled up by some chain of intermediate events, is not less evident. The same orders of succession, which to one set of men seem quite according to the natural course of things, and such as require no intermediate events to join them, shall to another appear altogether incoherent and disjointed, unless some such events be supposed: and this for no other reason, but because such orders of succession are familiar to the one, and strange to the other.

When we enter the work-houses of the most common artisans; such as dyers, brewers, distillers; we observe a number of appearances, which present themselves in an order that seems to us very strange and wonderful. Our thought cannot easily follow it, we feel an interval between every two of them, and require some chain of intermediate events, to fill it up, and link them together. But the artisan himself, who has been for many years familiar with the consequences of all the operations of his art, feels no such interval. They fall in with what custom has made the natural movement of his imagination: they no longer excite his Wonder, and if he is not a genius superior to his profession, so as to be capable of making the very easy reflection, that those things, though familiar to him, may be strange to us, he will be disposed rather to laugh at, than sympathize with our Wonder. He cannot conceive what occasion there is for any connecting events to unite those appearances, which seem to him to succeed each other very naturally. It is their nature, he tells us, to follow one another in this order, and that accordingly they always do so.

In the same manner bread has, since the world began, been the common nourishment of the human body, and men have so long seen it, every day, converted into flesh and bones, substances in all respects so unlike it, that they have seldom had the curiosity to inquire by what process of intermediate events this change is brought about. Because the passage of the thought from the one object to the other is by custom become quite smooth and easy, almost without the supposition of any such process. Philosophers, indeed, who often look for a chain of invisible objects to join together two events that occur in an order familiar to all the world, have endeavoured to find out a chain of this kind between the two events I have just now mentioned; in the same manner as they have endeavoured, by a like intermediate chain, to connect the gravity, the elasticity, and even the cohesion of natural bodies, with some of their other qualities. These, however, are all of them such combinations of events as give no stop to the imaginations of the bulk of mankind, as excite no Wonder, nor any apprehension that there is wanting the strictest connexion between them.

But as in those sounds, which to the greater part of men seem perfectly agreeable to measure and harmony, the nicer ear of a musician will discover a want, both of the most exact time, and of the most perfect coincidence: so the more practised thought of a philosopher, who has spent his whole life in the study of the connecting principles of nature, will often feel an interval between two objects, which, to more careless observers, seem very strictly conjoined. By long attention to all the connections which have ever been presented to his observation, by having often compared them with one another, he has, like the musician, acquired, if one may say so, a nicer ear, and a more delicate feeling with regard to things of this nature. And as to the one, that music seems dissonance which falls short of the most perfect harmony; so to the other, those events seem altogether separated and disjoined, which fall short of the strictest and most perfect connection.

Philosophy is the science of the connecting principles of nature. Nature, after the largest experience that common observation can acquire, seems to abound with events which appear solitary and incoherent with all that go before them, which therefore disturb the easy movement of the imagination; which make its ideas succeed each other, if one may say so, by irregular starts and sallies; and which thus tend, in some measure, to introduce those confusions and distractions we formerly mentioned. Philosophy, by representing the invisible chains which bind together all these disjointed objects, endeavours to introduce order into this chaos of jarring and discordant appearances, to allay this tumult of the imagination, and to restore it, when it surveys the great revolutions of the universe, to that tone of tranquillity and composure, which is both most agreeable in itself, and most suitable to its nature.

Philosophy, therefore, may be regarded as one of those arts which address themselves to the imagination; and whose theory and history, upon that account, fall properly within the circumference of our subject. Let us endeavour to trace it, from its first origin, up to that summit of perfection to which it is at present supposed to have arrived, and to which, indeed, it has equally been supposed to have arrived in almost all former times. It is the most sublime of all the agreeable arts, and its revolutions have been the greatest, the most frequent, and the most distinguished of all those that have happened in the literary world. Its history, therefore, must, upon all accounts, be the most entertaining and the most instructive. Let us examine, therefore, all the different systems of nature, which, in these western parts of the world, the only parts of whose history we know any thing, have successively been adopted by the

learned and ingenious; and, without regarding their absurdity or probability, their agreement or inconsistency with truth and reality, let us
consider them only in that particular point of view which belongs to our
subject; and content ourselves with inquiring how far each of them was
fitted to sooth the imagination, and to render the theatre of nature a
more coherent, and therefore a more magnificent spectacle, than otherwise it would have appeared to be. According as they have failed or
succeeded in this, they have constantly failed or succeeded in gaining
reputation and renown to their authors; and this will be found to be the
clue that is most capable of conducting us through all the labyrinths of
philosophical history: for, in the mean time, it will serve to confirm what
has gone before, and to throw light upon what is to come after, that we
observe, in general, that no system, how well soever in other respects
supported, has ever been able to gain any general credit on the world,
whose connecting principles were not such as were familiar to all mankind. . . .

[Smith's chronicle of the development of astronomy as a science has been
omitted. His concluding observations on the system of Sir Isaac Newton are
presented below. These capture both the astonishing technical scope and
the essential philosophical character of the excluded material.]

   The Earth had hitherto been regarded as perfectly globular, probably
for the same reason which had made men imagine, that the orbits of the
Planets must necessarily be perfectly circular. But Sir Isaac Newton,
from mechanical principles, concluded, that, as the parts of the Earth
must be more agitated by her diurnal revolution at the Equator, than at
the Poles, they must necessarily be somewhat elevated at the first, and
flattened at the second. The observation, that the oscillations of pendu-
lums were slower at the Equator than at the Poles, seeming to demonstrate that gravity was stronger at the Poles, and weaker at the Equator,
proved, he thought, that the Equator was further from the centre than
the Poles. All the measures, however, which had hitherto been made of
the Earth, seemed to show the contrary, that it was drawn out towards
the Poles, and flattened towards the Equator.
   Newton, however, preferred his mechanical computations to the former measures of Geographers and Astronomers; and in this he was confirmed by the observations of Astronomers on the figure of Jupiter, whose
diameter at the Pole seems to be to his diameter at the Equator, as twelve
to thirteen; a much greater inequality than could be supposed to take
place between the correspondent diameters of the Earth, but which was
exactly proportioned to the superior bulk of Jupiter, and the superior
rapidity with which he performs his diurnal revolutions. The observations of Astronomers at Lapland and Peru have fully confirmed Sir Isaac's
system, and have not only demonstrated that the figure of the Earth is,

in general, such as he supposed it; but that the proportion of its axis to the diameter of its Equator is almost precisely such as he had computed it. And of all the proofs that have ever been adduced of the diurnal revolution of the Earth, this perhaps is the most solid and satisfactory.

Hipparchus, by comparing his own observations with those of some former Astronomers, had found that the equinoxial points were not always opposite to the same part of the Heavens, but that they advanced gradually eastward by so slow a motion, as to be scarce sensible in one hundred years, and which would require thirty-six thousand to make a complete revolution of the Equinoxes, and to carry them successively through all the different points of the Ecliptic.

More accurate observations discovered that this precession of the Equinoxes was not so slow as Hipparchus had imagined it, and that it required somewhat less than twenty-six thousand years to give them a complete revolution. While the ancient system of Astronomy, which represented the Earth as the immoveable centre of the universe, took place, this appearance was necessarily accounted for, by supposing that the Firmament, besides its rapid diurnal revolution round the poles of the Equator, had likewise a slow periodical one round those of the Ecliptic. And when the system of Hipparchus was by the schoolmen united with the solid Spheres of Aristotle, they placed a new christaline Sphere above the Firmament, in order to join this motion to the rest. In the Copernican system, this appearance had hitherto been connected with the other parts of that hypothesis, by supposing a small revolution in the Earth's axis from east to west. Sir Isaac Newton connected this motion by the same principle of gravity, by which he had united all the others, and showed how the elevation of the parts of the Earth at the Equator must, by the attraction of the Sun, produce the same retrograde motion of the Nodes of the Ecliptic, which it produced of the Nodes of the Moon. He computed the quantity of motion which could arise from this action of the Sun, and his calculations here too entirely corresponded with the observations of Astronomers.

Comets had hitherto, of all the appearances in the Heavens, been the least attended to by Astronomers. The rarity and inconstancy of their appearance seemed to separate them entirely from the constant, regular, and uniform objects in the Heavens, and to make them resemble more the inconstant, transitory, and accidental phenomena of those regions that are in the neighbourhood of the Earth. Aristotle, Eudoxus, Hipparchus, Ptolemy, and Purbach, therefore, had all degraded them below the Moon, and ranked them among the meteors of the upper regions of the air. The observations of Tycho Brahe demonstrated that they ascended into the celestial regions, and were often higher than Venus or the Sun. Descartes, at random, supposed them to be always higher than even the orbit of Saturn; and seems, by the superior elevation he thus bestowed upon them, to have been willing to compensate that unjust degradation which they had suffered for so many ages before. The observations of some later Astronomers demonstrated, that they too revolved about the Sun, and might therefore be parts of the Solar System.

Newton accordingly applied his mechanical principle of gravity to explain the motions of these bodies. That they described equal areas in equal times, had been discovered by the observations of some later Astronomers; and Newton endeavoured to show how from this principle, and those observations, the nature and position of their several orbits might be ascertained, and their periodic times determined. His followers have, from his principles, ventured even to predict the returns of several of them, particularly of one which is to make its appearance in 1758.* We must wait for that time before we can determine whether his philosophy corresponds as happily to this part of the system as to all the others. In the meantime, however, the ductility of this principle, which applied itself so happily to these, the most irregular of all the celestial appearances, and which has introduced such complete coherence into the motions of all the Heavenly Bodies, has served not a little to recommend it to the imaginations of mankind.

But of all the attempts of the Newtonian Philosophy, that which would appear to be the most above the reach of human reason and experience, is the attempt to compute the weights and densities of the Sun, and of the Several Planets. An attempt, however, which was indispensibly necessary to complete the coherence of the Newtonian system. The power of attraction which, according to the theory of gravity, each body possesses, is in proportion to the quantity of matter contained in that body. But the periodic time in which one body, at a given distance, revolves round another that attracts it, is shorter in proportion as this power is greater, and consequently as the quantity of matter in the attracting body. If the densities of Jupiter and Saturn were the same with that of the Earth, the periodic times of their several Satellites would be shorter than by observation they are found to be. Because the quantity of matter, and consequently the attracting power of each of them, would be as the cubes of their diameters. By comparing the bulks of those Planets, and the periodic times of their Satellites, it is found that, upon the hypothesis of gravity, the density of Jupiter must be greater than that of Saturn, and the density of the Earth greater than that of Jupiter. This seems to establish it as a law in the system, that the nearer the several Planets approach to the Sun, the density of their matter is the greater: a constitution of things which would seem to be the most advantageous of any that could have been established; as water of the same density with that of our Earth, would freeze under the Equator of Saturn, and boil under that of Mercury.

Such is the system of Sir Isaac Newton, a system whose parts are all

---

*The mention of Halley's comet is a key fact in dating this essay as an "early" work.

more strictly connected together, than those of any other philosophical hypothesis. Allow his principle, the universality of gravity, and that it decreases as the squares of the distance increase, and all the appearances, which he joins together by it, necessarily follow. Neither is their connexion merely a general and loose connexion, as that of most other systems, in which either these appearances, or some such like appearances, might indifferently have been expected. It is everywhere the most precise and particular that can be imagined, and ascertains the time, the place, the quantity, the duration of each individual phenomenon, to be exactly such as, by observation, they have been determined to be. Neither are the principles of union, which it employs, such as the imagination can find any difficulty in going along with. The gravity of matter is, of all its qualities, after its inertness, that which is most familiar to us. We never act upon it without having occasion to observe this property.

The law too, by which it is supposed to diminish as it recedes from its centre, is the same which takes place in all other qualities which are propagated in rays from a centre, in light, and in every thing else of the same kind. It is such, that we not only find that it does take place in all such qualities, but we are necessarily determined to conceive that, from the nature of the thing, it must take place. The opposition which was made in France, and in some other foreign nations, to the prevalence of this system, did not arise from any difficulty which mankind naturally felt in conceiving gravity as an original and primary mover in the constitution of the universe. The Cartesian system, which had prevailed so generally before it, had accustomed mankind to conceive motion as never beginning, but in consequence of impulse, and had connected the descent of heavy bodies, near the surface of the Earth, and the other Planets, by this more general bond of union; and it was the attachment the world had conceived for this account of things, which indisposed them to that of Sir Isaac Newton.

His system, however, now prevails over all opposition, and has advanced to the acquisition of the most universal empire that was ever established in philosophy. His principles, it must be acknowledged, have a degree of firmness and solidity that we should in vain look for in any other system. The most sceptical cannot avoid feeling this. They not only connect together most perfectly all the phenomena of the Heavens, which had been observed before his time, but those also which the persevering industry and more perfect instruments of later Astronomers have made known to us; have been either easily and immediately explained by the application of his principles, or have been explained in consequence of more laborious and accurate calculations from these principles, than had been instituted before. And even we, while we have been endeavouring to represent all philosophical systems as mere inventions of the imagination, to connect together the otherwise disjointed and discordant phenomena of nature, have insensibly been drawn in, to make use of language expressing the connecting principles of this one, as if they were the real chains which Nature makes use of to bind together her several operations. Can we wonder then, that it should have gained the general and complete approbation of mankind, and that it should now be considered, not as an attempt to connect in the imagination the phenomena of the Heavens, but as the greatest discovery that ever was made by man, the discovery of an immense chain of the most important and sublime truths, all closely connected together, by one capital fact, of the reality of which we have daily experience.

JURIS PRUDENCE

or

Notes from the Lectures on Justice, Police, Revenue, and Arms delivered in the University of Glasgow

by

Adam Smith Professor of Moral Philosophy.

MDCCLXVI.

(frontispiece from original manuscript, dated 1766)

Lectures on Jurisprudence

Of Justice

Jurisprudence is the theory of the general principles of law and government.

The four great objects of law are justice, police, revenue, and arms.

The object of justice is the security from injury, and it is the foundation of civil government.

The objects of police are the cheapness of commodities, public security and cleanliness, if the two last were not too minute for a lecture of this kind. Under this head we will consider the opulence of a state.

It is likewise necessary that the magistrate who bestows his time and labour in the business of the state should be compensated for it. For this purpose, and for defraying the expences of government, some fund must be raised. Hence the origin of revenue. The subject of consideration under this head will be the proper means of levying revenue, which must come from the people by taxes, duties, etc. In general, whatever revenue can be raised most insensibly from the people ought to be preferred; and in the sequel it is proposed to be shown how far the laws of Britain and of other European nations are calculated for this purpose.

As the best police cannot give security unless the government can defend themselves from foreign injuries and attacks, the fourth thing appointed by law is for this purpose; and under this head will be shown the different species of arms with their advantages and disadvantages, the constitution of standing armies, militias, etc.

After these will be considered the laws of nations, under which are comprehended the demands which one independent society may have upon another, the privileges of aliens, and proper grounds for making war.

Of the Original Principles of Government

There are two principles which induce men to enter into a civil society, which we shall call the principles of authority and utility. At the head of every small society or association of men, we find a person of superior abilities. In a warlike society he is a man of superior strength, and in a polished one of superior mental capacity. Age and a long possession of power have also a tendency to strengthen authority. Age is naturally in our imagination connected with wisdom and experience, and a continuance in power bestows a kind of right to the exercise of it. But superior wealth still more than any of these qualities contributes to confer authority. This proceeds not from any dependence that the poor have upon the rich, for in general the poor are independent, and support themselves by their labour, yet, though they expect no benefit from them, they have a strong propensity to pay them respect. This principle is fully explained in the Theory of Moral Sentiments, where it is shown that it arises from our sympathy with our superiors being greater than that with our equals or inferiors: we admire their happy situation, enter into it with pleasure, and endeavour to promote it.

Among the great, as superior abilities of body and mind are not so easily judged of by others, it is more convenient, as it is more common, to give the preference to riches. It is evident that an old family, that is, one which has been long distinguished by its wealth, has more authority than any other. An upstart is always disagreeable, we envy his superiority over us and think ourselves as well entitled to wealth as he. If I am told that a man's grandfather was very poor and dependent on my family, I will grudge very much to see his grandson in a station above me, and will not be much disposed to submit to his authority. Superior age, superior abilities of body and of mind, ancient family, and superior wealth seem to be the four things that give one man authority over another.

The second principle which induces men to obey the civil magistrate is utility. Every one is sensible of the necessity of this principle to preserve justice and peace in the society. By civil institutions the poorest may get redress of injuries from the wealthiest and most powerful; and though there may be some irregularities in particular cases, as undoubtedly there are, yet we submit to them to avoid greater evils. It is the sense of public utility, more than of private, which influences men to obedience. It may sometimes be for my interest to disobey, and to wish government overturned, but I am sensible that other men are of a different opinion from me, and would not assist me in the enterprise. I therefore submit to its decision for the good of the whole.

If government has been of a long standing in a country, and if it be supported by proper revenues, and be at the same time in the hands of a man of great abilities, authority is then in perfection.

In all governments both these principles take place in some degree, but in a monarchy the principle of authority prevails, and in a democracy that of utility. . . .

Of the Nature of Government and its Progress in the first Ages of Society

. . . In a nation of hunters there is properly no government at all. The society consists of a few independent families who live in the same village and speak the same language, and have agreed among themselves to keep together for their mutual safety, but they have no authority one over another. The whole society interests itself in any offence; if possible they make it up between the parties, if not they banish from their society, kill or deliver up to the resentment of the injured him who has committed the crime. But this is no regular government, for though there may be some among them who are much respected, and have great influence in their determinations, yet he never can do anything without the consent of the whole.

Thus among hunters there is no regular government, they live according to the laws of nature.

The appropriation of herds and flocks which introduced an inequality of fortune, was that which first gave rise to regular government. Till there be property there can be no government, the very end of which is to secure wealth, and to defend the rich from the poor. In this age of shepherds, if one man possessed 500 oxen, and another had none at all, unless there were some government to secure them to him, he would not be allowed to possess them. This inequality of fortune, making a distinction between the rich and the poor, gave the former much influence over the latter, for they who had no flocks or herds must have depended on those who had them, because they could not now gain a subsistence from hunting, as the rich had made the game, now become tame, their own property. They therefore who had appropriated a number of flocks and herds, necessarily came to have great influence over the rest; and accordingly we find in the Old Testament that Abraham, Lot, and the other patriarchs were like little petty princes. It is to be observed that this inequality of fortune in a nation of shepherds occasioned greater influence than in any period after that. Even at present, a man may spend a great estate, and yet acquire no dependents. Arts and manufactures are increased by it, but it may make very few persons dependent. In a nation of shepherds it is quite otherways. They have no possible means of spending their property, having no domestic luxury, but by giving it in presents to the poor, and by this means they attain such influence over them as to make them, in a manner, their slaves.

We come now to explain how one man came to have more authority than the rest, and how chieftains were introduced. A nation consists of many families who have met together, and agreed to live with one another. At their public meetings there will always be one of superior influence to the rest, who will in a great measure direct and govern their resolutions, which is all the authority of a chieftain in a barbarous country. As the chieftain is the leader of the nation, his son naturally becomes the chief of the young people, and on the death of his father succeeds to his authority. Thus chieftainship becomes hereditary. This power of chieftainship comes in the progress of society to be increased by a variety of circumstances. The number of presents which he receives increase his fortune, and consequently his authority; for amongst barbarous nations nobody goes to the chieftain, or makes any application for his interest, without something in his hand. In a civilised nation the man who gives the present is superior to the person who receives it, but in a barbarous nation the case is directly opposite. . . .

We shall now make some observations on nations in the two first periods of society. Those, viz., of hunters and shepherds.

In a nation of hunters and fishers few people can live together, for in a short time any considerable number would destroy all the game in the country, and consequently would want a means of subsistence. Twenty or thirty families are the most that can live together, and these make up a village. But as they live together for their mutual defence, and to assist one another, their villages are not far distant from each other. When any controversy happens between persons of different villages, it is decided by a general assembly of both villages. As each particular village has its own leader, so there is one who is the leader of the whole nation. The nation consists of an alliance of the different villages, and the chieftains have great influence on their resolutions, especially among shepherds. In no age is antiquity of family more respected than in this. The principle of authority operates very strongly, and they have the liveliest sense of utility in the maintenance of law and government.

The difference of the conduct of these nations in peace and war, is worth our observation.

The exploits of hunters, though brave and gallant, are never very considerable. As few of them can march together, so their number seldom exceeds 200 men, and even these cannot be supported above fourteen days. There is therefore very little danger from a nation of hunters. Our colonies are much afraid of them without any just grounds. They may indeed give them some trouble by their inroads and excursions, but can never be very formidable. On the other hand a much greater number of shepherds can live together. There may be a thousand families in the same village. The Arabs and Tartars, who have always been shepherds, have on many occasions made the most dreadful havoc. A Tartar chief is extremely formidable, and when one of them gets the better of another, there always happens the most dreadful and violent revolutions. They take their whole flocks and herds into the field along with them, and whoever is overcome loses both his people and wealth. The victorious nation follows its flocks, and pursues its conquest, and if it comes into a cultivated country with such numbers of men, it is quite irresistible. It was in this manner that Mahomet ravaged all Asia.

How Liberty was lost

. . . When a country arrives at a certain degree of refinement it becomes less fit for war. When the arts arrive at a certain degree of improvement, the number of the people increases, yet that of fighting men becomes less. In a state of shepherds the whole nation can go out to war; and even when it becomes more refined, and the division of labour takes place, and everyone is possessed of a small farm, they can send out a great number. In such an age their campaigns are always in summer, and from seed time till harvest their young men have nothing ado but to serve in them. The whole business at home can be performed by the old men and women, and even these have sometimes beat the enemy in the absence of their soldiers. In a state where arts are carried on, and which consists chiefly of manufacturers, there cannot be sent out such numbers, because if a weaver or tailor be called away, nothing is done in his absence. Scarce one in an hundred can be spared from Britain and Holland. Of an hundred inhabitants fifty are women, and of fifty men twenty-five are unfit for war. In the last war Britain could not spare so many, as any one almost may be convinced, if he reflect whether among his acquaintances he missed one out of twenty-five. According to this principle Athens, though a small state, could once send out 30,000 fighting men, which made a very considerable figure; but after the improvement of arts, they could not send out more than 10,000, which was quite inconsiderable. Britain, notwithstanding the politeness and refinement at which it has arrived, on account of the largeness of its territories, can still send out a very formidable army, but a small state necessarily declines.

However, there is one advantage attending slavery in a small republic, which seems to be its only advantage, that it retards their declension. At Rome and Athens the arts were carried on by slaves, and the Lacedaemonians went so far as not to allow any freeman to be brought up to mechanic employments, because they imagined that they hurt the body. Accordingly we find that at the battle of Chaeronea, when the Athenians were come to a considerable degree of politeness, they were able to send out great numbers of men purely on this account, that all trades were carried on by slaves. We may observe that in the Italian republics, where slavery did not take place, they soon lost their liberty. When, in consequence of the improvement of arts, a state has become opulent, it must be reckoned a great hardship to go out to war, whereas among our ancestors it was thought no inconvenience to take the field. A knight (equus) was no more than a horseman, and a foot-soldier was a gentleman. They were inured to hardships at home, and therefore a campaign appeared no way dreadful. But when opulence and luxury increased, the rich would not take the field but on the most urgent account, and therefore it became necessary to employ mercenaries and the dregs of the people to serve in war. Such persons could never be trusted in war unless reduced to the form of a standing army, and subjected to rigid discipline, because their private interest was but little concerned, and therefore without such treatment they could not be expected to be very resolute in their undertakings. Gentlemen may carry on a war without much discipline, but this a mob can never do. As the citizens in Greece thought it below them to bear arms, and entrusted the republic to mercenaries, their military force was diminished, and consequently a means was provided for the fall of the government.

Another cause of their declension was the improvement of the art of war, which rendered everything precarious. In early ages it was very difficult to take a city, as it could only be done by a long blockade. The siege of Troy lasted ten years, and Athens once could withstand for two years a siege both by land and sea. In modern times the besiegers have an advantage over the besieged, and a good engineer can force almost any town to surrender in six weeks. But it was not so once. Philip of Macedon made great improvements in this art, which at last occasioned the dissolution of all the Greek governments and their subjection to foreign powers. Rome stood out much longer than Greece because the number of its citizens was daily increasing. At Rome any person might be made a citizen, as this was of little advantage. But at Athens the right of citizenship was given to very few, as it was itself a little estate. However, Rome itself after opulence and luxury increased, shared the fate of other republics, though the event was brought about in a different manner. Till the time of Marius, the better sort of free men went out to the field. Marius was the first that recruited slaves. He gathered the freed slaves into his army, and established a rigid military discipline. That army which before had consisted of gentlemen was now made up of runaway slaves and the lowest of the people. With such an army Marius conquered and kept in awe the provinces. He had the disposal of all offices and posts in this army. Every one among them owed his rise to him, and was consequently dependent upon him.

Whenever such a general was affronted he would naturally apply to his army for relief, who would easily be induced to side with their general against their own nation. This was the very expedient that Marius fell upon. By the influence of Sylla he was, in his absence, banished from Rome, and a price set upon him. Marius applied to his army, who were determined at all events to follow him, marched to Rome when Sylla was abroad on an expedition against Mithridates, took possession of the government and vanquished Sylla's party. Marius died soon after, and Sylla, having conquered Mithridates, returned to Rome, and in his turn beat the Marian party, changed the government into a monarchy, and made himself perpetual Dictator, though he afterwards had the generosity and magnanimity to resign it. About thirty or forty years afterwards the same thing happened between Caesar and Pompey. Caesar as well as Sylla got himself made perpetual Dictator, but had not enough of public spirit to resign it. His veteran troops which were settled in Italy, mindful of the favours which he conferred upon them, after his death gathered about Octavius, his adopted son, and invested him with the supreme authority. Much the same thing happened in our own country with respect to Oliver Cromwell. When the Parliament became jealous of this man, and disbanded the army, he applied to them in a manner indeed more canting than that of the Roman generals, and got the Parliament turned out and a new one appointed more suitable to his mind, with the whole authority vested in himself.

Thus we have seen how small republics, whether conquering or defensive, came at length to a dissolution from the improvements in mechanic arts, commerce, and the arts of war. . . .

PART II

Of Police

Police is the second general division of jurisprudence. The name is French, and is originally derived from the Greek πολιτεια,* which properly signified the policy of civil government, but now it only means the regulation of the inferior parts of government, viz:—cleanliness, security, and cheapness or plenty. The two former, to wit, the proper method of carrying dirt from the streets, and the execution of justice, so far as it regards regulations for preventing crimes or the method of keeping a city guard, though useful, are too mean to be considered in a general discourse of this kind. . . .

Of the Natural Wants of Mankind

In the following part of this discourse we are to confine ourselves to the consideration of cheapness or plenty, or, which is the same thing, the most proper way of procuring wealth and abundance. Cheapness is in fact the same thing with plenty. It is only on account of the plenty of water that it is so cheap as to be got for the lifting; and on account of the scarcity of diamonds (for their real use seems not yet to be discovered) that they are so dear. To ascertain the most proper method of obtaining these conveniences it will be necessary to show first wherein opulence consists, and still previous to this we must consider what are the natural wants of mankind which are to be supplied; and if we differ from common opinions, we shall at least give the reasons for our non-conformity.

Nature produces for every animal everything that is sufficient to support it without having recourse to the improvement of the original production. Food, clothes, and lodging are all the wants of any animal whatever, and most of the animal creation are sufficiently provided for by nature in all those wants to which their condition is liable. Such is the delicacy of man alone, that no object is produced to his liking. He finds that in everything there is need of improvement. Though the practise of savages shows that his food needs no preparation, yet being

* Politia.

acquainted with fire, he finds that it can be rendered more wholesome and easily digested, and thereby may preserve him from many diseases which are very violent among them. But it is not only his food that requires this improvement; his puny constitution is hurt also by the intemperature of the air he breathes in, which, though not very capable of improvement, must be brought to a proper temperament for his body, and an artificial atmosphere prepared for this purpose. The human skin cannot endure the inclemencies of the weather, and even in those countries where the air is warmer than the natural warmth of the constitution, and where they have no need of clothes, it must be stained and painted to be able to endure the hardships of the sun and rain. In general, however, the necessities of man are not so great but that they can be supplied by the unassisted labour of the individual. All the above necessities everyone can provide for himself, such as animals and fruits for his food, and skins for his clothing.

As the delicacy of a man's body requires much greater provision than that of any other animal, the same or rather the much greater delicacy of his mind requires a still greater provision to which all the different arts are subservient. Man is the only animal who is possessed of such a nicety that the very colour of an object hurts him. Among different objects a different division or arrangement of them pleases. The taste of beauty, which consists chiefly in the three following particulars, proper variety, easy connexion, and simple order, is the cause of all this niceness. Nothing without variety pleases us; a long uniform wall is a disagreeable object. Too much variety, such as the crowded objects of a parterre, is also disagreeable. Uniformity tires the mind; too much variety, too far increased, occasions an over-great dissipation of it. Easy connexion also renders objects agreeable; when we see no reason for the contiguity of the parts, when they are without any natural connexion, when they have neither a proper resemblance nor contrast, they never fail of being disagreeable. If simplicity of order be not observed, so as that the whole may be easily comprehended, it hurts the delicacy of our taste. Again, imitation and painting render objects more agreeable. To see upon a plain, trees, forests, and other such representations, is an agreeable surprise to the mind. Variety of objects also renders them agreeable. What we are every day accustomed to does but very indifferently affect us. Gems and diamonds are on this account much esteemed by us. In like manner our pinchbeck and many of our toys were so much valued by the Indians, that in bartering their jewels and diamonds for them they thought they had made by much the better bargain. . . .

That Opulence arises from the Division of Labour

In an uncivilised nation, and where labour is undivided, everything is provided for that the natural wants of mankind require; yet, when the nation is cultivated and labour divided, a more liberal provision is allotted them; and it is on this account that a common day labourer in Britain has more luxury in his way of living than an Indian sovereign. The woollen coat he wears requires very considerable preparations—the woolgatherer, the dresser, the spinster, the dyer, the weaver, the tailor, and many more, must all be employed before the labourer is clothed. The tools by which all this is effectuated employ a still greater number of artists—the loom-maker, mill-wright, rope-maker, not to mention the bricklayer, the tree-feller, the miner, the smelter, the forger, the smith, etc. Besides his dress, consider all his household furniture, his coarse linens, his shoes, his coals dug out of the earth or brought by sea, his kitchen utensils and different plates, those that are employed in providing his bread and beer, the sower, the brewer, the reaper, the baker, his glass windows and the art required in preparing them, without which our northern climate could hardly be inhabited. When we examine the conveniences of the day labourer, we find that even in his easy simple manner he cannot be accommodated without the assistance of a great number, and yet this is nothing compared with the luxury of the nobility. An European prince, however, does not so far exceed a commoner, as the latter does the chief of a savage nation. It is easy to conceive how the rich can be so well provided for, as they can direct so many hands to serve their purposes. They are supported by the industry of the peasant. In a savage nation every one enjoys the whole fruit of his own labour, yet their indigence is greater than anywhere.

It is the division of labour which increases the opulence of a country.

In a civilised society, though there is a division of labour, there is no equal division, for there are a good many who work none at all. The division of opulence is not according to the work. The opulence of the merchant is greater than that of all his clerks, though he works less; and they again have six times more than an equal number of artisans, who are more employed. The artisan who works at his ease within doors has far more than the poor labourer who trudges up and down without intermission. Thus, he who as it were bears the burden of society, has the fewest advantages.

How the Division of Labour Multiplies the Product

We shall next show how this division of labour occasions a multiplication of the product, or, which is the same thing, how opulence arises from it. In order to [do] this let us observe the effect of the division of labour in some manufactures. If all the parts of a pin were made by one man, if the same person dug the ore, smelted it, and split the wire, it would take him a whole year to make one pin, and this pin must therefore be sold at the expence of his maintenance for that time, which, taking it at a moderate computation, would at least be six pounds for a pin. If the labour is so far divided that the wire is ready-made, he will not make above twenty per day, which, allowing ten pence for wages, makes the pin a half-penny. The pin-maker therefore divides the labour among a great number of different persons; the cutting, pointing, heading, and gilding are all separate professions. Two or three are employed in making the head, one or two in putting it on, and so on, to the putting them in the paper, being in all eighteen. By this division every one can with great ease make 2000 a day. The same is the case in the linen and woollen manufactures. Some arts, however, there are which will not admit of this division, and therefore they cannot keep pace with other manufactures and arts. Such are farming and grazing. This is entirely owing to the return of the seasons, by which one man can only be for a short time employed in any one operation. In countries where the seasons do not make such alterations it is otherwise. In France the corn is better and cheaper than in England. But our toys, which have no dependence on the climate, and in which labour can be divided, are far superior to those of France.

When labour is thus divided, and so much done by one man in proportion, the surplus above their maintenance is considerable, which each man can exchange for a fourth of what he could have done if he had finished it alone. By this means the commodity becomes far cheaper, and the labour dearer. It is to be observed that the price of labour by no means determines the opulence of society; it is only when a little labour can procure abundance. . . .

But again, the quantity of work which is done by the division of labour is much increased by the three following articles: first, increase of dexterity; secondly, the saving of time lost in passing from one species of labour to another; and thirdly, the invention of machinery. Of these in order:

First, when any kind of labour is reduced to a simple operation, a frequency of action insensibly fits men to a dexterity in accomplishing it. A country smith not accustomed to make nails will work very hard for three or four hundred a day, and those too very bad; but a boy used to it will easily make two thousand, and those incomparably better; yet the improvement of dexterity in this very complex manufacture can never be equal to that in others. A nailmaker changes postures, blows the bellows, changes tools, etc., and therefore the quantity produced cannot be so great as in manufactures of pins and buttons, where the work is reduced to simple operations.

Secondly, there is always some time lost in passing from one species of labour to another, even when they are pretty much connected. When a person has been reading he must rest a little before he begin[s] to write. This is still more the case with the country weaver, who is possessed of a little farm; he must saunter a little when he goes from one to the other. This in general is the case with the country labourers, they are always the greatest saunterers; the country employments of sowing, reaping, threshing being so different, they naturally acquire a habit of indolence, and are seldom very dexterous. By fixing every man to his own operation, and preventing the shifting from one piece of labour to another, the quantity of work must be greatly increased.

Thirdly, the quantity of work is greatly increased by the invention of machines. Two men and three horses will do more in a day with the plough than twenty men without it. The miller and his servant will do more with the water mill than a dozen with the hand mill, though it, too, be a machine. The division of labour no doubt first gave occasion to the invention of machines. If a man's business in life is the performance of two or three things, the bent of his mind will be to find out the cleverest way of doing it; but when the force of his mind is divided it cannot be expected that he should be so successful. We have not, nor cannot have, any complete history of the invention of machines, because most of them are at first imperfect, and receive gradual improvements and increase of powers from those who use them. It was probably a farmer who made the original plough, though the improvements might be owing to some other. Some miserable slave who had perhaps been employed for a long time in grinding corn between two stones, probably first found out the method of supporting the upper stone by a spindle. A millwright perhaps found out the way of turning the spindle with the hand, but he who contrived that the outer wheel should go by water was a philosopher, whose business it is to do nothing, but observe everything. They must have extensive views of things, who, as in this case, bring in the assistance of new powers not formerly applied. Whether he was an artisan, or whatever he was who first executed this, he must have been a philosopher. Fire machines,* wind and water mills were the invention of philosophers, whose dexterity too is increased by a division of labour. They all divide themselves, according to the different branches, into the mechanical, moral, political, chemical philosophers.

Thus we have shown how the quantity of labour is increased by machines.

What gives Occasion to the Division of Labour

We have already shown that the division of labour is the immediate cause of opulence; we shall next consider what gives occasion to the division of labour, or from what principles in our nature it can best be accounted for. We cannot imagine this to be an effect of human prudence. It was indeed made a law by Sesostris that every man should follow the employment of his father, but this is by no means suitable to the dispositions of human nature, and can never long take place; every one is fond of being a gentleman, be his father what he would. They

* Steam engines.

who are strongest and, in the bustle of society, have got above the weak, must have as many under as to defend them in their station. From necessary causes, therefore, there must be as many in the lower stations as there is occasion for, there must be as many up as down, and no division can be overstretched. But it is not this which gives occasion to the division of labour; it flows from a direct propensity in human nature for one man to barter with another, which is common to all men, and known to no other animal. Nobody ever saw a dog, the most sagacious animal, exchange a bone with his companion for another. Two greyhounds, indeed, in running down a hare, seem to have something like compact or agreement between them, but this is nothing else but a concurrence of the same passions. If an animal intends to truck, as it were, or gain anything from man, it is by its fondness and kindness. Man, in the same manner, works on the self love of his fellows, by setting before them a sufficient temptation to get what he wants. The language of this disposition is, "Give me what I want, and you shall have what you want." It is not from benevolence, as the dogs, but from self-love that man expects anything. The brewer and the baker serve us not from benevolence, but from self-love. No man but a beggar depends on benevolence, and even they would die in a week were their entire dependence upon it.

By this disposition to barter and exchange the surplus of one's labour for that of other people, in a nation of hunters, if any one has a talent for making bows an*. arrows better than his neighbours, he will at first make presents of them, and in return get presents of their game. By continuing this practice he will live better than before, and will have no occasion to provide for himself, as the surplus of his own labour does it more effectually.

This disposition to barter is by no means founded upon different genius and talents. It is doubtful if there be any such difference at all, at least it is far less than we are aware of. Genius is more the effect of the division of labour than the latter is of it. The difference between a porter and a philosopher in the first four or five years of their life is, properly speaking, none at all. When they come to be employed in different occupations, their views widen and differ by degrees. As every one has this natural disposition to truck and barter, by which he provides for himself, there is no need for such different endowments; and accordingly, among savages there is always the greatest uniformity of character. In other animals of the same species we find a much greater difference than between the philosopher and porter, antecedent to custom. The mastiff and spaniel have quite different powers, but though these animals are possessed of talents they cannot, as it were, bring them into the common stock and exchange their productions, and therefore their different talents are of no use to them. It is quite otherwise among mankind; they can exchange their several productions according to their quantity or quality; the philosopher and the porter are both of advantage to each other. The porter is of use in carrying burdens for the philosopher, and in his turn he burns his coals cheaper by the philosopher's invention of the fire machine. Thus we have shown that different genius is not the foundation of this disposition to barter which is the cause of the division of labour. The real foundation of it is that principle to persuade which so much prevails in human nature. When any arguments are offered to persuade, it is always expected that they should have their proper effect. If a person asserts anything about the moon, though it should not be true, he will feel a kind of uneasiness in being contradicted, and would be very glad that the person he is endeavouring to persuade should be of the same way of thinking with himself. We ought then mainly to cultivate the power of persuasion, and indeed we do so without intending it. Since a whole life is spent in the exercise of it, a ready method of bargaining with each other must undoubtedly be attained. As was before observed, no animal can do this but by gaining the favour of those whom they would persuade. Sometimes, indeed, animals seem to act in concert, but there never is anything like bargain among them. Monkeys, when they rob a garden, throw the fruit from one to another, till they deposit it in the hoard, but there is always a scramble about the division of the booty, and usually some of them are killed.

That the Division of Labour must be Proportioned to the Extent of Commerce

From all that has been said we may observe that the division of labour must always be proportioned to the extent of commerce. If ten people only want a certain commodity, the manufacture of it will never be so divided as if a thousand wanted it. Again, the division of labour, in order to opulence, becomes always more perfect by the easy method of conveyance in a country. If the road be infested with robbers, if it be deep and conveyance not easy, the progress of commerce must be stopped. Since the mending of roads in England forty or fifty years ago, its opulence has increased extremely. Water carriage is another convenience, as by it 300 ton can be conveyed at the expence of the tear and wear of the vessel, and the wages of five or six men, and that too in a shorter time than by a hundred wagons which will take six horses and a man each. Thus the division of labour is the great cause of the increase of public opulence, which is always proportioned to the industry of the people, and not to the quantity of gold and silver, as is foolishly imagined, and the industry of the people is always proportioned to the division of labour.

Having thus shown what gives occasion to public opulence, in farther considering this subject we propose to consider:

First, what circumstances regulate the price of commodities:

Secondly, money in two different views, first as the measure of value, and then as the instrument of commerce:

Thirdly, the history of commerce, in which shall be taken notice of the causes of the slow progress of opulence, both in ancient and modern times, which causes shall be shown either to affect agriculture or arts and manufactures:

Lastly, the effects of a commercial spirit, on the government, temper, and manners of a people, whether good or bad, and the proper remedies. Of these in order.

What Circumstances Regulate the Price of Commodities

Of every commodity there are two different prices, which though apparently independent, will be found to have a necessary connexion, viz., the natural price and the market price. Both of these are regulated by certain circumstances. When men are induced to a certain species of industry, rather than any other, they must make as much by the employment as will maintain them while they are employed. An arrow maker must be sure to exchange as much surplus product as will maintain him during as long a time as he took to make them. But upon this principle in the different trades there must be a considerable difference, because some trades, such as those of the tailor and weaver, are not learned by casual observation and a little experience, like that of the day labourer, but take a great deal of time and pains before they are acquired. When a person begins them, for a considerable time his work is of no use to his master or any other person, and therefore his master must be compensated, both for what maintains him and for what he spoils. When he comes to exercise his trade, he must be repaid what he has laid out, both of expences and of apprentice fee, and as his life is not worth above ten or twelve years' purchase at most, his wages must be high on account of the risk he runs of not having the whole made up.

But again, there are many arts which require more extensive knowledge than is to be got during the time of an apprenticeship. A blacksmith and weaver may learn their business well enough without any previous knowledge of mathematics, but a watchmaker must be acquainted with several sciences in order to undertake his business well, such as arithmetic, geometry, and astronomy with regard to the equation of time, and their wages must be high in order to compensate the additional expence. In general, this is the case in all the liberal arts, because after they have spent a long time in their education, it is ten to one if ever they make anything by it. Their wages therefore must be higher in proportion to the expence they have been at, the risk of not living long enough, and the risk of not having dexterity enough to manage their business. Among the lawyers there is not one among twenty that attains such knowledge and dexterity in his business as enables him to get back the expences of his education, and many of them never make the price of their gown, as we say. The fees of lawyers are so far from being extravagant, as they are generally thought, that they are rather low in proportion. It is the eminence of the profession, and not the money made by it, that is the temptation for applying to it, and the dignity of that rank is to be considered as a part of what is made by it.

In the same manner we shall find that the price of gold and silver is not extravagant, if we consider it in this view, for in a gold or silver mine there is a great chance of missing it altogether. If we suppose an equal number of men employed in raising corn and digging silver, the former will make more than the latter, because perhaps of forty or fifty employed in a mine, only twenty make anything at all. Some of the rest may indeed make fortunes, but every corn man succeeds in his undertakings, so that upon the whole there is more made this way than the other. It is the ideal acquisition which is the principal temptation in a mine.

A man then has the natural price of his labour, when it is sufficient to maintain him during the time of labour, to defray the expence of education, and to compensate the risk of not living long enough, and of not succeeding in the business. When a man has this, there is sufficient encouragement to the labourer, and the commodity will be cultivated in proportion to the demand.

The market price of goods is regulated by quite other circumstances. When a buyer comes to the market, he never asks of the seller what expences he has been at in producing them. The regulation of the market price of goods depends on the three following articles:—

First, the demand, or need for the commodity. There is no demand for a thing of little use; it is not a rational object of desire.

Secondly, the abundance or scarcity of the commodity in proportion to the need of it. If the commodity be scarce, the price is raised, but if the quantity be more than is sufficient to supply the demand, the price falls. Thus it is that diamonds and other precious stones are dear, while iron, which is much more useful, is so many times cheaper, though this depends principally on the last cause, viz.:—

Thirdly, the riches or poverty of those who demand. When there is not enough produced to serve everybody, the fortune of the bidders is the only regulation of the price. The story which is told of the merchant and the carrier in the deserts of Arabia is an evidence of this. The merchant gave 10,000 ducats for a certain quantity of water. His fortune here regulated the price, for if he had not had them, he could not have given them, and if his fortune had been less, the water would have been cheaper. When the commodity is scarce, the seller must be content with that degree of wealth which they have who buy it. The case is much the same as in an auction. If two persons have an equal fondness for a book, he whose fortune is largest will carry it. Hence things that are very rare go always to rich countries. The King of France only could purchase that large diamond of so many thousand pounds value. Upon this principle, everything is dearer or cheaper according as it is the purchase of a higher or lower set of people. Utensils of gold are affordable only by persons in certain circumstances. Those of silver fall to another set of people, and their prices are regulated by what the majority can give. The prices of corn and beer are regulated by what all the world can give, and on this account the wages of the day-labourer have a great influence upon the price of corn. When the price of corn rises, wages rise also, and *vice versa*; when the quantity of corn falls short, as in a sea voyage, it always occasions a famine, and then the price becomes enormous. Corn then becomes the purchase of a higher set of people, and the lower must live on turnips and potatoes.

Thus we have considered the two prices, the natural and the market price, which every commodity is supposed to have. We observed before that however seemingly independent they appear to be, they are necessarily connected. This will appear from the following considerations. If the market price of any commodity is very great, and the labour very highly rewarded, the market is prodigiously crowded with it, greater quantities of it are produced, and it can be sold to the inferior ranks of people. If for every ten diamonds there were ten thousand, they would become the purchase of everybody, because they would become very cheap, and would sink to their natural price. Again, when the market is overstocked, and there is not enough got for the labour of the manufacture, nobody will bind to it, they cannot have a subsistence by it, because the market price falls then below the natural price. It is alleged that as the price of corn sinks, the wages of the labourer should sink, as he is then better rewarded. It is true that if provisions were long cheap, as more people would flock to this labour where the wages are high, through this concurrence of labour, the wages would come down, but we find that when the price of corn is doubled, the wages continue the same as before, because the labourers have no other way to turn themselves. The same is the case with menial servants.

From the above we may observe that whatever police tends to raise the market price above the natural, tends to diminish public opulence. Dearness and scarcity are in effect the same thing. When commodities are in abundance, they can be sold to the inferior ranks of people, who can afford to give less for them, but not if they are scarce. So far, therefore, as goods are a convenience to the society, the society lives less happy when only the few can possess them. Whatever therefore keeps goods above their natural price for a permanency, diminishes a nation's opulence. . . .

Of Money as the Measure of Value and Medium of Exchange

We come now to the second particular, to consider money, first as the measure of value and then as the medium of permutation or exchange. When people deal in many species of goods, one of them must be considered as the measure of value. Suppose there were only three commodities, sheep, corn, and oxen, we can easily remember them comparatively, but if we have a hundred different commodities, there are ninety-nine values of each arising from a comparison with each of the rest. As these cannot easily be remembered, men naturally fall upon one of them to be a common standard with which they compare all the rest. This will naturally at first be the commodity with which they are best acquainted. Accordingly we find that black cattle and sheep were the standard in Homer's time. The armour of one of his heroes was worth nine oxen, and that of another worth an hundred. Black cattle was the common standard in ancient Greece. In Italy, and particularly in Tuscany, everything was compared with sheep, as this was their principal commodity. This is what may be called the natural measure of value. In like manner there were natural measures of quantity, such as fathoms, cubits, inches, taken from the proportion of the human body, once in use with every nation. But by a little observation they found that one man's arm was longer or shorter than another's, and that one was not to be compared with the other, and therefore wise men who attended to these things would endeavour to fix upon some more accurate measure, that equal quantities might be of equal values. This method became absolutely necessary when people came to deal in many commodities, and in great quantities of them. Though an inch was altogether inconsiderable when their dealings were confined to a few yards, more accuracy was required when they came to deal in some thousands. We find, in countries where their dealings are small, the remains of this inaccuracy. The cast of the balance is nothing thought of in their coarse commodities.

Since, then, there must of necessity be a common standard of which equal quantities should be of equal values, metals in general seemed best to answer this purpose, and of these the value of gold and silver could best be ascertained. The temper of steel cannot be precisely known, but what degree of alloy is in gold and silver can be exactly found out. Gold and silver were therefore fixed upon as the most exact standard to compare goods with, and were therefore considered as the most proper measure of value.

In consequence of gold and silver becoming the measure of value, it came also to be the instrument of commerce. It soon became necessary that goods should be carried to market, and they could never be cleverly exchanged unless the measure of value was also the instrument of commerce. In the age of shepherds it might be no great inconvenience that cattle should be the medium of exchange, as the expence of maintaining them was nothing, the whole country being considered as one great common; but when lands came to be divided, and the division of labour introduced, this custom would be productive of very considerable inconveniences. The butcher and shoemaker might at times have no use for one another's commodities. The farmer very often cannot maintain upon his ground a cow more than he has. It would be a very great hardship on a Glasgow merchant to give him a cow for one of his commodities. To remedy this, those materials which were before considered as the measure of value, came also to be the instrument of exchange. Gold and silver had all advantages. They can be kept without expence, they do not waste, and they are very portable. Gold and silver, however, do not derive their whole utility from being the medium of exchange; though they never had been used as money, they are more valuable than any other metals. They have a superior beauty, are capable of a finer polish, and are more proper for making any instrument, except those with an edge. For all these reasons, gold and silver came to be the proper measure of value, and the instrument of exchange. . . .

Of the Causes of the slow Progress of Opulence

We come now to the next thing proposed, to examine the causes of the slow progress of opulence. When one considers the effects of the division of labour, what an immediate tendency it has to improve the arts, it appears somewhat surprising that every nation should continue so long in a poor and indigent state as we find it does. The causes of this may be considered under these two heads: first, natural impediments; and secondly, the oppression of civil government.

A rude and barbarous people are ignorant of the effects of the division of labour, and it is long before one person, by continually working at different things, can produce any more than is necessary for his daily subsistence. Before labour can be divided some accumulation of stock is necessary; a poor man with no stock can never begin a manufacture. Before a man can commence farming, he must at least have laid in a year's provision, because he does not receive the fruits of his labour till the end of the season. Agreeably to this, in a nation of hunters or shepherds no person can quit the common trade in which he is employed, and which affords him daily subsistence, till he have some stock to maintain him, and begin the new trade. Every one knows how difficult it is, even in a refined society, to raise one's self to moderate circumstances. It is still more difficult to raise one's self by those trades which require no art nor ingenuity. A porter or day-labourer must continue poor forever. In the beginnings of society this is still more difficult. Bare subsistence is almost all that a savage can procure, and having no stock to begin upon, nothing to maintain him but what is produced by the exertion of his own strength, it is no wonder he continues long in an indigent state. The meanest labourer in a polished society has in many respects an advantage over a savage: he has more assistance in his labour; he has only one particular thing to do, which, by assiduity, he attains a facility in performing; he has also machines and instruments which greatly assist him. An Indian has not so much as a pickaxe, a spade, or a shovel, nor anything else but his own labour. This is one great cause of the slow progress of opulence in every country; till some stock be produced there can be no division of labour, and before a division of labour takes place there can be very little accumulation of stock.

The other cause that was assigned was the nature of civil government. In the infancy of society, as has been often observed, government must be weak and feeble, and it is long before its authority can protect the industry of individuals from the rapacity of their neighbours. When people find themselves every moment in danger of being robbed of all they possess, they have no motive to be industrious. There could be little accumulation of stock, because the indolent, which would be the greatest number, would live upon the industrious, and spend whatever they produced. When the power of government becomes so great as to defend the produce of industry, another obstacle arises from a different quarter. Among neighbouring nations in a barbarous state there are perpetual wars, one continually invading and plundering the other, and though private property be secured from the violence of neighbours, it is in danger from hostile invasions. In this manner it is next to impossible that any accumulation of stock can be made. It is observable that among savage nations there are always more violent convulsions than among those farther advanced in refinement. Among the Tartars and Arabs, great bands of barbarians are always roaming from one place to another in quest of plunder, and they pillage every country as they go along. Thus large tracts of country are often laid waste, and all the effects carried away. Germany too was in the same condition about the fall of the Roman Empire; nothing can be more an obstacle to the progress of opulence. . . .

The Theory of Moral Sentiments

The Theory of Moral Sentiments was probably valued by Smith as highly as *The Wealth of Nations*. At least we know that he continued to revise it through six editions, the latest and most important being published in 1790, shortly before his death. Yet, compared with the immense fame of the later book, the earlier is shrouded in neglect. Few people have heard of the *Moral Sentiments*; fewer still have read it. But Smith was right. The book is a masterpiece, and its devotees make up for the fewness of their numbers by the fervor of their admiration.

Withal, *The Theory of Moral Sentiments* is not an easy book to read unless one knows in advance what to expect from it. To begin with, it is written in an ornamented and oratorical style very different from most modern books (and indeed, from Smith's *Wealth*). This is the consequence of the book's origin. Like the *Lectures on Jurisprudence*, the *Moral Sentiments* were delivered as lectures to an audience of fourteen- to sixteen-year-old students who must have required dramatic anecdotes and striking turns of phrase to grasp the argument, or perhaps simply to stay awake. If we read the book "aloud," allowing Smith's phrases to reverberate in our minds, it will speak to us as vividly as it did, by all accounts, to its original audience. Reading it in the modern manner will only reduce it to a blur.

It is, however, more than style and pace that must be understood if the book is to exert its charms. We must also understand what the book is about; and this is not a simple matter to explain because the *Sentiments* contains a number of distinct although intertwined themes. It is, as the title announces, a "theory" of "moral sentiments." By this we mean that it is a reasoned explanation of the manner in which we form moral judgments—the way in which we arrive at canons of virtue and criteria of vice. As we shall see, Smith has a novel and extremely interesting explanation to offer, one that can be easily translated from the old-fashioned language in which it is expressed into modern psychoanalytic and sociological terms.

Connected with this central problem is a discussion of the Invisible Hand, the name that Smith gives to the covert intervention of the Deity into the affairs of humankind. We are used to thinking of the Invisible Hand as a term that describes the manner in which a free market economy is kept on an even course despite the absence of any steersman. But as we shall see, the Invisible Hand plays a far more important role than that of a ghostly economic planner. Without it, neither morality nor social order would be possible.

This brings us to yet a third theme of the *Sentiments*, one that is directly connected with the Invisible Hand but only indirectly linked to the problem of morality. This is the issue of social stability and dependable hierarchy—a social condition that (we may recall) Smith deemed to be more important even than the relief of misery. A socially stable society is a prerequisite for an economically successful one. Thus Smith explores the basis for the society described in *The Wealth of Nations* in the pages of the *Sentiments*.

THE SYMPATHY PRINCIPLE

The Theory of Moral Sentiments is therefore a book that must be read at many levels. The first of these is undoubtedly Smith's explanation of morality. How can human beings, who are presumably captives of their own self-interest, suspend selfish considerations to form disinterested, "moral" judgments? Smith gives us his answer in the opening sentence of the first chapter: "How selfish soever man may be supposed, there are evidently some principles in his nature, which interest him in the fortune of others, and render their happiness necessary to him, though he derives nothing from it, except the pleasure of seeing it."

This is the famous sympathy principle on which Smith will build his theory of morality. We would call it "empathy" or perhaps give it the name of psychic projection or identification. Smith's vocabulary may be old-fashioned but there is no mistaking the propensity to which he calls attention: "When we see a stroke aimed, and just ready to fall upon the leg or arm of another person, we naturally shrink and draw back our own leg or our own arm; and when it does fall, we feel it in some measure, and are hurt by it as well as the sufferer."[1]

Sympathy is, however, only the "original passion"—or as we might describe it, the latent capacity, on which Smith will erect his theory of moral judgments. For it is immediately apparent that in many situations we do not spontaneously identify with the emotions of the actor. "The furious behavior of an angry man," Smith writes, "is more likely to exasperate us against himself than against his enemies."[2] The nature of our moral reaction therefore awaits our discovery of the causes for our fellow man's anger. To put it differently, our sympathy depends on our ability to approve of another's behavior because it is *appropriate* to the situation. Until we understand the context of another's behavior, we cannot know whether our own emotional response will be one of positive sympathy or negative revulsion, of approval or disgust.

Now we begin to come closer to Smith's explanation for our moral sentiments. Because our ability to extend sympathy depends so greatly on our being able to "go along with" the feelings of the actor, the latter will do everything possible to make his actions congenial to ourselves. The angry man will choke back his wrath to win the sympathy of his audience; the successful man will take care not to crow over his success, lest he alienate his friends. From here it is only a step to explain the manner in which *we* act, when it is ourselves who are the judged, not the judges. The answer is that we put ourselves in the position of a vicarious spectator, and "tune" our

---

1. Smith, *Moral Sentiments*, pp. 9, 10.   2. Ibid, p. 11.

behavior to the pitch that we know from experience will seem appropriate to others. Thus the extension of the sympathy principle leads to an explanation of moral sentiments. In a society of perfect liberty, we are no longer constrained by traditional moral codes any more than by an ordained social position. We are free to "realize" ourselves according to our capacities and ambitions. Does this not threaten us with social anarchy and moral disarray? No, says Smith, because the inescapable bond of sympathy will force upon us a socially approved mode of behavior. Sympathy will stabilize our social conduct, and it will normalize—literally "norm"-alize—our standards. At their crudest, these norms are no more than modes of behavior calculated to win approval. But gradually they become idealized modes—the behavior that an "impartial" spectator would find fitting. In this way, says Smith, we progress from the level of merely wishing to be praised to that of being *worthy* of praise, even though the actual spectator of our actions may condemn them because he does not know the full reasons for our behavior.

THE VOICE OF CONSCIENCE

The elaboration of the sympathy principle covers many pages in the *Moral Sentiments* as Smith explores its workings in different situations. Readers who follow his argument in the readings ahead will see how the principle applies in cases that involve our self-interest, in cases involving our benevolence, and in those concerning our determinations of justice. Smith helps us see how the principle of sympathy must be invoked in each category to determine the appropriate degree of self-interest, the proper display of benevolence, the desirable strictness of justice. Virtue—Smith's word for the embodiment of morality—is therefore not reducible to fixed rules. It is always mediated by the empathetic properties of human understanding. Morality is not given to us, but made by ourselves.

There are obviously attractive features to such a human view of moral sentiments, and it must be obvious as well that this view accords naturally with the Enlightenment project of freeing man from the thralldom of unexamined and oppressive standards of right and wrong. Nevertheless, it has grave difficulties. Perhaps the most important is that we have no way of explaining how or why humankind rises from the mere expediency of seeking praise to the genuine morality of seeking to be praiseworthy. Again and again Smith has to fall back on a higher standard of judgment than that of our desire to win sympathy, but he has no rationale for explaining why he does so.[3]

A marvelous story recounted in the *Moral Sentiments* brings out the point at issue. It concerns the reactions of a "man of humanity" in Europe on learning of a fearful earthquake that has swallowed up millions of Chinese. How would such a man behave? He would, Smith supposes, "make many melancholy reflections upon the precariousness of human life, and the vanity of all the labours of man, which could thus be annihilated in a moment. He would, too, perhaps, if he was a man of speculation, enter into many reasonings concerning the effects which this disaster might produce upon

3. See Alisdair MacIntyre, *After Virtue* (Notre Dame, Illinois; Notre Dame Press, 1981).

the commerce of Europe, and the trade and business of the world in general." And yet, when all this "fine philosophy" was over, would our man of humanity be much affected by this catastrophe? He would not. As Smith tells it, he would "pursue his business or his pleasure, take his repose or his diversion, with the same ease and tranquillity as if no such accident had happened."[4]

But now suppose, Smith says, that our man were told he was to lose his little finger on the morrow. A very different reaction would attend this "frivolous disaster." Our man will be put into a state of anguish and torment, whereas "provided he never saw them, he will snore with the most profound security over the ruin of a hundred millions of his brethren."[5]

At this point Smith asks the terrible question. Since the hurt to a finger bulks so large, and a catastrophe in China so small, does it not follow that a man of humanity, given his choice, would prefer the loss of a hundred million Chinese to that of his finger? Smith's answer must have awakened the sleepiest of his students. "Human nature startles with horror at the thought, and the world, in its greatest depravity, never produced such a villain as could be capable of entertaining it."[6]

What stays the hand of self-interest in favor of that of altruism? Smith calls on the rescuing force of a higher principle than that of immediate interest. "It is reason, principle, conscience, the inhabitant of the breast, the man within, the great judge and arbiter of our conduct."[7] But whence come these higher principles of nature? No satisfactory answer that can be derived from the sympathy principle alone. What is necessary is that we assume human nature to contain such a saving element. The imperatives of duty and the voice of conscience must be there from the start, available to us in critical situations. They must be part of the human makeup, placed there by the Deity that has arranged for our collective well-being.

FROM SYMPATHY TO THE INVISIBLE HAND

These considerations bring us to the theme of the Invisible Hand, a theme that runs through all of the *Moral Sentiments*. The idea behind it is simple and appealing. Man is by his human nature incapable of foreseeing the consequences of his actions beyond a very narrow range. How then does he know what course to follow, when he cannot use his faculties to anticipate the outcome of his own actions, much less those of his fellow actors? The question is answered in much the same way as the provision of a sense of duty and conscience. The Deity, when he created the world, gave to humankind a surer guide than reason. This was the call of its passions.

Thus the Invisible Hand refers to the means by which "the Author of nature" has assured that humankind will achieve His purposes despite the frailty of its reasoning powers. The means are a number of powerful instincts and promptings that the Deity has instilled within us, which we obey because we have to, quite unconscious of their long-term social purpose. In this way, "without intending it; without knowing it" the pursuit of our immediate desires brings us to follow courses of action that would otherwise require a Godlike intelligence to pursue.

4. Smith, *Moral Sentiments*, p. 136.
5. Ibid., p. 136.
6. Ibid., pp. 136, 137.
7. Ibid., p. 137.

Two of these manifestations of the Invisible Hand are of particular importance in making the *Moral Sentiments* a foundation for the *Wealth*. The first describes how individuals are led by the promptings of their passions to seek wealth. Smith poses the question in the form of a little morality tale. "The poor man's son, whom heaven in its anger has visited with ambition, when he begins to look around him, admires the condition of the rich. He finds the cottage of his father too small for his accommodation, and fancies that he should be lodged more at ease in a palace. . . . He is enchanted with the prospect of the felicity [that money can buy]."[8]

Accordingly the smitten fool devotes his life to the arduous, helath-sapping labor required to amass a fortune. Alas, too late he discovers that "wealth and greatness are mere trinkets of frivolous utility . . . , enormous and operose machines contrived to produce a few trifling conveniences to the body . . . , immense fabrics which it requires a labour of a life to raise, which threaten every moment to overwhelm the person who dwells in them."[9]

There is a more serious purpose here than is evident in the rather sententious illustration. For Smith quickly goes on to say "it is well that nature imposes upon us in this manner." Why *well*? Because the Author of nature, in making us vulnerable to the blandishments of wealth, arouses us to superhuman efforts. In pursuit of the will-o'-wisp of money, we "cultivate the ground, build houses, found cities and commonwealths, invent and improve all the sciences and arts . . . , turn the rude forests into agreeable and fertile plains."[10] In short, the Invisible Hand has arranged for us to carry out the very prodigies of capitalism that Marx will praise in the *Communist Manifesto*.

In this way the unsocial actions of acquisitiveness, undertaken solely for private gain, are transmuted into the social act of creating wealth that will benefit all. The rich, to be sure, will take for their own what is most precious, but (says Smith) their consumptions are little more than those of the poor—he speaks, perhaps, of their consumption of foodstuffs. And so, Smith writes, in the first use of the shining phrase, "[the rich] are led by an invisible hand to make nearly the same distribution of the necessaries of life, which would have been made, had the earth been divided into equal portions among all its inhabitants, and thus without knowing it, without intending it, advance the interest of the society, and afford means to the multiplication of the species."[11]

FROM ACQUISITIVENESS TO ACQUIESCENCE

There is a good deal of cant in Smith's description of the benign outcome of the acquisitive drive, and the extensive changes made in the last edition of the *Sentiments* reveal an uneasy awareness that the blandishments of a commercial society might prove too strong for the attainment of a high standard of virtue.[12] Nevertheless, the point was never better made that the accumulation of wealth, although undertaken for private motives, eventuates in a useful social outcome that is no part of the intention of the capitalist. Whether this outcome is the consequence of the intentions of the Diety or

8. Ibid., p. 181.
9. Ibid., pp. 182–183.
10. Ibid., p. 185.

11. Ibid., p. 184–185.
12. I am indebted for this point to an unpublished paper by Professor Lawrence Dickey.

of an elaborate functional system, Smith has identified a connection between private motives and public outcomes that continues to fascinate all students of a market economy.

Let us look at one last instance of the manner in which our passions guide us to unintended and useful social outcomes. It too involves the drive for wealth—this time not as a means to bring about the accumulation of social riches, but as a means to adduce the necessary acquiesence in hierarchy or "rank." For the illusions of happiness that drive the poor man's son to his exhausting labors are widely, perhaps even universally, held. The fascination for wealth and power is far greater than that for wisdom and virtue. But here too we find the Invisible Hand at work. For "Nature has wisely judged," Smith tells us, "that the distinction of ranks, the peace and order of society [that is, the acquiescence in class differences without which social order cannot obtain], would rest more securely upon the plain and palpable difference of birth and fortune, than upon the invisible and often uncertain difference of wisdom and virtue. The undistinguishing eyes of the great mob of mankind can well enough perceive the former: it is with difficulty that the nice discernment of the wise and virtuous can sometimes distinguish the latter. In the order of all these recommendations, the benevolent wisdom of nature is equally evident."[13]

In this explanation of the manner in which humankind becomes acquisitive for wealth and acquiescent in social rank Smith has touched on problems that go very deep. We would not accept the dispensations of an Invisible Hand in explaining the insatiable quality of the drive for wealth or the ubiquitous tendency to look up to and admire the wealthy and famous, but it is plain that Smith has identified a social problem of enormous consequence. Men do seek wealth and they do submit willingly to structures of social inequality. If this were not the case, civilized society as we know it would not exist, and certainly capitalism could not count on the motives or the cohesion necessary for its existence.

The Theory of Moral Sentiments is thus, in its largest focus, a book about the socialization of men and women who have emerged from the straitjacket of a traditional, often dogmatic social order, and must create a workable system of morality and social order in a new condition of "perfect" liberty. Smith shows us that the liberty is not perfect. There remain powerful constraints and impulses within us that impose an orderliness on society whether we will it or not. Whether that order owes its origins or its forms to the Deity or to elemental aspects of the human psyche, we can now begin to appreciate the ambitious reach of Smith's project and the extraordinary breadth of his second greatest book.

READINGS

All the readings that follow are from the *Moral Sentiments* in its sixth and last edition.* I shall not try to describe them in close detail, for that would require a running commentary much longer than this introductory over-

*The condensation that follows spans the first six parts of the *Sentiments*, but omits entirely Part VII, a review of "Systems of Moral Philosophy." Other editorial changes follow the guidelines of the previous readings.

13. Ibid., p. 226.

view. I would suggest that the casual reader begin by reading—*slowly* and "aloud"—the initial chapter on Sympathy, following thereafter with the various passions and situations that Smith describes, as long as his or her interest is sustained. One does not have to read it all to appreciate the work. There are a few sections not to be missed on any account. One of them is the full description of the "man of humanity" confronted with the choice between saving China or his finger, on page 106. Another is the passage about the poor man's son, visited by ambition, and his redemption by the Invisible Hand, page 119. A third is the wonderful chapter on "The Origin of Ambition, and of the Distinctions of Rank" (p. 78 following) and its successor chapter on "The Corruption of our Moral Sentiments," starting on page 86.

There are, I need hardly say, ten passages that are someone's favorite for every one that I have mentioned. Let me conclude by repeating what I have said at the outset. This is an extraordinary book, shot through with piercing social observations and intimate thrusts. It requires, but it will richly reward, a leisured reading, pencil in hand to mark the best parts. Above all, I should add, it is the perfect preparation for the book to follow.

THE

THEORY

OF

MORAL SENTIMENTS.

By ADAM SMITH,
PROFESSOR of MORAL PHILOSOPHY in the
Univerſity of GLASGOW.

LONDON:
Printed for A. MILLAR, in the STRAND;
And A. KINCAID and J. BELL, in EDINBURGH.
M DCC LIX.

Title-page of edition 1

OF THE PROPRIETY OF ACTION
CONSISTING OF THREE SECTIONS

SECTION I
Of the Sense of Propriety

CHAPTER I
Of Sympathy

How selfish soever man may be supposed, there are evidently some principles in his nature, which interest him in the fortune of others, and render their happiness necessary to him, though he derives nothing from it except the pleasure of seeing it. Of this kind is pity or compassion, the emotion which we feel for the misery of others, when we either see it, or are made to conceive it in a very lively manner. That we often derive sorrow from the sorrow of others, is a matter of fact too obvious to require any instances to prove it; for this sentiment, like all the other original passions of human nature, is by no means confined to the virtuous and humane, though they perhaps may feel it with the most exquisite sensibility. The greatest ruffian, the most hardened violator of the laws of society, is not altogether without it.

As we have no immediate experience of what other men feel, we can form no idea of the manner in which they are affected, but by conceiving what we ourselves should feel in the like situation. Though our brother is upon the rack, as long as we ourselves are at our ease, our senses will never inform us of what he suffers. They never did, and never can, carry us beyond our own person, and it is by the imagination only that we can form any conception of what are his sensations. Neither can that faculty help us to this any other way, than by representing to us what would be our own, if we were in his case. It is the impressions of our own senses only, not those of his, which our imaginations copy. By the imagination we place ourselves in his situation, we conceive ourselves enduring all the same torments, we enter as it were into his body, and become in some measure the same person with him, and thence form some idea of his sensations, and even feel something which, though weaker in degree, is not altogether unlike them. His agonies, when they are thus brought home to ourselves, when we have thus adopted and made them our own, begin at last to affect us, and we then tremble and shudder at the thought of what he feels. For as to be in pain or distress of any kind excites the most excessive sorrow, so to conceive or to imagine that we are in it, excites some degree of the same emotion, in proportion to the vivacity or dullness of the conception.

That this is the source of our fellow-feeling for the misery of others, that it is by changing places in fancy with the sufferer, that we come either to conceive or to be affected by what he feels, may be demonstrated by many obvious observations, if it should not be thought sufficiently evident of itself. When we see a stroke aimed and just ready to fall upon the leg or arm of another person, we naturally shrink and draw back our own leg or our own arm; and when it does fall, we feel it in some measure, and are hurt by it as well as the sufferer. The mob, when they are gazing at a dancer on the slack rope, naturally writhe and twist and balance their own bodies, as they see him do, and as they feel that they themselves must do if in his situation. Persons of delicate fibres and a weak constitution of body complain, that in looking on the sores and ulcers which are exposed by beggars in the streets, they are apt to feel an itching or uneasy sensation in the correspondent part of their own bodies. The horror which they conceive at the misery of those wretches affects that particular part in themselves more than any other; because that horror arises from conceiving what they themselves would suffer, if they really were the wretches whom they are looking upon, and if that particular part in themselves was actually affected in the same miserable manner. The very force of this conception is sufficient, in their feeble frames, to produce that itching or uneasy sensation complained of. Men of the most robust make, observe that in looking upon sore eyes they often feel a very sensible soreness in their own, which proceeds from the same reason; that organ being in the strongest man more delicate, than any other part of the body is in the weakest.

Neither is it those circumstances only, which create pain or sorrow, that call forth our fellow-feeling. Whatever is the passion which arises from any object in the person principally concerned, an analogous emotion springs up, at the thought of his situation, in the breast of every attentive spectator. Our joy for the deliverance of those heroes of tragedy or romance who interest us, is as sincere as our grief for their distress, and our fellow-feeling with their misery is not more real than that with their happiness. We enter into their gratitude towards those faithful friends who did not desert them in their difficulties; and we heartily go along with their resentment against those perfidious traitors who injured, abandoned, or deceived them. In every passion of which the mind of man is susceptible, the emotions of the bystander always correspond to what, by bringing the case home to himself, he imagines should be the sentiments of the sufferer.

Pity and compassion are words appropriated to signify our fellow-feeling with the sorrow of others. Sympathy, though its meaning was, perhaps, originally the same, may now, however, without much impropriety, be made use of to denote our fellow-feeling with any passion whatever.

Upon some occasions sympathy may seem to arise merely from the view of a certain emotion in another person. The passions, upon some occasions, may seem to be transfused from one man to another, instantaneously, and antecedent to any knowledge of what excited them in the person principally concerned. Grief and joy, for example, strongly expressed in the look and gestures of any one, at once affect the spectator with some degree of a like painful or agreeable emotion. A smiling face is, to every body that sees it, a cheerful object; as a sorrowful countenance, on the other hand, is a melancholy one.

This, however, does not hold universally, or with regard to every passion. There are some passions of which the expressions excite no sort of sympathy, but before we are acquainted with what gave occasion to them, serve rather to disgust and provoke us against them. The furious behaviour of an angry man is more likely to exasperate us against himself than against his enemies. As we are unacquainted with his provocation, we cannot bring his case home to ourselves, nor conceive any thing like the passions which it excites. But we plainly see what is the situation of those with whom he is angry, and to what violence they may be exposed from so enraged an adversary. We readily, therefore, sympathize with their fear or resentment, and are immediately disposed to take part against the man from whom they appear to be in so much danger.

If the very appearances of grief and joy inspire us with some degree of the like emotions, it is because they suggest to us the general idea of some good or bad fortune that has befallen the person in whom we observe them: and in these passions this is sufficient to have some little influence upon us. The effects of grief and joy terminate in the person who feels those emotions, of which the expressions do not, like those of resentment, suggest to us the idea of any other person for whom we are concerned, and whose interests are opposite to his. The general idea of good or bad fortune, therefore, creates some concern for the person who has met with it, but the general idea of provocation excites no sympathy with the anger of the man who has received it. Nature, it seems, teaches us to be more averse to enter into this passion, and, till informed of its cause, to be disposed rather to take part against it.

Even our sympathy with the grief or joy of another, before we are informed of the cause of either, is always extremely imperfect. General lamentations, which express nothing but the anguish of the sufferer, create rather a curiosity to inquire into his situation, along with some disposition to sympathize with him, than any actual sympathy that is very sensible. The first question which we ask is, What has befallen you? Till this be answered, though we are uneasy both from the vague idea of his misfortune, and still more from torturing ourselves with conjectures about what it may be, yet our fellow-feeling is not very considerable.

Sympathy, therefore, does not arise so much from the view of the passion, as from that of the situation which excites it. We sometimes feel for another, a passion of which he himself seems to be altogether incapable; because, when we put ourselves in his case, that passion arises in our breast from the imagination, though it does not in his from the reality. We blush for the impudence and rudeness of another, though he himself appears to have no sense of the impropriety of his own behaviour; because we cannot help feeling with what confusion we ourselves should be covered, had we behaved in so absurd a manner.

Of all the calamities to which the condition of mortality exposes mankind, the loss of reason appears, to those who have the least spark of humanity, by far the most dreadful, and they behold that last stage of human wretchedness with deeper commiseration than any other. But the poor wretch, who is in it, laughs and sings perhaps, and is altogether insensible of his own misery. The anguish which humanity feels, therefore, at the sight of such an object, cannot be the reflection of any sentiment of the sufferer. The compassion of the spectator must arise altogether from the consideration of what he himself would feel if he was reduced to the same unhappy situation, and, what perhaps is impossible, was at the same time able to regard it with his present reason and judgment.

What are the pangs of a mother, when she hears the moanings of her infant that during the agony of disease cannot express what it feels? In her idea of what it suffers, she joins, to its real helplessness, her own consciousness of that helplessness, and her own terrors for the unknown consequences of its disorder; and out of all these, forms, for her own sorrow, the most complete image of misery and distress. The infant, however, feels only the uneasiness of the present instant, which can never be great. With regard to the future, it is perfectly secure, and in its thoughtlessness and want of foresight, possesses an antidote against fear and anxiety, the great tormentors of the human breast, from which reason and philosophy will, in vain, attempt to defend it, when it grows up to a man.

We sympathize even with the dead, and overlooking what is of real importance in their situation, that awful futurity which awaits them, we are chiefly affected by those circumstances which strike our senses, but can have no influence upon their happiness. It is miserable, we think, to be deprived of the light of the sun; to be shut out from life and conversation; to be laid in the cold grave, a prey to corruption and the reptiles of the earth; to be no more thought of in this world, but to be obliterated, in a little time, from the affections, and almost from the memory, of their dearest friends and relations. Surely, we imagine, we can never feel too much for those who have suffered so dreadful a calamity. The tribute of our fellow-feeling seems doubly due to them now, when they are in danger of being forgot by every body; and, by the vain honours which we pay to their memory, we endeavour, for our own misery, artificially to keep alive our melancholy remembrance of their misfortune. That our sympathy can afford them no consolation seems to be an addition to their calamity; and to think that all we can do is unavailing, and that, what alleviates all other distress, the regret, the love, and the lamentations of their friends, can yield no comfort to them, serves only to exasperate our sense of their misery. The happiness of the dead, however, most assuredly, is affected by none of these circumstances; nor is it the thought of these things which can ever disturb the profound security of their repose. The idea of that dreary and endless melancholy, which the fancy naturally ascribes to their condition, arises altogether from our joining to the change which has been produced upon them, our own consciousness of that change, from our putting ourselves in their situation, and from our lodging, if I may be allowed to say so, our own living souls in their inanimated bodies, and thence conceiving what would be our emotions in this case. It is from this very illusion of the imagination, that the foresight of our own dissolution is so terrible to us, and that the idea of those circumstances, which undoubtedly can give us no pain when we are dead, makes us miserable while we are alive. And from thence arises one of the most important principles in human nature, the dread of death, the great poison to the happiness, but the great restraint upon the injustice of mankind, which, while it afflicts and mortifies the individual, guards and protects the society.

CHAPTER II

Of the pleasure of mutual sympathy

[This chapter expands on the theme of the title. The gist can be put in a single excerpt: "Nothing pleases us more than to observe in other men a fellow-feeling with all the emotions of our own breast."]

CHAPTER III

*Of the manner in which we judge of the propriety
or impropriety of the affections of other men, by their concord or
dissonance with our own*

When the original passions of the person principally concerned are in perfect concord with the sympathetic emotions of the spectator, they necessarily appear to this last just and proper, and suitable to their objects; and, on the contrary, when, upon bringing the case home to himself, he finds that they do not coincide with what he feels, they necessarily appear to him unjust and improper, and unsuitable to the causes which excite them.

To approve of the passions of another, therefore, as suitable to their objects, is the same thing as to observe that we entirely sympathize with them; and not to approve of them as such, is the same thing as to observe that we do not entirely sympathize with them. The man who resents the injuries that have been done to me, and observes that I resent them precisely as he does, necessarily approves of my resentment. The man whose sympathy keeps time to my grief, cannot but admit the reasonableness of my sorrow. He who admires the same poem, or the same picture, and admires them exactly as I do, must surely allow the justness of my admiration. He who laughs at the same joke, and laughs along with me, cannot well deny the propriety of my laughter. On the contrary, the person who, upon these different occasions, either feels no such emotion as that which I feel, or feels none that bears any proportion to mine, cannot avoid disapproving my sentiments on account of their dissonance with his own. If my animosity goes beyond what the indignation of my friend can correspond to; if my grief exceeds what his most tender compassion can go along with; if my admiration is either too high or too low to tally with his own; if I laugh loud and heartily when he only smiles, or, on the contrary, only smile when he laughs loud and heartily; in all these cases, as soon as he comes from considering the object, to observe how I am affected by it, according as there is more or less disproportion between his sentiments and mine, I must incur a greater or less degree of his disapprobation: and upon all occasions his own sentiments are the standards and measures by which he judges of mine.

To approve of another man's opinions is to adopt those opinions, and to adopt them is to approve of them. If the same arguments which convince you convince me likewise, I necessarily approve of your conviction; and if they do not, I necessarily disapprove of it: neither can I possibly conceive that I should do the one without the other. To approve or disapprove, therefore, of the opinions of others is acknowledged, by every body, to mean no more than to observe their agreement or disagreement with our own. But this is equally the case with regard to our approbation or disapprobation of the sentiments or passions of others.

There are, indeed, some cases in which we seem to approve without any sympathy or correspondence of sentiments, and in which, consequently, the sentiment of approbation would seem to be different from the perception of this coincidence. A little attention, however, will convince us that even in these cases our approbation is ultimately founded upon a sympathy or correspondence of this kind. I shall give an instance in things of a very frivolous nature, because in them the judgments of mankind are less apt to be perverted by wrong systems. We may often approve of a jest, and think the laughter of the company quite just and proper, though we ourselves do not laugh, because, perhaps, we are in a grave humour, or happen to have our attention engaged with other objects. We have learned, however, from experience, what sort of pleasantry is upon most occasions capable of making us laugh, and we observe that this is one of that kind. We approve, therefore, of the laughter of the company, and feel that it is natural and suitable to its object; because, though in our present mood we cannot easily enter into it, we are sensible that upon most occasions we should very heartily join in it.

The same thing often happens with regard to all the other passions. A stranger passes by us in the street with all the marks of the deepest affliction; and we are immediately told that he has just received the news of the death of his father. It is impossible that, in this case, we should not approve of his grief. Yet it may often happen, without any defect of humanity on our part, that, so far from entering into the violence of his sorrow, we should scarce conceive the first movements of concern upon his account. Both he and his father, perhaps, are entirely unknown to us, or we happen to be employed about other things, and do not take time to picture out in our imagination the different circumstances of distress which must occur to him. We have learned, however, from experience, that such a misfortune naturally excites such a degree of sorrow, and we know that if we took time to consider his situation, fully and in all its parts, we should, without doubt, most sincerely sympathize with him. It is upon the consciousness of this conditional sympathy, that our approbation of his sorrow is founded, even in those cases in which that sympathy does not actually take place; and the general rules derived from our preceding experience of what our sentiments would commonly correspond with, correct upon this, as upon many other occasions, the impropriety of our present emotions.

The sentiment or affection of the heart from which any action proceeds, and upon which its whole virtue or vice must ultimately depend, may be considered under two different aspects, or in two different relations; first, in relation to the cause which excites it, or the motive which gives occasion to it; and secondly, in relation to the end which it proposes, or the effect which it tends to produce.

In the suitableness or unsuitableness, in the proportion or disproportion which the affection seems to bear to the cause or object which excites it, consists the propriety or impropriety, the decency or ungracefulness of the consequent action.

In the beneficial or hurtful nature of the effects which the affection aims at, or tends to produce, consists the merit or demerit of the action, the qualities by which it is entitled to reward, or is deserving of punishment.

Philosophers have, of late years, considered chiefly the tendency of affections, and have given little attention to the relation which they stand in to the cause which excites them. In common life, however, when we judge of any person's conduct, and of the sentiments which directed it, we constantly consider them under both these aspects. When we blame in another man the excesses of love, of grief, of resentment, we not only consider the ruinous effects which they tend to produce, but the little occasion which was given for them. The merit of his favourite, we say, is not so great, his misfortune is not so dreadful, his provocation is not so extraordinary, as to justify so violent a passion. We should have indulged, we say; perhaps, have approved of the violence of his emotion, had the cause been in any respect proportioned to it.

When we judge in this manner of any affection, as proportioned or disproportioned to the cause which excites it, it is scarce possible that we should make use of any other rule or canon but the correspondent affection in ourselves. If, upon bringing the case home to our own breast, we find that the sentiments which it gives occasion to, coincide and tally with our own, we necessarily approve of them as proportioned and suitable to their objects; if otherwise, we necessarily disapprove of them, as extravagant and out of proportion.

Every faculty in one man is the measure by which he judges of the like faculty in another. I judge of your sight by my sight, of your ear by my ear, of your reason by my reason, of your resentment by my resentment, of your love by my love. I neither have, nor can have, any other way of judging about them.

CHAPTER IV

The same subject continued

We may judge of the propriety or impropriety of the sentiments of another person by their correspondence or disagreement with our own, upon two different occasions; either, first, when the objects which excite them are considered without any peculiar relation, either to ourselves or to the person whose sentiments we judge of; or, secondly, when they are considered as peculiarly affecting one or other of us.

1. With regard to those objects which are considered without any peculiar relation either to ourselves or to the person whose sentiments we judge of; wherever his sentiments entirely correspond with our own, we ascribe to him the qualities of taste and good judgment. The beauty of a plain, the greatness of a mountain, the ornaments of a building, the expression of a picture, the composition of a discourse, the conduct of a third person, the proportions of different quantities and numbers, the various appearances which the great machine of the universe is perpetually exhibiting, with the secret wheels and springs which produce them; all the general subjects of science and taste, are what we and our companion regard as having no peculiar relation to either of us. We both look at them from the same point of view, and we have no occasion for sympathy, or for that imaginary change of situations from which it arises, in order to produce, with regard to these, the most perfect harmony of sentiments and affections. If, notwithstanding, we are often differently affected, it arises either from the different degrees of attention, which our different habits of life allow us to give easily to the several parts of those complex objects, or from the different degrees of natural acuteness in the faculty of the mind to which they are addressed.

When the sentiments of our companion coincide with our own in things of this kind, which are obvious and easy, and in which, perhaps, we never found a single person who differed from us, though we, no doubt, must approve of them, yet he seems to deserve no praise or admiration on account of them. But when they not only coincide with our own, but lead and direct our own; when in forming them he appears to have attended to many things which we had overlooked, and to have adjusted them to all the various circumstances of their objects; we not only approve of them, but wonder and are surprised at their uncommon and unexpected acuteness and comprehensiveness, and he appears to deserve a very high degree of admiration and applause. For approbation heightened by wonder and surprise, constitutes the sentiment which is properly called admiration, and of which applause is the natural expression. The decision of the man who judges that exquisite beauty is preferable to the grossest deformity, or that twice two are equal to four, must certainly be approved of by all the world, but will not, surely, be much admired. It is the acute and delicate discernment of the man of taste, who distinguishes the minute, and scarce perceptible differences of beauty and deformity; it is the comprehensive accuracy of the experienced mathematician, who unravels, with ease, the most intricate and perplexed proportions; it is the great leader in science and taste, the man who directs and conducts our own sentiments, the extent and superior justness of whose talents astonish us with wonder and surprise, who excites our admiration, and seems to deserve our applause: and upon this foundation is grounded the greater part of the praise which is bestowed upon what are called the intellectual virtues.

The utility of those qualities, it may be thought, is what first recommends them to us; and, no doubt, the consideration of this, when we come to attend to it, gives them a new value. Originally, however, we approve of another man's judgement, not as something useful, but as right, as accurate, as agreeable to truth and reality: and it is evident we attribute those qualities to it for no other reason but because we find that it agrees with our own. Taste, in the same manner, is originally approved of, not as useful, but as just, as delicate, and as precisely suited to its object. The idea of the utility of all qualities of this kind, is plainly an afterthought, and not what first recommends them to our approbation.

2. With regard to those objects, which affect in a particular manner either ourselves or the person whose sentiments we judge of, it is at once more difficult to preserve this harmony and correspondence, and at the same time, vastly more important. My companion does not naturally look upon the misfortune that has befallen me, or the injury that has been done me, from the same point of view in which I consider them. They affect me much more nearly. We do not view them from the same station, as we do a picture, or a poem, or a system of philosophy, and are, therefore, apt to be very differently affected by them. But I can much more easily overlook the want of this correspondence of sentiments with regard to such indifferent objects as concern neither me nor my companion, than with regard to what interests me so much as the misfortune that has befallen me, or the injury that has been done me.

Though you despise that picture, or that poem, or even that system of philosophy, which I admire, there is little danger of our quarrelling upon that account. Neither of us can reasonably be much interested about them. They ought all of them to be matters of great indifference to us both; so that, though our opinions may be opposite, our affections may still be very nearly the same. But it is quite otherwise with regard to those objects by which either you or I are particularly affected. Though your judgments in matters of speculation, though your sentiments in matters of taste, are quite opposite to mine, I can easily overlook this opposition; and if I have any degree of temper, I may still find some entertainment in your conversation, even upon those very subjects. But if you have either no fellow-feeling for the misfortunes I have met with, or none that bears any proportion to the grief which distracts me; or if you have either no indignation at the injuries I have suffered, or none that bears any proportion to the resentment which transports me, we can no longer converse upon these subjects. We become intolerable to one another. I can neither support your company, nor you mine. You are confounded at my violence and passion, and I am enraged at your cold insensibility and want of feeling.

In all such cases, that there may be some correspondence of sentiments between the spectator and the person principally concerned, the spectator must, first of all, endeavour, as much as he can, to put himself in the situation of the other, and to bring home to himself every little circumstance of distress which can possibly occur to the sufferer. He must adopt the whole case of his companion with all its minutest incidents; and strive to render as perfect as possible, that imaginary change of situation upon which his sympathy is founded.

After all this, however, the emotions of the spectator will still be very apt to fall short of the violence of what is felt by the sufferer. Mankind, though naturally sympathetic, never conceive, for what has befallen another, that degree of passion which naturally animates the person principally concerned. That imaginary change of situation, upon which their sympathy is founded, is but momentary. The thought of their own safety, the thought that they themselves are not really the sufferers, continually intrudes itself upon them; and though it does not hinder them from conceiving a passion somewhat analogous to what is felt by the sufferer, hinders them from conceiving any thing that approaches to the same degree of violence. The person principally concerned is sensible of this, and at the same time passionately desires a more complete sympathy. He longs for that relief which nothing can afford him but the entire concord of the affections of the spectators with his own. To see the emotions of their hearts, in every respect, beat time to his own, in the violent and disagreeable passions, constitutes his sole consolation. But he can only hope to obtain this by lowering his passion to that pitch, in which the spectators are capable of going along with him. He must flatten, if I may be allowed to say so, the sharpness of its natural tone, in order to reduce it to harmony and concord with the emotions of those who are about him. What they feel, will, indeed, always be, in some respects, different from what he feels, and compassion can never be exactly the same with original sorrow; because the secret consciousness that the change of situations, from which the sympathetic sentiment arises, is but imaginary, not only lowers it in degree, but, in some measure, varies it in kind, and gives it a quite different modification. These two sentiments, however, may, it is evident, have such a correspondence with one another, as is sufficient for the harmony of society. Though they will never be unisons, they may be concords, and this is all that is wanted or required.

In order to produce this concord, as nature teaches the spectators to assume the circumstances of the person principally concerned, so she teaches this last in some measure to assume those of the spectators. As they are continually placing themselves in his situation, and thence conceiving emotions similar to what he feels; so he is as constantly placing himself in theirs, and thence conceiving some degree of that coolness about his own fortune, with which he is sensible that they will view it. As they are constantly considering what they themselves would feel, if they actually were the sufferers, so he is as constantly led to imagine in what manner he would be affected if he was only one of the spectators of his own situation. As their sympathy makes them look at it, in some measure, with his eyes, so his sympathy makes him look at it, in some measure, with theirs, especially when in their presence and acting under their observation: and as the reflected passion, which he thus conceives, is much weaker than the original one, it necessarily abates the violence of what he felt before he came into their presence, before he began to recollect in what manner they would be affected by it, and to view his situation in this candid and impartial light.

The mind, therefore, is rarely so disturbed, but that the company of a friend will restore it to some degree of tranquillity and sedateness. The breast is, in some measure, calmed and composed the moment we come into his presence. We are immediately put in mind of the light in which he will view our situation, and we begin to view it ourselves in the same light; for the effect of sympathy is instantaneous. We expect less sympathy from a common acquaintance than from a friend: we cannot open to the former all those little circumstances which we can unfold to the latter: we assume, therefore, more tranquillity before him, and endeavour to fix our thoughts upon those general outlines of our situation which he is willing to consider. We expect still less sympathy from an assembly of strangers, and we assume, therefore, still more tranquillity before them, and always endeavour to bring down our passion to that pitch, which the particular company we are in may be expected to go along with. Nor is this only an assumed appearance: for if we are at all masters of ourselves, the presence of a mere acquaintance will really compose us, still more than that of a friend; and that of an assembly of strangers still more than that of an acquaintance.

Society and conversation, therefore, are the most powerful remedies for restoring the mind to its tranquillity, if, at any time, it has unfortunately lost it; as well as the best preservatives of that equal and happy temper, which is so necessary to self-satisfaction and enjoyment. Men of retirement and speculation, who are apt to sit brooding at home over either grief or resentment, though they may often have more humanity, more generosity, and a nicer sense of honour, yet seldom possess that equality of temper which is so common among men of the world.

CHAPTER V

Of the amiable and respectable virtues

Upon these two different efforts, upon that of the spectator to enter into the sentiments of the person principally concerned, and upon that of the person principally concerned, to bring down his emotions to what the spectator can go along with, are founded two different sets of virtues. The soft, the gentle, the amiable virtues, the virtues of candid condescension and indulgent humanity, are founded upon the one: the great, the awful and respectable, the virtues of self-denial, of self-government, of that command of the passions which subjects all the movements of our nature to what our own dignity and honour, and the propriety of our own conduct require, take their origin from the other.

How amiable does he appear to be, whose sympathetic heart seems to reecho all the sentiments of those with whom he converses, who grieves for their calamities, who resents their injuries, and who rejoices at their good fortune! When we bring home to ourselves the situation of his companions, we enter into their gratitude, and feel what consolation they must derive from the tender sympathy of so affectionate a friend. And for a contrary reason, how disagreeable does he appear to be, whose hard and obdurate heart feels for himself only, but is altogether insensible to the happiness or misery of others! We enter, in this case too, into the pain which his presence must give to every mortal with whom he converses, to those especially with whom we are most apt to sympathize, the unfortunate and the injured.

On the other hand, what noble propriety and grace do we feel in the conduct of those who, in their own case, exert that recollection and self-command which constitute the dignity of every passion, and which bring it down to what others can enter into! We are disgusted with that clamorous grief, which, without any delicacy, calls upon our compassion with sighs and tears and importunate lamentations. But we reverence that reserved, that silent and majestic sorrow, which discovers itself only in the swelling of the eyes, in the quivering of the lips and cheeks, and in the distant, but affecting, coldness of the whole behavior. It imposes the like silence upon us. We regard it with respectful attention, and

watch with anxious concern over our whole behaviour, lest by any
impropriety we should disturb that concerted tranquillity, which it requires
so great an effort to support.

The insolence and brutality of anger, in the same manner, when we
indulge its fury without check or restraint, is, of all objects, the most
detestable. But we admire that noble and generous resentment which
governs its pursuit of the greatest injuries, not by the rage which they
are apt to excite in the breast of the sufferer, but by the indignation
which they naturally call forth in that of the impartial spectator; which
allows no word, no gesture, to escape it beyond what this more equitable
sentiment would dictate; which never, even in thought, attempts any
greater vengeance, nor desires to inflict any greater punishment, than
what every indifferent person would rejoice to see executed.

And hence it is, that to feel much for others and little for ourselves,
that to restrain our selfish, and to indulge our benevolent affections,
constitutes the perfection of human nature; and can alone produce among
mankind that harmony of sentiments and passions in which consists
their whole grace and propriety. As to love our neighbour as we love
ourselves is the great law of Christianity, so it is the great precept of
nature to love ourselves only as we love our neighbour, or what comes
to the same thing, as our neighbour is capable of loving us. . . .

SECTION II

Of the Degrees of the different Passions which are consistent with Propriety

CHAPTER I

Of the Passions which take their origin from the body

CHAPTER II

Of those Passions which take their origin from a particular turn or habit of the Imagination

CHAPTER III

Of the unsocial Passions

CHAPTER IV

Of the social Passions

CHAPTER V

Of the selfish Passions

[We have excluded all of Part I, Section II. The five chapters in this section
form a detailed taxonomy of what Smith takes to be the primary passions.
Chapter 1 enumerates the bodily passions—pain, sex, and hunger. While

these may overwhelm us physiologically, they are only fleeting in duration. As always, Smith has a telling example to drive home his point: "the loss of a leg may generally be regarded as a more real calamity than the loss of a mistress . . . [but] nothing is so soon forgot as pain."

Love, which thus tends to linger, is considered in chapter 2. "All serious and strong expressions [of it] . . . appear ridiculous to a third person" says Smith. In chapter 3 Smith abruptly turns to the "unsocial" passions which originate in the imagination—hatred and resentment. It is here that the sympathy principle assumes a decisive role. The capacity consciously to identify with the feelings of others—our fellow-feeling—intervenes to bring these passions "down to a pitch much lower than that to which undisciplined nature would raise them." Accordingly, it is the social passions which "please the indifferent spectator upon almost every occasion." These include generosity, humanity and kindness, and are discussed in chapter 4.

Chapter 5 concludes the review of the passions, juxtaposing what Smith terms the "selfish passions," namely grief (or sorrow), with joy. Smith's comparison continues in chapter 1 of Part I, Section III, preparing the way for what is to follow.]

SECTION III

Of the Effects of Prosperity and Adversity upon the Judgment of Mankind with regard to the Propriety of Action; and why it is more easy to obtain their Approbation in the one state than in the other

CHAPTER I

That though our sympathy with sorrow is generally a more lively sensation than our sympathy with joy, it commonly falls much more short of the violence of what is naturally felt by the person principally concerned

CHAPTER II

Of the origin of Ambition, and of the distinction of Ranks

It is because mankind are disposed to sympathize more entirely with our joy than with our sorrow, that we make parade of our riches, and conceal our poverty. Nothing is so mortifying as to be obliged to expose our distress to the view of the public, and to feel, that though our situation is open to the eyes of all mankind, no mortal conceives for us the half of what we suffer. Nay, it is chiefly from this regard to the sentiments of mankind, that we pursue riches and avoid poverty. For to what purpose is all the toil and bustle of this world? what is the end of avarice and ambition, of the pursuit of wealth, of power, and preeminence? Is it to supply the necessities of nature? The wages of the meanest labourer can supply them. We see that they afford him food and clothing, the comfort of a house, and of a family. If we examined his economy with rigour, we should find that he spends a great part of them upon conveniences, which may be regarded as superfluities, and that, upon extraordinary occasions, he can give something even to vanity and distinction.

What then is the cause of our aversion to his situation, and why should those who have been educated in the higher ranks of life, regard it as worse than death, to be reduced to live, even without labour, upon the same simple fare with him, to dwell under the same lowly roof, and to be clothed in the same humble attire? Do they imagine that their stomach is better, or their sleep sounder in a palace than in a cottage? The contrary has been so often observed, and, indeed, is so very obvious, though it had never been observed, that there is nobody ignorant of it.

From whence, then, arises that emulation which runs through all the different ranks of men, and what are the advantages which we propose by that great purpose of human life which we call bettering our condition? To be observed, to be attended to, to be taken notice of with sympathy, complacency, and approbation, are all the advantages which we can propose to derive from it. It is the vanity, not the ease, or the pleasure, which interests us. But vanity is always founded upon the belief of our being the object of attention and approbation. The rich man glories in his riches, because he feels that they naturally draw upon him the attention of the world, and that mankind are disposed to go along with him in all those agreeable emotions with which the advantages of his situation so readily inspire him. At the thought of this, his heart seems to swell and dilate itself within him, and he is fonder of his wealth, upon this account, than for all the other advantages it procures him.

The poor man, on the contrary, is ashamed of his poverty. He feels that it either places him out of the sight of mankind, or, that if they take any notice of him, they have, however, scarce any fellow-feeling with the misery and distress which he suffers. He is mortified upon both accounts; for though to be overlooked, and to be disapproved of, are things entirely different, yet as obscurity covers us from the daylight of honour and approbation, to feel that we are taken no notice of, necessarily damps the most agreeable hope, and disappoints the most ardent desire, of human nature. The poor man goes out and comes in unheeded, and when in the midst of a crowd is in the same obscurity as if shut up in his own hovel. Those humble cares and painful attentions which occupy those in his situation, afford no amusement to the dissipated and the gay. They turn away their eyes from him, or if the extremity of his distress forces them to look at him, it is only to spurn so disagreeable an object from among them. The fortunate and the proud wonder at the insolence of human wretchedness, that it should dare to present itself before them, and with the loathsome aspect of its misery presume to disturb the serenity of their happiness.

The man of rank and distinction, on the contrary, is observed by all the world. Every body is eager to look at him, and to conceive, at least by sympathy, that joy and exultation with which his circumstances naturally inspire him. His actions are the objects of the public care. Scarce a word, scarce a gesture, can fall from him that is altogether neglected. In a great assembly he is the person upon whom all direct their eyes; it is upon him that their passions seem all to wait with expectation, in order to receive that movement and direction which he shall impress upon them; and if his behaviour is not altogether absurd, he has, every moment, an opportunity of interesting mankind, and of rendering himself the object of the observation and fellow-feeling of every body about him. It is this, which, notwithstanding the restraint it imposes, notwithstanding the loss of liberty with which it is attended, renders greatness the object of envy, and compensates, in the opinion of mankind, all that toil, all that anxiety, all those mortifications which must be undergone in the pursuit of it; and what is of yet more consequence, all that leisure, all that ease, all that careless security, which are forfeited forever by the acquisition.

When we consider the condition of the great, in those delusive colours in which the imagination is apt to paint it, it seems to be almost the abstract idea of a perfect and happy state. It is the very state which, in all our waking dreams and idle reveries, we had sketched out to ourselves as the final object of all our desires. We feel, therefore, a peculiar sympathy with the satisfaction of those who are in it. We favour all their inclinations, and forward all their wishes. What pity, we think, that any thing should spoil and corrupt so agreeable a situation! We could even wish them immortal; and it seems hard to us, that death should at last put an end to such perfect enjoyment. It is cruel, we think, in Nature to compel them from their exalted stations to that humble, but hospitable home, which she has provided for all her children. Great King, live for ever! is the compliment, which, after the manner of eastern adulation, we should readily make them, if experience did not teach us its absurdity. Every calamity that befalls them, every injury that is done them, excites in the breast of the spectator ten times more compassion and resentment than he would have felt, had the same things happened to other men.

It is the misfortunes of Kings only which afford the proper subjects for tragedy. They resemble, in this respect, the misfortunes of lovers. Those two situations are the chief which interest us upon the theatre; because, in spite of all that reason and experience can tell us to the contrary, the prejudices of the imagination attach to these two states a happiness superior to any other. To disturb, or to put an end to such perfect enjoyment, seems to be the most atrocious of all injuries. The traitor who conspires against the life of his monarch, is thought a greater monster than any other murderer. All the innocent blood that was shed in the civil wars, provoked less indignation than the death of Charles I. A stranger to human nature, who saw the indifference of men about the misery of their inferiors, and the regret and indignation which they feel for the misfortunes and sufferings of those above them, would be apt to imagine, that pain must be more agonizing, and the convulsions of death more terrible to persons of higher rank, than to those of meaner stations.

Upon this disposition of mankind, to go along with all the passions of the rich and the powerful, is founded the distinction of ranks, and the order of society. Our obsequiousness to our superiors more frequently arises from our admiration for the advantages of their situation, than from any private expectations of benefit from their goodwill. Their benefits can extend but to a few; but their fortunes interest almost every body. We are eager to assist them in completing a system of happiness that approaches so near to perfection; and we desire to serve them for their own sake, without any other recompense but the vanity or the honour of obliging them. Neither is our deference to their inclinations founded chiefly, or altogether, upon a regard to the utility of such submission, and to the order of society, which is best supported by it. Even when the order of society seems to require that we should oppose them, we can hardly bring ourselves to do it.

That kings are the servants of the people, to be obeyed, resisted, deposed, or punished, as the public convenience may require, is the doctrine of reason and philosophy; but it is not the doctrine of Nature. Nature would teach us to submit to them for their own sake, to tremble and bow down before their exalted station, to regard their smile as a reward sufficient to compensate any services, and to dread their displeasure, though no other evil were to follow from it, as the severest of all mortifications. To treat them in any respect as men, to reason and dispute with them upon ordinary occasions, requires such resolution, that there are few men whose magnanimity can support them in it, unless they are likewise assisted by familiarity and acquaintance. The strongest motives, the most furious passions, fear, hatred, and resentment, are scarce sufficient to balance this natural disposition to respect them: and their conduct must, either justly or unjustly, have excited the highest degree of all those passions, before the bulk of the people can be brought to oppose them with violence, or to desire to see them either punished or deposed. Even when the people have been brought this length, they are apt to relent every moment, and easily relapse into their habitual state of deference to those whom they have been accustomed to look upon as their natural superiors. They cannot stand the mortification of their monarch. Compassion soon takes the place of resentment, they forget all past provocations, their old principles of loyalty revive, and they run to re-establish the ruined authority of their old masters, with the same violence with which they had opposed it. The death of Charles I brought about the Restoration of the royal family. Compassion for James II when he was seized by the populace in making his escape on shipboard had almost prevented the Revolution, and made it go on more heavily than before.

Do the great seem insensible of the easy price at which they may acquire the public admiration; or do they seem to imagine that to them, as to other men, it must be the purchase either of sweat or of blood? By what important accomplishments is the young nobleman instructed to support the dignity of his rank, and to render himself worthy of that superiority over his fellow-citizens, to which the virtue of his ancestors had raised them? Is it by knowledge, by industry, by patience, by self-denial, or by virtue of any kind? As all his words, as all his motions are attended to, he learns an habitual regard to every circumstance of ordinary behaviour, and studies to perform all those small duties with the most exact propriety. As he is conscious how much he is observed, and how much mankind are disposed to favour all his inclinations, he acts, upon the most indifferent occasions, with that freedom and elevation which the thought of this naturally inspires. His air, his manner, his deportment, all mark that elegant and graceful sense of his own superiority, which those who are born to inferior stations can hardly ever arrive at. These are the arts by which he proposes to make mankind more easily submit to his authority, and to govern their inclinations according to his own pleasure: and in this he is seldom disappointed. These arts, supported by rank and preeminence are, upon ordinary occasions, sufficient to govern the world.

Louis XIV during the greater part of his reign, was regarded, not only in France, but over all Europe, as the most perfect model of a great prince. But what were the talents and virtues by which he acquired this great reputation? Was it by the scrupulous and inflexible justice of all his undertakings, by the immense dangers and difficulties with which they were attended, or by the unwearied and unrelenting application with which he pursued them? Was it by his extensive knowledge, by his exquisite judgment, or by his heroic valour? It was by none of these qualities. But he was, first of all, the most powerful prince in Europe, and consequently held the highest rank among kings; and then, says his historian, "he surpassed all his courtiers in the gracefulness of his shape, and the majestic beauty of his features. The sound of his voice, noble and affecting, gained those hearts which his presence intimidated. He had a step and a deportment which could suit only him and his rank, and which would have been ridiculous in any other person. The embarrassment which he occasioned to those who spoke to him, flattered that secret satisfaction with which he felt his own superiority. The old officer, who was confounded and faltered in asking him a favour, and not being able to conclude his discourse, said to him: Sir, your majesty, I hope, will believe that I do not tremble thus before your enemies: had no difficulty to obtain what he demanded."

These frivolous accomplishments, supported by his rank, and, no doubt too, by a degree of other talents and virtues, which seems, however, not to have been much above mediocrity, established this prince in the esteem of his own age, and have drawn, even from posterity, a good deal of respect for his memory. Compared with these, in his own times, and in his own presence, no other virtue, it seems, appeared to have any merit. Knowledge, industry, valour, and beneficence, trembled, were abashed, and lost all dignity before them.

But it is not by accomplishments of this kind, that the man of inferior rank must hope to distinguish himself. Politeness is so much the virtue of the great, that it will do little honour to anybody but themselves. The coxcomb, who imitates their manner, and affects to be eminent by the superior propriety of his ordinary behaviour, is rewarded with a double share of contempt for his folly and presumption. Why should the man, whom nobody thinks it worthwhile to look at, be very anxious about the manner in which he holds up his head, or disposes of his arms while he walks through a room? He is occupied surely with a very superfluous attention, and with an attention too that marks a sense of his own importance, which no other mortal can go along with.

The most perfect modesty and plainness, joined to as much negligence as is consistent with the respect due to the company, ought to be the chief characteristics of the behaviour of a private man. If ever he hopes to distinguish himself, it must be by more important virtues. He must acquire dependants to balance the dependants of the great, and he has no other fund to pay them from, but the labour of his body, and the activity of his mind. He must cultivate these therefore: he must acquire superior knowledge in his profession, and superior industry in the exercise of it. He must be patient in labour, resolute in danger, and firm in distress. These talents he must bring into public view, by the difficulty, importance, and, at the same time, good judgment of his undertakings, and by the severe and unrelenting application with which he pursues them. Probity and prudence, generosity and frankness, must characterize his behaviour upon all ordinary occasions; and he must, at the same time, be forward to engage in all those situations, in which it requires the greatest talents and virtues to act with propriety, but in which the greatest applause is to be acquired by those who can acquit themselves with honour.

With what impatience does the man of spirit and ambition, who is depressed by his situation, look round for some great opportunity to distinguish himself? No circumstances, which can afford this, appear to him undesirable. He even looks forward with satisfaction to the prospect of foreign war, or civil dissension; and, with secret transport and delight, sees through all the confusion and bloodshed which attend them, the probability of those wished-for occasions presenting themselves, in which he may draw upon himself the attention and admiration of mankind.

The man of rank and distinction, on the contrary, whose whole glory consists in the propriety of his ordinary behaviour, who is contented with the humble renown which this can afford him, and has no talents to acquire any other, is unwilling to embarrass himself with what can be attended either with difficulty or distress. To figure at a ball is his great triumph, and to succeed in an intrigue of gallantry, his highest exploit. He has an aversion to all public confusions, not from the love of mankind, for the great never look upon their inferiors as their fellow-creatures; nor yet from want of courage, for in that he is seldom defective; but from a consciousness that he possesses none of the virtues which are required in such situations, and that the public attention will certainly be drawn away from him by others. He may be willing to expose himself to some little danger, and to make a campaign when it happens to be the fashion. But he shudders with horror at the thought of any situation which demands the continual and long exertion of patience, industry, fortitude, and application of thought. These virtues are hardly ever to be met with in men who are born to those high stations. In all governments accordingly, even in monarchies, the highest offices are generally possessed, and the whole detail of the administration conducted, by men who were educated in the middle and inferior ranks of life, who have been carried forward by their own industry and abilities, though loaded with the jealousy, and opposed by the resentment, of all those who were born their superiors, and to whom the great, after having regarded them first with contempt, and afterwards with envy, are at last contented to truckle with the same abject meanness with which they desire that the rest of mankind should behave to themselves.

It is the loss of this easy empire over the affections of mankind which renders the fall from greatness so insupportable. When the family of the king of Macedon was led in triumph by Paulus Aemilius, their misfortunes, it is said, made them divide with their conqueror the attention of the Roman people. The sight of the royal children, whose tender age rendered them insensible of their situation, struck the spectators, amidst the public rejoicings and prosperity, with the tenderest sorrow and compassion. The king appeared next in the procession; and seemed like one confounded and astonished, and bereft of all sentiment, by the greatness of his calamities. His friends and ministers followed after him. As they moved along, they often cast their eyes upon their fallen sovereign, and always burst into tears at the sight; their whole behaviour demonstrating that they thought not of their own misfortunes, but were occupied entirely by the superior greatness of his. The generous Romans, on the contrary, beheld him with disdain and indignation, and regarded as unworthy of all compassion the man who could be so mean-spirited as to bear to live under such calamities.

Yet what did those calamities amount to? According to the greater part of historians, he was to spend the remainder of his days, under the protection of a powerful and humane people, in a state which in itself should seem worthy of envy, a state of plenty, ease, leisure, and security, from which it was impossible for him even by his own folly to fall. But he was no longer to be surrounded by that admiring mob of fools, flatterers, and dependants, who had formerly been accustomed to attend upon all his motions. He was no longer to be gazed upon by multitudes, nor to have it in his power to render himself the object of their respect, their gratitude, their love, their admiration. The passions of nations were no longer to mould themselves upon his inclinations. This was that insupportable calamity which bereaved the king of all sentiment; which made his friends forget their own misfortunes; and which the Roman magnanimity could scarce conceive how any man could be so meanspirited as to bear to survive.

"Love," says my Lord Rochefoucauld, "is commonly succeeded by ambition; but ambition is hardly ever succeeded by love." That passion, when once it has got entire possession of the breast, will admit neither a rival nor a successor. To those who have been accustomed to the possession, or even to the hope of public admiration, all other pleasures sicken and decay. Of all the discarded statesmen who for their own ease have studied to get the better of ambition, and to despise those honours which they could no longer arrive at, how few have been able to succeed? The greater part have spent their time in the most listless and insipid indolence, chagrined at the thoughts of their own insignificancy, incapable of being interested in the occupations of private life, without enjoyment, except when they talked of their former greatness, and without satisfaction, except when they were employed in some vain project to recover it. Are you in earnest resolved never to barter your liberty for the lordly servitude of a court, but to live free, fearless, and independent? There seems to be one way to continue in that virtuous resolution; and perhaps but one. Never enter the place from whence so few have been able to return; never come within the circle of ambition; nor ever bring yourself into comparison with those masters of the earth who have already engrossed the attention of half mankind before you.

Of such mighty importance does it appear to be, in the imaginations of men, to stand in that situation which sets them most in the view of general sympathy and attention. And thus, place, that great object which divides the wives of aldermen, is the end of half the labours of human life; and is the cause of all the tumult and bustle, all the rapine and injustice, which avarice and ambition have introduced into this world. People of sense, it is said, indeed despise place; that is, they despise sitting at the head of the table, and are indifferent who it is that is pointed out to the company by that frivolous circumstance, which the smallest advantage is capable of overbalancing. But rank, distinction, preeminence, no man despises, unless he is either raised very much above, or sunk very much below, the ordinary standard of human nature; unless he is either so confirmed in wisdom and real philosophy, as to be satisfied that, while the propriety of his conduct renders him the just object of approbation, it is of little consequence though he be neither attended to, nor approved of; or so habituated to the idea of his own meanness, so sunk in slothful and sottish indifference, as entirely to have forgot the desire, and almost the very wish, for superiority. . . .

CHAPTER III

Of the corruption of our moral sentiments, which is occasioned by this disposition to admire the rich and the great, and to despise or neglect persons of poor and mean condition

This disposition to admire, and almost to worship, the rich and the powerful, and to despise, or, at least, to neglect persons of poor and mean condition, though necessary both to establish and to maintain the distinction of ranks and the order of society, is, at the same time, the great and most universal cause of the corruption of our moral sentiments. That wealth and greatness are often regarded with the respect and admiration which are due only to wisdom and virtue; and that the contempt, of which vice and folly are the only proper objects, is often most unjustly bestowed upon poverty and weakness, has been the complaint of moralists in all ages.

We desire both to be respectable and to be respected. We dread both to be contemptible and to be contemned. But, upon coming into the world, we soon find that wisdom and virtue are by no means the sole objects of respect; nor vice and folly, of contempt. We frequently see the respectful attentions of the world more strongly directed towards the rich and the great, than towards the wise and the virtuous. We see frequently the vices and follies of the powerful much less despised than the poverty and weakness of the innocent. To deserve, to acquire, and to enjoy the respect and admiration of mankind, are the great objects of ambition and emulation. Two different roads are presented to us, equally leading to the attainment of this so much desired object; the one, by the study of wisdom and the practice of virtue; the other, by the acquisition of wealth and greatness. Two different characters are presented to our emulation; the one, of proud ambition and ostentatious avidity; the other, of humble modesty and equitable justice. Two different models, two different pictures, are held out to us, according to which we may fashion our own character and behaviour; the one more gaudy and glittering in its colouring; the other more correct and more exquisitely beautiful in its outline: the one forcing itself upon the notice of every wandering eye; the other, attracting the attention of scarce any body but the most studious and careful observer. They are the wise and the virtuous chiefly, a select, though, I am afraid, but a small party, who are the real and steady admirers of wisdom and virtue. The great mob of mankind are the admirers and worshippers, and, what may seem more extraordinary, most frequently the disinterested admirers and worshippers, of wealth and greatness.

The respect which we feel for wisdom and virtue is, no doubt, different from that which we conceive for wealth and greatness; and it requires no very nice discernment to distinguish the difference. But, notwithstanding this difference, those sentiments bear a very considerable resemblance to one another. In some particular features they are, no doubt, different, but, in the general air of the countenance, they seem to be so very nearly the same, that inattentive observers are very apt to mistake the one for the other.

In equal degrees of merit there is scarce any man who does not respect more the rich and the great, than the poor and the humble. With most men the presumption and vanity of the former are much more admired, than the real and solid merit of the latter. It is scarce agreeable to good morals, or even to good language, perhaps, to say, that mere wealth and greatness, abstracted from merit and virtue, deserve our respect. We must acknowledge, however, that they almost constantly obtain it; and that they may, therefore, be considered as, in some respects, the natural objects of it. Those exalted stations may, no doubt, be completely degraded by vice and folly. But the vice and folly must be very great, before they can operate this complete degradation. The profligacy of a man of fashion is looked upon with much less contempt and aversion, than that of a man of meaner condition. In the latter, a single transgression of the rules of temperance and propriety, is commonly more resented, than the constant and avowed contempt of them ever is in the former.

In the middling and inferior stations of life, the road to virtue and that to fortune, to such fortune, at least, as men in such stations can reasonably expect to acquire, are, happily in most cases, very nearly the same. In all the middling and inferior professions, real and solid professional abilities, joined to prudent, just, firm, and temperate conduct, can very seldom fail of success. Abilities will even sometimes prevail where the conduct is by no means correct. Either habitual imprudence, however, or injustice, or weakness, or profligacy, will always cloud, and sometimes depress altogether, the most splendid professional abilites. Men in the inferior and middling stations of life, besides, can never be great enough to be above the law, which must generally overawe them into some sort of respect for, at least, the more important rules of justice. The success of such people, too, almost always depends upon the favour and good opinion of their neighbours and equals; and without a tolerably regular conduct these can very seldom be obtained. The good old proverb, therefore, That honesty is the best policy, holds, in such situations, almost always perfectly true. In such situations, therefore, we may generally expect a considerable degree of virtue; and, fortunately for the good morals of society, these are the situations of by far the greater part of mankind.

In the superior stations of life the case is unhappily not always the same. In the courts of princes, in the drawing-rooms of the great, where success and preferment depend, not upon the esteem of intelligent and

well-informed equals, but upon the fanciful and foolish favour of ignorant, presumptuous, and proud superiors; flattery and falsehood too often
prevail over merit and abilities. In such societies the abilities to please,
are more regarded than the abilities to serve. In quiet and peaceable
times, when the storm is at a distance, the prince, or great man, wishes
only to be amused, and is even apt to fancy that he has scarce any
occasion for the service of any body, or that those who amuse him are
sufficiently able to serve him. The external graces, the frivolous accomplishments of that impertinent and foolish thing called a man of fashion,
are commonly more admired than the solid and masculine virtues of a
warrior, a statesman, a philosopher, or a legislator. All the great and
awful virtues, all the virtues which can fit, either for the council, the
senate, or the field, are, by the insolent and insignificant flatterers, who
commonly figure the most in such corrupted societies, held in the utmost
contempt and derision. When the duke of Sully was called upon by
Lewis the Thirteenth, to give his advice in some great emergency, he
observed the favourites and courtiers whispering to one another, and
smiling at his unfashionable appearance. "Whenever your majesty's
father," said the old warrior and statesman, "did me the honour to consult me, he ordered the buffoons of the court to retire into the antecham-
ber." . . .

PART II
OF MERIT AND DEMERIT; OR, OF THE OBJECTS OF REWARD AND PUNISHMENT CONSISTING OF THREE SECTIONS

SECTION I
Of the Sense of Merit and Demerit

CHAPTER I
*That whatever appears to be the proper object of gratitude,
appears to deserve reward; and that, in the same manner,
whatever appears to be the proper object of resentment, appears to
deserve punishment*

CHAPTER II
Of the proper objects of gratitude and resentment

CHAPTER III
*That where there is no approbation of the conduct of the
person who confers the benefit, there is little sympathy with*

the gratitude of him who receives it: and that, on the contrary,
where there is no disapprobation of the motives of the person who
does the mischief, there is no sort of sympathy with the resentment
of him who suffers it

[The first three, very short chapters of Part II, Section I, are omitted. Chapter 4 nicely summarizes the common theme: The impartial spectator determines whether the actions of individuals deserve our reward or punishment.]

CHAPTER IV

Recapitulation of the foregoing chapters

1. We do not, therefore, thoroughly and heartily sympathize with the gratitude of one man towards another, merely because this other has been the cause of his good fortune, unless he has been the cause of it from motives which we entirely go along with. Our heart must adopt the principles of the agent, and go along with all the affections which influenced his conduct, before it can entirely sympathize with, and beat time to, the gratitude of the person who has been benefited by his actions. If in the conduct of the benefactor there appears to have been no propriety, how beneficial soever its effects, it does not seem to demand, or necessarily to require, any proportionable recompense.

But when to the beneficent tendency of the action is joined the propriety of the affection from which it proceeds, when we entirely sympathize and go along with the motives of the agent, the love which we conceive for him upon his own account, enhances and enlivens our fellow-feeling with the gratitude of those who owe their prosperity to his good conduct. His actions seem then to demand, and, if I may say so, to call aloud for a proportionable recompense. We then entirely enter into that gratitude which prompts to bestow it. The benefactor seems then to be the proper object of reward, when we thus entirely sympathize with, and approve of, that sentiment which prompts to reward him. When we approve of, and go along with, the affection from which the action proceeds, we must necessarily approve of the action, and regard the person towards whom it is directed, as its proper and suitable object.

2. In the same manner, we cannot at all sympathize with the resentment of one man against another, merely because this other has been the cause of his misfortune, unless he has been the cause of it from motives which we cannot enter into. Before we can adopt the resentment of the sufferer, we must disapprove of the motives of the agent, and feel that our heart renounces all sympathy with the affections which influenced his conduct. If there appears to have been no impropriety in these, how fatal soever the tendency of the action which proceeds from them to those against whom it is directed, it does not seem to deserve any punishment, or to be the proper object of any resentment.

But when to the hurtfulness of the action is joined the impropriety of the affection from whence it proceeds, when our heart rejects with abhorrence all fellow-feeling with the motives of the agent, we then heartily and entirely sympathize with the resentment of the sufferer. Such actions seem then to deserve, and, if I may say so, to call aloud for, a proportionable punishment; and we entirely enter into, and thereby approve of, that resentment which prompts to inflict it. The offender necessarily seems then to be the proper object of punishment, when we thus entirely sympathize with, and thereby approve of, that sentiment which prompts to punish. In this case too, when we approve, and go along with, the affection from which the action proceeds, we must necessarily approve of the action, and regard the person against whom it is directed, as its proper and suitable object. . . .

CHAPTER V

The analysis of the sense of Merit and Demerit

[Chapter 5 provides few additional insights into the circumstances of reward and punishment and is excluded. At the end of the chapter, however a lengthy, somewhat curious note contains one of the most significant passages in the book. Nowhere else in Smith's writings is there a more succinct statement of what enforces systematic order in society. His bold allusion to the Invisible Hand—an indirect intervention of the Divinity into everyday life—is perhaps his most forthright acknowledgment of the limits of human reason in the realization of social cohesion and harmony.]

. . . Let it be considered too, that the present inquiry is not concerning a matter of right, if I may say so, but concerning a matter of fact. We are not at present examining upon what principles a perfect being would approve of the punishment of bad actions; but upon what principles so weak and imperfect a creature as man actually and in fact approves of it. The principles which I have just now mentioned, it is evident, have a very great effect upon his sentiments; and it seems wisely ordered that it should be so. The very existence of society requires that unmerited and unprovoked malice should be restrained by proper punishments; and consequently, that to inflict those punishments should be regarded as a proper and laudable action. Though man, therefore, be naturally endowed with a desire of the welfare and preservation of society, yet the Author of nature has not entrusted it to his reason to find out that a certain application of punishments is the proper means of attaining this end; but has endowed him with an immediate and instinctive approbation of that very application which is most proper to attain it.

The economy of nature is in this respect exactly of a piece with what it is upon many other occasions. With regard to all those ends which, upon account of their peculiar importance, may be regarded, if such an expression is allowable, as the favourite ends of nature, she has con-

stantly in this manner not only endowed mankind with an appetite for
the end which she proposes, but likewise with an appetite for the means
by which alone this end can be brought about, for their own sakes, and
independent of their tendency to produce it. Thus self-preservation, and
the propagation of the species, are the great ends which Nature seems to
have proposed in the formation of all animals. Mankind are endowed
with a desire of those ends, and an aversion to the contrary; with a love
of life, and a dread of dissolution; with a desire of the continuance and
perpetuity of the species, and with an aversion to the thoughts of its
entire extinction.

But though we are in this manner endowed with a very strong desire
of those ends, it has not been entrusted to the slow and uncertain determinations of our reason, to find out the proper means of bringing them
about. Nature has directed us to the greater part of these by original and
immediate instincts. Hunger, thirst, the passion which unites the two
sexes, the love of pleasure, and the dread of pain, prompt us to apply
those means for their own sakes, and without any consideration of their
tendency to those beneficent ends which the great Director of nature
intended to produce by them . . .

SECTION II

Of Justice and Beneficence

CHAPTER I

Comparison of those two virtues

Actions of a beneficent tendency, which proceed from proper motives,
seem alone to require reward; because such alone are the approved objects
of gratitude, or excite the sympathetic gratitude of the spectator.

Actions of a hurtful tendency, which proceed from improper motives,
seem alone to deserve punishment; because such alone are the appoved
objects of resentment, or excite the sympathetic resentment of the spectator.

Beneficence is always free, it cannot be extorted by force, the mere
want of it exposes to no punishment; because the mere want of beneficence tends to do no real positive evil. It may disappoint of the good
which might reasonably have been expected, and upon that account it
may justly excite dislike and disapprobation: it cannot, however, provoke
any resentment which mankind will go along with. The man who does
not recompense his benefactor, when he has it in his power, and when
his benefactor needs his assistance, is, no doubt, guilty of the blackest
ingratitude. The heart of every impartial spectator rejects all fellow-feeling with the selfishness of his motives, and he is the proper object of the
highest disapprobation.

But still he does no positive hurt to any body. He only does not do that good which in propriety he ought to have done. He is the object of hatred, a passion which is naturally excited by impropriety of sentiment and behaviour; not of resentment, a passion which is never properly called forth but by actions which tend to do real and positive hurt to some particular persons. His want of gratitude, therefore, cannot be punished. To oblige him by force to perform what in gratitude he ought to perform, and what every impartial spectator would approve of him for performing, would, if possible, be still more improper than his neglecting to perform it. His benefactor would dishonour himself if he attempted by violence to constrain him to gratitude, and it would be impertinent for any third person, who was not the superior of either, to intermeddle.

But of all the duties of beneficence, those which gratitude recommends to us approach nearest to what is called a perfect and complete obligation. What friendship, what generosity, what charity, would prompt us to do with universal approbation, is still more free, and can still less be extorted by force than the duties of gratitude. We talk of the debt of gratitude, not of charity, or generosity, nor even of friendship, when friendship is me-e esteem, and has not been enhanced and complicated with gratitude for good offices.

Resentment seems to have been given us by nature for defence, and for defence only. It is the safeguard of justice and the security of innocence. It prompts us to beat off the mischief which is attempted to be done to us, and to retaliate that which is already done; that the offender may be made to repent of his injustice, and that others, through fear of the like punishment, may be terrified from being guilty of the like offence. It must be reserved therefore for these purposes, nor can the spectator ever go along with it when it is exerted for any other. But the mere want of the beneficent virtues, though it may disappoint us of the good which might reasonably be expected, neither does, not attempts to do, any mischief from which we can have occasion to defend ourselves.

There is, however, another virtue, of which the observance is not left to the freedom of our own wills, which may be extorted by force, and of which the violation exposes to resentment, and consequently to punishment. This virtue is justice: the violation of justice is injury: it does real and positive hurt to some particular persons, from motives which are naturally disapproved of. It is, therefore, the proper object of resentment, and of punishment, which is the natural consequence of resentment. As mankind go along with, and approve of the violence employed to avenge the hurt which is done by injustice, so they much more go along with, and approve of, that which is employed to prevent and beat off the injury, and to restrain the offender from hurting his neighbours. The person himself who meditates an injustice is sensible of this, and feels that force may, with the utmost propriety, be made use of, both by the person whom he is about to injure, and by others, either to obstruct the execution of his crime, or to punish him when he has executed it. And upon this is founded that remarkable distinction between justice and all the other social virtues, which has of late been particularly insisted upon by an author of very great and original genius,* that we feel ourselves to be under a stricter obligation to act according to justice, than agreeably to friendship, charity, or generosity; that the practise of these last mentioned virtues seems to be left in some measure to our own choice, but that, somehow or other, we feel ourselves to be in a peculiar manner tied, bound, and obliged to the observation of justice. We feel, that is to say, that force may, with the utmost propriety, and with the approbation of all mankind, be made use of to constrain us to observe the rules of the one, but not to follow the precepts of the other. . . .

CHAPTER II

*Of the sense of Justice, of Remorse,
and of the consciousness of Merit*

There can be no proper motive for hurting our neighbour, there can be no incitement to do evil to another, which mankind will go along with, except just indignation for evil which that other has done to us. To disturb his happiness merely because it stands in the way of our own, to take from him what is of real use to him merely because it may be of equal or of more use to us, or to indulge, in this manner, at the expence of other people, the natural preference which every man has for his own happiness above that of other people, is what no impartial spectator can go along with. Every man is, no doubt, by nature, first and principally recommended to his own care; and as he is fitter to take care of himself than of any other person, it is fit and right that it should be so. Every man, therefore, is much more deeply interested in whatever immediately concerns himself, than in what concerns any other man: and to hear, perhaps, of the death of another person, with whom we have no particular connection, will give us less concern, will spoil our stomach, or break our rest much less than a very insignificant disaster which has befallen ourselves.

But though the ruin of our neighbour may affect us much less than a very small misfortune of our own, we must not ruin him to prevent that small misfortune, nor even to prevent our own ruin. We must, here, as in all other cases, view ourselves not so much according to that light in which we may naturally appear to ourselves, as according to that in which we naturally appear to others. Though every man may, according to the proverb, be the whole world to himself, to the rest of mankind he is a most insignificant part of it. Though his own happiness may be of more importance to him than that of all the world besides, to every other person it is of no more consequence than that of any other man. Though

*Lord Kames, *Essays on the Principles of Morality and Natural Religion*, 1751.

it may be true, therefore, that every individual, in his own breast, naturally prefers himself to all mankind, yet he dares not look mankind in the face, and avow that he acts according to this principle. He feels that in this preference they can never go along with him, and that how natural soever it may be to him, it must always appear excessive and extravagant to them.

When he views himself in the light in which he is conscious that others will view him, he sees that to them he is but one of the multitude in no respect better than any other in it. If he would act so as that the impartial spectator may enter into the principles of his conduct, which is what of all things he has the greatest desire to do, he must, upon this, as upon all other occasions, humble the arrogance of his self-love, and bring it down to something which other men can go along with. They will indulge it so far as to allow him to be more anxious about, and to pursue with more earnest assiduity, his own happiness than that of any other person. Thus far, whenever they place themselves in his situation, they will readily go along with him. In the race for wealth, and honours, and preferments, he may run as hard as he can, and strain every nerve and every muscle, in order to outstrip all his competitors. But if he should justle, or throw down any of them, the indulgence of the spectators is entirely at an end. It is a violation of fair play, which they cannot admit of. This man is to them, in every respect, as good as he: they do not enter into that self-love by which he prefers himself so much to this other, and cannot go along with the motive from which he hurt him. They readily, therefore, sympathize with the natural resentment of the injured, and the offender becomes the object of their hatred and indignation. He is sensible that he becomes so, and feels that those sentiments are ready to burst out from all sides against him.

As the greater and more irreparable the evil that is done, the resentment of the sufferer runs naturally the higher; so does likewise the sympathetic indignation of the spectator, as well as the sense of guilt in the agent. Death is the greatest evil which one man can inflict upon another, and excites the highest degree of resentment in those who are immediately connected with the slain. Murder, therefore, is the most atrocious of all crimes which affect individuals only, in the sight both of mankind, and of the person who has committed it. To be deprived of that which we are possessed of, is a greater evil than to be disappointed of what we have only the expectation. Breach of property, therefore, theft and robbery, which take from us what we are possessed of, are greater crimes than breach of contract, which only disappoints us of what we expected. The most sacred laws of justice, therefore, those whose violation seems to call loudest for vengeance and punishment, are the laws which guard the life and person of our neighbour; the next are those which guard his property and possessions; and last of all come those which guard what are called his personal rights, or what is due to him from the promises of others.

The violator of the more sacred laws of justice can never reflect on the sentiments which mankind must entertain with regard to him, without feeling all the agonies of shame, and horror, and consternation. When his passion is gratified, and he begins coolly to reflect on his past conduct, he can enter into none of the motives which influenced it. They appear now as detestable to him as they did always to other people. By sympathizing with the hatred and abhorrence which other men must entertain for him, he becomes in some measure the object of his own hatred and abhorrence. The situation of the person, who suffered by his injustice, now calls upon his pity. He is grieved at the thought of it; regrets the unhappy effects of his own conduct, and feels at the same time that they have rendered him the proper object of the resentment and indignation of mankind, and of what is the natural consequence of resentment, vengeance and punishment. The thought of this perpetually haunts him, and fills him with terror and amazement. He dares no longer look society in the face, but imagines himself as it were rejected, and thrown out from the affections of all mankind. He cannot hope for the consolation of sympathy in this his greatest and most dreadful distress. The remembrance of his crimes has shut out all fellow-feeling with him from the hearts of his fellow-creatures. The sentiments which they entertain with regard to him, are the very thing which he is most afraid of. Every thing seems hostile, and he would be glad to fly to some inhospitable desert, where he might never more behold the face of a human creature, nor read in the countenance of mankind the condemnation of his crimes.

But solitude is still more dreadful than society. His own thoughts can present him with nothing but what is black, unfortunate, and disastrous, the melancholy forebodings of incomprehensible misery and ruin. The horror of solitude drives him back into society, and he comes again into the presence of mankind, astonished to appear before them, loaded with shame and distracted with fear, in order to supplicate some little protection from the countenance of those very judges, who he knows have already all unanimously condemned him. Such is the nature of that sentiment, which is properly called remorse; of all the sentiments which can enter the human breast the most dreadful. It is made up of shame from the sense of the impropriety of past conduct; of grief for the effects of it; of pity for those who suffer by it; and of the dread and terror of punishment from the consciousness of the justly provoked resentment of all rational creatures.

The opposite behaviour naturally inspires the opposite sentiment. The man who, not from frivolous fancy, but from proper motives, has performed a generous action, when he looks forward to those whom he has served, feels himself to be the natural object of their love and gratitude, and, by sympathy with them, of the esteem and approbation of all mankind. And when he looks backward to the motive from which he acted, and surveys it in the light in which the indifferent spectator will survey it, he still continues to enter into it, and applauds himself by sympathy with the approbation of this supposed impartial judge. In both these points of view his own conduct appears to him every way agreeable. His mind, at the thought of it, is filled with cheerfulness, serenity, and composure. He is in friendship and harmony with all mankind, and looks upon his fellow creatures with confidence and benevolent satisfaction, secure that he has rendered himself worthy of their most favourable regards. In the combination of all these sentiments consists the consciousness of merit, or of deserved reward.

CHAPTER III

Of the utility of this constitution of Nature

It is thus that man, who can subsist only in society, was fitted by nature to that situation for which he was made. All the members of human society stand in need of each others assistance, and are likewise exposed to mutual injuries. Where necessary assistance is reciprocally afforded from love, from gratitude, from friendship, and esteem, the society flourishes and is happy. All the different members of it are bound together by the agreeable bands of love and affection, and are, as it were, drawn to one common centre of mutual good offices.

But though the necessary assistance should not be afforded from such generous and disinterested motives, though among the different members of the society there should be no mutual love and affection, the society, though less happy and agreeable, will not necessarily be dissolved. Society may subsist among different men, as among different merchants, from a sense of its utility, without any mutual love or affection; and though no man in it should owe any obligation, or be bound in gratitude to any other, it may still be upheld by a mercenary exchange of good offices according to an agreed valuation.

Society, however, cannot subsist among those who are at all times ready to hurt and injure one another. The moment that injury begins, the moment that mutual resentment and animosity take place, all the bonds of it are broke asunder, and the different members of which it consisted are, as it were, dissipated and scattered abroad by the violence and opposition of their discordant affections. If there is any society among robbers and murderers, they must at least, according to the trite observation, abstain from robbing and murdering one another. Beneficence, therefore, is less essential to the existence of society than justice. Society may subsist, though not in the most comfortable state, without beneficence; but the prevalence of injustice must utterly destroy it.

Though Nature, therefore, exhorts mankind to acts of beneficence, by the pleasing consciousness of deserved reward, she has not thought it necessary to guard and enforce the practise of it by the terrors of merited punishment in case it should be neglected. It is the ornament which embellishes, not the foundation which supports the building, and which it was, therefore, sufficient to recommend, but by no means necessary to impose. Justice, on the contrary, is the main pillar that upholds the whole edifice. If it is removed, the great, the immense fabric of human society, that fabric which to raise and support seems in this world, if I may say so, to have been the peculiar and darling care of Nature, must in a moment crumble into atoms. In order to enforce the observation of justice, therefore, Nature has implanted in the human breast that consciousness of ill desert, those terrors of merited punishment which attend upon its violation, as the great safeguards of the association of mankind, to protect the weak, to curb the violent, and to chastise the guilty. Men, though naturally sympathetic, feel so little for another, with whom they have no particular connexion, in comparison of what they feel for themselves; the misery of one, who is merely their fellow creature, is of so little importance to them in comparison even of a small convenience of their own; they have it so much in their power to hurt him, and may have so many temptations to do so, that if this principle did not stand up within them in his defence, and overawe them into a respect for his innocence, they would, like wild beasts, be at all times ready to fly upon him; and a man would enter an assembly of men as he enters a den of lions.

In every part of the universe we observe means adjusted with the nicest artifice to the ends which they are intended to produce; and in the mechanism of a plant, or animal body, admire how every thing is contrived for advancing the two great purposes of nature, the support of the individual, and the propagation of the species. But in these, and in all such objects, we still distinguish the efficient from the final cause of their several motions and organizations. The digestion of the food, the circulation of the blood, and the secretion of the several juices which are drawn from it, are operations all of them necessary for the great purposes of animal life. Yet we never endeavour to account for them from those purposes as from their efficient causes, nor imagine that the blood circulates, or that the food digests of its own accord, and with a view or intention to the purposes of circulation or digestion. The wheels of the watch are all admirably adjusted to the end for which it was made, the pointing of the hour. All their various motions conspire in the nicest manner to produce this effect. If they were endowed with a desire and intention to produce it, they could not do it better. Yet we never ascribe any such desire or intention to them, but to the watchmaker, and we know that they are put into motion by a spring, which intends the effect it produces as little as they do. But though, in accounting for the operations of bodies, we never fail to distinguish in this manner the efficient from the final cause, in accounting for those of the mind we are very apt to confound these two different things with one another. When by natural principles we are led to advance those ends, which a refined and enlightened reason would recommend to us, we are very apt to impute to that reason, as to their efficient cause, the sentiments and actions by which we advance those ends, and to imagine that to be the wisdom of man, which in reality is the wisdom of God. Upon a superficial view, this cause seems sufficient to produce the effects which are ascribed to it; and the system of human nature seems to be more simple and agreeable when all its different operations are in this manner deduced from a single principle. . . .

SECTION III

Of the Influence of Fortune upon the Sentiments of Mankind, with regard to the Merit or Demerit of Actions

CHAPTER I

Of the causes of this Influence of Fortune

CHAPTER II

Of the extent of this Influence of Fortune

[Section III considers the social consequences of individual action. We exclude chapters 1 and 2, where Smith takes up the question of actions that are intended to bring about preconceived results. These *intended consequences* "show some agreeable or disagreeable quality in the intention of the heart." A circumstance of a different order is raised at the end of chapter 2. Here, when seeking to determine the appropriate punishment for negligence, the *unintended consequences* of individual actions must also be weighed. "Thus, if a person should throw a large stone into a public street without giving warning to those who might be passing by . . . he would undoubtedly deserve some chastisement. [If] a person happens to occasion some damage to another, he is often by the law obliged to compensate it," even where the harm caused was *unintended*.

The following excerpt from chapter 3 summarizes the entire section and shows how the mechanism of the Invisible Hand explains both this regularity and irregularity in the actions of individuals.]

CHAPTER III

Of the final cause of this Irregularity of Sentiments

Such is the effect of the good or bad consequences of actions upon the sentiments both of the person who performs them, and of others; and thus, Fortune, which governs the world, has some influence where we should be least willing to allow her any, and directs in some measure the sentiments of mankind, with regard to the character and conduct both of themselves and others. That the world judges by the event, and not by the design, has been in all ages the complaint, and is the great discouragement of virtue. Every body agrees to the general maxim, that as the event does not depend on the agent, it ought to have no influence upon our sentiments, with regard to the merit or propriety of his conduct. But when we come to particulars, we find that our sentiments are scarce in any one instance exactly conformable to what this equitable maxim would direct. The happy or unprosperous event of any action, is not only apt to give us a good or bad opinion of the prudence with which it was conducted, but almost always too animates our gratitude or resentment, our sense of the merit or demerit of the design.

Nature, however, when she implanted the seeds of this irregularity in the human breast, seems, as upon all other occasions, to have intended the happiness and perfection of the species. If the hurtfulness of the design, if the malevolence of the affection, were alone the causes which excited our resentment, we should feel all the furies of that passion against any person in whose breast we suspected or believed such designs or affections were harboured, though they had never broke out into any action. Sentiments, thoughts, intentions, would become the objects of punishment; and if the indignation of mankind run as high against them as against actions; if the baseness of the thought which had given birth to no action, seemed in the eyes of the world as much to call aloud for vengeance as the baseness of the action, every court of judicature would become a real inquisition. There would be no safety for the most innocent and circumspect conduct. Bad wishes, bad views, bad designs, might still be suspected; and while these excited the same indignation with bad conduct, while bad intentions were as much resented as bad actions, they would equally expose the person to punishment and resentment.

Actions, therefore, which either produce actual evil, or attempt to produce it, and thereby put us in the immediate fear of it, are by the Author of nature rendered the only proper and approved objects of human punishment and resentment. Sentiments, designs, affections, though it is from these that according to cool reason human actions derive their whole merit or demerit, are placed by the great Judge of hearts beyond the limits of every human jurisdiction, and are reserved for the cognizance of his own unerring tribunal. That necessary rule of justice, therefore, that men in this life are liable to punishment for their actions only, not for their designs and intentions, is founded upon this salutary and useful irregularity in human sentiments concerning merit or demerit, which at first sight appears so absurd and unaccountable. But every part of nature, when attentively surveyed, equally demonstrates the providential care of its Author, and we may admire the wisdom and goodness of God even in the weakness and folly of man.

Nor is that irregularity of sentiments altogether without its utility, by which the merit of an unsuccessful attempt to serve, and much more that of mere good inclinations and kind wishes, appears to be imperfect. Man was made for action, and to promote by the exertion of his faculties such changes in the external circumstances both of himself and others, as may seem most favourable to the happiness of all. He must not be satisfied with indolent benevolence, nor fancy himself the friend of mankind, because in his heart he wishes well to the prosperity of the world. That he may call forth the whole vigour of his soul, and strain every nerve, in order to produce those ends which it is the purpose of his being to advance, Nature has taught him, that neither himself nor mankind can be fully satisfied with his conduct, nor bestow upon it the full measure of applause, unless he has actually produced them. . . .

PART III

Of the Foundation of our Judgments concerning our own Sentiments and Conduct, and of the Sense of Duty Consisting of One Section

CHAPTER I

Of the Principle of Self-approbation and of Self-disapprobation

In the two foregoing parts of this discourse, I have chiefly considered the origin and foundation of our judgments concerning the sentiments and conduct of others. I come now to consider more particularly the origin of those concerning our own.

The principle by which we naturally either approve or disapprove of our own conduct, seems to be altogether the same with that by which we exercise the like judgments concerning the conduct of other people. We either approve or disapprove of the conduct of another man according as we feel that, when we bring his case home to ourselves, we either can or cannot entirely sympathize with the sentiments and motives which directed it. And, in the same manner, we either approve or disapprove of our own conduct, according as we feel that, when we place ourselves in the situation of another man, and view it, as it were, with his eyes and from his station, we either can or cannot entirely enter into and sympathize with the sentiments and motives which influenced it. We can never survey our own sentiments and motives, we can never form any judgment concerning them; unless we remove ourselves, as it were, from our own natural station, and endeavour to view them as at a certain distance from us. But we can do this in no other way than by endeavouring to view them with the eyes of other people, or as other people are likely to view them. Whatever judgment we can form concerning them, accordingly, must always bear some secret reference, either to what are, or to what, upon a certain condition, would be, or to what, we imagine, ought to be the judgment of others. We endeavour to examine our own conduct as we imagine any other fair and impartial spectator would examine it. If, upon placing ourselves in his situation, we thoroughly enter into all the passions and motives which influenced it, we approve of it, by sympathy with the approbation of this supposed equitable judge. If otherwise, we enter into his disapprobation, and condemn it.

Were it possible that a human creature could grow up to manhood in some solitary place, without any communication with his own species, he could no more think of his own character, of the propriety or demerit of his own sentiments and conduct, of the beauty or deformity of his own mind, than of the beauty or deformity of his own face. All these are objects which he cannot easily see, which naturally he does not look at, and with regard to which he is provided with no mirror which can present them to his view. Bring him into society, and he is immediately provided with the mirror which he wanted before. It is placed in the countenance and behaviour of those he lives with, which always mark when they enter into, and when they disapprove of his sentiments; and it is here that he first views the propriety and impropriety of his own passions, the beauty and deformity of his own mind. To a man who from his birth was a stranger to society, the objects of his passions, the external bodies which either pleased or hurt him, would occupy his whole attention. The passions themselves, the desires or aversions, the joys or sorrows, which those objects excited, though of all things the most immediately present to him, could scarce ever be the objects of his thoughts. The idea of them could never interest him so much as to call upon his attentive consideration. The consideration of his joy could in him excite no new joy, nor that of his sorrow any new sorrow, though the consideration of the causes of those passions might often excite both. Bring him into society, and all his own passions will immediately become the causes of new passions. He will observe that mankind approve of some of them, and are disgusted by others. He will be elevated in the one case, and cast down in the other; his desires and aversions, his joys and sorrows, will now often become the causes of new desires and new aversions, new joys and new sorrows: they will now, therefore, interest him deeply, and often call upon his most attentive consideration.

Our first ideas of personal beauty and deformity, are drawn from the shape and appearance of others, not from our own. We soon become sensible, however, that others exercise the same criticism upon us. We are pleased when they approve of our figure, and are disobliged when they seem to be disgusted. We become anxious to know how far our appearance deserves either their blame or approbation. We examine our persons limb by limb, and by placing ourselves before a looking-glass, or by some such expedient, endeavour, as much as possible, to view ourselves at the distance and with the eyes of other people. If, after this examination, we are satisfied with our own appearance, we can more easily support the most disadvantageous judgments of others. If, on the contrary, we are sensible that we are the natural objects of distaste, every appearance of their disapprobation mortifies us beyond all measure. A man who is tolerably handsome, will allow you to laugh at any little irregularity in his person; but all such jokes are commonly unsupportable to one who is really deformed. It is evident, however, that we are anxious about our own beauty and deformity, only upon account of its effect upon others. If we had no connexion with society, we should be altogether indifferent about either.

In the same manner our first moral criticisms are exercised upon the characters and conduct of other people; and we are all very forward to observe how each of these affects us. But we soon learn, that other people are equally frank with regard to our own. We become anxious to know how far we deserve their censure or applause, and whether to them we must necessarily appear those agreeable or disagreeable creatures which they represent us. We begin, upon this account, to examine our own passions and conduct, and to consider how these must appear to them, by considering how they would appear to us if in their situation. We suppose ourselves the spectators of our own behaviour, and endeavour to imagine what effect it would, in this light, produce upon us. This is the only looking-glass by which we can, in some measure, with the eyes of other people, scrutinize the propriety of our own conduct. If in this view it pleases us, we are tolerably satisfied. We can be more indifferent about the applause, and, in some measure, despise the censure of the world; secure that, however misunderstood or misrepresented, we are the natural and proper objects of approbation. On the contrary, if we are doubtful about it, we are often, upon that very account, more anxious to gain their approbation, and, provided we have not already, as they say, shaken hands with infamy, we are altogether distracted at the thoughts of their censure, which then strikes us with double severity.

When I endeavour to examine my own conduct, when I endeavour to pass sentence upon it, and either to approve or condemn it, it is evident that, in all such cases, I divide myself, as it were, into two persons; and that I, the examiner and judge, represent a different character from that other I, the person whose conduct is examined into and judged of. The first is the spectator, whose sentiments with regard to my own conduct I endeavour to enter into, by placing myself in his situation, and by considering how it would appear to me, when seen from that particular point of view. The second is the agent, the person whom I properly call myself, and of whose conduct, under the character of a spectator, I was endeavouring to form some opinion. The first is the judge; the second the person judged of. But that the judge should, in every respect, be the same with the person judged of, is as impossible, as that the cause should, in every respect, be the same with the effect.

To be amiable and to be meritorious; that is, to deserve love and to deserve reward, are the great characters of virtue; and to be odious and punishable, of vice. But all these characters have an immediate reference to the sentiments of others. Virtue is not said to be amiable, or to be meritorious, because it is the object of its own love, or of its own gratitude; but because it excites those sentiments in other men. The consciousness that it is the object of such favourable regards, is the source of that inward tranquillity and self-satisfaction with which it is naturally attended, as the suspicion of the contrary gives occasion to the torments of vice. What so great happiness as to be beloved, and to know that we deserve to be beloved? What so great misery as to be hated, and to know that we deserve to be hated?

CHAPTER II

Of the love of Praise, and of that of Praise-worthiness; and of the dread of Blame, and of that of Blame-worthiness

Man naturally desires, not only to be loved, but to be lovely; or to be that thing which is the natural and proper object of love. He naturally dreads, not only to be hated, but to be hateful; or to be that thing which is the natural and proper object of hatred. He desires, not only praise, but praise-worthiness; or to be that thing which, though it should be praised by nobody, is, however, the natural and proper object of praise. He dreads, not only blame, but blame-worthiness; or to be that thing which, though it should be blamed by nobody, is, however, the natural and proper object of blame.

The love of praise-worthiness is by no means derived altogether from the love of praise. Those two principles, though they resemble one another, though they are connected, and often blended with one another, are yet, in many respects, distinct and independent of one another.

The love and admiration which we naturally conceive for those whose character and conduct we approve of, necessarily dispose us to desire to become ourselves the objects of the like agreeable sentiments, and to be as amiable and as admirable as those whom we love and admire the most. Emulation, the anxious desire that we ourselves should excel, is originally founded in our admiration of the excellence of others. Neither can we be satisfied with being merely admired for what other people are admired. We must at least believe ourselves to be admirable for what they are admirable. But, in order to attain this satisfaction, we must become the impartial spectators of our own character and conduct. We must endeavour to view them with the eyes of other people, or as other people are likely to view them. When seen in this light, if they appear to us as we wish, we are happy and contented. But it greatly confirms this happiness and contentment when we find that other people, viewing them with those very eyes with which we, in imagination only, were endeavouring to view them, see them precisely in the same light in which we ourselves had seen them. Their approbation necessarily confirms our own self-approbation. Their praise necessarily strengthens our own sense of our own praise-worthiness. In this case, so far is the love of praise-worthiness from being derived altogether from that of praise; that the love of praise seems, at least in a great measure, to be derived from that of praise-worthiness.

The most sincere praise can give little pleasure when it cannot be considered as some sort of proof of praise-worthiness. It is by no means sufficient that, from ignorance or mistake, esteem and admiration should, in some way or other, be bestowed upon us. If we are conscious that we do not deserve to be so favourably thought of, and that if the truth were known, we should be regarded with very different sentiments, our satisfaction is far from being complete. The man who applauds us either for actions which we did not perform, or for motives which had no sort of influence upon our conduct, applauds not us, but another person. We can derive no sort of satisfaction from his praises. To us they should be more mortifying than any censure, and should perpetually call to our minds, the most humbling of all reflections, the reflection of what we ought to be, but what we are not. A woman who paints,* could derive, one should imagine, but little vanity from the compliments that are paid to her complexion. These, we should expect, ought rather to put her in mind of the sentiments which her real complexion would excite, and mortify her the more by the contrast. To be pleased with such groundless applause is a proof of the most superficial levity and weakness. It is what is properly called vanity, and is the foundation of the most ridiculous and contemptible vices, the vices of affectation and common lying; follies which, if experience did not teach us how common they are, one should imagine the least spark of common sense would save us from.

The foolish liar, who endeavours to excite the admiration of the company by the relation of adventures which never had any existence; the important coxcomb, who gives himself airs of rank and distinction which he well knows he has no just pretensions to; are both of them, no doubt, pleased with the applause which they fancy they meet with. But their vanity arises from so gross an illusion of the imagination, that it is difficult to conceive how any rational creature should be imposed upon by it. When they place themselves in the situation of those whom they fancy they have deceived, they are struck with the highest admiration for their own persons. They look upon themselves, not in that light in which, they know, they ought to appear to their companions, but in that in which they believe their companions actually look upon them. Their superficial weakness and trivial folly hinder them from ever turning their eyes inwards, or from seeing themselves in that despicable point of view in which their own consciences must tell them that they would appear to every body, if the real truth should ever come to be known. . . .

---

* Applies makeup.

CHAPTER III

Of the Influence and Authority of Conscience

But though the approbation of his own conscience can scarce, upon some extraordinary occasions, content the weakness of man; though the testimony of the supposed impartial spectator, of the great inmate of the breast, cannot always alone support him; yet the influence and authority of this principle is, upon all occasions, very great; and it is only by consulting this judge within, that we can ever see what relates to ourselves in its proper shape and dimensions; or that we can ever make any proper comparison between our own interests and those of other people.

As to the eye of the body, objects appear great or small, not so much according to their real dimensions, as according to the nearness or distance of their situation; so do they likewise to what may be called the natural eye of the mind: and we remedy the defects of both these organs pretty much in the same manner. In my present situation an immense landscape of lawns, and woods, and distant mountains, seems to do no more than cover the little window which I write by, and to be out of all proportion less than the chamber in which I am sitting. I can form a just comparison between those great objects and the little objects around me, in no other way, than by transporting myself, at least in fancy, to a different station, from whence I can survey both at nearly equal distances, and thereby form some judgment of their real proportions. Habit and experience have taught me to do this so easily and so readily, that I am scarce sensible that I do it; and a man must be, in some measure, acquainted with the philosophy of vision, before he can be thoroughly convinced, how little those distant objects would appear to the eye, if the imagination, from a knowledge of their real magnitudes, did not swell and dilate them.

In the same manner, to the selfish and original passions of human nature, the loss or gain of a very small interest of our own, appears to be of vastly more importance, excites a much more passionate joy or sorrow, a much more ardent desire or aversion, than the greatest concern of another with whom we have no particular connexion. His interests, as long as they are surveyed from this station, can never be put into the balance with our own, can never restrain us from doing whatever may tend to promote our own, how ruinous soever to him. Before we can make any proper comparison of those opposite interests, we must change our position. We must view them, neither from our own place nor yet from his, neither with our own eyes nor yet with his, but from the place and with the eyes of a third person, who has no particular connexion with either, and who judges with impartiality between us. Here, too, habit and experience have taught us to do this so easily and so readily, that we are scarce sensible that we do it; and it requires, in this case too, some degree of reflection, and even of philosophy, to convince us, how little interest we should take in the greatest concerns of our neighbour, how little we should be affected by whatever relates to him, if the sense of propriety and justice did not correct the otherwise natural inequality of our sentiments.

Let us suppose that the great empire of China, with all its myriads of inhabitants, was suddenly swallowed up by an earthquake, and let us consider how a man of humanity in Europe, who had no sort of connexion with that part of the world, would be affected upon receiving intelligence of this dreadful calamity. He would, I imagine, first of all, express very strongly his sorrow for the misfortune of that unhappy people, he would make many melancholy reflections upon the precariousness of human life, and the vanity of all the labours of man, which could thus be annihilated in a moment. He would too, perhaps, if he was a man of speculation, enter into many reasonings concerning the effects which this disaster might produce upon the commerce of Europe, and the trade and business of the world in general. And when all this fine philosophy was over, when all these humane sentiments had been once fairly expressed, he would pursue his business or his pleasure, take his repose or his diversion, with the same ease and tranquillity, as if no such accident had happened.

The most frivolous disaster which could befall himself would occasion a more real disturbance. If he was to lose his little finger tomorrow, he would not sleep tonight; but, provided he never saw them, he will snore with the most profound security over the ruin of a hundred millions of his brethren, and the destruction of that immense multitude seems plainly an object less interesting to him, than this paltry misfortune of his own. To prevent, therefore, this paltry misfortune to himself, would a man of humanity be willing to sacrifice the lives of a hundred millions of his brethren, provided he had never seen them? Human nature startles with horror at the thought, and the world, in its greatest depravity and corruption, never produced such a villain as could be capable of entertaining it. But what makes this difference? When our passive feelings are almost always so sordid and so selfish, how comes it that our active principles should often be so generous and so noble? When we are always so much more deeply affected by whatever concerns ourselves, than by whatever concerns other men; what is it which prompts the generous, upon all occasions, and the mean upon many, to sacrifice their own interests to the greater interests of others? It is not the soft power of humanity, it is not that feeble spark of benevolence which Nature has lighted up in the human heart, that is thus capable of counteracting the strongest impulses of self-love. It is a stronger power, a more forcible motive, which exerts itself upon such occasions. It is reason, principle, conscience, the inhabitant of the breast, the man within, the great judge and arbiter of our conduct. It is he who, whenever we are about to act so as to affect the happiness of others, calls to us, with a voice capable

of astonishing the most presumptuous of our passions, that we are but
one of the multitude, in no respect better than any other in it; and that
when we prefer ourselves so shamefully and so blindly to others, we
become the proper objects of resentment, abhorrence, and execration.
It is from him only that we learn the real littleness of ourselves, and of
whatever relates to ourselves, and the natural misrepresentations of self–
love can be corrected only by the eye of this impartial spectator. It is he
who shows us the propriety of generosity and the deformity of injustice;
the propriety of resigning the greatest interests of our own, for the yet
greater interests of others, and the deformity of doing the smallest injury
to another, in order to obtain the greatest benefit to ourselves. It is not
the love of our neighbour, it is not the love of mankind, which upon
many occasions prompts us to the practise of those divine virtues. It is a
stronger love, a more powerful affection, which generally takes place
upon such occasions; the love of what is honourable and noble, of the
grandeur, and dignity, and superiority of our own characters.

When the happiness or misery of others depends in any respect upon
our conduct, we dare not, as self-love might suggest to us, prefer the
interest of one to that of many. The man within immediately calls to
us, that we value ourselves too much and other people too little, and
that, by doing so, we render ourselves the proper object of the contempt
and indignation of our brethren. Neither is this sentiment confined to
men of extraordinary magnanimity and virtue. It is deeply impressed
upon every tolerably good soldier, who feels that he would become the
scorn of his companions, if he could be supposed capable of shrinking
from danger, or of hesitating, either to expose or to throw away his life,
when the good of the service required it.

One individual must never prefer himself so much even to any other
individual, as to hurt or injure that other, in order to benefit himself,
though the benefit to the one should be much greater than the hurt or
injury to the other. The poor man must neither defraud nor steal from
the rich, though the acquisition might be much more beneficial to the
one than the loss could be hurtful to the other. The man within immediately calls to him, in this case too, that he is no better than his neighbour, and that by this unjust preference he renders himself the proper
object of the contempt and indignation of mankind; as well as of the
punishment which that contempt and indignation must naturally dispose them to inflict, for having thus violated one of those sacred rules,
upon the tolerable observation of which depend the whole security and
peace of human society. There is no commonly honest man who does
not more dread the inward disgrace of such an action, the indelible stain
which it would forever stamp upon his own mind, than the greatest
external calamity which, without any fault of his own, could possibly
befall him; and who does not inwardly feel the truth of that great stoical
maxim, that for one man to deprive another unjustly of any thing, or

unjustly to promote his own advantage by the loss or disadvantage of another, is more contrary to nature, than death, than poverty, than pain, than all the misfortunes which can affect him, either in his body, or in his external circumstances.

When the happiness or misery of others, indeed, in no respect depends upon our conduct, when our interests are altogether separated and detached from theirs, so that there is neither connexion nor competition between them, we do not always think it so necessary to restrain, either our natural and, perhaps, improper anxiety about our own affairs, or our natural and, perhaps, equally improper indifference about those of other men. The most vulgar education teaches us to act, upon all important occasions, with some sort of impartiality between ourselves and others, and even the ordinary commerce of the world is capable of adjusting our active principles to some degree of propriety. But it is the most artifical and refined education only, it has been said, which can correct the inequalities of our passive feelings; and we must for this purpose, it has been pretended, have recourse to the severest, as well as to the profoundest philosophy. . . .

Our sensibility to the feelings of others, so far from being inconsistent with the manhood of self-command, is the very principle upon which that manhood is founded. The very same principle or instinct which, in the misfortune of our neighbour, prompts us to compassionate his sorrow; in our own misfortune, prompts us to restrain the abject and miserable lamentations of our own sorrow. The same principle or instinct which, in his prosperity and success, prompts us to congratulate his joy; in our own prosperity and success, prompts us to restrain the levity and intemperance of our own joy. In both cases, the propriety of our own sentiments and feelings seems to be exactly in proportion to the vivacity and force with which we enter into and conceive his sentiments and feelings.

The man of the most perfect virtue, the man whom we naturally love and revere the most, is he who joins, to the most perfect command of his own original and selfish feelings, the most exquisite sensibility both to the original and sympathetic feelings of others. The man who, to all the soft, the amiable, and the gentle virtues, joins all the great, the awful, and the respectable, must surely be the natural and proper object of our highest love and admiration.

The person best fitted by nature for acquiring the former of those two sets of virtues, is likewise best fitted for acquiring the latter. The man who feels the most for the joys and sorrows of others, is best fitted for acquiring the most complete control of his own joys and sorrows. The man of the most exquisite humanity, is naturally the most capable of acquiring the highest degree of self-command. He may not, however, always have acquired it; and it very frequently happens that he has not. He may have lived too much in ease and tranquillity. He may have never been exposed to the violence of faction, or to the hardships and hazards of war. He may have never experienced the insolence of his superiors, the jealous and malignant envy of his equals, or the pilfering injustice of his inferiors. When, in an advanced age, some accidental change of fortune exposes him to all these, they all make too great an impression upon him. He has the disposition which fits him for acquiring the most perfect self-command; but he has never had the opportunity of acquiring it. Exercise and practise have been wanting; and without these no habit can ever be tolerably established. Hardships, dangers, injuries, misfortunes, are the only masters under whom we can learn the exercise of this virtue. But these are all masters to whom nobody willingly puts himself to school. . . .

CHAPTER IV

Of the Nature of Self-deceit, and of the Origin and Use of general Rules

. . . Self-deceit, this fatal weakness of mankind, is the source of half the disorders of human life. If we saw ourselves in the light in which others see us, or in which they would see us if they knew all, a reformation would generally be unavoidable. We could not otherwise endure the sight.

Nature, however, has not left this weakness, which is of so much importance, altogether without a remedy; nor has she abandoned us entirely to the delusions of self-love. Our continual observations upon the conduct of others, insensibly lead us to form to ourselves certain general rules concerning what is fit and proper either to be done or to be avoided. Some of their actions shock all our natural sentiments. We hear every body about us express the like detestation against them. This still further confirms, and even exasperates our natural sense of their deformity. It satisfies us that we view them in the proper light, when we see other people view them in the same light. We resolve never to be guilty of the like, nor ever, upon any account, to render ourselves in this manner the objects of universal disapprobation. We thus naturally lay down to ourselves a general rule, that all such actions are to be avoided, as tending to render us odious, contemptible, or punishable, the objects of all those sentiments for which we have the greatest dread and aversion. Other actions, on the contrary, call forth our approbation, and we hear every body around us express the same favourable opinion concerning them. Every body is eager to honour and reward them. They excite all those sentiments for which we have by nature the strongest desire; the love, the gratitude, the admiration of mankind. We become ambitious of performing the like; and thus naturally lay down to ourselves a rule of another kind, that every opportunity of acting in this manner is carefully to be sought after.

It is thus that the general rules of morality are formed. They are ultimately founded upon experience of what, in particular instances, our moral faculties, our natural sense of merit and propriety, approve, or disapprove of. We do not originally approve or condemn particular actions; because, upon examination, they appear to be agreeable or inconsistent with a certain general rule. The general rule, on the contrary, is formed, by finding from experience, that all actions of a certain kind, or circumstanced in a certain manner, are approved or disapproved of. To the man who first saw an inhuman murder, committed from avarice, envy, or unjust resentment, and upon one too that loved and trusted the murderer, who beheld the last agonies of the dying person, who heard him, with his expiring breath, complain more of the perfidy and ingratitude of his false friend, than of the violence which had been done to him, there could be no occasion, in order to conceive how horrible such an action was, that he should reflect, that one of the most sacred rules of conduct was what prohibited the taking away the life of an innocent person, that this was a plain violation of that rule, and consequently a very blamable action. His detestation of this crime, it is evident, would arise instantaneously and antecedent to his having formed to himself any such general rule. The general rule, on the contrary, which he might afterwards form, would be founded upon the detestation which he felt necessarily arise in his own breast, at the thought of this, and every other particular action of the same kind. . . .

CHAPTER V

Of the influence and authority of the general Rules of Morality, and that they are justly regarded as the Laws of the Deity

The regard to those general rules of conduct, is what is properly called a sense of duty, a principle of the greatest consequence in human life, and the only principle by which the bulk of mankind are capable of directing their actions. Many men behave very decently, and through the whole of their lives avoid any considerable degree of blame, who yet, perhaps, never felt the sentiment upon the propriety of which we found our approbation of their conduct, but acted merely from a regard to what they saw were the established rules of behaviour. The man who has received great benefits from another person, may, by the natural coldness of his temper, feel but a very small degree of the sentiment of gratitude. If he has been virtuously educated, however, he will often have been made to observe how odious those actions appear which denote a want of this sentiment, and how amiable the contrary. Though his heart therefore is not warmed with any grateful affection, he will strive to act as if it was, and will endeavour to pay all those regards and attentions to his patron which the liveliest gratitude could suggest. He will visit him regularly; he will behave to him respectfully; he will never talk of him but with expressions of the highest esteem, and of the many obligations which he owes to him. And what is more, he will carefully embrace every opportunity of making a proper return for past services. He may do all this too without any hypocrisy or blamable dissimulation, without any selfish intention of obtaining new favours, and without any design of imposing either upon his benefactor or the public. The motive of his actions may be no other than a reverence for the established rule of duty, a serious and earnest desire of acting, in every respect, according to the law of gratitude. A wife, in the same manner, may sometimes not feel that tender regard for her husband which is suitable to the relation that subsists between them. If she has been virtuously educated, however, she will endeavour to act as if she felt it, to be careful, officious, faithful, and sincere, and to be deficient in none of those attentions which the sentiment of conjugal affection could have prompted her to perform. Such a friend, and such a wife, are neither of them, undoubtedly, the very best of their kinds: and though both of them may have the most serious and earnest desire to fulfill every part of their duty, yet they will fail in many nice and delicate regards, they will miss many opportunities of obliging, which they could never have overlooked if they had possessed the sentiment that is proper to their situation. Though not the very first of their kinds, however, they are perhaps the second; and if the regard to the general rules of conduct has been very strongly impressed upon them, neither of them will fail in any very essential part of their duty. None but those of the happiest mould are capable of suiting, with exact justness, their sentiments and behaviour to the smallest difference of situation, and of acting upon all occasions with the most delicate and accurate propriety. The coarse clay of which the bulk of mankind are formed, cannot be wrought up to such perfection. There is scarce any man, however, who by discipline, education, and example, may not be so impressed with a regard to general rules, as to act upon almost every occasion with tolerable decency, and through the whole of his life to avoid any considerable degree of blame.

Without this sacred regard to general rules, there is no man whose conduct can be much depended upon. It is this which constitutes the most essential difference between a man of principle and honour and a worthless fellow. The one adheres, on all occasions, steadily and resolutely to his maxims, and preserves through the whole of his life one even tenor of conduct. The other, acts variously and accidentally, as humour, inclination, or interest chance to be uppermost. Nay, such are the inequalities of humour to which all men are subject, that without this principle, the man who, in all his cool hours, had the most delicate sensibility to the propriety of conduct, might often be led to act absurdly upon the most frivolous occasions, and when it was scarce possible to assign any serious motive for his behaving in this manner. Your friend makes you a visit when you happen to be in a humour which makes it disagreeable to receive him: in your present mood his civility is very apt to appear an impertinent intrusion; and if you were to give way to the views of things which at this time occur, though civil in your temper, you would behave to him with coldness and contempt. What renders you incapable of such a rudeness, is nothing but a regard to the general rules of civility and hospitality, which prohibit it. That habitual reverence which your former experience has taught you for these, enables you to act, upon all such occasions, with nearly equal propriety, and hinders those inequalities of temper, to which all men are subject, from influencing your conduct in any very sensible degree. But if without regard to these general rules, even the duties of politeness, which are so easily observed, and which one can scarce have any serious motive to violate, would yet be so frequently violated, what would become of the duties of justice, of truth, of chastity, of fidelity, which it is often so difficult to observe, and which there may be so many strong motives to violate? But upon the tolerable observance of these duties, depends the very existence of human society, which would crumble into nothing if mankind were not generally impressed with a reverence for those important rules of conduct.

This reverence is still further enhanced by an opinion which is first impressed by nature, and afterwards confirmed by reasoning and philosophy, that those important rules of morality are the commands and laws of the Deity, who will finally reward the obedient, and punish the transgressors of their duty.

This opinion or apprehension, I say, seems first to be impressed by nature. Men are naturally led to ascribe to those mysterious beings, whatever they are, which happen, in any country, to be the objects of religious fear, all their own sentiments and passions. They have no other, they can conceive no other to ascribe to them. Those unknown intelligences which they imagine but see not, must necessarily be formed with some sort of resemblance to those intelligences of which they have experience. During the ignorance and darkness of pagan superstition, mankind seem to have formed the ideas of their divinities with so little delicacy, that they ascribed to them, indiscriminately, all the passions of human nature, those not excepted which do the least honour to our species, such as lust, hunger, avarice, envy, revenge. They could not fail, therefore, to ascribe to those beings, for the excellence of whose nature they still conceived the highest admiration, those sentiments and qualities which are the great ornaments of humanity, and which seem to raise it to a resemblance of divine perfection, the love of virtue and beneficence, and the abhorrence of vice and injustice.

The man who was injured, called upon Jupiter to be witness of the wrong that was done to him, and could not doubt, but that divine being would behold it with the same indignation which would animate the meanest of mankind, who looked on when injustice was committed. The man who did the injury, felt himself to be the proper object of the detestation and resentment of mankind; and his natural fears led him to impute the same sentiments to those awful beings, whose presence he could not avoid, and whose power he could not resist. These natural hopes and fears, and suspicions, were propagated by sympathy, and confirmed by education; and the gods were universally represented and believed to be the rewarders of humanity and mercy, and the avengers of perfidy and injustice. And thus religion, even in its rudest form, gave a sanction to the rules of morality, long before the age of artificial reasoning and philosophy. That the terrors of religion should thus enforce the natural sense of duty, was of too much importance to the happiness of mankind, for nature to leave it dependent upon the slowness and uncertainty of philosophical researches.

These researches, however, when they came to take place, confirmed those original anticipations of nature. Upon whatever we suppose that our moral faculties are founded, whether upon a certain modification of reason, upon an original instinct, called a moral sense, or upon some other principle of our nature, it cannot be doubted, that they were given us for the direction of our conduct in this life. They carry along with them the most evident badges of this authority, which denote that they were set up within us to be the supreme arbiters of all our actions, to superintend all our senses, passions, and appetites, and to judge how far each of them was either to be indulged or restrained.

Our moral faculties are by no means, as some have pretended, upon a level in this respect with the other faculties and appetites of our nature, endowed with no more right to restrain these last, than these last are to restrain them. No other faculty or principle of action judges of any other. Love does not judge of resentment, nor resentment of love. Those two passions may be opposite to one another, but cannot, with any propriety, be said to approve or disapprove of one another. But it is the peculiar office of those faculties now under our consideration to judge, to bestow censure or applause upon all the other principles of our nature. They may be considered as a sort of senses of which those principles are the objects. Every sense is supreme over its own objects. There is no appeal from the eye with regard to the beauty of colours, nor from the ear with regard to the harmony of sounds, nor from the taste with regard to the agreeableness of flavours. Each of those senses judges in the last resort of its own objects. Whatever gratifies the taste is sweet, whatever pleases the eye is beautiful, whatever soothes the ear is harmonious. The very essence of each of those qualities consists in its being fitted to please the sense to which it is addressed. It belongs to our moral faculties, in the same manner to determine when the ear ought to be soothed, when the eye ought to be indulged, when the taste ought to be gratified, when and how far every other principle of our nature ought either to be indulged or restrained. What is agreeable to our moral faculties, is fit, and right, and proper to be done; the contrary wrong, unfit, and improper. The sentiments which they approve of, are graceful and becoming: the contrary, ungraceful and unbecoming. The very words, right, wrong, fit, improper, graceful, unbecoming, mean only what pleases or displeases those faculties.

Since these, therefore, were plainly intended to be the governing principles of human nature, the rules which they prescribe are to be regarded as the commands and laws of the Deity, promulgated by those vicegerents which he has thus set up within us. All general rules are commonly denominated laws: thus the general rules which bodies observe in the communication of motion, are called the laws of motion. But those general rules which our moral faculties observe in approving or condemning whatever sentiment or action is subjected to their examination, may much more justly be denominated such. They have a much greater resemblance to what are properly called laws, those general rules which the sovereign lays down to direct the conduct of his subjects. Like them they are rules to direct the free actions of men: they are prescribed most surely by a lawful superior, and are attended too with the sanction of rewards and punishments. Those vicegerents of God within us, never fail to punish the violation of them, by the torments of inward shame, and self–condemnation; and on the contrary, always reward obedience with tranquillity of mind, with contentment, and self-satisfaction.

There are innumerable other considerations which serve to confirm the same conclusion. The happiness of mankind, as well as of all other rational creatures, seems to have been the original purpose intended by the Author of nature, when he brought them into existence. No other end seems worthy of that supreme wisdom and divine benignity which we necessarily ascribe to him; and this opinion, which we are led to by the abstract consideration of his infinite perfections, is still more confirmed by the examination of the works of nature, which seem all intended to promote happiness, and to guard against misery. But by acting according to the dictates of our moral faculties, we necessarily pursue the most effectual means for promoting the happiness of mankind, and may therefore be said, in some sense, to cooperate with the Deity, and to advance as far as in our power the plan of Providence. By acting otherways, on the contrary, we seem to obstruct, in some measure, the scheme which the Author of nature has established for the happiness and perfection of the world, and to declare ourselves, if I may say so, in some measure the enemies of God. Hence we are naturally encouraged to hope for his extraordinary favour and reward in the one case, and to dread his vengeance and punishment in the other.

There are besides many other reasons, and many other natural principles, which all tend to confirm and inculcate the same salutary doctrine. If we consider the general rules by which external prosperity and adversity are commonly distributed in this life, we shall find, that notwithstanding the disorder in which all things appear to be in this world, yet even here every virtue naturally meets with its proper reward, with the recompense which is most fit to encourage and promote it; and this too so surely, that it requires a very extraordinary concurrence of circumstances entirely to disappoint it. What is the reward most proper for encouraging industry, prudence, and circumspection? Success in every sort of business. And is it possible that in the whole of life these virtues should fail of attaining it? Wealth and external honours are their proper recompense, and the recompense which they can seldom fail of acquiring. What reward is most proper for promoting the practise of truth, justice, and humanity? The confidence, the esteem, and love of those we live with. Humanity does not desire to be great, but to be beloved. It is not in being rich that truth and justice would rejoice, but in being trusted and believed, recompenses which those virtues must almost always acquire.

By some very extraordinary and unlucky circumstance, a good man may come to be suspected of a crime of which he was altogether incapable, and upon that account be most unjustly exposed for the remaining part of his life to the horror and aversion of mankind. By an accident of this kind he may be said to lose his all, notwithstanding his integrity and justice; in the same manner as a cautious man, notwithstanding his utmost circumspection, may be ruined by an earthquake or an inundation. Accidents of the first kind, however, are perhaps still more rare, and still more contrary to the common course of things than those of the second; and it still remains true, that the practise of truth, justice, and humanity is a certain and almost infallible method of acquiring what those virtues chiefly aim at, the confidence and love of those we live with. A person may be very easily misrepresented with regard to a particular action; but it is scarce possible that he should be so with regard to the general tenor of his conduct. An innocent man may be believed to have done wrong: this, however, will rarely happen. On the contrary, the established opinion of the innocence of his manners, will often lead us to absolve him where he has really been in the fault, notwithstanding very strong presumptions. A knave, in the same manner, may escape censure, or even meet with applause, for a particular knavery, in which his conduct is not understood. But no man was ever habitually such, without being almost universally known to be so, and without being even frequently suspected of guilt, when he was in reality perfectly innocent. And so far as vice and virtue can be either punished or rewarded by the sentiments and opinions of mankind, they both, according to the common course of things, meet even here with something more than exact and impartial justice.

But though the general rules by which prosperity and adversity are commonly distributed, when considered in this cool and philosophical light, appear to be perfectly suited to the situation of mankind in this life, yet they are by no means suited to some of our natural sentiments. Our natural love and admiration for some virtues is such, that we should

wish to bestow on them all sorts of honours and rewards, even those
which we must acknowledge to be the proper recompenses of other qualities, with which those virtues are not always accompanied. Our detestation, on the contrary, for some vices is such, that we should desire to
heap upon them every sort of disgrace and disaster, those not excepted
which are the natural consequences of very different qualities. Magnanimity, generosity, and justice, command so high a degree of admiration,
that we desire to see them crowned with wealth, and power, and honours of every kind, the natural consequences of prudence, industry, and
application; qualities with which those virtues are not inseparably connected. Fraud, falsehood, brutality, and violence, on the other hand,
excite in every human breast such scorn and abhorrence, that our indignation rouses to see them possess those advantages which they may in
some sense be said to have merited, by the diligence and industry with
which they are sometimes attended. The industrious knave cultivates the
soil; the indolent good man leaves it uncultivated. Who ought to reap
the harvest? who starve, and who live in plenty? The natural course of
things decides it in favour of the knave: the natural sentiments of mankind in favour of the man of virtue.

Man judges, that the good qualities of the one are greatly over-recom-
pensed by those advantages which they tend to procure him, and that
the omissions of the other are by far too severely punished by the distress
which they naturally bring upon him; and human laws, the consequences of human sentiments, forfeit the life and the estate of the industrious and cautious traitor, and reward, by extraordinary recompenses,
the fidelity and public spirit of the improvident and careless good citizen. Thus man is by Nature directed to correct, in some measure, that
distribution of things which she herself would otherwise have made. The
rules which for this purpose she prompts him to follow, are different
from those which she herself observes. She bestows upon every virtue,
and upon every vice, that precise reward or punishment which is best
fitted to encourage the one, or to restrain the other. She is directed by
this sole consideration, and pays little regard to the different degrees of
merit and demerit, which they may seem to possess in the sentiments
and passions of man. Man, on the contrary, pays regard to this only,
and would endeavour to render the state of every virtue precisely proportioned to that degree of love and esteem, and of every vice to that
degree of contempt and abhorrence, which he himself conceives for it.
The rules which she follows are fit for her, those which he follows for
him: but both are calculated to promote the same great end, the order
of the world, and the perfection and happiness of human nature.

But though man is thus employed to alter that distribution of things
which natural events would make, if left to themselves; though, like the
gods of the poets, he is perpetually interposing, by extraordinary means,
in favour of virtue, and in opposition to vice, and, like them, endeavours

to turn away the arrow that is aimed at the head of the righteous, but to accelerate the sword of destruction that is lifted up against the wicked; yet he is by no means able to render the fortune of either quite suitable to his own sentiments and wishes. The natural course of things cannot be entirely controlled by the impotent endeavours of man: the current is too rapid and too strong for him to stop it; and though the rules which direct it appear to have been established for the wisest and best purposes, they sometimes produce effects which shock all his natural sentiments. That a great combination of men should prevail over a small one; that those who engage in an enterprise with forethought and all necessary preparation, should prevail over such as oppose them without any; and that every end should be acquired by those means only which Nature has established for acquiring it, seems to be a rule not only necessary and unavoidable in itself, but even useful and proper for rousing the industry and attention of mankind. Yet, when, in consequence of this rule, violence and artifice prevail over sincerity and justice, what indignation does it not excite in the breast of every human spectator? What sorrow and compassion for the sufferings of the innocent, and what furious resentment against the success of the oppressor? We are equally grieved and enraged at the wrong that is done, but often find it altogether out of our power to redress it. When we thus despair of finding any force upon earth which can check the triumph of injustice, we naturally appeal to heaven, and hope, that the great Author of our nature will himself execute hereafter, what all the principles which he has given us for the direction of our conduct, prompt us to attempt even here; that he will complete the plan which he himself has thus taught us to begin; and will, in a life to come, render to every one according to the works which he has performed in this world. And thus we are led to the belief of a future state, not only by the weaknesses, by the hopes and fears of human nature, but by the noblest and best principles which belong to it, by the love of virtue, and by the abhorrence of vice and injustice. . . .

CHAPTER VI

In what cases the Sense of Duty ought to be the sole principle of our conduct; and in what cases it ought to concur with other motives

[Chapter 6 discusses the diversity of religious interpretations found in the world.]

PART IV

OF THE EFFECT OF UTILITY UPON THE SENTIMENT OF APPROBATION CONSISTING OF ONE SECTION

CHAPTER I

Of the beauty which the appearance of Utility bestows upon all the productions of art, and of the extensive influence of this species of Beauty

That utility is one of the principal sources of beauty has been observed by every body, who has considered with any attention what constitutes the nature of beauty. The convenience of a house gives pleasure to the spectator as well as its regularity, and he is as much hurt when he observes the contrary defect, as when he sees the correspondent windows of different forms, or the door not placed exactly in the middle of the building. That the fitness of any system or machine to produce the end for which it was intended, bestows a certain propriety and beauty upon the whole, and renders the very thought and contemplation of it agreeable, is so very obvious that nobody has overlooked it.

The cause too, why utility pleases, has of late been assigned by an ingenious and agreeable philosopher, * who joins the greatest depth of thought to the greatest elegance of expression, and possesses the singular and happy talent of treating the abstrusest subjects not only with the most perfect perspicuity, but with the most lively eloquence. The utility of any object, according to him, pleases the master by perpetually suggesting to him the pleasure or convenience which it is fitted to promote. Every time he looks at it, he is put in mind of this pleasure; and the object in this manner becomes a source of perpetual satisfaction and enjoyment. The spectator enters by sympathy into the sentiments of the master, and necessarily views the object under the same agreeable aspect. When we visit the palaces of the great, we cannot help conceiving the satisfaction we should enjoy if we ourselves were the masters, and were possessed of so much artful and ingeniously contrived accommodation. A similar account is given why the appearance of inconvenience should render any object disagreeable both to the owner and to the spectator.

But that this fitness, this happy contrivance of any production of art, should often be more valued, than the very end for which it was intended; and that the exact adjustment of the means for attaining any convenience or pleasure should frequently be more regarded, than that very convenience or pleasure, in the attainment of which their whole merit would seem to consist, has not, so far as I know, been yet taken notice

* David Hume.

of by any body. That this however is very frequently the case, may be observed in a thousand instances, both in the most frivolous and in the most important concerns of human life.

When a person comes into his chamber, and finds the chairs all standing in the middle of the room, he is angry with his servant, and rather than see them continue in that disorder, perhaps takes the trouble himself to set them all in their places with their backs to the wall. The whole propriety of this new situation arises from its superior convenience in leaving the floor free and disengaged. To attain this convenience he voluntarily puts himself to more trouble than all he could have suffered from the want of it; since nothing was more easy, than to have set himself down upon one of them, which is probably what he does when his labour is over. What he wanted therefore, it seems, was not so much this convenience, as that arrangement of things which promotes it. Yet it is this convenience which ultimately recommends that arrangement, and bestows upon it the whole of its propriety and beauty.

A watch, in the same manner, that falls behind above two minutes in a day, is despised by one curious in watches. He sells it perhaps for a couple of guineas, and purchases another at fifty, which will not lose above a minute in a fortnight. The sole use of watches however, is to tell us what o'clock it is, and to hinder us from breaking any engagement, or suffering any other inconvenience by our ignorance in that particular point. But the person so nice with regard to this machine will not always be found either more scrupulously punctual than other men, or more anxiously concerned upon any other account, to know precisely what time of day it is. What interests him is not so much the attainment of this piece of knowledge, as the perfection of the machine which serves to attain it.

How many people ruin themselves by laying out money on trinkets of frivolous utility? What pleases these lovers of toys is not so much the utility as the aptness of the machines which are fitted to promote it. All their pockets are stuffed with little conveniences. They contrive new pockets, unknown in the clothes of other people, in order to carry a greater number. They walk about loaded with a multitude of baubles, in weight and sometimes in value not inferior to an ordinary Jew's-box, some of which may sometimes be of some little use, but all of which might at all times be very well spared, and of which the whole utility is certainly not worth the fatigue of bearing the burden.

Nor is it only with regard to such frivolous objects that our conduct is influenced by this principle; it is often the secret motive of the most serious and important pursuits of both private and public life.

The poor man's son, whom heaven in its anger has visited with ambition, when he begins to look around him, admires the condition of the rich. He finds the cottage of his father too small for his accommodation, and fancies he should be lodged more at his ease in a palace. He is displeased with being obliged to walk a-foot, or to endure the fatigue of riding on horseback. He sees his superiors carried about in machines, and imagines that in one of these he could travel with less inconvenience. He feels himself naturally indolent, and willing to serve himself with his own hands as little as possible; and judges, that a numerous retinue of servants would save him from a great deal of trouble. He thinks if he had attained all these, he would sit still contentedly, and be quiet, enjoying himself in the thought of the happiness and tranquillity of his situation. He is enchanted with the distant idea of this felicity. It appears in his fancy like the life of some superior rank of beings, and, in order to arrive at it, he devotes himself forever to the pursuit of wealth and greatness.

To obtain the conveniences which these afford, he submits in the first year, nay in the first month of his application, to more fatigue of body and more uneasiness of mind than he could have suffered through the whole of his life from the want of them. He studies to distinguish himself in some laborious profession. With the most unrelenting industry he labours night and day to acquire talents superior to all his competitors. He endeavours next to bring those talents into public view, and with equal assiduity solicits every opportunity of employment. For this purpose he makes his court to all mankind; he serves those whom he hates, and is obsequious to those whom he despises. Through the whole of his life he pursues the idea of a certain artificial and elegant repose which he may never arrive at, for which he sacrifices a real tranquillity that is at all times in his power, and which, if in the extremity of old age he should at last attain to it, he will find to be in no respect preferable to that humble security and contentment which he had abandoned for it.

It is then, in the last dregs of life, his body wasted with toil and diseases, his mind galled and ruffled by the memory of a thousand injuries and disappointments which he imagines he has met with from the injustice of his enemies, or from the perfidy and ingratitude of his friends, that he begins at last to find that wealth and greatness are mere trinkets of frivolous utility, no more adapted for procuring ease of body or tranquillity of mind that the tweezer cases of the lover of toys; and like them too, more troublesome to the person who carries them about with him than all the advantages they can afford him are commodious. There is no other real difference between them, except that the conveniences of the one are somewhat more observable than those of the other. The palaces, the gardens, the equipage, the retinue of the great are objects of which the obvious convenience strikes every body. They do not require that their masters should point out to us wherein consists their utility. Of our own accord we readily enter into it, and by sympathy enjoy and thereby applaud the satisfaction which they are fitted to afford him.

But the curiosity of a toothpick, of an ear-picker, of a machine for cutting the nails, or of any other trinket of the same kind, is not so obvious. Their convenience may perhaps be equally great, but it is not so striking, and we do not so readily enter into the satisfaction of the man who possesses them. They are therefore less reasonable subjects of vanity than the magnificence of wealth and greatness; and in this consists the sole advantage of these last. They more effectually gratify that love of distinction so natural to man. To one who was to live alone in a desolate island it might be a matter of doubt, perhaps, whether a palace, or a collection of such small conveniences as are commonly contained in a tweezer case, would contribute most to his happiness and enjoyment. If he is to live in society, indeed, there can be no comparison, because in this, as in all other cases, we constantly pay more regard to the sentiments of the spectator, than to those of the person principally concerned, and consider rather how his situation will appear to other people, than how it will appear to himself.

If we examine, however, why the spectator distinguishes with such admiration the condition of the rich and the great, we shall find that it is not so much upon account of the superior ease or pleasure which they are supposed to enjoy, as of the numberless artificial and elegant contrivances for promoting this ease or pleasure. He does not even imagine that they are really happier than other people: but he imagines that they possess more means of happiness. And it is the ingenious and artful adjustment of those means to the end for which they were intended, that is the principal source of his admiration. But in the languor of disease and the weariness of old age, the pleasures of the vain and empty distinctions of greatness disappear. To one, in this situation, they are no longer capable of recommending those toilsome pursuits in which they had formerly engaged him. In his heart he curses ambition, and vainly regrets the ease and the indolence of youth, pleasures which are fled forever, and which he has foolishly sacrificed for what, when he has got it, can afford him no real satisfaction. In this miserable aspect does greatness appear to every man when reduced either by spleen or disease to observe with attention his own situation, and to consider what it is that is really wanting to his happiness. Power and riches appear then to be, what they are, enormous and operose machines contrived to produce a few trifling conveniences to the body, consisting of springs the most nice and delicate, which must be kept in order with the most anxious attention, and which in spite of all our care are ready every moment to burst into pieces, and to crush in their ruins their unfortunate possessor. They are immense fabrics, which it requires the labour of a life to raise, which threaten every moment to overwhelm the person that dwells in them, and which while they stand, though they may save him from some smaller inconveniences, can protect him from none of the severer inclemencies of the season. They keep off the summer shower, not the winter storm, but leave him always as much, and sometimes more exposed than before, to anxiety, to fear, and to sorrow; to diseases, to danger, and to death.

But though this splenetic philosophy, which in time of sickness or low spirits is familiar to every man, thus entirely depreciates those great objects of human desire, when in better health and in better humour, we never fail to regard them under a more agreeable aspect. Our imagination, which in pain and sorrow seems to be confined and cooped up within our own persons, in times of ease and prosperity expands itself to every thing around us. We are then charmed with the beauty of that accommodation which reigns in the palaces and economy of the great; and admire how every thing is adapted to promote their ease, to prevent their wants, to gratify their wishes, and to amuse and entertain their most frivolous desires. If we consider the real satisfaction which all these things are capable of affording, by itself and separated from the beauty of that arrangement which is fitted to promote it, it will always appear in the highest degree contemptible and trifling. But we rarely view it in this abstract and philosophical light. We naturally confound it in our imagination with the order, the regular and harmonious movement of the system, the machine or economy by means of which it is produced. The pleasures of wealth and greatness, when considered in this complex view, strike the imagination as something grand and beautiful and noble, of which the attainment is well worth all the toil and anxiety which we are so apt to bestow upon it.

And it is well that nature imposes upon us in this manner. It is this deception which rouses and keeps in continual motion the industry of mankind. It is this which first prompted them to cultivate the ground, to build houses, to found cities and commonwealths, and to invent and improve all the sciences and arts, which ennoble and embellish human life; which have entirely changed the whole face of the globe, have turned the rude forests of nature into agreeable and fertile plains, and made the trackless and barren ocean a new fund of subsistence, and the great high road of communication to the different nations of the earth. The earth by these labours of mankind has been obliged to redouble her natural fertility, and to maintain a greater multitude of inhabitants. It is to no purpose, that the proud and unfeeling landlord views his extensive fields, and without a thought for the wants of his brethren, in imagination consumes himself the whole harvest that grows upon them. The homely and vulgar proverb, that the eye is larger than the belly, never was more fully verified than with regard to him. The capacity of his stomach bears no proportion to the immensity of his desires, and will receive no more than that of the meanest peasant. The rest he is obliged to distribute among those, who prepare, in the nicest manner, that little which he himself makes use of, among those who fit up the palace in which this little is to be consumed, among those who provide and keep in order all the different baubles and trinkets, which are employed in the economy of greatness; all of whom thus derive from his luxury and caprice, that share of the necessaries of life, which they would in vain have expected from his humanity or his justice.

The produce of the soil maintains at all times nearly that number of inhabitants which it is capable of maintaining. The rich only select from the heap what is most precious and agreeable. They consume little more than the poor, and in spite of their natural selfishness and rapacity, though they mean only their own convenience, though the sole end which they propose from the labours of all the thousands whom they employ, be the gratification of their own vain and insatiable desires, they divide with the poor the produce of all their improvements. They are led by an invisible hand to make nearly the same distribution of the necessaries of life, which would have been made, had the earth been divided into equal portions among all its inhabitants, and thus without intending it, without knowing it, advance the interest of the society, and afford means to the multiplication of the species. When Providence divided the earth among a few lordly masters, it neither forgot nor abandoned those who seemed to have been left out in the partition. These last too enjoy their share of all that it produces. In what constitutes the real happiness of human life, they are in no respect inferior to those who would seem so much above them. In ease of body and peace of mind, all the different ranks of life are nearly upon a level, and the beggar, who suns himself by the side of the highway, possesses that security which kings are fighting for. . . .

CHAPTER II

Of the beauty which the appearance of Utility bestows upon the characters and actions of men; and how far the perception of this beauty may be regarded as one of the original principles of approbation

[Chapter 2 elaborates further on the concept and role of utility in our ordinary conduct.]

PART V

OF THE INFLUENCE OF CUSTOM AND FASHION UPON THE SENTIMENTS OF MORAL APPROBATION AND DISAPPROBATION CONSISTING OF ONE SECTION

CHAPTER I

Of the Influence of Custom and Fashion upon our Notions of Beauty and Deformity

There are other principles besides those already enumerated, which have a considerable influence upon the moral sentiments of mankind, and are the chief causes of the many irregular and discordant opinions which prevail in different ages and nations concerning what is blamable or praise-worthy. These principles are custom and fashion, principles which extend their dominion over our judgments concerning beauty of every kind.

When two objects have frequently been seen together, the imagination acquires a habit of passing easily from the one to the other. If the first appear, we lay our account that the second is to follow. Of their own accord they put us in mind of one another, and the attention glides easily along them. Though, independent of custom, there should be no real beauty in their union, yet when custom has thus connected them together, we feel an impropriety in their separation. The one we think is awkward when it appears without its usual companion. We miss something which we expected to find, and the habitual arrangement of our ideas is disturbed by the disappointment. A suit of clothes, for example, seems to want something if they are without the most insignificant ornament which usually accompanies them, and we find a meanness or awkwardness in the absence even of a haunch button. When there is any natural propriety in the union, custom increases our sense of it, and makes a different arrangement appear still more disagreeable than it would otherwise seem to be. Those who have been accustomed to see things in a good taste are more disgusted by whatever is clumsy or awkward. Where the conjunction is improper, custom either diminishes, or takes away altogether, our sense of the impropriety. Those who have been accustomed to slovenly disorder lose all sense of neatness or elegance. The modes of furniture or dress which seem ridiculous to strangers, give no offence to the people who are used to them.

Fashion is different from custom, or rather is a particular species of it. That is not the fashion which every body wears, but which those wear who are of a high rank, or character. The graceful, the easy, and commanding manners of the great, joined to the usual richness and magnificence of their dress, give a grace to the very form which they happen to bestow upon it. As long as they continue to use this form, it is connected in our imaginations with the idea of something that is genteel and magnificent, and though in itself it should be indifferent, it seems, on account of this relation, to have something about it that is genteel and magnificent too. As soon as they drop it, it loses all the grace, which it had appeared to possess before, and being now used only by the inferior ranks of people, seems to have something of their meanness and awkwardness.

Dress and furniture are allowed by all the world to be entirely under the dominion of custom and fashion. The influence of those principles, however, is by no means confined to so narrow a sphere, but extends itself to whatever is in any respect the object of taste, to music, to poetry, to architecture. The modes of dress and furniture are continually changing, and that fashion appearing ridiculous today which was admired five years ago, we are experimentally convinced that it owed its vogue chiefly or entirely to custom and fashion. Clothes and furniture are not made of very durable materials. A well-fancied coat is done in a twelve-month, and cannot continue longer to propagate, as the fashion, that form according to which it was made. The modes of furniture change less rapidly than those of dress; because furniture is commonly more durable. In five or six years, however, it generally undergoes an entire revolution, and every man in his own time sees the fashion in this respect change many different ways.

The productions of the other arts are much more lasting, and, when happily imagined, may continue to propagate the fashion of their make for a much longer time. A well-contrived building may endure many centuries: a beautiful air may be delivered down by a sort of tradition, through many successive generations: a well-written poem may last as long as the world; and all of them continue for ages together, to give the vogue to that particular style, to that particular taste or manner, according to which each of them was composed. Few men have an opportunity of seeing in their own times the fashion in any of these arts change very considerably. Few men have so much experience and acquaintance with the different modes which have obtained in remote ages and nations, as to be thoroughly reconciled to them, or to judge with impartiality between them, and what takes place in their own age and country. Few men therefore are willing to allow, that custom or fashion have much influence upon their judgments concerning what is beautiful, or otherwise, in the productions of any of those arts; but imagine, that all the rules, which they think ought to be observed in each of them, are founded upon reason and nature, not upon habit or prejudice. A very little attention, however, may convince them of the contrary, and satisfy them, that the influence of custom and fashion over dress and furniture, is not more absolute than over architecture, poetry, and music.

Can any reason, for example, be assigned why the Doric capital should be appropriated to a pillar whose height is equal to eight diameters; the Ionic volute to one of nine; and the Corinthian foliage to one of ten? The propriety of each of those appropriations can be founded upon nothing but habit and custom. The eye having been used to see a particular proportion connected with a particular ornament, would be offended if they were not joined together. Each of the five orders has its peculiar ornaments, which cannot be changed for any other, without giving offence to all those who know any thing of the rules of architecture. According to some architects, indeed, such is the exquisite judgment with which the ancients have assigned to each order its proper ornaments, that no others can be found which are equally suitable. It seems, however, a little difficult to be conceived that these forms, though, no doubt, extremely agreeable, should be the only forms which can suit those proportions, or that there should not be five hundred others which, antecedent to established custom, would have fitted them equally well. When custom, however, has established particular rules of building, provided they are not absolutely unreasonable, it is absurd to think of altering them for others which are only equally good, or even for others which, in point of elegance and beauty, have naturally some little advantage over them. A man would be ridiculous who should appear in public with a suit of clothes quite different from those which are commonly worn, though the new dress should in itself be ever so graceful or convenient. And there seems to be an absurdity of the same kind in ornamenting a house after a quite different manner from that which custom and fashion have prescribed; though the new ornaments should in themselves be somewhat superior to the common ones. . . .

Neither is it only over the productions of the arts, that custom and fashion exert their dominion. They influence our judgments, in the same manner, with regard to the beauty of natural objects. What various and opposite forms are deemed beautiful in different species of things? The proportions which are admired in one animal, are altogether different from those which are esteemed in another. Every class of things has its own peculiar conformation, which is approved of, and has a beauty of its own, distinct from that of every other species. It is upon this account that a learned Jesuit, father Buffier, has determined that the beauty of every object consists in that form and colour, which is most usual among things of that particular sort to which it belongs. Thus, in the human form, the beauty of each feature lies in a certain middle, equally removed from a variety of other forms that are ugly. A beautiful nose, for example, is one that is neither very long, nor very short, neither very straight, nor very crooked, but a sort of middle among all these extremes, and less different from any one of them, than all of them are from one another. It is the form which Nature seems to have aimed at in them all, which, however, she deviates from in a great variety of ways, and very seldom hits exactly; but to which all those deviations still bear a very strong resemblance.

When a number of drawings are made after one pattern, though they may all miss it in some respects, yet they will all resemble it more than they resemble one another; the general character of the pattern will run through them all; the most singular and odd will be those which are most wide of it; and though very few will copy it exactly, yet the most accurate delineations will bear a greater resemblance to the most careless, than the careless ones will bear to one another.

In the same manner, in each species of creatures, what is most beautiful bears the strongest characters of the general fabric of the species, and has the strongest resemblance to the greater part of the individuals with which it is classed. Monsters, on the contrary, or what is perfectly deformed, are always most singular and odd, and have the least resemblance to the generality of that species to which they belong. And thus the beauty of each species, though in one sense the rarest of all things, because few individuals hit this middle form exactly, yet in another, is the most common, because all the deviations from it resemble it more than they resemble one another. The most customary form, therefore, is in each species of things, according to him, the most beautiful. And hence it is that a certain practise and experience in contemplating each species of objects is requisite, before we can judge of its beauty, or know wherein the middle and most usual form consists. The nicest judgment concerning the beauty of the human species, will not help us to judge of that of flowers, or horses, or any other species of things.

It is for the same reason that in different climates, and where different customs and ways of living take place, as the generality of any species receives a different conformation from those circumstances, so different ideas of its beauty prevail. The beauty of a Moorish is not exactly the same with that of an English horse. What different ideas are formed in different nations concerning the beauty of the human shape and countenance? A fair complexion is a shocking deformity upon the coast of Guinea. Thick lips and a flat nose are a beauty. In some nations long ears that hang down upon the shoulders are the objects of universal admiration. In China if a lady's foot is so large as to be fit to walk upon, she is regarded as a monster of ugliness. Some of the savage nations in North America tie four boards round the heads of their children, and thus squeeze them, while the bones are tender and gristly, into a form that is almost perfectly square. Europeans are astonished at the absurd barbarity of this practise, to which some missionaries have imputed the singular stupidity of those nations among whom it prevails. But when they condemn those savages, they do not reflect that the ladies in Europe had, till within these very few years, been endeavouring, for near a century past, to squeeze the beautiful roundness of their natural shape into a square form of the same kind. And that, notwithstanding the many distortions and diseases which this practise was known to occasion, custom had rendered it agreeable among some of the most civilised nations which, perhaps, the world ever beheld. . . .

CHAPTER II

Of the Influence of Custom and Fashion upon Moral Sentiments

Since our sentiments concerning beauty of every kind are so much influenced by custom and fashion, it cannot be expected, that those, concerning the beauty of conduct, should be entirely exempted from the dominion of those principles. Their influence here, however, seems to be much less than it is everywhere else. There is, perhaps, no form of external objects, how absurd and fantastical soever, to which custom will not reconcile us, or which fashion will not render even agreeable. But the characters and conduct of a Nero, or a Claudius, are what no custom will ever reconcile us to, what no fashion will ever render agreeable; but the one will always be the object of dread and hatred; the other of scorn and derision. The principles of the imagination, upon which our sense of beauty depends, are of a very nice and delicate nature, and may easily be altered by habit and education: but the sentiments of moral appro-bation and disapprobation, are founded on the strongest and most vig-orous passions of human nature; and though they may be somewhat warped, cannot be entirely perverted.

But though the influence of custom and fashion upon moral senti-ments, is not altogether so great, it is however perfectly similar to what it is everywhere else. When custom and fashion coincide with the nat-ural principles of right and wrong, they heighten the delicacy of our sentiments, and increase our abhorrence for every thing which approaches to evil. Those who have been educated in what is really good company, not in what is commonly called such, who have been accustomed to see nothing in the persons whom they esteemed and lived with, but justice, modesty, humanity, and good order; are more shocked with whatever seems to be inconsistent with the rules which those virtues prescribe. Those, on the contrary, who have had the misfortune to be brought up amidst violence, licentiousness, falsehood, and injustice; lose, though not all sense of the impropriety of such conduct, yet all sense of its dreadful enormity, or of the vengeance and punishment due to it. They have been familiarized with it from their infancy, custom has rendered it habitual to them, and they are very apt to regard it as, what is called, the way of the world, something which either may, or must be practised, to hinder us from being the dupes of our own integrity. . . .

The different situations of different ages and countries are apt, in the same manner, to give different characters to the generality of those who live in them, and their sentiments concerning the particular degree of each quality, that is either blamable or praise-worthy, vary, according to that degree which is usual in their own country, and in their own times. That degree of politeness, which would be highly esteemed, perhaps would be thought effeminate adulation, in Russia, would be regarded as rudeness and barbarism at the court of France. That degree of order and frugality, which, in a Polish nobleman, would be considered as exces-sive parsimony, would be regarded as extravagance in a citizen of Amsterdam. Every age and country look upon that degree of each qual-ity, which is commonly to be met within those who are esteemed among themselves, as the golden mean of that particular talent or virtue. And as this varies, according as their different circumstances render different qualities more or less habitual to them, their sentiments concerning the exact propriety of character and behaviour vary accordingly.

Among civilised nations, the virtues which are founded upon human-ity, are more cultivated than those which are founded upon self-denial and the command of the passions. Among rude and barbarous nations, it is quite otherwise, the virtues of self-denial are more cultivated than those of humanity. The general security and happiness which prevail in ages of civility and politeness, afford little exercise to the contempt of danger, to patience in enduring labour, hunger, and pain. Poverty may easily be avoided, and the contempt of it therefore almost ceases to be a virtue. The abstinence from pleasure becomes less necessary, and the mind is more at liberty to unbend itself, and to indulge its natural inclinations in all those particular respects.

Among savages and barbarians it is quite otherwise. Every savage undergoes a sort of Spartan discipline, and by the necessity of his situation is inured to every sort of hardship. He is in continual danger: he is often exposed to the greatest extremities of hunger, and frequently dies of pure want. His circumstances may not habituate him to every sort of distress, but teach him to give way to none of the passions which that distress is apt to excite. He can expect from his countrymen no sympathy or indulgence for such weakness. Before we can feel much for others, we must in some measure be at ease ourselves. If our own misery pinches us very severely, we have no leisure to attend to that of our neighbour: and all savages are too much occupied with their own wants and necessities, to give much attention to those of another person. A savage, therefore, whatever be the nature of his distress, expects no sympathy from those about him, and disdains, upon that account, to expose himself, by allowing the least weakness to escape him. His passions, how furious and violent soever, are never permitted to disturb the serenity of his countenance or the composure of his conduct and behaviour. The savages in North America, we are told, assume upon all occasions the greatest indifference, and would think themselves degraded if they should ever appear in any respect to be overcome, either by love, or grief, or resentment. Their magnanimity and self-command, in this respect, are almost beyond the conception of Europeans.

In a country in which all men are upon a level, with regard to rank and fortune, it might be expected that the mutual inclinations of the two parties should be the only thing considered in marriages, and should be indulged without any sort of control. This, however, is the country in which all marriages, without exception, are made up by the parents, and in which a young man would think himself disgraced forever, if he showed the least preference of one woman above another, or did not express the most complete indifference, both about the time when, and the person to whom, he was to be married. The weakness of love, which is so much indulged in ages of humanity and politeness, is regarded among savages as the most unpardonable effeminacy. Even after the marriage, the two parties seem to be ashamed of a connexion which is founded upon so sordid a necessity. They do not live together. They see one another by stealth only. They both continue to dwell in the houses of their respective fathers, and the open cohabitation of the two sexes, which is permitted without blame in all other countries, is here considered as the most indecent and unmanly sensuality. Nor is it only over this agreeable passion that they exert their absolute self-command. They often bear, in the sight of all their countrymen, with injuries, reproach, and the grossest insults, with the appearance of the greatest insensibility, and without expressing the smallest resentment.

When a savage is made prisoner of war, and receives, as is usual, the sentence of death from his conquerors, he hears it without expressing any emotion, and afterwards submits to the most dreadful torments, without ever bemoaning himself, or discovering any other passion but contempt of his enemies. While he is hung by the shoulders over a slow fire, he derides his tormentors, and tells them with how much more ingenuity he himself had tormented such of their countrymen as had fallen into his hands. After he has been scorched and burnt, and lacerated in all the most tender and sensible parts of his body for several hours together, he is often allowed, in order to prolong his misery, a short respite, and is taken down from the stake: he employs this interval in talking upon all indifferent subjects, inquires after the news of the country, and seems indifferent about nothing but his own situation. The spectators express the same insensibility; the sight of so horrible an object seems to make no impression upon them; they scarce look at the prisoner, except when they lend a hand to torment him. At other times they smoke tobacco, and amuse themselves with any common object, as if no such matter was going on.

Every savage is said to prepare himself from his earliest youth for this dreadful end. He composes, for this purpose, what they call the song of death, a song which he is to sing when he has fallen into the hands of his enemies, and is expiring under the tortures which they inflict upon him. It consists of insults upon his tormentors, and expresses the highest contempt of death and pain. He sings this song upon all extraordinary occasions, when he goes out to war, when he meets his enemies in the field, or whenever he has a mind to show that he has familiarized his imagination to the most dreadful misfortunes, and that no human event can daunt his resolution, or alter his purpose. The same contempt of death and torture prevails among all other savage nations. There is not a negro from the coast of Africa who does not, in this respect, possess a degree of magnanimity which the soul of his sordid master is too often scarce capable of conceiving. Fortune never exerted more cruelly her empire over mankind, than when she subjected those nations of heroes to the refuse of the jails of Europe, to wretches who possess the virtues neither of the countries which they come from, nor of those which they go to, and whose levity, brutality, and baseness, so justly expose them to the contempt of the vanquished. . . .

All of these effects of custom and fashion, however, upon the moral sentiments of mankind, are inconsiderable, in comparison of those which they give occasion to in some other cases; and it is not concerning the general style of character and behaviour, that those principles produce the greatest perversion of judgment, but concerning the propriety or impropriety of particular usages.

The different manners which custom teaches us to approve of in the different professions and states of life, do not concern things of the greatest importance. We expect truth and justice from an old man as well as from a young, from a clergyman as well as from an officer; and it is in matters of small moment only that we look for the distinguishing marks of their respective characters. With regard to these too, there is often some unobserved circumstance which, if it was attended to, would show us, that, independent of custom, there was a propriety in the character which custom had taught us to allot to each profession. We cannot complain, therefore, in this case, that the perversion of natural sentiment is very great. Though the manners of different nations require different degrees of the same quality, in the character which they think worthy of esteem, yet the worst that can be said to happen even here, is that the duties of one virtue are sometimes extended so as to encroach a little upon the precincts of some other. The rustic hospitality that is in fashion among the Poles encroaches, perhaps, a little upon economy and good order; and the frugality that is esteemed in Holland, upon generosity and good-fellowship. The hardiness demanded of savages diminishes their humanity; and, perhaps, the delicate sensibility required in civilised nations sometimes destroys the masculine firmness of the character. In general, the style of manners which takes place in any nation, may commonly upon the whole be said to be that which is most suitable to its situation. Hardiness is the character most suitable to the circumstances of a savage; sensibility to those of one who lives in a very civilised society. Even here, therefore, we cannot complain that the moral sentiments of men are very grossly perverted.

It is not therefore in the general style of conduct or behaviour that custom authorizes the widest departure from what is the natural propriety of action. With regard to particular usages, its influence is often much more destructive of good morals, and it is capable of establishing, as lawful and blameless, particular actions, which shock the plainest principles of right and wrong.

Can there be greater barbarity, for example, than to hurt an infant? Its helplessness, its innocence, its amiableness, call forth the compassion, even of an enemy, and not to spare that tender age is regarded as the most furious effort of an enraged and cruel conqueror. What then should we imagine must be the heart of a parent who could injure that weakness which even a furious enemy is afraid to violate? Yet the exposition, that is, the murder of newborn infants, was a practise allowed of in almost all the states of Greece, even among the polite and civilised Athenians; and whenever the circumstances of the parent rendered it inconvenient to bring up the child, to abandon it to hunger, or to wild beasts, was regarded without blame or censure. This practise had probably begun in times of the most savage barbarity. The imaginations of men had been first made familiar with it in that earliest period of society, and the uniform continuance of the custom had hindered them afterwards from perceiving its enormity. We find, at this day, that this practise prevails among all savage nations; and in that rudest and lowest state of society it is undoubtedly more pardonable than in any other.

The extreme indigence of a savage is often such that he himself is frequently exposed to the greatest extremity of hunger, he often dies of pure want, and it is frequently impossible for him to support both himself and his child. We cannot wonder, therefore, that in this case he should abandon it. One who, in flying from an enemy, whom it was impossible to resist, should throw down his infant, because it retarded his flight, would surely be excusable; since, by attempting to save it, he could only hope for the consolation of dying with it. That in this state of society, therefore, a parent should be allowed to judge whether he can bring up his child, ought not to surprise us so greatly.

In the latter ages of Greece, however, the same thing was permitted from views of remote interest or convenience, which could by no means excuse it. Uninterrupted custom had by this time so thoroughly authorized the practise, that not only the loose maxims of the world tolerated this barbarous prerogative, but even the doctrine of philosophers, which ought to have been more just and accurate, was led away by the established custom, and upon this, as upon many other occasions, instead of censuring, supported the horrible abuse, by far-fetched considerations of public utility. Aristotle talks of it as of what the magistrate ought upon many occasions to encourage. The humane Plato is of the same opinion, and, with all that love of mankind which seems to animate all his writings, nowhere marks this practise with disapprobation. When custom can give sanction to so dreadful a violation of humanity, we may well imagine that there is scarce any particular practise so gross which it cannot authorize. Such a thing, we hear men every day saying, is commonly done, and they seem to think this a sufficient apology for what, in itself, is the most unjust and unreasonable conduct.

There is an obvious reason why custom should never pervert our sentiments with regard to the general style and character of conduct and behaviour, in the same degree as with regard to the propriety or unlawfulness of particular usages. There never can be any such custom. No society could subsist a moment, in which the usual strain of men's conduct and behaviour was of a piece with the horrible practise I have just now mentioned.

PART VI

OF THE CHARACTER OF VIRTUE
CONSISTING OF THREE SECTIONS

SECTION I

Of the Character of the Individual, so far as it affects his own Happiness; or of Prudence

. . . The care of the health, of the fortune, of the rank and reputation of the individual, the objects upon which his comfort and happiness in this life are supposed principally to depend, is considered as the proper business of that virtue which is commonly called Prudence.

We suffer more, it has already been observed, when we fall from a better to a worse situation, than we ever enjoy when we rise from a worse to a better. Security, therefore, is the first and the principal object of prudence. It is averse to expose our health, our fortune, our rank, or reputation, to any sort of hazard. It is rather cautious than enterprising, and more anxious to preserve the advantages which we already possess, than forward to prompt us to the acquisition of still greater advantages. The methods of improving our fortune, which it principally recommends to us, are those which expose to no loss or hazard; real knowledge and skill in our trade or profession, assiduity and industry in the exercise of it, frugality, and even some degree of parsimony, in all our expences.

The prudent man always studies seriously and earnestly to understand whatever he professes to understand, and not merely to persuade other people that he understands it; and though his talents may not always be very brilliant, they are always perfectly genuine. He neither endeavours to impose upon you by the cunning devices of an artful impostor, nor by the arrogant airs of an assuming pedant, nor by the confident assertions of a superficial and imprudent pretender. He is not ostentatious even of the abilities which he really possesses. His conversation is simple and modest, and he is averse to all the quackish arts by which other people so frequently thrust themselves into public notice and reputation. For reputation in his profession he is naturally disposed to rely a good deal upon the solidity of his knowledge and abilities; and he does not always think of cultivating the favour of those little clubs and cabals, who, in the superior arts and sciences, so often erect themselves into the supreme judges of merit; and who make it their business to celebrate the talents and virtues of one another, and to decry whatever can come into competition with them. If he ever connects himself with any society of this kind, it is merely in self-defence, not with a view to impose upon the public, but to hinder the public from being imposed upon, to his disadvantage, by the clamours, the whispers, or the intrigues, either of that particular society, or of some other of the same kind.

The prudent man is always sincere, and feels horror at the very thought of exposing himself to the disgrace which attends upon the detection of falsehood. But though always sincere, he is not always frank and open; and though he never tells any thing but the truth, he does not always think himself bound, when not properly called upon, to tell the whole truth. As he is cautious in his actions, so he is reserved in his speech; and never rashly or unnecessarily obtrudes his opinion concerning either things or persons.

The prudent man, though not always distinguished by the most exquisite sensibility, is always very capable of friendship. But his friendship is not that ardent and passionate, but too often transitory affection, which appears so delicious to the generosity of youth and inexperience. It is a sedate, but steady and faithful attachment to a few well-tried and well-chosen companions; in the choice of whom he is not guided by the giddy admiration of shining accomplishments, but by the sober esteem of modesty, discretion, and good conduct. But though capable of friendship, he is not always much disposed to general sociality. He rarely frequents, and more rarely figures in those convivial societies which are distinguished for the jollity and gaiety of their conversation. Their way of life might too often interfere with the regularity of his temperance, might interrupt the steadiness of his industry, or break in upon the strictness of his frugality. . . .

The man who lives within his income, is naturally contented with his situation, which, by continual, though small accumulations, is growing better and better every day. He is enabled gradually to relax, both in the rigour of his parsimony and in the severity of his application; and he feels with double satisfaction this gradual increase of ease and enjoyment, from having felt before the hardship which attended the want of them. He has no anxiety to change so comfortable a situation, and does not go in quest of new enterprises and adventures, which might endanger, but could not well increase, the secure tranquillity which he actually enjoys. If he enters into any new projects or enterprises, they are likely to be well concerted and well prepared. He can never be hurried or driven into them by any necessity, but has always time and leisure to deliberate soberly and coolly concerning what are likely to be their consequences.

The prudent man is not willing to subject himself to any responsibility which his duty does not impose upon him. He is not a bustler in business where he has no concern; is not a meddler in other people's affairs; is not a professed counsellor or adviser, who obtrudes his advice where nobody is asking it. He confines himself, as much as his duty will permit, to his own affairs, and has no taste for that foolish importance which many people wish to derive from appearing to have some influence in the management of those of other people. He is averse to enter into any party disputes, hates faction, and is not always very forward to listen to the voice even of noble and great ambition. When distinctly called upon, he will not decline the service of his country, but he will not cabal in order to force himself into it, and would be much better pleased that the public business were well managed by some other person, than that he himself should have the trouble, and incur the responsibility, of managing it. In the bottom of his heart he would prefer the undisturbed enjoyment of secure tranquillity, not only to all the vain splendour of successful ambition, but to the real and solid glory of performing the greatest and most magnanimous actions.

Prudence, in short, when directed merely to the care of the health, of the fortune, and of the rank and reputation of the individual, though it is regarded as a most respectable and even, in some degree, as an amiable and agreeable quality, yet it never is considered as one, either of the most endearing, or of the most ennobling of the virtues. It commands a certain cold esteem, but seems not entitled to any very ardent love or admiration.

Wise and judicious conduct, when directed to greater and nobler purposes than the care of the health, the fortune, the rank and reputation of the individual, is frequently and very properly called prudence. We talk of the prudence of the great general, of the great statesman, of the great legislator. Prudence is, in all these cases, combined with many greater and more splendid virtues, with valour, with extensive and strong benevolence, with a sacred regard to the rules of justice, and all these supported by a proper degree of self-command. This superior prudence, when carried to the highest degree of perfection, necessarily supposes the art, the talent, and the habit or disposition of acting with the most perfect propriety in every possible circumstance and situation. It necessarily supposes the utmost perfection of all the intellectual and of all the moral virtues. It is the best head joined to the best heart. It is the most perfect wisdom combined with the most perfect virtue. It constitutes very nearly the character of the Academical or Peripatetic sage, as the inferior prudence does that of the Epicurean. . . .

SECTION II

Of the Character of the Individual, so far as it can affect the Happiness of other People

CHAPTER I

Of the Order in which Individuals are recommended by Nature to our care and attention

Every man, as the Stoics used to say, is first and principally recommended to his own care; and every man is certainly, in every respect, fitter and abler to take care of himself than of any other person. Every man feels his own pleasures and his own pains more sensibly than those of other people. The former are the original sensations; the latter the reflected or sympathetic images of those sensations. The former may be said to be the substance; the latter the shadow.

After himself, the members of his own family, those who usually live in the same house with him, his parents, his children, his brothers and sisters, are naturally the objects of his warmest affections. They are naturally and usually the persons upon whose happiness or misery his conduct must have the greatest influence. He is more habituated to sympathize with them. He knows better how every thing is likely to affect them, and his sympathy with them is more precise and determinate, than it can be with the greater part of other people. It approaches nearer, in short, to what he feels for himself. . . .

After the persons who are recommended to our beneficence, either by their connexion with ourselves, by their personal qualities, or by their past services, come those who are pointed out, not indeed to, what is called, our friendship, but to our benevolent attention and good offices; those who are distinguished by their extraordinary situation; the greatly fortunate and the greatly unfortunate, the rich and the powerful, the poor and the wretched. The distinction of ranks, the peace and order of society, are, in a great measure, founded upon the respect which we naturally conceive for the former. The relief and consolation of human misery depend altogether upon our compassion for the latter. The peace and order of society, is of more importance than even the relief of the miserable. Our respect for the great, accordingly, is most apt to offend by its excess; our fellow-feeling for the miserable, by its defect. Moralists exhort us to charity and compassion. They warn us against the fascination of greatness. This fascination, indeed, is so powerful, that the rich and the great are too often preferred to the wise and the virtuous. Nature has wisely judged that the distinction of ranks, the peace and order of society, would rest more securely upon the plain and palpable difference of birth and fortune, than upon the invisible and often uncertain difference of wisdom and virtue. The undistinguishing eyes of the great mob of mankind can well enough perceive the former: it is with difficulty that the nice discernment of the wise and the virtuous can sometimes distinguish the latter. In the order of all those recommendations, the benevolent wisdom of nature is equally evident. . . .

CHAPTER II

Of the order in which Societies are by nature recommended to our Beneficence

The same principles that direct the order in which individuals are recommended to our beneficence, direct that likewise in which societies are recommended to it. Those to which it is, or may be of most importance, are first and principally recommended to it.

The state or sovereignty in which we have been born and educated, and under the protection of which we continue to live, is, in ordinary cases, the greatest society upon whose happiness or misery, our good or bad conduct can have much influence. It is accordingly, by nature, most strongly recommended to us. Not only we ourselves, but all the objects of our kindest affections, our children, our parents, our relations, our friends, our benefactors, all those whom we naturally love and revere the most, are commonly comprehended within it; and their prosperity and safety depend in some measure upon its prosperity and safety. It is by nature, therefore, endeared to us, not only by all our selfish, but by all our private benevolent affections. Upon account of our own connexion with it, its prosperity and glory seem to reflect some sort of honour upon ourselves. When we compare it with other societies of the same kind, we are proud of its superiority, and mortified in some degree, if it appears in any respect below them.

All the illustrious characters which it has produced in former times (for against those of our own times envy may sometimes prejudice us a little), its warriors, its statesmen, its poets, its philosophers, and men of letters of all kinds; we are disposed to view with the most partial admiration, and to rank them (sometimes most unjustly) above those of all other nations. The patriot who lays down his life for the safety, or even for the vain-glory of this society, appears to act with the most exact propriety. He appears to view himself in the light in which the impartial spectator naturally and necessarily views him, as but one of the multitude, in the eye of that equitable judge, of no more consequence than any other in it, but bound at all times to sacrifice and devote himself to the safety, to the service, and even to the glory of the greater number. But though this sacrifice appears to be perfectly just and proper, we know how difficult it is to make it, and how few people are capable of making it. His conduct, therefore, excites not only our entire approbation, but our highest wonder and admiration, and seems to merit all the applause which can be due to the most heroic virtue. The traitor, on the contrary, who, in some peculiar situation, fancies he can promote his own little interest by betraying to the public enemy that of his native country; who, regardless of the judgment of the man within the breast, prefers himself, in this respect so shamefully and so basely, to all those with whom he has any connexion; appears to be of all villains the most detestable. . . .

The love of our own country seems not to be derived from the love of mankind. The former sentiment is altogether independent of the latter, and seems sometimes even to dispose us to act inconsistently with it. France may contain, perhaps, near three times the number of inhabitants which Great Britain contains. In the great society of mankind, therefore, the prosperity of France should appear to be an object of much greater importance than that of Great Britain. The British subject, however, who, upon that account, should prefer upon all occasions the prosperity of the former to that of the latter country, would not be thought a good citizen of Great Britain. We do not love our country merely as a part of the great society of mankind: we love it for its own sake, and independently of any such consideration. That wisdom which contrived the system of human affections, as well as that of every other part of nature, seems to have judged that the interest of the great society of mankind would be best promoted by directing the principal attention of each individual to that particular portion of it, which was most within the sphere both of his abilities and of his understanding.

National prejudices and hatreds seldom extend beyond neighbouring nations. We very weakly and foolishly, perhaps, call the French our natural enemies; and they perhaps, as weakly and foolishly, consider us in the same manner. Neither they nor we bear any sort of envy to the prosperity of China or Japan. It very rarely happens, however, that our good-will towards such distant countries can be exerted with much effect. . . .

The love of our country seems, in ordinary cases, to involve in it two different principles; first, a certain respect and reverence for that constitution or form of government which is actually established; and secondly, an earnest desire to render the condition of our fellow-citizens as safe, respectable, and happy as we can. He is not a citizen who is not disposed to respect the laws and to obey the civil magistrate; and he is certainly not a good citizen who does not wish to promote, by every means in his power, the welfare of the whole society of his fellow-citizens.

In peaceable and quiet times, those two principles generally coincide and lead to the same conduct. The support of the established government seems evidently the best expedient for maintaining the safe, respectable, and happy situation of our fellow-citizens; when we see that this government actually maintains them in that situation. But in times of public discontent, faction, and disorder, those two different principles may draw different ways, and even a wise man may be disposed to think some alteration necessary in that constitution or form of government, which, in its actual condition, appears plainly unable to maintain the public tranquillity. In such cases, however, it often requires, perhaps, the highest effort of political wisdom to determine when a real patriot ought to support and endeavour to re-establish the authority of the old system, and when he ought to give way to the more daring, but often dangerous spirit of innovation. . . .

Amidst the turbulence and disorder of faction, a certain spirit of system is apt to mix itself with that public spirit which is founded upon the love of humanity, upon a real fellow-feeling with the inconveniences and distresses to which some of our fellow-citizens may be exposed. This spirit of system commonly takes the direction of that more gentle public spirit; always animates it, and often inflames it even to the madness of fanaticism. The leaders of the discontented party seldom fail to hold out some plausible plan of reformation which, they pretend, will not only remove the inconveniences and relieve the distresses immediately complained of, but will prevent, in all time coming, any return of the like inconveniences and distresses. They often propose, upon this account, to remodel the constitution, and to alter, in some of its most essential parts, that system of government under which the subjects of a great empire have enjoyed, perhaps, peace, security, and even glory, during the course of several centuries together.

The great body of the party are commonly intoxicated with the imaginary beauty of this ideal system, of which they have no experience, but which has been represented to them in all the most dazzling colours in which the eloquence of their leaders could paint it. Those leaders themselves, though they originally may have meant nothing but their own aggrandizement, become many of them in time the dupes of their own sophistry, and are as eager for this great reformation as the weakest and foolishest of their followers. Even though the leaders should have preserved their own heads, as indeed they commonly do, free from this fanaticism, yet they dare not always disappoint the expectation of their followers; but are often obliged, though contrary to their principle and their conscience, to act as if they were under the common delusion. The violence of the party, refusing all palliatives, all temperaments, all reasonable accommodations, by requiring too much frequently obtains nothing; and those inconveniences and distresses which, with a little moderation, might in a great measure have been removed and relieved, are left altogether without the hope of a remedy.

The man whose public spirit is prompted altogether by humanity and benevolence, will respect the established powers and privileges even of individuals, and still more those of the great orders and societies, into which the state is divided. Though he should consider some of them as in some measure abusive, he will content himself with moderating, what he often cannot annihilate without great violence. When he cannot conquer the rooted prejudices of the people by reason and persuasion, he will not attempt to subdue them by force; but will religiously observe what, by Cicero, is justly called the divine maxim of Plato, never to use violence to his country no more than to his parents. He will accommodate, as well as he can, his public arrangements to the confirmed habits and prejudices of the people; and will remedy as well as he can, the inconveniences which may flow from the want of those regulations which the people are averse to submit to. When he cannot establish the right, he will not disdain to ameliorate the wrong; but like Solon, when he cannot establish the best system of laws, he will endeavour to establish the best that the people can bear.

The man of system, on the contrary, is apt to be very wise in his own conceit; and is often so enamoured with the supposed beauty of his own ideal plan of government, that he cannot suffer the smallest deviation from any part of it. He goes on to establish it completely and in all its parts, without any regard either to the great interests, or to the strong prejudices which may oppose it. He seems to imagine that he can arrange the different members of a great society with as much ease as the hand arranges the different pieces upon a chessboard. He does not consider that the pieces upon the chessboard have no other principle of motion besides that which the hand impresses upon them; but that, in the great chessboard of human society, every single piece has a principle of motion of its own, altogether different from that which the legislature might choose to impress upon it. If those two principles coincide and act in the same direction, the game of human society will go on easily and harmoniously, and is very likely to be happy and successful. If they are opposite or different, the game will go on miserably, and the society must be at all times in the highest degree of disorder.

Some general, and even systematical, idea of the perfection of policy and law, may no doubt be necessary for directing the views of the statesman. But to insist upon establishing, and upon establishing all at once, and in spite of all opposition, every thing which that idea may seem to require, must often be the highest degree of arrogance. It is to erect his own judgment into the supreme standard of right and wrong. It is to fancy himself the only wise and worthy man in the commonwealth, and that his fellow-citizens should accommodate themselves to him and not he to them. It is upon this account, that of all political speculators, sovereign princes are by far the most dangerous. This arrogance is perfectly familiar to them. They entertain no doubt of the immense superiority of their own judgment. When such imperial and royal reformers, therefore, condescend to contemplate the constitution of the country which is committed to their government, they seldom see any thing so wrong in it as the obstructions which it may sometimes oppose to the execution of their own will. They hold in contempt the divine maxim of Plato, and consider the state as made for themselves, not themselves for the state. The great object of their reformation, therefore, is to remove those obstructions; to reduce the authority of the nobility; to take away the privileges of cities and provinces, and to render both the greatest individuals and the greaterst orders of the state, as incapable of opposing their commands, as the weakest and most insignificant.

CHAPTER III

Of universal Benevolence

Though our effectual good offices can very seldom be extended to any wider society than that of our own country; our good-will is circumscribed by no boundary, but may embrace the immensity of the universe. We cannot form the idea of any innocent and sensible being, whose happiness we should not desire, or to whose misery, when distinctly brought home to the imagination, we should not have some degree of aversion. The idea of a mischievous, though sensible, being, indeed, naturally provokes our hatred: but the ill-will which, in this case, we bear to it, is really the effect of our universal benevolence. It is the effect of the sympathy which we feel with the misery and resentment of those other innocent and sensible beings, whose happiness is disturbed by its malice.

This universal benevolence, how noble and generous soever, can be the source of no solid happiness to any man who is not thoroughly convinced that all the inhabitants of the universe, the meanest as well as the greatest, are under the immediate care and protection of that great, benevolent, and all-wise Being, who directs all the movements of nature; and who is determined, by his own unalterable perfections, to maintain in it, at all times, the greatest possible quantity of happiness. To this universal benevolence, on the contrary, the very suspicion of a fatherless world, must be the most melancholy of all reflections; from the thought that all the unknown regions of infinite and incomprehensible space may be filled with nothing but endless misery and wretchedness. All the splendour of the highest prosperity can never enlighten the gloom with which so dreadful an idea must necessarily overshadow the imagination; nor, in a wise and virtuous man, can all the sorrow of the most afflicting adversity ever dry up the joy which necessarily springs from the habitual and thorough conviction of the truth of the contrary system.

The wise and virtuous man is at all times willing that his own private interest should be sacrificed to the public interest of his own particular order or society. He is at all times willing, too, that the interest of this order or society should be sacrificed to the greater interest of the state or sovereignty, of which it is only a subordinate part. He should, therefore, be equally willing that all those inferior interests should be sacrificed to the greater interest of the universe, to the interest of that great society of all sensible and intelligent beings, of which God himself is the immediate administrator and director. If he is deeply impressed with the habitual and thorough conviction that this benevolent and all-wise Being can admit into the system of his government, no partial evil which is not necessary for the universal good, he must consider all the misfortunes which may befall himself, his friends, his society, or his country, as necessary for the prosperity of the universe, and therefore as what he ought, not only to submit to with resignation, but as what he himself, if he had known all the connexions and dependencies of things, ought sincerely and devoutly to have wished for.

Nor does this magnanimous resignation to the will of the greater Director of the universe, seem in any respect beyond the reach of human nature. Good soldiers, who both love and trust their general, frequently march with more gaiety and alacrity to the forlorn station, from which they never expect to return, than they would to one where there was neither difficulty nor danger. In marching to the latter, they could feel no other sentiment than that of the dullness of ordinary duty: in marching to the former, they feel that they are making the noblest exertion which it is possible for man to make. They know that their general would not have ordered them upon this station, had it not been necessary for the safety of the army, for the success of the war. They cheerfully sacrifice their own little systems to the prosperity of a greater system. They take an affectionate leave of their comrades, to whom they wish all happiness and success; and march out, not only with submissive obedience, but often with shouts of the most joyful exultation, to that fatal, but splendid and honourable station to which they are appointed. No conductor of an army can deserve more unlimited trust, more ardent and zealous affection, than the great Conductor of the universe. In the greatest public as well as private disasters, a wise man ought to consider that he himself, his friends and countrymen, have only been ordered upon the forlorn station of the universe; that had it not been necessary for the good of the whole, they would not have been so ordered; and that it is their duty, not only with humble resignation to submit to this allotment, but to endeavour to embrace it with alacrity and joy. A wise man should surely be capable of doing what a good soldier holds himself at all times in readiness to do.

The idea of that divine Being, whose benevolence and wisdom have, from all eternity, contrived and conducted the immense machine of the universe, so as at all times to produce the greatest possible quantity of happiness, is certainly of all the objects of human contemplation by far the most sublime. Every other thought necessarily appears mean in the comparison. The man whom we believe to be principally occupied in this sublime contemplation, seldom fails to be the object of our highest veneration; and though his life should be altogether contemplative, we often regard him with a sort of religious respect much superior to that with which we look upon the most active and useful servant of the commonwealth. The Meditations of Marcus Antoninus,* which turn principally upon this subject, have contributed more, perhaps, to the general admiration of his character, than all the different transactions of his just, merciful, and beneficent reign.

The administration of the great system of the universe, however, the care of the universal happiness of all rational and sensible beings, is the business of God and not of man. To man is allotted a much humbler department, but one much more suitable to the weakness of his powers, and to the narrowness of his comprehension; the care of his own happiness, of that of his family, his friends, his country: that he is occupied in contemplating the more sublime, can never be an excuse for his neglecting the more humble department; and he must not expose himself to the charge which Avidius Cassius is said to have brought, perhaps unjustly, against Marcus Antoninus; that while he employed himself in

---

*Marcus Aurelius.

philosophical speculations, and contemplated the prosperity of the universe, he neglected that of the Roman empire. The most sublime speculation of the contemplative philosopher can scarce compensate the neglect of the smallest active duty.

SECTION III
Of Self-command

The man who acts according to the rules of perfect prudence, of strict justice, and of proper benevolence, may be said to be perfectly virtuous. But the most perfect knowledge of those rules will not alone enable him to act in this manner: his own passions are very apt to mislead him; sometimes to drive him and sometimes to seduce him to violate all the rules which he himself, in all his sober and cool hours, approves of. The most perfect knowledge, if it is not supported by the most perfect self-command, will not always enable him to do his duty.

Some of the best of the ancient moralists seem to have considered those passions as divided into two different classes: first, into those which it requires a considerable exertion of self-command to restrain even for a single moment; and secondly, into those which it is easy to restrain for a single moment, or even for a short period of time; but which, by their continual and almost incessant solicitations, are, in the course of a life, very apt to mislead into great deviations.

Fear and anger, together with some other passions which are mixed or connected with them, constitute the first class. The love of ease, of pleasure, of applause, and of many other selfish gratifications, constitute the second. Extravagant fear and furious anger, it is often difficult to restrain even for a single moment. The love of ease, of pleasure, of applause, and other selfish gratifications, it is always easy to restrain for a single moment, or even for a short period of time; but, by their continual solicitations, they often mislead us into many weaknesses which we have afterwards much reason to be ashamed of. The former set of passions may often be said to drive, the latter, to seduce us from our duty. The command of the former was, by the ancient moralists above alluded to, denominated fortitude, manhood, and strength of mind; that of the latter, temperance, decency, modesty, and moderation.

The command of each of those two sets of passions, independent of the beauty which it derives from its utility; from its enabling us upon all occasions to act according to the dictates of prudence, of justice, and of proper benevolence; has a beauty of its own, and seems to deserve for its own sake a certain degree of esteem and admiration. In the one case, the strength and greatness of the exertion excites some degree of that esteem and admiration. In the other, the uniformity, the equality and unremitting steadiness of that exertion.

The man who, in danger, in torture, upon the approach of death, preserves his tranquillity unaltered, and suffers no word, no gesture to escape him which does not perfectly accord with the feelings of the most indifferent spectator, necessarily commands a very high degree of admiration. If he suffers in the cause of liberty and justice, for the sake of humanity and the love of his country, the most tender compassion for his sufferings, the strongest indignation against the injustice of his persecutors, the warmest sympathetic gratitude for his beneficent intentions, the highest sense of his merit, all join and mix themselves with the admiration of his magnanimity, and often inflame that sentiment into the most enthusiastic and rapturous veneration. The heroes of ancient and modern history, who are remembered with the most peculiar favour and affection, are, many of them, those who, in the cause of truth, liberty, and justice, have perished upon the scaffold, and who behaved there with that ease and dignity which became them. Had the enemies of Socrates suffered him to die quietly in his bed, the glory even of that great philosopher might possibly never have acquired that dazzling splendour in which it has been beheld in all succeeding ages. In the English history, when we look over the illustrious heads which have been engraved by Vertue and Howbraken, there is scarce any body, I imagine, who does not feel that the axe, the emblem of having been beheaded, which is engraved under some of the most illustrious of them; under those of the Sir Thomas Mores, of the Raleighs, the Russels, the Sydneys, etc., sheds a real dignity and interestingness over the characters to which it is affixed, much superior to what they can derive from all the futile ornaments of heraldry, with which they are sometimes accompanied.

Nor does this magnanimity give lustre only to the characters of innocent and virtuous men. It draws some degree of favourable regard even upon those of the greatest criminals; and when a robber or highwayman is brought to the scaffold, and behaves there with decency and firmness, though we perfectly approve of his punishment, we often cannot help regretting that a man who possessed such great and noble powers should have been capable of such mean enormities.

War is the great school both for acquiring and exercising this species of magnanimity. Death, as we say, is the king of terrors; and the man who has conquered the fear of death, is not likely to lose his presence of mind at the approach of any other natural evil. In war, men become familiar with death, and are thereby necessarily cured of that superstitious horror with which it is viewed by the weak and unexperienced. They consider it merely as the loss of life, and as no further the object of aversion than as life may happen to be that of desire. They learn from experience, too, that many seemingly great dangers are not so great as they appear; and that, with courage, activity, and presence of mind, there is often a good probability of extricating themselves with honour from situations where at first they could see no hope. The dread of death is thus greatly diminished; and the confidence or hope of escaping it, augmented. They learn to expose themselves to danger with less reluctance. They are less anxious to get out of it, and less apt to lose their presence of mind while they are in it. It is this habitual contempt of danger and death which ennobles the profession of a soldier, and bestows upon it, in the natural apprehensions of mankind, a rank and dignity superior to that of any other profession. The skillful and successful exercise of this profession, in the service of their country, seems to have constituted the most distinguishing feature in the character of the favourite heroes of all ages. . . .

To act according to the dictates of prudence, of justice, and proper beneficence, seems to have no great merit where there is no temptation to do otherwise. But to act with cool deliberation in the midst of the greatest dangers and difficulties; to observe religiously the sacred rules of justice in spite both of the greatest interests which might tempt, and the greatest injuries which might provoke us to violate them; never to suffer the benevolence of our temper to be damped or discouraged by the malignity and ingratitude of the individuals towards whom it may have been exercised; is the character of the most exalted wisdom and virtue. Self-command is not only itself a great virtue, but from it all the other virtues seem to derive their principal lustre . . .

CONCLUSION *of the* SIXTH PART

Concern for our own happiness recommends to us the virtue of prudence: concern for that of other people, the virtues of justice and beneficence; of which, the one restrains us from hurting, the other prompts us to promote that happiness. Independent of any regard either to what are, or to what ought to be, or to what upon a certain condition would be, the sentiments of other people, the first of those three virtues is originally recommended to us by our selfish, the other two by our benevolent affections. Regard to the sentiments of other people, however, comes afterwards both to enforce and to direct the practise of all those virtues; and no man during, either the whole of his life, or that of any considerable part of it, ever trod steadily and uniformly in the paths of prudence, of justice, or of proper beneficence, whose conduct was not principally directed by a regard to the sentiments of the supposed impartial spectator, of the great inmate of the breast, the great judge and arbiter of conduct.

If in the course of the day we have swerved in any respect from the rules which he prescribes to us; if we have either exceeded or relaxed in our frugality; if we have either exceeded or relaxed in our industry; if, through passion or inadvertence, we have hurt in any respect the interest or happiness of our neighbour; if we have neglected a plain and proper opportunity of promoting that interest and happiness; it is this inmate who, in the evening, calls us to an account for all those omissions and violations, and his reproaches often make us blush inwardly both for our folly and inattention to our own happiness, and for our still greater indifference and inattention, perhaps, to that of other people.

But though the virtues of prudence, justice, and beneficence, may, upon different occasions, be recommended to us almost equally by two different principles; those of self-command are, upon most occasions, principally and almost entirely recommended to us by one; by the sense of propriety, by regard to the sentiments of the supposed impartial spectator. Without the restraint which this principle imposes, every passion would, upon most occasions, rush headlong, if I may say so, to its own gratification. Anger would follow the suggestions of its own fury; fear those of its own violent agitations. Regard to no time or place would induce vanity to refrain from the loudest and most impertinent ostentation; or voluptuousness from the most open, indecent, and scandalous indulgence. Respect for what are, or for what ought to be, or for what upon a certain condition would be, the sentiments of other people, is the sole principle which, upon most occasions, overawes all those mutinous and turbulent passions into that tone and temper which the impartial spectator can enter into and sympathize with.

Upon some occasions, indeed, those passions are restrained, not so much by a sense of their impropriety, as by prudential considerations of the bad consequences which might follow from their indulgence. In such cases, the passions, though restrained, are not always subdued, but often remain lurking in the breast with all their original fury. The man whose anger is restrained by fear, does not always lay aside his anger, but only reserves its gratification for a more safe opportunity. But the man who, in relating to some other person the injury which has been done to him, feels at once the fury of his passion cooled and becalmed by sympathy with the more moderate sentiments of his companion, who at once adopts those more moderate sentiments, and comes to view that injury, not in the black and atrocious colours in which he had originally beheld it, but in the much milder and fairer light in which his companion naturally views it; not only restrains, but in some measure subdues, his anger. The passion becomes really less than it was before, and less capable of exciting him to the violent and bloody revenge which at first, perhaps, he might have thought of inflicting.

Those passions which are restrained by the sense of propriety, are all in some degree moderated and subdued by it. But those which are restrained only by prudential considerations of any kind, are, on the contrary, frequently inflamed by the restraint, and sometimes (long after the provocation given, and when nobody is thinking about it) burst out absurdly and unexpectedly, and with tenfold fury and violence.

Anger, however, as well as every other passion, may, upon many occasions, be very properly restrained by prudential considerations. Some exertion of manhood and self-command is even necessary for this sort of restraint; and the impartial spectator may sometimes view it with that sort of cold esteem due to that species of conduct which he considers as a mere matter of vulgar prudence; but never with that affectionate admiration with which he surveys the same passions, when, by the sense of propriety, they are moderated and subdued to what he himself can readily enter into. In the former species of restraint, he may frequently discern some degree of propriety, and, if you will, even of virtue; but it is a propriety and virtue of a much inferior order to those which he always feels with transport and admiration in the latter.

The virtues of prudence, justice, and beneficence, have no tendency to produce any but the most agreeable effects. Regard to those effects, as it originally recommends them to the actor, so does it afterwards to the impartial spectator. In our approbation of the character of the prudent man, we feel, with peculiar complacency, the security which he must enjoy while he walks under the safeguard of that sedate and deliberate virtue. In our approbation of the character of the just man, we feel, with equal complacency, the security which all those connected with him, whether in neighbourhood, society, or business, must derive from his scrupulous anxiety never either to hurt or offend. In our approbation of the character of the beneficent man, we enter into the gratitude of all those who are within the sphere of his good offices, and conceive with them the highest sense of his merit. In our approbation of all those virtues, our sense of their agreeable effects, of their utility, either to the person who exercises them, or to some other persons, joins with our sense of their propriety, and constitutes always a considerable, frequently the greater part of that approbation.

But in our approbation of the virtues of self-command, complacency with their effects sometimes constitutes no part, and frequently but a small part, of that approbation. Those effects may sometimes be agreeable, and sometimes disagreeable; and though our approbation is no doubt stronger in the former case, it is by no means altogether destroyed in the latter. The most heroic valour may be employed indifferently in the cause either of justice or of injustice; and though it is no doubt much more loved and admired in the former case, it still appears a great and respectable quality even in the latter. In that, and in all the other virtues of self-command, the splendid and dazzling quality seems always to be the greatness and steadiness of the exertion, and the strong sense of propriety which is necessary in order to make and to maintain that exertion. The effects are too often but too little regarded.

The Wealth of Nations

The Wealth of Nations is much more than a treatise on economics. It is Smith's magnum opus—his vision of a society of perfect liberty as a full-blown stage of history. The *Wealth* can be, and often is, read as a demonstration of how such a society arranges its economic affairs but that is to understate its significance. For the *Wealth of Nations* is a study of the broad historic tendencies of human society, once that society has wrested itself free of its earlier encumbrances and entrusted itself to new, self-generated, self-determined processes of social interaction. As we shall see, the outcome of these tendencies is by no means blandly reassuring. On the contrary, Smith's book—like his total vision—achieves its greatness because it mixes expectations of progress with a sobering recognition of the limitations of human capability.

THEMATIC HISTORY

It is not an easy matter to provide a Baedeker's tour of *The Wealth of Nations*, especially for someone who has never read any of it. * Rather than retracing its long and sometimes rambling course, I shall start by trying to give coherence to the book as a whole. I shall do so by setting out a few large themes—some of them discussed in a single portion of the text, others woven into the exposition almost from start to finish.

The first of these is the theme of historic evolution. Although the entire text is pervaded by a sense of history, we do not arrive at a systematic consideration of the subject until Book III—page 248 below—when Smith takes up the "Progress of Opulence in different Nations." At that point he examines the origins of commercial society within the crevices of the feudal order. Here he is describing the manner in which the insinuation of merchant activity undermined that order:

> What all the violence of the feudal institutions could never have effected, the silent and insensible operation of foreign commerce and manufactures gradually brought about. These gradually furnished the great proprietors with something for which they could exchange the whole surplus produce of their lands, and which they could consume themselves without sharing it either with tenants or retainers. All for ourselves, and nothing for other people, seems, in every age of the world, to have been the vile maxim of the masters of mankind. As soon, therefore, as they could find a method of consuming the whole value of their rents themselves,

---

* For the benefit of those who would like a short "treasury" of Smith's well-known aphorisms, I have added a brief selection at the end of the readings.

they had no disposition to share them with any other person. For a pair of diamond buckles perhaps . . . they exchanged the maintenance of a thousand men for a year. . . . [T]hus, for the gratification of the most childish, the meanest and the most sordid of vanities, they gradually bartered their whole power and authority."[1]

Perhaps we can see the Invisible Hand once more at work. "A revolution of the greatest importance to the public," Smith writes, "was in this manner brought about by two different orders of people, who had not the slightest intention to serve the public. To gratify the most childish vanity was the sole motive of the great proprietors. The merchants and artificers, much less ridiculous, acted merely with a view to their own interest, and in pursuit of their pedlar principle of turning a penny wherever a penny was to be got. Neither of them had either knowledge of foresight of that great revolution which the folly of one, and the industry of the other, was gradually bringing about."[2]

Smith thus shows us how commercial society arrived on the scene. But the larger historic theme does not appear until we reach Book V, a portion of the *Wealth* dedicated to a discussion of a government. Now Smith picks up the thread he has first placed in our hands at the outset of the *Lectures on Jurisprudence*, where he discussed the "stages" of social history and their determination by the material basis of existence. In Book V we meet the stadial treatment of history in a much more fully developed form. Smith discusses how each level of material capability calls into being a different form of military organization, a different natural degree of inequality, and therefore a different form of "the magistrate" (government).

"Among nations of hunters," he writes, "there is scarce any property, or at least none that exceeds the value of two or three days labour; so there is seldom any established magistrate or any regular administration of justice. . . . It is in the age of shepherds, in the second period of society, that the inequality of fortune first begins to take place, and introduces among men a degree of authority and subordination which could not possibly exist before. . . . The rich, in particular, are necessarily interested to support that order of things, which can alone secure them in the possession of their advantages. . . . Civil government, so far as it is instituted for the security of property, is in reality instituted for the defence of the rich against the poor, or of those who have some property against those who have none at all."[3]

Thus the *Wealth* encloses its discussion of "economics" within a broad historical framework. The specific institutions of commercial society are therefore seen as the outcome of a process of social conflict—merchant against feudal lord—rather than presumed to have existed from all time, or to have sprung into being full blown, like Minerva from the brow of Jupiter. In addition, because of the historical perspective, the society of perfect liberty is never depicted in unrealistic terms. Because commercial society remains a society of inequality, it presupposes what Smith calls "a certain subordination."[4] This subordination is provided in part by the propensity of the poor to look up to and admire the rich, a propensity whose origins we have stud-

1. Smith, *Wealth*, pp. 418–419.   3. Ibid., p. 709, 715.
2. Ibid., p. 422.   4. Ibid., p. 710.

ied in the *Moral Sentiments*. But in addition, we now also see the "magistrate" standing in the background, vigilant in the protection of property should the spontaneous mechanisms of order fail. It is these considerations of power and psychology that lift *The Wealth of Nations* from the arid soil of economics to the rich terrain of political economy.

ECONOMIC ORDER

We turn now to the next major theme within the work—a theme that many economists consider to be its central message. This is the capacity of a society of perfect liberty to maintain internal order and cohesion. In the *Wealth*, this problem is not initially considered from the viewpoint of subordination to which we have just paid heed. Rather, the question focuses on the *economic* problems of a society in which stability and order can no longer be presumed to result from the directives imposed on its members from above.

Here the *Wealth* brings to full maturity the embryonic system of order sketched out in the Glasgow lectures on "police." For Smith has found the secret of a self-regulating economy in the very attribute of a society of perfect liberty that seemed at first to pose the greatest threat to order. This was its social and spatial mobility—characteristics that appeared to many contemporary observers to be the source of potential disruption and disorder. It was Smith's great achievement to show how the mechanism of *competition* would bring about a state of economic provisioning as dependable as any provided by state command, and·a great deal more flexible and dynamic.

The secret of competition lay in two aspects of a commercial society. The first was its encouragement of the drive for wealth, of which we will hear more when we consider economic growth in our next section. The second attribute was the dismantling of the structure of social and economic rules and regulations left over from mercantilism, the still feudal-minded, but intricately state-controlled predecessor of commercial society. For Smith now shows how competition will attract labor and capital into the production of any commodity whose market price is above its "natural price"—that is, its normal costs of production. In the same way, competition will motivate labor and capital to move elsewhere when market prices are below natural prices. In this way, the quantity of production of different commodities will accommodate itself ɯ the demand for those commodities—*provided that nothing interferes with the movement of land and capital into or out of various employments.*

Here is where we encounter Smith's conception of the role of government in a society of perfect liberty. Smith is certainly not "against" government— we have already seen how central he considers its order-bestowing functions to be. In a society of perfect liberty the government will have three essential functions to perform—not merely the provision of law and order, and defense, but also the construction of essential public works. What Smith *is* against is the meddling of government in the workings of the free market. The "pretensions" of statesmen, against which Smith likes to rail, do not refer only to their deficiencies of character or intelligence (although there is plenty of that), but to the presumption that they can better manage the affairs of the country than the remarkable capacities of the market system.

These capabilities are again evidence of the Invisible Hand. No participant in the market has in mind—or if he did have in mind, has the power to effect—the orderly provisioning of society. Like the butcher and the baker, each is concerned only with his private interest. But the pressure of competition nonetheless turns this self-oriented process toward a socially useful goal. Because many marketers seek their self interest, society is rescued from the extortions that a few "monopolists" could exact. (Monopolists, as well as government, are a particular bane of Smith's.) And because the setting of natural liberty has removed the hobbles and inhibitions of earlier societies, the flow of labor and capital can move into all fields and be barred from none.

I need hardly add that Smith's vision of a self-regulating market has provided the substance for economic debate ever since the *Wealth* appeared, a debate that is still far from settled. In many ways Smith's vision of a self-regulating market has been shown to be deeper and more complete than even he could have known. Here indeed are proper grounds for considering Smith to be a founding father of economic conservatism. But in two respects, the present debate is far removed from the grounds on which Smith originally conceived of it. One difference is that economic activity in the modern world is in the hands of high-technology, large-scale business, not low-technology, small-scale enterprise. This change brings far-reaching differences to the working of a market system. The quick adaptation of supply to demand, and the immediate pull of personal interest that are necessary for Smith's market mechanism to work, do not appear in vast managerial entities, saddled with expensive fixed equipment and forced to plan months or even years in advance. A large-scale industrial economy is a very different kind of "commercial society" from the small-scale economy of Smith's time. Smith's earlier form of capitalism can still be observed within the structure of modern industrial capitalism, tucked away in the listings of the Yellow Pages of the phone book, but it is no longer an accurate description of the organized power, the massive institutions, and the often ponderous workings of the system in its modern form.

A second difference is that modern technology brings startling and sometimes awesome side effects as the unintended consequences of industrial production. It is difficult to champion the unfettered operation of a free market when the Invisible Hand reveals itself in the form of noxious fumes or poisoned waters or resource exhaustion—not to mention technological unemployment. Thus Smith's analysis of the market mechanism cannot be considered the last word on the subject. But in some ways it is more important than that: it is the "first word" on the subject—the pioneering exploration of the market *as a system*. As such, it is still the conception to which we turn when we explain how a market economy works.

ECONOMIC GROWTH

Smith's analysis of the process of internal order is far more extensive than this initial overview can indicate. But the attainment of internal order is only one of two major economic themes in the *Wealth of Nations*, and perhaps not the most important one. For a society of natural liberty exhibits another tendency in addition to that of stability and order. This is its tendency to grow, to increase the production of those "necessaries and conveniences" which themselves constitute the wealth of a nation.

Growth comes about in Smith's model of an economy as the consequence of both psychological and technological considerations. At the core of the process is the drive to amass wealth with whose roots in the human psyche we are familiar from the *Moral Sentiments*. In the *Wealth* this all-important drive is ascribed to the "desire of bettering our condition, a desire, which though generally calm and dispassionate, comes with us from the womb, and never leaves us till we go into the grave. . . . An augmentation of fortune is the means by which the greater part of men propose and wish to better their condition. It is the means the most vulgar and the most obvious; and the most likely way of augmenting their fortune is to save and accumulate some part of what they acquire."[5]

Thus growth starts as a consequence of the Invisible Hand, which has implanted within us that all-important confusion of wealth with betterment. Now Smith turns his attention to the social class whose actions will be strategic for growth. A manufacturing capitalist normally seeks to better his condition by saving and accumulating the revenue from his enterprise. He uses his profits to buy additional machinery to expand output—and thereby sets into motion a train of economic consequences.

The first of these is that the addition of equipment will improve the division of labor. In the early pages of the *Wealth*, Smith describes a "small manufactory," where ten persons were employed making pins—the very example he had already spoken of in his *Lectures on Jurisprudence*. By dividing the task into its constituent parts and assisting each task with machinery, the manufactory was able to produce forty-eight thousand pins a day, whereas each person, working separately, could not have made twenty, perhaps not a single pin.[6] This sets the stage for the process of economic growth—the division of labor enormously enhancing the technical capacity to produce wealth, and the saving and investing of revenue providing the economic basis for the wealth–expanding process. What Joseph Schumpeter has called a prospect of "hitchless" expansion is thereby opened up.[7]

But a hitch appears nonetheless. As many manufacturers seek to expand their revenues, they also expand their demand for labor. This is because Smith, unlike Marx, is analyzing the effects of preindustrial, not industrial, technology, and does not therefore consider machinery as displacing labor. As Smith's manufacturers seek to mechanize their operations, they increase their number of workmen. As a result, the demand for labor rises, and with it, the general level of wages. And as wages rise, profits shrink. The process of expansion, in other words, is threatened because the funds needed for accumulation are forced to buy more expensive labor power.

All is not lost, however. For the increased demand for labor will now increase the supply of labor: "The demand for men, like that for any other commodity, necessarily regulates the production of men, writes Smith.[8] It regulates it because the higher level of wages enables the working class to rear more of its children to working age—Smith has some chilling statistics as to the mortality rate of children born into the working class. So the hitch is circumvented. The increased number of workers dampens or halts the upward tendency of wages, just as the increased supply of any commodity

5. Ibid., pp. 341–342.
6. Ibid., p. 15.
7. Joseph Schumpeter, A *History of Economic*

Analysis (New York, Oxford University Press, 1954), pp. 572, 640.
8. Smith, *Wealth*, p. 98.

works to soften its price. Revenues can therefore once again be used to buy more labor and machine power, not to pay higher wages. The division of labor continues, and with it, economic growth. The system of perfect liberty thus brings its greatest benefit—a steady increase in the wealth of nations.

DECLINE AND DECAY

The great message of the *Wealth* is therefore a positive and hopeful one. Left to itself the system will generate wealth; and this wealth will diffuse throughout society down to its lowliest members. "Observe the accomodation of the most common artificer or day labourer in a civilized and thriving country," writes Smith. "Compared, indeed, with the most extravagant luxury of the great, his accomodations must no doubt appear extremely simple and easy; and yet it may be true, perhaps, that the accomodation of an European prince does not always so much exceed that of an industrious and frugal peasant, as the accomodation of the latter exceeds that of many an African king, the absolute master of lives and liberties of ten thousand naked savages."[9]

There is more than a little hyperbole, not to say cant, in this famous passage, but the underlying message retains its validity. Whatever dislocations and other difficulties it may introduce into society, the market system—capitalism—is an unparalleled means of accumulating social wealth.

It would be wrong, however to leave our introduction to the *Wealth of Nations* having stressed only its affirmative aspects. For there remains a last theme to be taken into account. It is a theme of historical limitation, of a deeply conservative pessimism, that elevates the book into a commentary on the human condition.

We meet the first intimations of this sobering darker side to the *Wealth* in chapter 9, when Smith speaks of "Profits of Stock" (capital). There we consider what will happen to a nation that acquired all the capital which its soil and climate and international position permitted. In such a nation, "both the wages of labour and the profits of stock would probably be very low. In a country fully peopled in proportion to what either its territory could maintain or its stock employ, the competition for employment would necessarily be so great as to reduce the wages of labour to what was barely sufficient to keep up the number of labourers. . . . In a country fully stocked in proportion to all the business it had to transact . . . the competition would everywhere be as great, and consequently the ordinary profit, as low as possible."[10]

Smith makes it clear that no country has yet reached this condition of a "full complement" of capital, and it is evident that he does not envisage the dynamism of technology that makes such a vision even more remote in our day than in his. What is remarkable, nonetheless, is that the gradient of progress foreseen by Smith is not one of endless improvement. It is, rather, a projection of a widely held Enlightenment expectation that nations, like individuals, had their times of youth and old age. Thus the buoyant prospects for a society of perfect liberty come to an "end." They do not stretch endlessly into the future.

We encounter a second jarring note within the *Wealth* much later in the

9. Ibid., pp. 23–24.   10. Ibid., pp. 111.

book, when we have reached the chapters in which the "stages" of progress are laid out. For then it becomes apparent that the progress to which Smith directs our attention is material, not spiritual or mental. From the nonmaterial point of view, not progress but retrogression has taken place. The division of labor, on which material progress has been based, has sapped, not enhanced, the mental capabilities of its users. Writes Smith:

> In the progress of the division of labour, the employment of the far greater part of those who live by labour . . . comes to be confined to a few very simple operations; frequently to one or two. But the understandings of the greater part of men are necessarily formed by their employments. The man whose whole life is spent in performing a few simple operations, of which the effects, too, are always the same, or very nearly the same, has no occasion to exert his understanding. . . . He naturally loses, therefore, the habit of such exertion, and generally becomes as stupid and ignorant as it is possible for a human creature to become. . . . In every improved and civilised society this is the state into which the labouring poor, that is, the great body of the people, must necessarily fall, unless government takes some pains to prevent it.[11]

Material progress, in other words, brings moral decay. Smith makes us doubly aware of this by contrasting the condition of civilized society with that which preceded it. In the "barbarous societies, as they are commonly called," Smith writes, ". . . the varied occupations of every man oblige every man to exert his capacity, and to invent expedients for removing the difficulties which are continually occurring. Invention is kept alive, and the mind is not suffered to fall into that drowsy stupidity, which, in a civilized society, seems to benumb the understanding of almost all the inferior ranks of the people."[12]

What is perhaps the most sobering note of all is the absence of any transcendent vision in Smith—an absence that prevents him from offering his readers the utopian hope that glimmers, ever so faintly, in Marx. No utopia beckons in Smith. Nor is there any effort to portray the existing state of things in very hopeful terms. Discussing the interests of the three orders, and their capacity to govern wisely, Smith passes a poor judgment on all of them. The landlord class, enjoying its rents in "indolence", is "incapable of that application of mind which is necessary to foresee and understand the consequences of any public regulation." The laborer, for reasons that we have seen, is "incapable either of comprehending [the interest of society], or of understanding its connexion with his own." As for the "third order" of manufacturers and merchants, it comes, as we may remember from the earlier pages of this book, "from an order of men whose interest is never exactly the same with that of the public, who generally have an interest to deceive and even to oppress the public, and who accordingly have, upon many occasions, both deceived and oppressed it."[13]

11. Ibid., pp. 781–82.
12. Ibid., pp. 782–83.
13. Ibid., pp. 265, 266, 267.

Thus beneath the surface assurance of the book there lurk portents of a far less reassuring kind. It would misrepresent the *Wealth* to place these in the foreground of Smith's panorama, but it would misrepresent it even more to pretend that they were not an integral part of that panorama.

READINGS

The readings that follow are entirely from the *Wealth*. It would be tedious to review the book, chapter by chapter, but it may help if I provide a quick guide through and to important sections.

Every fresh student of the *Wealth* will want to read the Introduction, and and more important, the first chapter on The Division of Labour. Here is the pin factory, and a magnificent passage at the end of the chapter on the social division of tasks whose origins we can see in the "Early Draft." Chapter 2 contains the immortal phrases about "trucking and bartering," and "No one ever saw a dog make a fair and deliberate exchange," as well as the passage about the butcher, the brewer, and the baker. It is quintessential Smith. Chapter 3, "That the Division of Labour is Limited by the Extent of the Market," contains its message in its title. Despite its title, chapter 4, "On the Origin and Use of Money," has little of importance except an introduction to the question of value. Smith warns that "some obscurity may still appear to remain" about this subject, despite the next three chapters to be devoted to it: Professor Mark Blaug has written that "most readers would put this remark down as the greatest understatement in the history of economic thought."[14]

Chapters 5 and 6, which are concerned with the questions of value, are rich for the economist, perhaps less so for the general reader. Chapter 7 contains the analysis of market and natural prices, and is full of striking bits of analysis—"A public mourning raises the price of black cloth." Chapter 8, on wages, speaks unforgettably about the struggle between workmen and their masters, as well of the poverty of the working classes. The next chapter, on profits, is less interesting although it contains the passages referred to above about the "full complement" of riches. Many economists consider chapter 10 on "Inequalities of Wages and Profits" to be one of Smith's triumphs; it is certainly worth looking at. We have reduced the following chapter on rent to a few pages, in which Smith presents three confused explanations of the origins of rent: the monopoly power of landlords; the intrinsic productivity of the soil; and the differential income that accrues to land of greater marginal fertility; and we have omitted a lengthy "Digression on Silver" that mainly contains matters of interest to scholars. We have, of course, included and very much recommend, the discussion of the interests of the three orders of society referred to above.

Book II is about accumulation. Chapter 3 brings up the important distinction between productive and unproductive labor, and expounds on the virtues of parsimony: do not miss page 234. There follows the passage on "bettering our condition" and on "the impertinence and presumption" of kings and ministers who interfere with the workings of a market society. It is certainly "essential" Smith. The remaining chapters of the book are not.

14. Mark Blaug, *Economic Theory in Retrospect*, 3rd ed. (Cambridge, Cambridge University Press, 1978), p. 39.

Book III is about history. Its first chapter on "The Natural Progress of Opulence" is interesting; the next two less so for a general audience; the fourth of great interest and containing the sections we have quoted about the merchants unknowingly subverting feudalism.

Book IV covers many subjects besides its announced "Systems of Political Economy." It begins with a chapter critically analyzing mercantilism, and goes on in chapter 2 to inveigh against protectionism. This is a rich chapter which contains (on page 265) the *only* reference to the Invisible Hand in the *Wealth of Nations!* In addition to a great deal of acute analysis, this chapter also contains two much quoted apothegms, "What is prudence in the conduct of every private family, can scarce be folly in that of a great kingdom" (p. 266), and a reference to statesmen and politicians as "crafty and insidious animal[s]" (p. 266). The following chapter has another gem, aimed at monopolists who seek to advance their private interests the basis for public policy: "The sneaking arts of underlying tradesmen are thus erected into the political maxims of a great empire" (p. 268). Chapter 7, "Of Colonies," is celebrated but very lengthy. We have included what we believe to be its essence, including the ringing section on the American colonies (p. 278–279). Chapter 8 concludes Smith's dissection of the Mercantile System. We have retained only the famous passage beginning "Consumption is the sole end and purpose of all production" (p. 284). The concluding chapter of this book concerns Physiocracy ("The Agricultural System") and will mainly interest historians of economic thought. We have kept enough to convey the criticism that Smith makes of Physiocracy, as well as the last stunning paragraphs (p. 289) announcing the system of natural liberty.

The final Book V is essentially about the economic role of government in a society of natural liberty. Accordingly the book covers the main kinds of expenditures that Smith believes such a government should undertake, and the basic forms of taxation by which its revenue should be raised. Before taking up these matters, chapter 1 gives us a tour of "stadial" history, in which institutions alter as the material basis of society changes; a discussion of the roots of social authority; and (in the lengthy section on education) the telling passages about the adverse effects of the division of labor. As a result that chapter contains some of the most interesting material in the *Wealth.* (See pages 290–312).

The remainder of Book V is of less interest, save for three passages. One of these are his famous four maxims of taxation set out on pp. 313–314. A second is a polemic against the public debt, reproduced on p. 318, and often quoted by opponents of national debts. Last, we end with a superb short statement about the futility of England's dreams of an American empire. These words conclude The *Wealth of Nations*, but they still reverberate wherever empires have been built on little more than the imagination.

In addition, I have added a few pages of famous sentences or short paragraphs that cull the essence of Smith's message and style. Page references are to the Glasgow edition, and in brackets to the pages of this book, whenever the sentences have already appeared in the readings.

A N

I N Q U I R Y

INTO THE

Nature and Caufes

OF THE

WEALTH OF NATIONS.

By ADAM SMITH, LL. D. and F. R. S.
Formerly Profeffor of Moral Philofophy in the Univerfity of GLASGOW.

IN TWO VOLUMES.

VOL. I.

LONDON:

PRINTED FOR W. STRAHAN; AND T. CADELL, IN THE STRAND.
MDCCLXXVI.

Introduction and Plan of the Work

The annual labour of every nation is the fund which originally supplies it with all the necessaries and conveniences of life which it annually consumes, and which consist always, either in the immediate produce of that labour, or in what is purchased with that produce from other nations.

According therefore, as this produce, or what is purchased with it, bears a greater or smaller proportion to the number of those who are to consume it, the nation will be better or worse supplied with all the necessaries and conveniences for which it has occasion.

But this proportion must in every nation be regulated by two different circumstances; first, by the skill, dexterity, and judgment with which its labour is generally applied; and, secondly, by the proportion between the number of those who are employed in useful labour, and that of those who are not so employed. Whatever be the soil, climate, or extent of territory of any particular nation, the abundance or scantiness of its annual supply must, in that particular situation, depend upon those two circumstances.

The abundance or scantiness of this supply too seems to depend more upon the former of those two circumstances than upon the latter. Among the savage nations of hunters and fishers, every individual who is able to work, is more or less employed in useful labour, and endeavours to provide, as well as he can, the necessaries and conveniences of life, for himself, or such of his family or tribe as are either too old, or too young, or too infirm to go a hunting and fishing. Such nations, however, are so miserably poor, that, from mere want, they are frequently reduced, or, at least, think themselves reduced, to the necessity sometimes of directly destroying, and sometimes of abandoning their infants, their old people, and those afflicted with lingering diseases, to perish with hunger, or to be devoured by wild beasts. Among civilised and thriving nations, on the contrary, though a great number of people do not labour at all, many of whom consume the produce of ten times, frequently of a hundred times more labour than the greater part of those who work; yet the produce of the whole labour of the society is so great, that all are often abundantly supplied, and a workman, even of the lowest and poorest order, if he is frugal and industrious, may enjoy a greater share of the

---

*To guide the reader through the Glasgow text we have added most but not all of Edwin Cannan's famous margin notes from the Modern Library edition of the *Wealth of Nations* (Random House, New York, 1937.) Of them Cannan wrote in his introduction:

> I have felt like an architect commissioned to place a new building alongside some ancient masterpiece: I have endeavoured to avoid on the one hand an impertinent adoption of Smith's words and style, and on the other an obtrusively modern phraseology which might contrast unpleasantly with the text. (p. xx.)

As before, we have modernized spellings and introduced some additional paragraphing for ease of reading.

necessaries and conveniences of life than it is possible for any savage to acquire.

The causes of this improvement, in the productive powers of labour, and the order, according to which its produce is naturally distributed among the different ranks and conditions of men in the society, make the subject of the First Book of this Inquiry.

Whatever be the actual state of the skill, dexterity, and judgment with which labour is applied in any nation, the abundance or scantiness of its annual supply must depend, during the continuance of that state, upon the proportion between the number of those who are annually employed in useful labour, and that of those who are not so employed. The number of useful and productive labourers, it will hereafter appear, is everywhere in proportion to the quantity of capital stock which is employed in setting them to work, and to the particular way in which it is so employed. The Second Book, therefore, treats of the nature of capital stock, of the manner in which it is gradually accumulated, and of the different quantities of labour which it puts into motion, according to the different ways in which it is employed.

Nations tolerably well advanced as to skill, dexterity, and judgment, in the application of labour, have followed very different plans in the general conduct or direction of it; and those plans have not all been equally favourable to the greatness of its produce. The policy of some nations has given extraordinary encouragement to the industry of the country; that of others to the industry of towns. Scarce any nation has dealt equally and impartially with every sort of industry. Since the downfall of the Roman empire, the policy of Europe has been more favourable to arts, manufactures, and commerce, the industry of towns; than to agriculture, the industry of the country. The circumstances which seem to have introduced and established this policy are explained in the Third Book.

Though those different plans were, perhaps, first introduced by the private interests and prejudices of particular orders of men, without any regard to, or foresight of, their consequences upon the general welfare of the society; yet they have given occasion to very different theories of political economy; of which some magnify the importance of that industry which is carried on in towns, others of that which is carried on in the country. Those theories have had a considerable influence, not only upon the opinions of men of learning, but upon the public conduct of princes and sovereign states. I have endeavoured, in the Fourth Book, to explain, as fully and distinctly as I can, those different theories, and the principal effects which they have produced in different ages and nations.

To explain in what has consisted the revenue of the great body of the people, or what has been the nature of those funds which, in different ages and nations, have supplied their annual consumption, is the object of these Four first Books. The Fifth and last Book treats of the revenue of the sovereign, or commonwealth. In this book I have endeavoured to show; first, what are the necessary expences of the sovereign, or commonwealth; which of those expences ought to be defrayed by the general contribution of the whole society; and which of them, by that of some particular part only, or of some particular members of it; secondly, what are the different methods in which the whole society may be made to contribute towards defraying the expences incumbent on the whole society, and what are the principal advantages and inconveniences of each of those methods: and, thirdly and lastly, what are the reasons and causes which have induced almost all modern governments to mortgage some part of this revenue, or to contract debts, and what have been the effects of those debts upon the real wealth, the annual produce of the land and labour of the society.

BOOK I
OF THE CAUSES OF IMPROVEMENT IN THE PRODUCTIVE POWERS OF LABOUR, AND OF THE ORDER ACCORDING TO WHICH ITS PRODUCE IS NATURALLY DISTRIBUTED AMONG THE DIFFERENT RANKS OF THE PEOPLE

CHAPTER I
Of the Division of Labour

The greatest improvement in the productive powers of labour, and the greater part of the skill, dexterity, and judgment with which it is anywhere directed, or applied, seem to have been the effects of the division of labour.

Division of labour is the great cause of its increased powers, as may be better understood from a particular example, such as pin making.

The effects of the division of labour, in the general business of society, will be more easily understood, by considering in what manner it operates in some particular manufactures. It is commonly supposed to be carried furthest in some very trifling ones; not perhaps that it really is carried further in them than in others of more importance: but in those trifling manufactures which are destined to supply the small wants of but a small number of people, the whole number of workmen must necessarily be small; and those employed in every different branch of the work can often be collected into the same workhouse, and placed at once under the view of the spectator. In those great manufactures, on the contrary, which are destined to supply the great wants of the great body of the people, every different branch of the work employs so great a number of workmen, that it is impossible to collect them all into the same workhouse. We can seldom see more, at one time, than those employed in one single branch. Though in such manufactures, therefore, the work may really be divided into a much greater number of parts, than in those of a more trifling nature, the division is not near so obvious, and has accordingly been much less observed.

To take an example, therefore, from a very trifling manufacture; but one in which the division of labour has been very often taken notice of, the trade of the pin maker; a workman not educated to this business (which the division of labour has rendered a distinct trade), nor acquainted with the use of the machinery employed in it (to the invention of which the same division of labour has probably given occasion), could scarce, perhaps, with his utmost industry, make one pin in a day, and certainly could not make twenty. But in the way in which this business is now carried on, not only the whole work is a peculiar trade, but it is divided into a number of branches, of which the greater part are likewise peculiar trades. One man draws out the wire, another straightens it, a third cuts it, a fourth points it, a fifth grinds it at the top for receiving the head; to make the head requires two or three distinct operations; to put it on, is a peculiar business, to whiten the pins is another; it is even a trade by itself to put them into the paper; and the important business of making a pin is, in this manner, divided into about eighteen distinct operations, which, in some manufactories, are all performed by distinct hands, though in others the same man will sometimes perform two or three of them. I have seen a small manufactory of this kind where ten men only were employed, and where some of them consequently performed two or three distinct operations. But though they were very poor, and therefore but indifferently accommodated with the necessary machinery, they could, when they exerted themselves, make among them about twelve pounds of pins in a day. There are in a pound upwards of four thousand pins of a middling size. Those ten persons, therefore, could make among them upwards of forty-eight thousand pins in a day. Each person, therefore, making a tenth part of forty-eight thousand pins, might be considered as making four thousand eight hundred pins in a day. But if they had all wrought separately and independently, and without any of them having been educated to this peculiar business, they certainly could not each of them have made twenty, perhaps not one pin in a day; that is, certainly not the two hundred and fortieth, perhaps not the four thousand eight hundredth part of what they are at present capable of performing, in consequence of a proper division and combination of their different operations.

In every other art and manufacture, the effects of
the division of labour are similar to what they are in
this very trifling one; though, in many of them, the
labour can neither be so much subdivided, nor

The effect is similar in
all trades and also in the
division of employ-
ments.

reduced to so great a simplicity of operation. The division of labour,
however, so far as it can be introduced, occasions, in every art, a proportionable increase of the productive powers of labour. The separation
of different trades and employments from one another, seems to have
taken place, in consequence of this advantage. This separation too is
generally carried furthest in those countries which enjoy the highest degree
of industry and improvement; what is the work of one man, in a rude
state of society, being generally that of several in an improved one. In
every improved society, the farmer is generally nothing but a farmer; the
manufacturer, nothing but a manufacturer. The labour too which is
necessary to produce any one complete manufacture, is almost always
divided among a great number of hands. How many different trades are
employed in each branch of the linen and woollen manufactures, from
the growers of the flax and the wool, to the bleachers and smoothers of
the linen, or to the dyers and dressers of the cloth! The nature of agriculture, indeed, does not admit of so many subdivisions of labour, nor
of so complete a separation of one business from another, as manufactures. It is impossible to separate so entirely, the business of the grazier
from that of the corn farmer, as the trade of the carpenter is commonly
separated from that of the smith. The spinner is almost always a distinct
person from the weaver; but the ploughman, the harrower, the sower of
the seed, and the reaper of the corn, are often the same. The occasions
for those different sorts of labour returning with the different seasons of
the year, it is impossible that one man should be constantly employed
in any one of them.

This impossibility of making so complete and entire a separation of
all the different branches of labour employed in agriculture, is perhaps
the reason why the improvement of the productive powers of labour in
this art, does not always keep pace with their improvement in manufactures. The most opulent nations, indeed, generally excel all their neighbours in agriculture as well as in manufactures; but they are commonly
more distinguished by their superiority in the latter than in the former.
Their lands are in general better cultivated, and having more labour and
expence bestowed upon them, produce more, in proportion to the extent
and natural fertility of the ground. But this superiority of produce is
seldom much more than in proportion to the superiority of labour and
expence. In agriculture, the labour of the rich country is not always
much more productive than that of the poor; or, at least, it is never so
much more productive, as it commonly is in manufactures. The corn
of the rich country, therefore, will not always, in the same degree of
goodness, come cheaper to market than that of the poor. The corn of

Poland, in the same degree of goodness, is as cheap as that of France, notwithstanding the superior opulence and improvement of the latter country. The corn of France is, in the corn provinces, fully as good, and in most years nearly about the same price with the corn of England, though, in opulence and improvement, France is perhaps inferior to England. The corn lands of England, however, are better cultivated than those of France, and the corn lands of France are said to be much better cultivated than those of Poland. But though the poor country, notwithstanding the inferiority of its cultivation, can, in some measure, rival the rich in the cheapness and goodness of its corn, it can pretend to no such competition in its manufactures; at least if those manufactures suit the soil, climate, and situation of the rich country. The silks of France are better and cheaper than those of England, because the silk manufacture, at least under the present high duties upon the importation of raw silk, does not so well suit the climate of England as that of France. But the hardware and the coarse woollens of England are beyond all comparison superior to those of France, and much cheaper too in the same degree of goodness. In Poland there are said to be scarce any manufactures of any kind, a few of those coarser household manufactures excepted, without which no country can well subsist.

This great increase of the quantity of work, which, in consequence of the division of labour, the same number of people are capable of performing, is owing to three different circumstances; first, to the increase of dexterity in every particular workman; secondly, to the saving of the time which is commonly lost in passing from one species of work to another; and lastly, to the invention of a great number of machines which facilitate and abridge labour, and enable one man to do the work of many.

The advantage is due to three circumstances, (1) improved dexterity, (2) saving of time, and (3) application of machinery, invented by workmen, or by machine-makers and philosophers.

First, the improvement of the dexterity of the workman necessarily increases the quantity of the work he can perform, and the division of labour, by reducing every man's business to some one simple operation, and by making this operation the sole employment of his life, necessarily increases very much the dexterity of the workman. A common smith, who, though accustomed to handle the hammer, has never been used to make nails, if upon some particular occasion he is obliged to attempt it, will scarce, I am assured, be able to make above two or three hundred nails in a day, and those too very bad ones. A smith who has been accustomed to make nails, but whose sole or principal business has not been that of a nailer, can seldom with his utmost diligence make more than eight hundred or a thousand nails in a day. I have seen several boys under twenty years of age who had never exercised any other trade but that of making nails, and who, when they exerted themselves, could make, each of them, upwards of two thousand three hundred nails in a day. The making of a nail, however, is by no means one of the simplest operations. The same person blows the bellows, stirs or mends the fire as there is occasion, heats the iron, and forges every part of the nail: In forging the head too he is obliged to change his tools. The different operations into which the making of a pin, or of a metal button, is subdivided, are all of them much more simple, and the dexterity of the person, of whose life it has been the sole business to perform them, is usually much greater. The rapidity with which some of the operations of those manufactures are performed, exceeds what the human hand could, by those who had never seen them, be supposed capable of acquiring.

Secondly, the advantage which is gained by saving the time commonly lost in passing from one sort of work to another, is much greater than we should at first view be apt to imagine it. It is impossible to pass very quickly from one kind of work to another, that is carried on in a different place, and with quite different tools. A country weaver, who cultivates a small farm, must lose a good deal of time in passing from his loom to the field, and from the field to his loom. When the two trades can be carried on in the same workhouse, the loss of time is no doubt much less. It is even in this case, however, very considerable. A man commonly saunters a little in turning his hand from one sort of employment to another. When he first begins the new work he is seldom very keen and hearty; his mind, as they say, does not go to it, and for some time he rather trifles than applies to good purpose. The habit of sauntering and of indolent careless application, which is naturally, or rather necessarily acquired by every country workman who is obliged to change his work and his tools every half hour, and to apply his hand in twenty different ways almost every day of his life; renders him almost always slothful and lazy, and incapable of any vigorous application even on the most pressing occasions. Independent, therefore, of his deficiency in point of dexterity, this cause alone must always reduce considerably the quantity of work which he is capable of performing.

Thirdly, and lastly, every body must be sensible how much labour is facilitated and abridged by the application of proper machinery. It is unnecessary to give any example. I shall only observe, therefore, that the invention of all those machines by which labour is so much facilitated and abridged, seems to have been originally owing to the division of labour. Men are much more likely to discover easier and readier methods of attaining any object, when the whole attention of their minds is directed towards that single object, than when it is dissipated among a great variety of things. But in consequence of the division of labour, the whole of every man's attention comes naturally to be directed towards some one very simple object. It is naturally to be expected, therefore, that some one or other of those who are employed in each particular branch of labour should soon find out easier and readier methods of performing their own particular work, wherever the nature of it admits of such improvement.

A great part of the machines made use of in those manufactures in which labour is most subdivided, were originally the inventions of common workmen, who, being each of them employed in some very simple operation, naturally turned their thoughts towards finding out easier and readier methods of performing it. Whoever has been much accustomed to visit such manufactures, must frequently have been shown very pretty machines, which were the inventions of such workmen, in order to facilitate and quicken their own particular part of the work. In the first fire engines,* a boy was constantly employed to open and shut alternately the communication between the boiler and the cylinder, according as the piston either ascended or descended. One of those boys, who loved to play with his companions, observed that, by tying a string from the handle of the valve, which opened this communication, to another part of the machine, the valve would open and shut without his assistance, and leave him at liberty to divert himself with his play-fellows. One of the greatest improvements that has been made upon this machine, since it was first invented, was in this manner the discovery of a boy who wanted to save his own labour.

All the improvements in machinery, however, have by no means been the inventions of those who had occasion to use the machines. Many improvements have been made by the ingenuity of the makers of the machines, when to make them became the business of a peculiar trade; and some by that of those who are called philosophers or men of speculation, whose trade it is, not to do any thing, but to observe every thing; and who, upon that account, are often capable of combining together the powers of the most distant and dissimilar objects. In the progress of society, philosophy or speculation becomes, like every other employment, the principal or sole trade and occupation of a particular class of citizens. Like every other employment too, it is subdivided into a great number of different branches, each of which affords occupation to a peculiar tribe or class of philosophers; and this subdivision of employment in philosophy, as well as in every other business, improves dexterity, and saves time. Each individual becomes more expert in his own peculiar branch, more work is done upon the whole, and the quantity of science is considerably increased by it.

It is the great multiplication of the productions of all the different arts, in consequence of the division of labour, which occasions, in a well-governed society, that universal opulence which extends itself to the lowest ranks of the people. Every workman has a great quantity of his own work to dispose of beyond what he himself has occasion for; and every other workman being exactly in the same situation, he is enabled to exchange a great quantity of his

Hence the universal opulence of a well-governed society; even the day-labourer's coat being the produce of a vast number of workmen.

*Steam engines.

own goods for a great quantity, or, what comes to the same thing, for the price of a great quantity of theirs. He supplies them abundantly with what they have occasion for, and they accommodate him as amply with what he has occasion for, and a general plenty diffuses itself through all the different ranks of the society.

Observe the accommodation of the most common artificer or day-labourer in a civilised and thriving country, and you will perceive that the number of people of whose industry a part, though but a small part, has been employed in procuring him this accommodation, exceeds all computation. The woollen coat, for example, which covers the day-labourer, as coarse and rough as it may appear, is the produce of the joint labour of a great multitude of workmen. The shepherd, the sorter of the wool, the wool-comber or carder, the dyer, the scribbler, the spinner, the weaver, the fuller, the dresser, with many others, must all join their different arts in order to complete even this homely production. How many merchants and carriers, besides, must have been employed in transporting the materials from some of those workmen to others who often live in a very distant part of the country! How much commerce and navigation in particular, how many shipbuilders, sailors, sailmakers, ropemakers, must have been employed in order to bring together the different drugs made use of by the dyer, which often come from the remotest corners of the world! What a variety of labour too is necessary in order to produce the tools of the meanest of those workmen! To say nothing of such complicated machines as the ship of the sailor, the mill of the fuller, or even the loom of the weaver, let us consider only what a variety of labour is requisite in order to form that very simple machine, the shears with which the shepherd clips the wool. The miner, the builder of the furnace for smelting the ore, the feller of the timber, the burner of the charcoal to be made use of in the smelting house, the brickmaker, the bricklayer, the workmen who attend the furnace, the millwright, the forger, the smith, must all of them join their different arts in order to produce them.

Were we to examine, in the same manner, all the different parts of his dress and household furniture, the coarse linen shirt which he wears next his skin, the shoes which cover his feet, the bed which he lies on, and all the different parts which compose it, the kitchen grate at which he prepares his victuals, the coals which he makes use of for that purpose, dug from the bowels of the earth, and brought to him perhaps by a long sea and a long land carriage, all the other utensils of his kitchen, all the furniture of his table, the knives and forks, the earthen or pewter plates upon which he serves up and divides his victuals, the different hands employed in preparing his bread and his beer, the glass window which lets in the heat and the light, and keeps out the wind and the rain, with all the knowledge and art requisite for preparing that beautiful and happy invention, without which these northern parts of the world could scarce have afforded a very comfortable habitation, together with the tools of all the different workmen employed in producing those different conveniences; if we examine, I say, all these things, and consider what a variety of labour is employed about each of them, we shall be sensible that without the assistance and cooperation of many thousands, the very meanest person in a civilised country could not be provided, even according to, what we very falsely imagine, the easy and simple manner in which he is commonly accommodated. Compared, indeed, with the more extravagant luxury of the great, his accommodation must no doubt appear extremely simple and easy; and yet it may be true, perhaps, that the accommodation of an European prince does not always so much exceed that of an industrious and frugal peasant, as the accommodation of the latter exceeds that of many an African king, the absolute master of the lives and liberties of ten thousand naked savages.

CHAPTER II

Of the Principle which gives occasion to the Division of Labour

This division of labour, from which so many advantages are derived, is not originally the effect of any human wisdom, which foresees and intends that general opulence to which it gives occasion. It is the necessary, though very slow and gradual consequence of a certain propensity in human nature which has in view no such extensive utility; the propensity to truck, barter, and exchange one thing for another.

The division of labour arises from a propensity in human nature to exchange.

This propensity is found in man alone.

Whether this propensity be one of those original principles in human nature, of which no further account can be given; or whether, as seems more probable, it be the necessary consequence of the faculties of reason and speech, it belongs not to our present subject to enquire. It is common to all men, and to be found in no other race of animals, which seem to know neither this nor any other species of contracts. Two greyhounds, in running down the same hare, have sometimes the appearance of acting in some sort of concert. Each turns her towards his companion, or endeavours to intercept her when his companion turns her towards himself.

This, however, is not the effect of any contract, but of the accidental concurrence of their passions in the same object at that particular time. Nobody ever saw a dog make a fair and deliberate exchange of one bone for another with another dog. Nobody ever saw one animal by its gestures and natural cries signify to another, this is mine, that yours; I am willing to give this for that. When an animal wants to obtain something either of a man or of another animal, it has no other means of persuasion but to gain the favour of those whose service it requires. A puppy fawns upon its dam, and a spaniel endeavours by a thousand attractions to engage the attention of its master who is at dinner, when it wants to be fed by him. Man sometimes uses the same arts with his brethren, and when he has no other means of engaging them to act according to his inclinations, endeavours by every servile and fawning attention to obtain their good will. He has not time, however, to do this upon every occasion. In civilised society he stands at all times in need of the cooperation and assistance of great multitudes, while his whole life is scarce sufficient to gain the friendship of a few persons.

In almost every other race of animals each individual, when it is grown up to maturity, is entirely independent, and in its natural state has occasion for the assistance of no other living creature. But man has almost constant occasion for the help of his brethren, and it is in vain for him to expect it from their benevolence only. He will be more likely to prevail if he can interest their self-love in his favour, and show them that it is for their own advantage to do for him what he requires of them. Whoever offers to another a bargain of any kind, proposes to do this. Give me that which I want, and you shall have this which you want, is the meaning of every such offer; and it is in this manner that we obtain from one another the far greater part of those good offices which we stand in need of. It is not from the benevolence of the butcher, the brewer, or the baker, that we expect our dinner, but from their regard to their own interest. We address ourselves, not to their humanity but to their self-love, and never talk to them of our own necessities but of their advantages. Nobody but a beggar chooses to depend chiefly upon the benevolence of his fellow-citizens. Even a beggar does not depend upon it entirely. The charity of well-disposed people, indeed, supplies him with the whole fund of his subsistence. But though this principle ultimately provides him with all the necessaries of life which he has occasion for, it neither does nor can provide him with them as he has occasion for them. The greater part of his occasional wants are supplied in the same manner as those of other people, by treaty, by barter, and by purchase. With the money which one man gives him he purchases food. The old clothes which another bestows upon him he exchanges for other old clothes which suit him better, or for lodging, or for food, or for money, with which he can buy either food, clothes, or lodging, as he has occasion.

As it is by treaty, by barter, and by purchase, that we obtain from one another the greater part of those mutual good offices which we stand in need of, so it is this same trucking disposition which originally gives occasion to the division of labour. In a tribe of hunters or shepherds a particular person makes bows and arrows, for example, with more readiness and

It is encouraged by self-interest and leads to division of labour, thus giving rise to differences of talent more important than the natural differences, and rendering those differences useful.

dexterity than any other. He frequently exchanges them for cattle or for venison with his companions; and he finds at last that he can in this manner get more cattle and venison, than if he himself went to the field to catch them. From a regard to his own interest, therefore, the making of bows and arrows grows to be his chief business, and he becomes a sort of armourer. Another excels in making the frames and covers of their little huts or moveable houses. He is accustomed to be of use in this way to his neighbours, who reward him in the same manner with cattle and with venison, till at last he finds it his interest to dedicate himself entirely to this employment, and to become a sort of house-carpenter. In the same manner a third becomes a smith or a brazier, a fourth a tanner or dresser of hides or skins, the principal part of the clothing of savages. And thus the certainty of being able to exchange all that surplus part of the produce of his own labour, which is over and above his own consumption, for such parts of the produce of other men's labour as he may have occasion for, encourages every man to apply himself to a particular occupation, and to cultivate and bring to perfection whatever talent or genius he may possess for that particular species of business.

The difference of natural talents in different men is, in reality, much less than we are aware of; and the very different genius which appears to distinguish men of different professions, when grown up to maturity, is not upon many occasions so much the cause, as the effect of the division of labour. The difference between the most dissimilar characters, between a philosopher and a common street porter, for example, seems to arise not so much from nature, as from habit, custom, and education. When they came into the world, and for the first six or eight years of their existence, they were, perhaps, very much alike, and neither their parents nor play-fellows could perceive any remarkable difference. About that age, or soon after, they come to be employed in very different occupations. The difference of talents comes then to be taken notice of, and widens by degrees, till at last the vanity of the philosopher is willing to acknowledge scarce any resemblance. But without the disposition to truck, barter, and exchange, every man must have procured to himself every necessary and convenience of life which he wanted. All must have had the same duties to perform, and the same work to do, and there could have been no such difference of employment as could alone give occasion to any great difference of talents.

As it is this disposition which forms that difference of talents, so remarkable among men of different professions, so it is this same disposition which renders that difference useful. Many tribes of animals acknowledged to be all of the same species, derive from nature a much more remarkable distinction of genius, than what, antecedent to custom and education, appears to take place among men. By nature a philosopher is not in genius and disposition half so different from a street porter, as a mastiff is from a greyhound, or a greyhound from a spaniel, or this last from a shepherd's dog. Those different tribes of animals, however, though all of the same species, are of scarce any use to one another. The strength of the mastiff is not, in the least, supported either by the swiftness of the greyhound, or by the sagacity of the spaniel, or by the docility of the shepherd's dog. The effects of those different geniuses and talents, for want of the power or disposition to barter and exchange, cannot be brought into a common stock, and do not in the least contribute to the better accommodation and convenience of the species. Each animal is still obliged to support and defend itself, separately and independently, and derives no sort of advantage from that variety of talents with which nature has distinguished its fellows. Among men, on the contrary, the most dissimilar geniuses are of use to one another; the different produces of their respective talents, by the general disposition to truck, barter, and exchange, being brought, as it were, into a common stock, where every man may purchase whatever part of the produce of other men's talents he has occasion for.

CHAPTER III

That the Division of Labour is limited by the Extent of the Market

As it is the power of exchanging that gives occasion to the division of labour, so the extent of this division must always be limited by the extent of that power, or, in other words, by the extent of the market. When the market is very small, no person can have any encouragement to dedicate himself entirely to one employment, for want of the power to exchange all that surplus part of the produce of his own labour, which is over and above his own consumption, for such parts of the produce of other men's labour as he has occasion for.

Division of labour is limited by the extent of the power of exchanging.

Various trades cannot be carried on except in towns.

There are some sorts of industry, even of the lowest kind, which can be carried on nowhere but in a great town. A porter, for example, can find employment and subsistence in no other place. A village is by much too narrow a sphere for him; even an ordinary market town is scarce large enough to afford him constant occupation. In the lone houses and very small villages which are scattered about in so desert a country as the Highlands of Scotland, every farmer must be butcher, baker and brewer for his own family. In such situations we can scarce expect to find even a smith, a carpenter, or a mason, within less than twenty miles of another of the same trade. The scattered families that live at eight or ten miles distance from the nearest of them, must learn to perform themselves a great number of little pieces of work, for which, in more populous countries, they would call in the assistance of those workmen.

Country workmen are almost everywhere obliged to apply themselves to all the different branches of industry that have so much affinity to one another as to be employed about the same sort of materials. A country carpenter deals in every sort of work that is made of wood: a country smith in every sort of work that is made of iron. The former is not only a carpenter, but a joiner, a cabinetmaker, and even a carver in wood, as well as a wheelwright, a ploughwright, a cart and wagon maker. The employments of the latter are still more various. It is impossible there should be such a trade as even that of a nailer in the remote and inland parts of the Highlands of Scotland. Such a workman at the rate of a thousand nails a day, and three hundred working days in the year, will make three hundred thousand nails in the year. But in such a situation it would be impossible to dispose of one thousand, that is, of one day's work in the year. . . .

[The remainder of the chapter, a skeletal history of water transport from ancient Egypt to the eighteenth century, has been omitted.]

CHAPTER IV

Of the Origin and Use of Money

When the division of labour has been once thoroughly established, it is but a very small part of a man's wants which the produce of his own labour can supply. He supplies the far greater part of them by exchanging that surplus part of the produce of his own labour, which is over and above his own consumption, for such parts of the produce of other men's labour as he has occasion for. Every man thus lives by exchanging, or becomes in some measure a merchant, and the society itself grows to be what is properly a commercial society.

Division of labour being established, every man lives by exchanging.

But when the division of labour first began to take place, this power of exchanging must frequently have been very much clogged and embarrassed in its operations. One man, we shall suppose, has more of a certain commodity than he himself has occasion for, while another has less. The former consequently would be glad to dispose of, and the latter to purchase, a part of this superfluity. But if this latter should chance to have nothing that the former stands in need of, no exchange can be made between them.

Difficulties of barter lead to the selection of one commodity as money, for example, cattle, salt, shells, cod, tobacco, sugar, leather and nails.

The butcher has more meat in his shop than he himself can consume, and the brewer and the baker would each of them be willing to purchase a part of it. But they have nothing to offer in exchange, except the different productions of their respective trades, and the butcher is already provided with all the bread and beer which he has immediate occasion for. No exchange can, in this case, be made between them. He cannot be their merchant, nor they his customers; and they are all of them thus mutually less serviceable to one another. In order to avoid the inconvenience of such situations, every prudent man in every period of society, after the first establishment of the division of labour, must naturally have endeavoured to manage his affairs in such a manner, as to have at all times by him, besides the peculiar produce of his own industry, a certain quantity of some one commodity or other, such as he imagined few people would be likely to refuse in exchange for the produce of their industry.

Many different commodities, it is probable, were successively both thought of and employed for this purpose. In the rude ages of society, cattle are said to have been the common instrument of commerce; and, though they must have been a most inconvenient one, yet in old times we find things were frequently valued according to the number of cattle which had been given in exchange for them. The armour of Diomede, says Homer, cost only nine oxen; but that of Glaucus cost an hundred oxen. Salt is said to be the common instrument of commerce and exchanges in Abyssinia; a species of shells in some parts of the coast of India; dried cod at Newfoundland; tobacco in Virginia; sugar in some of our West India colonies; hides or dressed leather in some other countries; and there is at this day a village in Scotland where it is not uncommon, I am told, for a workman to carry nails instead of money to the baker's shop or the alehouse.

In all countries, however, men seem at last to have been determined by irresistible reasons to give the preference, for this employment, to metals above every other commodity. Metals cannot only be kept with as little loss as any other commodity, scarce any thing being less perishable that they are, but they can likewise, without any loss, be divided into any number of parts, as by fusion those parts can easily be reunited again; a quality which no other equally durable commodities possess, and which more than any other quality renders them fit to be the instruments of commerce and circulation. The man who wanted to buy salt, for example, and had nothing but cattle to give in exchange for it, must have been obliged to buy salt to the value of a whole ox, or a whole sheep at a time. He could seldom buy less than this, because what he was to give for it could seldom be divided without loss; and if he had a mind to buy more, he must, for the same reasons, have been obliged to buy double or triple the quantity, the value, to wit, of two or three oxen, or of two or three sheep. If, on the contrary, instead of sheep or oxen, he had metals to give in exchange for it, he could easily proportion the quantity of the metal to the precise quantity of the commodity which he had immediate occasion for.

Metals were eventually preferred because durable and divisible.

Different metals have been made use of by different nations for this purpose. Iron was the common instrument of commerce among the ancient Spartans; copper among the ancient Romans; and gold and silver among all rich and commercial nations.

Iron, copper, gold and silver, were at first used in unstamped bars, and coinage to show weight later.

Those metals seem originally to have been made use of for this purpose in rude bars, without any stamp or coinage. Thus we are told by Pliny, upon the authority of Timaeus, an ancient historian, that, till the time of Servius Tullius, the Romans had no coined money, but made use of unstamped bars of copper to purchase whatever they had occasion for. These rude bars, therefore, performed at this time the function of money. . . .

The inconvenience and difficulty of weighing those metals with exactness gave occasion to the institution of coins, of which the stamp, covering entirely both sides of the piece and sometimes the edges too, was supposed to ascertain not only the fineness, but the weight of the metal. Such coins, therefore, were received by tale as at present, without the trouble of weighing. . . .

It is in this manner that money has become in all civilised nations the universal instrument of commerce, by the intervention of which goods of all kinds are bought and sold, or exchanged for one another.

What are the rules which men naturally observe in exchanging them either for money or for one another, I shall now proceed to examine. These rules determine what may be called the relative or exchangeable value of goods.

The next inquiry is what rules determine exchangeable value.

Value may mean either value in use or value or value in exchange.

The word VALUE, it is to be observed, has two different meanings, and sometimes expresses the utility of some particular object, and sometimes the power of purchasing other goods which the possession of that object conveys. The one may be called value in use; the other, value in exchange. The things which have the greatest value in use have frequently little or no value in exchange; and, on the contrary, those which have the greatest value in exchange have frequently little or no value in use. Nothing is more useful than water: but it will purchase scarce any thing; scarce any thing can be had in exchange for it. A diamond, on the contrary, has scarce any value in use; but a very great quantity of other goods may frequently be had in exchange for it.

In order to investigate the principles which regulate the exchangeable value of commodities, I shall endeavour to show,

First, what is the real measure of this exchangeable value; or, wherein consists the real price of all commodities,

Secondly, what are the different parts of which this real price is composed or made up.

And, lastly, what are the different circumstances which sometimes

raise some or all of these different parts of price above, and sometimes
sink them below their natural or ordinary rate; or, what are the causes
which sometimes hinder the market price, that is, the actual price of
commodities, from coinciding exactly with what may be called their
natural price.

I shall endeavour to explain, as fully and distinctly as I can, those
three subjects in the three following chapters, for which I must very
earnestly entreat both the patience and attention of the reader: his patience
in order to examine a detail which may perhaps in some places appear
unnecessarily tedious; and his attention in order to understand what may,
perhaps, after the fullest explication which I am capable of giving of it,
appear still in some degree obscure. I am always willing to run some
hazard of being tedious in order to be sure that I am perspicuous; and
after taking the utmost pains that I can to be perspicuous, some obscurity
may still appear to remain upon a subject in its own nature extremely
abstracted.

CHAPTER V

Of the real and nominal Price of Commodities, or of their Price in Labour, and their Price in Money

Every man is rich or poor according to the degree
in which he can afford to enjoy the necessaries,
conveniences, and amusements of human life. But
after the division of labour has once thoroughly taken

*Labour is the real mea-
sure of exchangeable
value, and the first price
paid for all things.*

place, it is but a very small part of these with which a man's own labour
can supply him. The far greater part of them he must derive from the
labour of other people, and he must be rich or poor according to the
quantity of that labour which he can command, or which he can afford
to purchase. The value of any commodity, therefore, to the person who
possesses it, and who means not to use or consume it himself, but to
exchange it for other commodities, is equal to the quantity of labour
which it enables him to purchase or command. Labour, therefore, is
the real measure of the exchangeable value of all commodities.

The real price of every thing, what every thing really costs to the man
who wants to acquire it, is the toil and trouble of acquiring it. What
every thing is really worth to the man who has acquired it, and who
wants to dispose of it or exchange it for something else, is the toil and
trouble which it can save to himself, and which it can impose upon
other people. What is bought with money or with goods is purchased by
labour as much as what we acquire by the toil of our own body. That
money or those goods indeed save us this toil. They contain the value
of a certain quantity of labour which we exchange for what is supposed
at the time to contain the value of an equal quantity. Labour was the

first price, the original purchase money that was paid for all things. It was not by gold or by silver, but by labour, that all the wealth of the world was originally purchased; and its value, to those who possess it and who want to exchange it for some new productions, is precisely equal to the quantity of labour which it can enable them to purchase or command.

Wealth, as Mr. Hobbes says, is power. But the person who either acquires, or succeeds to a great fortune, does not necessarily acquire or succeed to any political power, either civil or military. His fortune may, perhaps, afford him the means of acquiring both, but the mere possession of that fortune does not necessarily convey to him either. The power which that possession immediately and directly conveys to him, is the power of purchasing; a certain command over all the labour, or over all the produce of labour which is then in the market. His fortune is greater or less, precisely in proportion to the extent of this power; or to the quantity either of other men's labour, or, what is the same thing, of the produce of other men's labour, which it enables him to purchase or command. The exchangeable value of every thing must always be precisely equal to the extent of this power which it conveys to its owner.

Wealth is power of purchasing labour.

But though labour be the real measure of the exchangeable value of all commodities, it is not that by which their value is commonly estimated. It is often difficult to ascertain the proportion between two different quantities of labour. The time spent in two different sorts of work will not always alone determine this proportion. The different degrees of hardship endured, and of ingenuity exercised, must likewise be taken into account. There may be more labour in an hour's hard work than in two hours easy business; or in an hour's application to a trade which it cost ten years labour to learn, than in a month's industry at an ordinary and obvious employment. But it is not easy to find any accurate measure either of hardship or ingenuity. In exchanging indeed the different productions of different sorts of labour for one another, some allowance is commonly made for both. It is adjusted, however, not by any accurate measure, but by the higgling and bargaining of the market, according to that sort of rough equality which, though not exact, is sufficient for carrying on the business of common life.

But value is not commonly estimated by labour, because labour is difficult to measure, and commodities are more frequently exchanged for other commodities, especially money, which is therefore more frequently used in estimating value.

Every commodity besides, is more frequently exchanged for, and thereby compared with, other commodities than with labour. It is more natural, therefore, to estimate its exchangeable value by the quantity of some other commodity than by that of the labour which it can purchase. The greater part of people too understand better what is meant by a quantity of a particular commodity, than by a quantity of labour. The one is a plain palpable object; the other an abstract notion, which, though it can be made sufficiently intelligible, is not altogether so natural and obvious.

But when barter ceases, and money has become the common instrument of commerce, every particular commodity is more frequently exchanged for money than for any other commodity. The butcher seldom carries his beef or his mutton to the baker, or the brewer, in order to exchange them for bread or for beer, but he carries them to the market, where he exchanges them for money, and afterwards exchanges that money for bread and for beer. The quantity of money which he gets for them regulates too the quantity of bread and beer which he can afterwards purchase. It is more natural and obvious to him, therefore, to estimate their value by the quantity of money, the commodity for which he immediately exchanges them, than by that of bread and beer, the commodities for which he can exchange them only by the intervention of another commodity; and rather to say that his butcher's meat is worth threepence or fourpence a pound, than that it is worth three or four pounds of bread, or three or four quarts of small beer. Hence it comes to pass, that the exchangeable value of every commodity is more frequently estimated by the quantity of money, than by the quantity either of labour or of any other commodity which can be had in exchange for it.

Gold and silver, however, like every other commodity, vary in their value, are sometimes cheaper and sometimes dearer, sometimes of easier and sometimes of more difficult purchase. The quantity of labour which any particular quantity of them can purchase or command, or the quantity of other goods which it will exchange for, depends always upon the fertility or barrenness of the mines which happen to be known about the time when such exchanges are made. The discovery of the abundant mines of America reduced, in the sixteenth century, the value of gold and silver in Europe to about a third of what it had been before. As it cost less labour to bring those metals from the mine to the market, so when they were brought thither they could purchase or command less labour; and this revolution in their value, though perhaps the greatest, is by no means the only one of which history gives some account. But as a measure of quantity, such as the natural foot, fathom, or handful, which is continually varying in its own quantity, can never be an accurate measure of the quantity of other things; so a commodity which is itself continually varying in its own value, can never be an accurate measure of the value of other commodities.

> But gold and silver vary in value, sometimes costing more and sometimes less labour, whereas equal labour always means equal sacrifice to the labourer, although the employer regards labour as varying in value.

Equal quantities of labour, at all times and places, may be said to be of equal value to the labourer. In his ordinary state of health, strength and spirits; in the ordinary degree of his skill and dexterity, he must always lay down the same portion of his ease, his liberty, and his happiness. The price which he pays must always be the same, whatever may be the quantity of goods which he receives in return for it. Of these, indeed, it may sometimes purchase a greater and sometimes a smaller quantity; but it is their value which varies, not that of the labour which purchases them. At all times and places that is dear which it is difficult to come at, or which it costs much labour to acquire; and that cheap which is to be had easily, or with very little labour. Labour alone, therefore, never varying in its own value, is alone the ultimate and real standard by which the value of all commodities can at all times and places be estimated and compared. It is their real price; money is their nominal price only.

But though equal quantities of labour are always of equal value to the labourer, yet to the person who employs him they appear sometimes to be of greater and sometimes of smaller value. He purchases them sometimes with a greater and sometimes with a smaller quantity of goods, and to him the price of labour seems to vary like that of all other things. It appears to him dear in the one case, and cheap in the other. In reality, however, it is the goods which are cheap in the one case, and dear in the other.

In this popular sense, therefore, labour, like commodities, may be said to have a real and a nominal price. Its real price may be said to consist in the quantity of the necessaries and conveniences of life which are given for it; its nominal price, in the quantity of money. The labourer is rich or poor, is well or ill rewarded, in proportion to the real, not to the nominal price of his labour.

So regarded, labour has a real and a nominal price.

The distinction between the real and the nominal price of commodities and labour, is not a matter of mere speculation, but may sometimes be of considerable use in practice. The same real price is always of the same value; but on account of the variations in the value of gold and silver, the same nominal price is sometimes of very different values. When a landed estate, therefore, is sold with a reservation of a perpetual rent, if it is intended that this rent should always be of the same value, it is of importance to the family in whose favour it is reserved, that it should not consist in a particular sum of money. Its value would in this case be liable to variations of two different kinds; first, to those which arise from the different quantities of gold and silver which are contained at different times in coin of the same denomination; and, secondly, to those which arise from the different values of equal quantities of gold and silver at different times. . . .

The distinction between real and nominal is sometimes useful in practice.

Equal quantities of labour will at distant times be purchased more nearly with equal quantities of corn, the subsistence of the labourer, than with equal quantities of gold and silver, or perhaps of any other commodity. Equal quantities of corn, therefore, will,

Corn rents are more stable than money rents, but liable to much larger annual variations, so that labour is the only universal standard.

at distant times, be more nearly of the same real value, or enable the possessor to purchase or command more nearly the same quantity of the labour of other people. They will do this, I say, more nearly than equal quantities of almost any other commodity; for even equal quantities of corn will not do it exactly. The subsistence of the labourer, or the real price of labour, as I shall endeavour to show hereafter, is very different upon different occasions; more liberal in a society advancing to opulence than in one that is standing still; and in one that is standing still than in one that is going backwards. Every other commodity, however, will at any particular time purchase a greater or smaller quantity of labour in proportion to the quantity of subsistence which it can purchase at that time. A rent therefore reserved in corn is liable only to the variations in the quantity of labour which a certain quantity of corn can purchase. But a rent reserved in any other commodity is liable, not only to the variations in the quantity of labour which any particular quantity of corn can purchase, but to the variations in the quantity of corn which can be purchased by any particular quantity of that commodity.

Though the real value of a corn rent, it is to be observed however, varies much less from century to century than that of a money rent, it varies much more from year to year. The money price of labour, as I shall endeavour to show hereafter, does not fluctuate from year to year with the money price of corn, but seems to be everywhere accommodated, not to the temporary or occasional, but to the average or ordinary price of that necessary of life. The average or ordinary price of corn again is regulated, as I shall likewise endeavour to show hereafter, by the value of silver, by the richness or barrenness of the mines which supply the market with that metal, or by the quantity of labour which must be employed, and consequently of corn which must be consumed, in order to bring any particular quantity of silver from the mine to the market. But the value of silver, though it sometimes varies greatly from century to century, seldom varies much from year to year, but frequently continues the same, or very nearly the same, for half a century or a century together. The ordinary or average money price of corn, therefore, may, during so long a period, continue the same or very nearly the same too, and along with it the money price of labour, provided, at least, the society continues, in other respects, in the same or nearly in the same condition. In the meantime the temporary and occasional price of corn may frequently be double, one year, of what it had been the year before, or fluctuate, for example, from five and twenty to fifty shillings the quarter. But when corn is at the latter price, not only the nominal, but the real value of a corn rent will be double of what it is when at the former, or will command double the quantity either of labour or of the greater part of other commodities; the money price of labour, and along with it that of most other things, continuing the same during all these fluctuations.

Labour, therefore, it appears evidently, is the only universal, as well as the only accurate measure of value, or the only standard by which we can compare the values of different commodities at all times and at all places. We cannot estimate, it is allowed, the real value of different commodities from century to century by the quantities of silver which were given for them. We cannot estimate it from year to year by the quantities of corn. By the quantities of labour we can, with the greatest accuracy, estimate it both from century to century and from year to year. From century to century, corn is a better measure than silver, because, from century to century, equal quantities of corn will command the same quantity of labour more nearly than equal quantities of silver. From year to year, on the contrary, silver is a better measure than corn, because equal quantities of it will more nearly command the same quantity of labour. . . .

As it is the nominal or money price of goods, therefore, which finally determines the prudence or imprudence of all purchases and sales, and thereby regulates almost the whole business of common life in which price is concerned, we cannot wonder that it should have been so much more attended to than the real price.

In such a work as this, however, it may sometimes be of use to compare the different real values of a particular commodity at different times and places, or the different degrees of power over the labour of other people which it may, upon different occasions, have given to those who possessed it. We must in this case compare, not so much the different quantities of silver for which it was commonly sold, as the different quantities of labour which those different quantities of silver could have purchased. But the current prices of labour at distant times and places can scarce ever be known with any degree of exactness. Those of corn, though they have in few places been regularly recorded, are in general better known and have been more frequently taken notice of by historians and other writers. We must generally, therefore, content ourselves with them, not as being always exactly in the same proportion as the current prices of labour, but as being the nearest approximation which can commonly be had to that proportion. I shall hereafter have occasion to make several comparisons of this kind. . . .

CHAPTER VI

Of the component Parts of the Price of Commodities

In that early and rude state of society which precedes both the accumulation of stock and the appropriation of land, the proportion between the quantities of labour necessary for acquiring different objects seems to be the only circumstance which can afford any rule for exchanging them for one

Quantity of labour is originally the only rule of value, allowance being made for superior hardship, and for uncommon dexterity and ingenuity.

another. If among a nation of hunters, for example, it usually costs twice the labour to kill a beaver which it does to kill a deer, one beaver should naturally exchange for or be worth two deer. It is natural that what is usually the produce of two days or two hours labour, should be worth double of what is usually the produce of one day's or one hour's labour.

If the one species of labour should be more severe than the other, some allowance will naturally be made for this superior hardship; and the produce of one hour's labour in the one way may frequently exchange for that of two hours labour in the other.

Or if the one species of labour requires an uncommon degree of dexterity and ingenuity, the esteem which men have for such talents will naturally give a value to their produce, superior to what would be due to the time employed about it. Such talents can seldom be acquired but in consequence of long application, and the superior value of their produce, may frequently be no more than a reasonable compensation for the time and labour which must be spent in acquiring them. In the advanced state of society, allowances of this kind, for superior hardship and superior skill, are commonly made in the wages of labour; and something of the same kind must probably have taken place in its earliest and rudest period.

In this state of things, the whole produce of labour belongs to the labourer; and the quantity of labour commonly employed in acquiring or producing any commodity, is the only circumstance which can regulate the quantity of labour which it ought commonly to purchase, command, or exchange for.

> The whole produce then belongs to the labourer, but when stock is used, something must be given for the profits of the undertaker, and the value of work resolves itself into wages and profits.

As soon as stock has accumulated in the hands of particular persons, some of them will naturally employ it in setting to work industrious people, whom they will supply with materials and subsistence, in order to make a profit by the sale of their work, or by what their labour adds to the value of the materials. In exchanging the complete manufacture either for money, for labour, or for other goods, over and above what may be sufficient to pay the price of the materials, and the wages of the workmen, something must be given for the profits of the undertaker of the work who hazards his stock in this adventure. The value which the workmen add to the materials, therefore, resolves itself in this case into two parts, of which the one pays their wages, the other the profits of their employer upon the whole stock of materials and wages which he advanced. He could have no interest to employ them, unless he expected from the sale of their work something more than what was sufficient to replace his stock to him; and he could have no interest to employ a great stock rather than a small one, unless his profits were to bear some proportion to the extent of his stock.

The profits of stock, it may perhaps be thought, are only a different name for the wages of a particular sort of labour, the labour of inspection and

> Profits are not merely wages of inspection and direction.

direction. They are, however, altogether different, are regulated by quite different principles, and bear no proportion to the quantity, the hardship, or the ingenuity of this supposed labour of inspection and direction. They are regulated altogether by the value of the stock employed, and are greater or smaller in proportion to the extent of this stock. Let us suppose, for example, that in some particular place, where the common annual profits of manufacturing stock are ten percent there are two different manufactures, in each of which twenty workmen are employed at the rate of fifteen pounds a year each, or at the expence of three hundred a year in each manufactory. Let us suppose too, that the coarse materials annually wrought up in the one cost only seven hundred pounds, while the finer materials in the other cost seven thousand. The capital annually employed in the one will in this case amount only to one thousand pounds; whereas that employed in the other will amount to seven thousand three hundred pounds. At the rate of ten percent therefore, the undertaker of the one will expect an yearly profit of about one hundred pounds only; while that of the other will expect about seven hundred and thirty pounds. But though their profits are so very different, their labour of inspection and direction may be either altogether or very nearly the same. In many great works, almost the whole labour of this kind is committed to some principal clerk. His wages properly express the value of this labour of inspection and direction. Though in settling them some regard is had commonly, not only to his labour and skill, but to the trust which is reposed in him, yet they never bear any regular proportion to the capital of which he oversees the management; and the owner of this capital, though he is thus discharged of almost all labour, still expects that his profits should bear a regular proportion to his capital. In the price of commodities, therefore, the profits of stock constitute a component part altogether different from the wages of labour, and regulated by quite different principles.

In this state of things, the whole produce of labour does not always belong to the labourer. He must in most cases share it with the owner of the stock which employs him. Neither is the quantity of labour commonly employed in acquiring or producing any commodity, the only circumstance which can regulate the quantity which it ought commonly to purchase, command, or exchange for. An additional quantity, it is evident, must be due for the profits of the stock which advanced the wages and furnished the materials of that labour.

The labourer shares with the employer, and labour alone no longer regulates value.

As soon as the land of any country has all become private property, the landlords, like all other men, love to reap where they never sowed, and demand a rent even for its natural produce. The wood of the forest, the grass of the field, and all the natural fruits of the earth, which, when land was in common, cost the labourer only

When land has all become private property, rent constitutes a third component part of the price of most commodities.

the trouble of gathering them, come, even to him, to have an additional price fixed upon them. He must then pay for the licence to gather them; and must give up to the landlord a portion of what his labour either collects or produces. This portion, or, what comes to the same thing, the price of this portion, constitutes the rent of land, and in the price of the greater part of commodities makes a third component part.

The real value of all the different component parts of price, it must be observed, is measured by the quantity of labour which they can, each of them, purchase or command. Labour measures the value not only of that part of price which resolves itself into labour, but of that which resolves itself into rent, and of that which resolves itself into profit.

The real value of all three parts is measured by labour

In every society the price of every commodity finally resolves itself into some one or other, or all of those three parts; and in every improved society, all the three enter more or less, as component parts, into the price of the far greater part of commodities.

In an improved society all three parts are generally present, for example, in corn, in flour or meal, and in flax.

In the price of corn, for example, one part pays the rent of the landlord, another pays the wages or maintenance of the labourers and labouring cattle employed in producing it, and the third pays the profit of the farmer. These three parts seem either immediately or ultimately to make up the whole price of corn. A fourth part, it may perhaps be thought, is necessary for replacing the stock of the farmer, or for compensating the wear and tear of his labouring cattle, and other instruments of husbandry. But it must be considered that the price of any instrument of husbandry, such as a labouring horse, is itself made up of the same three parts; the rent of the land upon which he is reared, the labour of tending and rearing him, and the profits of the farmer who advances both the rent of this land, and the wages of this labour. Though the price of the corn, therefore, may pay the price as well as the maintenance of the horse, the whole price still resolves itself either immediately or ultimately into the same three parts of rent, labour, and profit.

In the price of flour or meal, we must add to the price of the corn, the profits of the miller, and the wages of his servants; in the price of the bread, the profits of the baker, and the wages of his servants; and in the price of both, the labour of transporting the corn from the house of the farmer to that of the miller, and from that of the miller to that of the baker, together with the profits of those who advance the wages of that labour.

The price of flax resolves itself into the same three parts as that of corn. In the price of linen we must add to this price the wages of the flax dresser, of the spinner, of the weaver, of the bleacher, etc., together with the profits of their respective employers.

As any particular commodity comes to be more manufactured, that part of the price which resolves itself into wages and profit, comes to be greater in proportion to that which resolves itself into rent. In the progress of the manufacture, not only the number of profits increase, but every subsequent profit is greater than the foregoing; because the capital from which it is derived must always be greater. The capital which employs the weavers, for example, must be greater than that which employs the spinners; because it not only replaces that capital with its profits, but pays, besides, the wages of the weavers; and the profits must always bear some proportion to the capital.

In the most improved societies, however, there are always a few commodities of which the price resolves itself into two parts only, the wages of labour, and the profits of stock; and a still smaller number in which it consists altogether in the wages of labour. In the price of sea-fish, for example, one part pays the labour of the fishermen, and the other the profits of the capital employed in the fishery. Rent very seldom makes any part of it, though it does sometimes, as I shall show hereafter. It is otherwise, at least through the greater part of Europe, in river fisheries. A salmon fishery pays a rent, and rent, though it cannot well be called the rent of land, makes a part of the price of a salmon as well as wages and profit. In some parts of Scotland a few poor people make a trade of gathering, along the seashore, those little variegated stones commonly known by the name of Scotch Pebbles. The price which is paid to them by the stonecutter is altogether the wages of their labour; neither rent nor profit make any part of it.

A few commodities have only two or even one of the three component parts.

But the whole price of any commodity must still finally resolve itself into some one or other, or all of those three parts; as whatever part of it remains after paying the rent of the land, and the price of the whole labour employed in raising, manufacturing, and bringing it to market, must necessarily be profit to somebody.

But all must have at least one, and the price of the whole annual produce resolves itself into wages, profits and rent, which are the only original kinds of revenue.

As the price or exchangeable value of every particular commodity, taken separately, resolves itself into some one or other or all of those three parts; so that of all the commodities which compose the whole annual produce of the labour of every country, taken complexly, must resolve itself into the same three parts, and be parcelled out among different inhabitants of the country, either as the wages of their labour, the profits of their stock, or the rent of their land. The whole of what is annually either collected or produced by the labour of every society, or what comes to the same thing, the whole price of it, is in the manner originally distributed among some of its different members. Wages, profit, and rent are the three original sources of all revenue as well as of all exchangeable value. All other revenue is ultimately derived from some one or other of these.

Whoever derives his revenue from a fund which is his own, must draw it either from his labour, from his stock, or from his land. The revenue derived from labour is called wages. That derived from stock, by the person who manages or employs it, is called profit. That derived from it by the person who does not employ it himself, but lends it to another, is called the interest or the use of money. It is the compensation which the borrower pays to the lender, for the profit which he has an opportunity of making by the use of the money. Part of that profit naturally belongs to the borrower, who runs the risk and takes the trouble of employing it; and part to the lender, who affords him the opportunity of making this profit. The interest of money is always a derivative revenue, which, if it is not paid from the profit which is made by the use of the money, must be paid from some other source of revenue, unless perhaps the borrower is a spendthrift, who contracts a second debt in order to pay the interest of the first. The revenue which proceeds altogether from land, is called rent, and belongs to the landlord. The revenue of the farmer is derived partly from his labour, and partly from his stock. To him, land is only the instrument which enables him to earn the wages of this labour, and to make the profits of this stock. All taxes, and all the revenue which is founded upon them, all salaries, pensions, and annuities of every kind, are ultimately derived from some one or other of those three original sources of revenue, and are paid either immediately or mediately from the wages of labour, the profits of stock, or the rent of land.

They are sometimes confounded; for example, a gentleman farmer's rent is called profit, a common farmer's wages are called profit, and so are an independent manufacturer's wages, while the rent and profit of a gardener cultivating his own land are considered earnings of labour.

When those three different sorts of revenue belong to different persons, they are readily distinguished; but when they belong to the same they are sometimes confounded with one another, at least in common language.

A gentleman who farms a part of his own estate, after paying the expence of cultivation, should gain both the rent of the landlord and the profit of the farmer. He is apt to denominate, however, his whole gain, profit, and thus confounds rent with profit, at least in common language. The greater part of our North American and West Indian planters are in this situation. They farm, the greater part of them, their own estates, and accordingly we seldom hear of the rent of a plantation, but frequently of its profit.

Common farmers seldom employ any overseer to direct the general operations of the farm. They generally too work a good deal with their own hands, as ploughmen, harrowers, etc. What remains of the crop after paying the rent, therefore, should not only replace to them their stock employed in cultivation, together with its ordinary profits, but pay them the wages which are due to them, both as labourers and overseers. Whatever remains, however, after paying the rent and keeping up the stock, is called profit. But wages evidently make a part of it. The farmer, by saving these wages, must necessarily gain them. Wages, therefore, are in this case confounded with profit.

An independent manufacturer, who has stock enough both to purchase materials, and to maintain himself till he can carry his work to market, should gain both the wages of a journeyman who works under a master, and the profit which that master makes by the sale of the journeyman's work. His whole gains, however, are commonly called profit, and wages are, in this case too, confounded with profit.

A gardener who cultivates his own garden with his own hands, unites in his own person the three different characters, of landlord, farmer, and labourer. His produce, therefore, should pay him the rent of the first, the profit of the second, and the wages of the third. The whole, however, is commonly considered as the earnings of his labour. Both rent and profit are, in this case, confounded with wages.

As in a civilised country there are but few commodities of which the exchangeable value arises from labour only, rent and profit contributing largely to that of the far greater part of them, so the annual produce of its labour will always be sufficient to purchase or command a much greater quantity of labour than what was employed in raising, preparing, and bringing that produce to market. If the society was annually to employ all the labour which it can annually purchase, as the quantity of labour would increase greatly every year, so the produce of every succeeding year would be of vastly greater value than that of the foregoing. But there is no country in which the whole annual produce is employed in maintaining the industrious. The idle everywhere consume a great part of it; and according to the different proportions in which it is annually divided between those two different orders of people, its ordinary or average value must either annually increase, or diminish, or continue the same from one year to another.

A great part of the annual produce goes to the idle; the proportion regulates the increase or diminution of the produce.

CHAPTER VII

Of the natural and market Price of Commodities

There is in every society or neighbourhood an ordinary or average rate both of wages and profit in every different employment of labour and stock. This rate is naturally regulated, as I shall show hereafter, partly by the general circumstances of the society, their riches or poverty, their advancing, stationary, or declining condition; and partly by the particular nature of each employment.

Ordinary or average rates of wages, profit, and rent may be called natural rates, to pay which a commodity is sold at its natural price, or for what it really costs, which includes profit, since no one will go on selling without profit.

There is likewise in every society or neighbourhood an ordinary or average rate of rent, which is regulated too, as I shall show hereafter, partly by the general circumstances of the society or neighbourhood in which the land is situated, and partly by the natural or improved fertility of the land.

These ordinary or average rates may be called the natural rates of wages, profit, and rent, at the time and place in which they commonly prevail.

When the price of any commodity is neither more nor less than what is sufficient to pay the rent of the land, the wages of the labour, and the profits of the stock employed in raising, preparing, and bringing it to market, according to their natural rates, the commodity is then sold for what may be called its natural price.

The commodity is then sold precisely for what it is worth, or for what it really costs the person who brings it to market; for though in common language what is called the prime cost of any commodity does not comprehend the profit of the person who is to sell it again, yet if he sells it at a price which does not allow him the ordinary rate of profit in his neighbourhood, he is evidently a loser by the trade; since by employing his stock in some other way he might have made that profit. His profit, besides, is his revenue, the proper fund of his subsistence. As, while he is preparing and bringing the goods to market, he advances to his workmen their wages, or their subsistence; so he advances to himself, in the same manner, his own subsistence, which is generally suitable to the profit which he may reasonably expect from the sale of his goods. Unless they yield him this profit, therefore, they do not repay him what they may very properly be said to have really cost him.

Though the price, therefore, which leaves him this profit, is not always the lowest at which a dealer may sometimes sell his goods, it is the lowest at which he is likely to sell them for any considerable time; at least where there is perfect liberty, or where he may change his trade as often as he pleases.

The actual price at which any commodity is commonly sold is called its market price. It may either be above, or below, or exactly the same with its natural price.

Market price is regulated by the quantity brought to market and the effectual demand.

The market price of every particular commodity is regulated by the proportion between the quantity which is actually brought to market, and the demand of those who are willing to pay the natural price of the commodity, or the whole value of the rent, labour, and profit, which must be paid in order to bring it thither. Such people may be called the effectual demanders, and their demand the effectual demand; since it may be sufficient to effectuate the bringing of the commodity to market. It is different from the absolute demand. A very poor man may be said in some sense to have a demand for a coach and six; he might like to have it; but his demand is not an effectual demand, as the commodity can never be brought to market in order to satisfy it.

When the quantity of any commodity which is brought to market falls short of the effectual demand, all those who are willing to pay the whole value of the rent, wages, and profit, which must be paid in order to bring it thither, cannot be supplied with the quantity which they want. Rather than want it altogether, some of them will be willing to give more. A competition will immediately begin among them, and the market price will rise more or less above the natural price, according as either the greatness of the deficiency, or the wealth and wanton luxury of the competitors, happen to animate more or less the eagerness of the competition. Among competitors of equal wealth and luxury the same deficiency will generally occasion a more or less eager competition, according as the acquisition of the commodity happens to be of more or less importance to them. Hence the exorbitant price of the necessaries of life during the blockade of a town or in a famine.

When the quantity brought falls short of the effectual demand, the market price rises above the natural; when it exceeds the effectual demand the market price falls below the natural; when it is just equal to the effectual demand the market and natural price coincide.

When the quantity brought to market exceeds the effectual demand, it cannot be all sold to those who are willing to pay the whole value of the rent, wages and profit, which must be paid in order to bring it thither. Some part must be sold to those who are willing to pay less, and the low price which they give for it must reduce the price of the whole. The market price will sink more or less below the natural price, according as the greatness of the excess increases more or less the competition of the sellers, or according as it happens to be more or less important to them to get immediately rid of the commodity. The same excess in the importation of perishable, will occasion a much greater competition than in that of durable commodities; in the importation of oranges, for example, than in that of old iron.

When the quantity brought to market is just sufficient to supply the effectual demand and no more, the market price naturally comes to be either exactly, or as nearly as can be judged of, the same with the natural price. The whole quantity upon hand can be disposed of for this price, and cannot be disposed of for more. The competition of the different dealers obliges them all to accept of this price, but does not oblige them to accept of less.

The quantity of every commodity brought to market naturally suits itself to the effectual demand. It is the interest of all those who employ their land, labour, or stock, in bringing any commodity to market, that the quantity never should exceed the effectual demand; and it is the interest of all other people that it never should fall short of that demand.

It naturally suits itself to the effectual demand.

When it exceeds that demand, some of the component parts of its price are below their natural rate; when it falls short, some of the component parts are above their natural rate.

If at any time it exceeds the effectual demand,

some of the component parts of its price must be paid below their natural rate. If it is rent, the interest of the landlords will immediately prompt them to withdraw a part of their land; and if it is wages or profit, the interest of the labourers in the one case, and of their employers in the other, will prompt them to withdraw a part of their labour or stock from this employment. The quantity brought to market will soon be no more than sufficient to supply the effectual demand. All the different parts of its price will rise to their natural rate, and the whole price to its natural price.

If, on the contrary, the quantity brought to market should at any time fall short of the effectual demand, some of the component parts of its price must rise above their natural rate. If it is rent, the interest of all other landlords will naturally prompt them to prepare more land for the raising of this commodity; if it is wages or profit, the interest of all other labourers and dealers will soon prompt them to employ more labour and stock in preparing and bringing it to market. The quantity brought thither will soon be sufficient to supply the effectual demand. All the different parts of its price will soon sink to their natural rate, and the whole price to its natural price.

The natural price, therefore, is, as it were, the central price, to which the prices of all commodities are continually gravitating. Different accidents may sometimes keep them suspended a good deal above it, and sometimes force them down even somewhat below it. But whatever may be the obstacles which hinder them from settling in this center of repose and continuance, they are constantly tending towards it.

Natural price is the central price to which actual prices gravitate.

Industry suits itself to the effectual demand, but the quantity produced by a given amount of industry sometimes fluctuates.

The whole quantity of industry annually employed in order to bring any commodity to market, naturally suits itself in this manner to the effectual demand. It naturally aims at bringing always that precise quantity thither which may be sufficient to supply, and no more than supply, that demand.

But in some employments the same quantity of industry will in different years produce very different quantities of commodities; while in others it will produce always the same, or very nearly the same. The same number of labourers in husbandry will, in different years, produce very different quantities of corn, wine, oil, hops, etc. But the same number of spinners and weavers will every year produce the same or very nearly the same quantity of linen and woollen cloth. It is only the average produce of the one species of industry which can be suited in any respect to the effectual demand; and as its actual produce is frequently much greater and frequently much less than its average produce, the quantity of the commodities brought to market will sometimes exceed a good deal, and sometimes fall short a good deal of the effectual demand. Even though that demand therefore should continue always the same, their market price will be liable to great fluctuations, will sometimes fall a good deal below, and sometimes rise a good deal above their natural price. In the other species of industry, the produce of equal quantities of labour being always the same or very nearly the same, it can be more exactly suited to the effectual demand. While that demand continues the same, therefore, the market price of the commodities is likely to do so too, and to be either altogether, or as nearly as can be judged of, the same with the natural price. That the price of linen and woollen cloth is liable neither to such frequent nor to such great variations as the price of corn, every man's experience will inform him. The price of the one species of commodities varies only with the variations in the demand: That of the other varies, not only with the variations in the demand, but with the much greater and more frequent variations in the quantity of what is brought to market in order to supply that demand.

The occasional and temporary fluctuations in the market price of any commodity fall chiefly upon those parts of its price which resolve themselves into wages and profit. That part which resolves itself into rent is less affected by them. A rent certain in money is not in the least affected by them either in its rate or in its value. A rent which consists either in a certain proportion or in a certain quantity of the rude produce, is no doubt affected in its yearly value by all the occasional and temporary fluctuations in the market price of that rude produce: but it is seldom affected by them in its yearly rate. In settling the terms of the lease, the landlord and farmer endeavour, according to their best judgment, to adjust that rate, not to the temporary and occasional, but to the average and ordinary price of the produce.

The fluctuations fall on wages and profit more than on rent, affecting them in different proportions according to the supply of commodities and labour.

Such fluctuations affect both the value and the rate either of wages or of profit, according as the market happens to be either overstocked or understocked with commodities or with labour; with work done, or with work to be done. A public mourning raises the price of black cloth (with which the market is almost always understocked upon such occasions) and augments the profits of the merchants who possess any considerable quantity of it. It has no effect upon the wages of the weavers. The market is understocked with commodities, not with labour; with work done, not with work to be done. It raises the wages of journeymen tailors. The market is here understocked with labour. There is an effectual demand for more labour, for more work to be done than can be had. It sinks the price of coloured silks and cloths, and thereby reduces the profits of the merchants who have any considerable quantity of them upon hand. It sinks too the wages of the workmen employed in preparing such commodities, for which all demand is stopped for six months, perhaps for a twelvemonth. The market is here overstocked both with commodities and with labour.

But though the market price of every particular commodity is in this manner continually gravitating, if one may say so, towards the natural price, yet sometimes particular accidents, sometimes natural causes, and sometimes particular regulations of police, may, in many commodities, keep up the market price, for a long time together, a good deal above the natural price.

But market price may be kept above natural for a long time, in consequence of want of general knowledge of high profits, or in consequence of secrets in manufactures, which may operate for long periods, or in consequence of scarcity of peculiar soils, which may continue forever.

When by an increase in the effectual demand, the market price of some particular commodity happens to rise a good deal above the natural price, those who employ their stocks in supplying that market are generally careful to conceal this change. If it was commonly known, their great profit would tempt so many new rivals to employ their stocks in the same way, that, the effectual demand being fully supplied, the market price would soon be reduced to the natural price, and perhaps for some time even below it. If the market is at a great distance from the residence of those who supply it, they may sometimes be able to keep the secret for several years together, and may so long enjoy their extraordinary profits without any new rivals. Secrets of this kind, however, it must be acknowledged, can seldom be long kept; and the extraordinary profit can last very little longer than they are kept.

Secrets in manufactures are capable of being longer kept than secrets in trade. A dyer who has found the means of producing a particular colour with materials which cost only half the price of those commonly made use of, may, with good management, enjoy the advantage of his discovery as long as he lives, and even leave it as a legacy to his posterity. His extraordinary gains arise from the high price which is paid for his private labour. They properly consist in the high wages of that labour. But as they are repeated upon every part of his stock, and as their whole amount bears, upon that account, a regular proportion to it, they are commonly considered as extraordinary profits of stock.

Such enhancements of the market price are evidently the effects of particular accidents, of which, however, the operation may sometimes last for many years together.

Some natural productions require such a singularity of soil and situation, that all the land in a great country, which is fit for producing them, may not be sufficient to supply the effectual demand. The whole quantity brought to market, therefore, may be disposed of to those who are willing to give more than what is sufficient to pay the rent of the land which produced them, together with the wages of the labour, and the profits of the stock which were employed in preparing and bringing them to market, according to their natural rates. Such commodities may continue for whole centuries together to be sold at this high price; and that part of it which resolves itself into the rent of land is in this case the part which is generally paid above its natural rate. The rent of the land which affords such singular and esteemed productions, like the rent of some vineyards in France of a peculiarly happy soil and situation, bears no regular proportion to the rent of other equally fertile and equally well-cultivated land in its neighbourhood. The wages of the labour and the profits of the stock employed in bringing such commodities to market, on the contrary, are seldom out of their natural proportion to those of the other employments of labour and stock in their neighbourhood.

Such enhancements of the market price are evidently the effect of natural causes which may hinder the effectual demand from ever being fully supplied, and which may continue, therefore, to operate forever.

A monopoly granted either to an individual or to a trading company has the same effect as a secret in trade or manufactures. The monopolists, by keeping the market constantly understocked, by never fully supplying the effectual demand, sell their commodities much above the natural price, and raise their emoluments, whether they consist in wages or profit, greatly above their natural rate.

A monopoly has the same effect as a trade secret, the price of monopoly being the highest which can be got.

The price of monopoly is upon every occasion the highest which can be got. The natural price, or the price of free competition, on the contrary, is the lowest which can be taken, not upon every occasion, indeed, but for any considerable time together. The one is upon every occasion the highest which can be squeezed out of the buyers, or which, it is supposed, they will consent to give: The other is the lowest which the sellers can commonly afford to take, and at the same time continue their business.

The exclusive privileges of corporations, statutes of apprenticeship, and all those laws which restrain, in particular employments, the competition to a smaller number than might otherwise go into them, have the same tendency, though in a less degree. They are a sort of enlarged monopolies, and may frequently, for ages together and in whole classes of employments, keep up the market price of particular commodities above the natural price, and maintain both the wages of the labour and the profits of the stock employed about them somewhat above their natural rate.

Corporation privileges, etc., are enlarged monopolies.

Such enhancements of the market price may last as long as the regulations of police which give occasion to them.

The market price of any particular commodity, though it may continue long above, can seldom continue long below its natural price. Whatever part of it was paid below the natural rate, the persons whose interest it affected would immediately feel the loss, and would immediately withdraw either so much land, or so much labour, or so much stock, from being employed about it, that the quantity brought to market would soon be no more than sufficient to supply the effectual demand. Its market price, there-

Market price is seldom long below natural price, though apprenticeship and corporation laws sometimes reduce wages much below the natural rate for a certain period.

fore, would soon rise to the natural price. This at least would be the case where there was perfect liberty.

The same statutes of apprenticeship and other corporation laws indeed, which, when a manufacture is in prosperity, enable the workman to raise his wages a good deal above their natural rate, sometimes oblige him, when it decays, to let them down a good deal below it. As in the one case they exclude many people from his employment, so in the other they exclude him from many employments. The effect of such regulations, however, is not near so durable in sinking the workman's wages below, as in raising them above their natural rate. Their operation in the one way may endure for many centuries, but in the other it can last no longer than the lives of some of the workmen who were bred to the business in the time of its prosperity. When they are gone, the number of those who are afterwards educated to the trade will naturally suit itself to the effectual demand. The police must be as violent as that of Indostan or ancient Egypt (where every man was bound by a principle of religion to follow the occupation of his father, and was supposed to commit the most horrid sacrilege if he changed it for another) which can in any particular employment, and for several generations together, sink either the wages of labour or the profits of stock below their natural rate.

This is all that I think necessary to be observed at present concerning the deviations, whether occasional or permanent, of the market price of commodities from the natural price.

The natural price itself varies with the natural rate of each of its component parts, of wages, profit, and rent; and in every society this rate varies according *Natural price varies with the natural rate of wages, profit and rent.* to their circumstances, according to their riches or poverty, their advancing, stationary, or declining condition. I shall, in the four following chapters, endeavour to explain, as fully and distinctly as I can, the causes of those different variations.

First, I shall endeavour to explain what are the circumstances which naturally determine the rate of wages, and in what manner those circumstances are affected by the riches or poverty, by the advancing, stationary, or declining state of the society.

Secondly, I shall endeavour to show what are the circumstances which naturally determine the rate of profit, and in what manner too those circumstances are affected by the like variations in the state of the society.

Though pecuniary wages and profit are very different in the different employments of labour and stock; yet a certain proportion seems commonly to take place between both the pecuniary wages in all the different employments of labour, and the pecuniary profits in all the different employments of stock. This proportion, it will appear hereafter, depends partly upon the nature of the different employments, and partly upon the different laws and policy of the society in which they are carried on. But though in many respects dependent upon the laws and policy, this proportion seems to be little affected by the riches or poverty of that society; by its advancing, stationary, or declining condition; but to remain the same or very nearly the same in all those different states. I shall, in the third place, endeavour to explain all the different circumstances which regulate this proportion.

In the fourth and last place, I shall endeavour to show what are the circumstances which regulate the rent of land, and which either raise or lower the real price of all the different substances which it produces.

CHAPTER VIII
Of the Wages of Labour

The produce of labour constitutes the natural recompence or wages of labour.

Produce is the natural wages of labour.

In that original state of things, which precedes both the appropriation of land and the accumulation of stock, the whole produce of labour belongs to the labourer. He has neither landlord nor master to share with him.

Originally the whole belonged to the labourer.

If this had continued, all things would have become cheaper, though in appearance many things might have become dearer.

Had this state continued, the wages of labour would have augmented with all those improvements in its productive powers, to which the division of labour gives occasion. All things would gradually have become cheaper. They would have been produced by a smaller quantity of labour; and as the commodities produced by equal quantities of labour would naturally in this state of things be exchanged for one another, they would have been purchased likewise with the produce of a smaller quantity.

But though all things would have become cheaper in reality, in appearance many things might have become dearer than before, or have been exchanged for a greater quantity of other goods. Let us suppose, for example, that in the greater part of employments the productive powers of labour had been improved to tenfold, or that a day's labour could produce ten times the quantity of work which it had done originally; but that in a particular employment they had been improved only to double, or that a day's labour could produce only twice the quantity of work which it had done before. In exchanging the produce of a day's labour in the greater part of employments, for that of a day's labour in this particular one, ten times the original quantity of work in them would purchase only twice the original quantity in it. Any particular quantity in it, therefore, a pound weight, for example, would appear to be five times dearer than before. In reality, however, it would be twice as cheap.

Though it required five times the quantity of other goods to purchase it, it would require only half the quantity of labour either to purchase or to produce it. The acquisition, therefore, would be twice as easy as before.

But this original state of things, in which the labourer enjoyed the whole produce of his own labour, could not last beyond the first introduction of the appropriation of land and the accumulation of stock. It was at an end, therefore, long before the most considerable improvements were made in the productive powers of labour, and it would be to no purpose to trace farther what might have been its effects upon the recompence or wages of labour.

This state was ended by the appropriation of land and accumulation of stock, rent being the first deduction, and profit the second, both in agriculture, and other arts and manufactures.

As soon as land becomes private property, the landlord demands a share of almost all the produce which the labourer can either raise, or collect from it. His rent makes the first deduction from the produce of the labour which is employed upon land.

It seldom happens that the person who tills the ground has wherewithal to maintain himself till he reaps the harvest. His maintenance is generally advanced to him from the stock of a master, the farmer who employs him, and who would have no interest to employ him, unless he was to share in the produce of his labour, or unless his stock was to be replaced to him with a profit. This profit makes a second deduction from the produce of the labour which is employed upon land.

The produce of almost all other labour is liable to the like deduction of profit. In all arts and manufactures the greater part of the workmen stand in need of a master to advance them the materials of their work, and their wages and maintenance till it be completed. He shares in the produce of their labour, or in the value which it adds to the materials upon which it is bestowed; and in this share consists his profit.

It sometimes happens, indeed, that a single independent workman has stock sufficient both to purchase the materials of his work, and to maintain himself till it be completed. He is both master and workman, and enjoys the whole produce of his own labour, or the whole value which it adds to the materials upon which it is bestowed. It includes what are usually two distinct revenues, belonging to two distinct persons, the profits of stock, and the wages of labour.

The independent workman gets profits as well as wages, but this case is infrequent.

Such cases, however, are not very frequent, and in every part of Europe, twenty workmen serve under a master for one that is independent; and the wages of labour are everywhere understood to be, what they usually are, when the labourer is one person, and the owner of the stock which employs him another.

What are the common wages of labour depends everywhere upon the contract usually made between those two parties, whose interests are by no means the same. The workmen desire to get as much, the masters to give as

Wages depend on contract between masters and workmen.

little as possible. The former are disposed to combine in order to raise, the latter in order to lower the wages of labour.

It is not, however, difficult to foresee which of the two parties must, upon all ordinary occasions, have the advantage in the dispute, and force the other into a compliance with their terms. The masters, being fewer in number, can combine much more easily; and the law, besides, authorizes, or at least does not prohibit their combinations, while it prohibits those of the workmen. We have no acts of parliament against combining to lower the price of work; but many against combining to raise it. In all such disputes the masters can hold out much longer. A landlord, a farmer, a master manufacturer, or merchant, though they did not employ a single workman, could generally live a year or two upon the stocks which they have already acquired. Many workmen could not subsist a week, few could subsist a month, and scarce any a year without employment. In the long run the workman may be as necessary to his master as his master is to him; but the necessity is not so immediate.

The masters have the advantage, though less is heard of masters' combinations than of workmen's.

We rarely hear, it has been said, of the combinations of masters; though frequently of those of workmen. But whoever imagines, upon this account, that masters rarely combine, is as ignorant of the world as of the subject. Masters are always and everywhere in a sort of tacit, but constant and uniform combination, not to raise the wages of labour above their actual rate. To violate this combination is everywhere a most unpopular action, and a sort of reproach to a master among his neighbours and equals. We seldom, indeed, hear of this combination, because it is the usual, and one may say, the natural state of things which nobody ever hears of. Masters too sometimes enter into particular combinations to sink the wages of labour even below this rate. These are always conducted with the utmost silence and secrecy, till the moment of execution, and when the workmen yield, as they sometimes do, without resistance, though severely felt by them, they are never heard of by other people. Such combinations, however, are frequently resisted by a contrary defensive combination of the workmen; who sometimes too, without any provocation of this kind, combine of their own accord to raise the price of their labour. Their usual pretences are, sometimes the high price of provisions; sometimes the great profit which their masters make by their work. But whether their combinations be offensive or defensive, they are always abundantly heard of. In order to bring the point to a speedy decision, they have always recourse to the loudest clamour, and sometimes to the most shocking violence and outrage. They are desperate, and act with the folly and extravagance of desperate men, who must either starve, or frighten their masters into an immediate compliance with their demands. The masters upon these occasions are just as clamorous upon the other side, and never cease to call aloud for the assistance of the civil magistrate, and the rigorous execution of those laws which have been enacted with so much severity against the combinations of servants, labourers, and journeymen. The workmen, accordingly, very seldom derive any advantage from the violence of those tumultuous combinations, which, partly from the interposition of the civil magistrate, partly from the superior steadiness of the masters, partly from the necessity which the greater part of the workmen are under of submitting for the sake of present subsistence, generally end in nothing, but the punishment or ruin of the ringleaders.

But though in disputes with their workmen, masters must generally have the advantage, there is however a certain rate below which it seems impossible to reduce, for any considerable time, the ordinary wages even of the lowest species of labour.

But masters cannot reduce wages below a certain rate, namely, subsistence for a man and something over for a family.

A man must always live by his work, and his wages must at least be sufficient to maintain him. They must even upon most occasions be somewhat more; otherwise it would be impossible for him to bring up a family, and the race of such workmen could not last beyond the first generation. Mr. Cantillon* seems, upon this account, to suppose that the lowest species of common labourers must everywhere earn at least double their own maintenance, in order that one with another they may be enabled to bring up two children; the labour of the wife, on account of her necessary attendance on the children, being supposed no more than sufficient to provide for herself. But one half the children born, it is computed, die before the age of manhood. The poorest labourers, therefore, according to this account, must, one with another, attempt to rear at least four children, in order that two may have an equal chance of living to that age. But the necessary maintenance of four children, it is supposed, may be nearly equal to that of one man. The labour of an able-bodied slave, the same author adds, is computed to be worth double his maintenance; and that of the meanest labourer, he thinks, cannot be worth less than that of an able-bodied slave. Thus far at least seems certain, that, in order to bring up a family, the labour of the husband and wife together must, even in the lowest species of common labour, be able to earn something more than what is precisely necessary for their own maintenance; but in what proportion, whether in that abovementioned, or in any other, I shall not take upon me to determine.

There are certain circumstances, however, which sometimes give the labourers an advantage, and enable them to raise their wages considerably above this rate; evidently the lowest which is consistent with common humanity.

When in any country the demand for those who live by wages; labourers, journeymen, servants of every kind, is continually increasing; when every year

Wages may be considerably above this rate, when there is an increasing demand for labourers, which is caused by an increase of the funds destined for the payment of wages. The funds consist of surplus revenue, and surplus stock.

* Richard Cantillon (1680?–1734?), Paris banker, author of the *Essai sur la nature du commerce en général* (1730?).

furnishes employment for a greater number than had been employed the year before, the workmen have no occasion to combine in order to raise their wages. The scarcity of hands occasions a competition among masters, who bid against one another, in order to get workmen, and thus voluntarily break through the natural combination of masters not to raise wages.

The demand for those who live by wages, it is evident, cannot increase but in proportion to the increase of the funds which are destined for the payment of wages. These funds are of two kinds; first, the revenue which is over and above what is necessary for the maintenance; and, secondly, the stock which is over and above what is necessary for the employment of their masters.

When the landlord, annuitant, or monied man, has a greater revenue than what he judges sufficient to maintain his own family, he employs either the whole or a part of the surplus in maintaining one or more menial servants. Increase this surplus, and he will naturally increase the number of those servants.

When an independent workman, such as a weaver or shoemaker, has got more stock than what is sufficient to purchase the materials of his own work, and to maintain himself till he can dispose of it, he naturally employs one or more journeymen with the surplus, in order to make a profit by their work. Increase this surplus, and he will naturally increase the number of his journeymen.

The demand for those who live by wages, therefore, necessarily increases with the increase of the revenue and stock of every country, and cannot possibly increase without it. The increase of revenue and stock is the increase of national wealth. The demand for those who live by wages, therefore, naturally increases with the increase of national wealth, and cannot possibly increase without it. . . .

The demand for labourers therefore increases with the increase of national wealth.

Wages are not high in a stationary country however rich.

Though the wealth of a country should be very great, yet if it has been long stationary, we must not expect to find the wages of labour very high in it. The funds destined for the payment of wages, the revenue and stock of its inhabitants, may be of the greatest extent, but if they have continued for several centuries of the same, or very nearly of the same extent, the number of labourers employed every year could easily supply, and even more than supply, the number wanted the following year. There could seldom be any scarcity of hands, nor could the masters be obliged to bid against one another in order to get them. The hands, on the contrary, would, in this case, naturally multiply beyond their employment. There would be a constant scarcity of employment, and the labourers would be obliged to bid against one another in order to get it. If in such a country the wages of labour had ever been more than sufficient to maintain the labourer, and to enable him to bring up a family, the competition of the labourers and the interest of the masters would soon reduce them to this lowest rate which is consistent with common humanity.

China has been long one of the richest, that is, one of the most fertile, best cultivated, most industrious, and most populous countries in the world. It seems, however, to have been long stationary. Marco Polo, who visited it more than five hundred years ago, describes its cultivation, industry, and populousness, almost in the same terms in which they are described by travellers in the present times. It had perhaps, even long before his time, acquired that full complement of riches which the nature of its laws and institutions permits it to acquire. The accounts of all travellers, inconsistent in many other respects, agree in the low wages of labour, and in the difficulty which a labourer finds in bringing up a family in China. If by digging the ground a whole day he can get what will purchase a small quantity of rice in the evening, he is contented. The condition of artificers is, if possible, still worse. Instead of waiting indolently in their workhouses, for the calls of their customers, as in Europe, they are continually running about the streets with the tools of their respective trades, offering their service, and as it were begging employment. The poverty of the lower ranks of people in China far surpasses that of the most beggarly nations in Europe. In the neighbourhood of Canton many hundred, it is commonly said, many thousand families have no habitation on the land, but live constantly in little fishing boats upon the rivers and canals. The subsistence which they find there is so scanty that they are eager to fish up the nastiest garbage thrown overboard from any European ship. Any carrion, the carcase of a dead dog or cat, for example, though half putrid and stinking, is as welcome to them as the most wholesome food to the people of other countries. Marriage is encouraged in China, not by the profitableness of children, but by the liberty of destroying them. In all great towns several are every night exposed in the street, or drowned like puppies in the water. The performance of this horrid office is even said to be the avowed business by which some people earn their subsistence.

China, however, though it may perhaps stand still, does not seem to go backwards. Its towns are nowhere deserted by their inhabitants. The lands which had once been cultivated are nowhere neglected. The *China is not going backwards and labourers there keep up their numbers.* same or very nearly the same annual labour must therefore continue to be performed, and the funds destined for maintaining it must not, consequently, be sensibly diminished. The lowest class of labourers, therefore, notwithstanding their scanty subsistence, must some way or another make shift to continue their race so far as to keep up their usual numbers.

But it would be otherwise in a country where the funds destined for the maintenance of labour were sensibly decaying. Every year the demand for servants and labourers would, in all the different classes of employments, *In a declining country this would not be the case.*

be less than it had been the year before. Many who had been bred in the superior classes, not being able to find employment in their own business, would be glad to seek it in the lowest. The lowest class being not only overstocked with its own workmen, but with the overflowings of all the other classes, the competition for employment would be so great in it, as to reduce the wages of labour to the most miserable and scanty subsistence of the labourer. Many would not be able to find employment even upon these hard terms, but would either starve, or be driven to seek a subsistence either by begging, or by the perpetration perhaps of the greatest enormities. Want, famine, and mortality would immediately prevail in that class, and from thence extend themselves to all the superior classes, till the number of inhabitants in the country was reduced to what could easily be maintained by the revenue and stock which remained in it, and which had escaped either the tyranny or calamity which had destroyed the rest. This perhaps is nearly the present state of Bengal, and of some other of the English settlements in the East Indies. In a fertile country which had before been much depopulated, where subsistence, consequently, should not be very difficult, and where, notwithstanding, three or four hundred thousand people die of hunger in one year, we may be assured that the funds destined for the maintenance of the labouring poor are fast decaying. The difference between the genius of the British constitution which protects and governs North America, and that of the mercantile company which oppresses and domineers in the East Indies, cannot perhaps be better illustrated than by the different state of those countries.

The liberal reward of labour, therefore, as it is the necessary effect, so it is the natural symptom of increasing national wealth. The scanty maintenance of the labouring poor, on the other hand, is the natural symptom that things are at a stand, and their starving condition that they are going fast backwards.

In Great Britain the wages of labour seem, in the present times, to be evidently more than what is precisely necessary to enable the labourer to bring up a family. In order to satisfy ourselves upon this point it will not be necessary to enter into any tedious or doubtful calculation of what may be the lowest sum upon which it is possible to do this. There are many plain symptoms that the wages of labour are nowhere in this country regulated by this lowest rate which is consistent with common humanity.

First, in almost every part of Great Britain there is a distinction, even in the lowest species of labour, between summer and winter wages. Summer wages are always highest. But on account of the extraordinary expence of fuel, the maintenance of a family is most expensive

In Great Britain wages are above the lowest rate, since (1) there is a difference between winter and summer wages, (2) wages do not fluctuate with the price of provisions, (3) wages vary more from place to place than the price of provisions, and (4) frequently wages and the price of provisions vary in opposite directions, as grain is cheaper and wages are higher in England than in Scotland.

in winter. Wages, therefore, being highest when this expence is lowest, it seems evident that they are not regulated by what is necessary for this expence; but by the quantity and supposed value of the work. A labourer, it may be said indeed, ought to save part of his summer wages in order to defray his winter expence; and that through the whole year they do not exceed what is necessary to maintain his family through the whole year. A slave, however, or one absolutely dependent on us for immediate subsistence, would not be treated in this manner. His daily subsistence would be proportioned to his daily necessities.

Secondly, the wages of labour do not in Great Britain fluctuate with the price of provisions. These vary everywhere from year to year, frequently from month to month. But in many places the money price of labour remains uniformly the same sometimes for half a century together. If in these places, therefore, the labouring poor can maintain their families in dear years, they must be at their ease in times of moderate plenty, and in affluence in those of extraordinary cheapness. The high price of provisions during these ten years past has not in many parts of the kingdom been accompanied with any sensible rise in the money price of labour. It has, indeed, in some; owing probably more to the increase of the demand for labour, than to that of the price of provisions.

Thirdly, as the price of provisions varies more from year to year than the wages of labour, so, on the other hand, the wages of labour vary more from place to place than the price of provisions. The prices of bread and butcher's meat are generally the same or very nearly the same through the greater part of the united kingdom. These and most other things which are sold by retail, the way in which the labouring poor buy all things, are generally fully as cheap or cheaper in great towns than in the remoter parts of the country, for reasons which I shall have occasion to explain hereafter. But the wages of labour in a great town and its neighbourhood are frequently a fourth or a fifth part, twenty or five-and-twenty percent higher than at a few miles distance. Eighteen pence a day may be reckoned the common price of labour in London and its neighbourhood. At a few miles distance it falls to fourteen and fifteen pence. Ten pence may be reckoned its price in Edinburgh and its neighbourhood. At a few miles distance it falls to eight pence, the usual price of common labour through the greater part of the low country of Scotland, where it varies a good deal less than in England. Such a difference of prices, which it seems is not always sufficient to transport a man from one parish to another, would necessarily occasion so great a transportation of the most bulky commodities, not only from one parish to another, but from one end of the kingdom, almost from one end of the world to the other, as would soon reduce them more nearly to a level. After all that has been said of the levity and inconstancy of human nature, it appears evidently from experience that a man is of all sorts of luggage the most difficult to be transported. If the labouring poor, therefore, can maintain their families in those parts of the kingdom where the price of labour is lowest, they must be in affluence where it is highest.

Fourthly, the variations in the price of labour not only do not correspond either in place or time with those in the price of provisions, but they are frequently quite opposite.

Grain, the food of the common people, is dearer in Scotland than in England, whence Scotland receives almost every year very large supplies. But English corn must be sold dearer in Scotland, the country to which it is brought, than in England, the country from which it comes; and in proportion to its quality it cannot be sold dearer in Scotland than the Scotch corn that comes to the same market in competition with it. The quality of grain depends chiefly upon the quantity of flour or meal which it yields at the mill, and in this respect English grain is so much superior to the Scotch, that, though often dearer in appearance, or in proportion to the measure of its bulk, it is generally cheaper in reality, or in proportion to its quality, or even to the measure of its weight. The price of labour, on the contrary, is dearer in England than in Scotland. If the labouring poor, therefore, can maintain their families in the one part of the united kingdom, they must be in affluence in the other. Oatmeal indeed supplies the common people in Scotland with the greatest and the best part of their food, which is in general much inferior to that of their neighbours of the same rank in England. This difference, however, in the mode of their subsistence is not the cause, but the effect of the difference in their wages; though, by a strange misapprehension, I have frequently heard it represented as the cause. It is not because one man keeps a coach while his neighbor walks a-foot, that the one is rich and the other poor; but because the one is rich he keeps a coach, and because the other is poor he walks a-foot. . . .

The real recompence of labour, the real quantity of the necessaries and conveniences of life which it can procure to the labourer, has, during the course of the present century, increased perhaps in a still greater proportion than its money price. Not only grain has become somewhat cheaper, but many other things from which the industrious poor derive an agreeable and wholesome variety of food, have become a great deal cheaper. Potatoes, for example, do not at present, through the greater part of the kingdom, cost half the price which they used to do thirty or forty years ago. The same thing may be said of turnips, carrots, cabbages; things which were formerly never raised but by the spade, but which are now commonly raised by the plough. All sort of garden stuff too has become cheaper. The greater part of the apples and even of the onions consumed in Great Britain were in the last century imported from Flanders. The great improvements in the coarser manufactures of both linen and woollen cloth furnish the labourers with cheaper and better clothing; and those in the manufactures of the coarser metals, with cheaper and better

Other necessaries and conveniences have also become cheaper.

instruments of trade, as well as with many agreeable and convenient pieces of household furniture. Soap, salt, candles, leather, and fermented liquors have, indeed, become a good deal dearer; chiefly from the taxes which have been laid upon them. The quantity of these, however, which the labouring poor are under any necessity of consuming, is so very small, that the increase in their price does not compensate the diminution in that of so many other things. The common complaint that luxury extends itself even to the lowest ranks of the people, and that the labouring poor will not now be contented with the same food, clothing and lodging which satisfied them in former times, may convince us that it is not the money price of labour only, but its real recompence, which has augumented.

Is this improvement in the circumstances of the lower ranks of the people to be regarded as an advantage or as an inconvenience to the society? The answer seems at first sight abundantly plain. Servants, labourers, and workmen of different kinds, make up the far greater part of every great political society. But what improves the circumstances of the greater part can never be regarded as an inconvenience to the whole. No society can surely be flourishing and happy, of which the far greater part of the members are poor and miserable. It is but equity, besides, that they who feed, clothe, and lodge the whole body of the people, should have such a share of the produce of their own labour as to be themselves tolerably well fed, clothed, and lodged.

High earnings of labour are an advantage to the society.

Poverty, though it no doubt discourages, does not always prevent marriage. It seems even to be favourable to generation. A half-starved Highland woman frequently bears more than twenty children, while a pampered fine lady is often incapable of bearing any, and is generally exhausted by two or three. Barrenness, so frequent among women of fashion, is very rare among those of inferior station. Luxury in the fair sex, while it enflames perhaps the passion for enjoyment, seems always to weaken, and frequently to destroy altogether, the powers of generation.

Poverty does not prevent births, but is unfavourable to the rearing of children, and so restrains multiplication, while the liberal reward of labour encourages it, as the wear and tear of the free man must be paid for just like that of the slave, though not so extravagantly.

But poverty, though it does not prevent the generation, is extremely unfavourable to the rearing of children. The tender plant is produced, but in so cold a soil and so severe a climate, soon withers and dies. It is not uncommon, I have been frequently told, in the Highlands of Scotland for a mother who has borne twenty children not to have two alive. Several officers of great experience have assured me, that so far from recruiting their regiment, they have never been able to supply it with drums and fifes from all the soldiers' children that were born in it. A greater number of fine children, however, is seldom seen anywhere than about a barrack of soldiers. Very few of them, it seems, arrive at the age of thirteen or fourteen. In some places one half the children born die before they are four years of age; in many places before they are seven; and in almost all places before they are nine or ten. This great mortality, however, will everywhere be found chiefly among the children of the common people, who cannot afford to tend them with the same care as those of better station. Though their marriages are generally more fruitful than those of people of fashion, a smaller proportion of their children arrive at maturity. In foundling hospitals, and among the children brought up by parish charities, the mortality is still greater than among those of the common people.

Every species of animals naturally multiplies in proportion to the means of their subsistence, and no species can ever multiply beyond it. But in civilised society it is only among the inferior ranks of people that the scantiness of subsistence can set limits to the further multiplication of the human species; and it can do so in no other way than by destroying a great part of the children which their fruitful marriages produce.

The liberal reward of labour, by enabling them to provide better for their children, and consequently to bring up a greater number, naturally tends to widen and extend those limits. It deserves to be remarked too, that it necessarily does this as nearly as possible in the proportion which the demand for labour requires. If this demand is continually increasing, the reward of labour must necessarily encourage in such a manner the marriage and multiplication of labourers, as may enable them to supply that continually increasing demand by a continually increasing population. If the reward should at any time be less than what was requisite for this purpose, the deficiency of hands would soon raise it; and if it should at any time be more, their excessive multiplication would soon lower it to this necessary rate. The market would be so much understocked with labour in the one case, and so much overstocked in the other, as would soon force back its price to that proper rate which the circumstances of the society required. It is in this manner that the demand for men, like that for any other commodity, necessarily regulates the production of men; quickens it when it goes on too slowly, and stops it when it advances too fast. It is this demand which regulates and determines the state of propagation in all the different countries of the world, in North America, in Europe, and in China; which renders it rapidly progressive in the first, slow and gradual in the second, and altogether stationary in the last.

The wear and tear of a slave, it has been said, is at the expence of his master; but that of a free servant is at his own expence. The wear and tear of the latter, however, is, in reality, as much at the expence of his master as that of the former. The wages paid to journeymen and servants of every kind must be such as may enable them, one with another, to continue the race of journeymen and servants, according as the increasing, diminishing, or stationary demand of the society may happen to require. But though the wear and tear of a free servant be equally at the expence of his master, it generally costs him much less than that of a slave. The fund destined for replacing or repairing, if I may say so, the wear and tear of the slave, is commonly managed by a negligent master or careless overseer. That destined for performing the same office with regard to the free man, is managed by the free man himself. The disorders which generally prevail in the economy of the rich, naturally introduce themselves into the management of the former: The strict frugality and parsimonious attention of the poor as naturally establish themselves in that of the latter. Under such different management, the same purpose must require very different degrees of expence to execute it. It appears, accordingly, from the experience of all ages and nations, I believe, that the work done by freemen comes cheaper in the end than that performed by slaves. It is found to do so even at Boston, New York, and Philadelphia, where the wages of common labour are so very high.

The liberal reward of labour, therefore, as it is the effect of increasing wealth, so it is the cause of increasing population. To complain of it is to lament over the necessary effect and cause of the greatest public prosperity.

It deserves to be remarked, perhaps, that it is in the progressive state, while the society is advancing to the further acquisition, rather than when it has acquired its full complement of riches, that the condition of the labouring poor, of the great body of the people, seems to be the happiest and the most comfortable. It is hard in the stationary, and miserable in the declining state. The progressive state is in reality the cheerful and the hearty state to all the different orders of the society. The stationary is dull; the declining, melancholy.

The liberal reward of labour, as it encourages the propagation, so it increases the industry of the common people. The wages of labour are the encouragement of industry, which, like every other human quality, improves in proportion to the encouragement it receives. A plentiful subsistence increases the bodily strength of the labourer, and the comfortable hope of bettering his condition, and of ending his days perhaps in ease and plenty, animates him to exert that strength to the utmost. Where wages are high, accordingly, we shall always find the workmen more active, diligent, and expeditious, than where they are low; in England, for example, than in Scotland; in the neighbourhood of great towns, than in remote country places. Some workmen, indeed, when they can earn in four days what will maintain them through the week, will be idle the other three. This, however, is by no means the case with the greater part. Workmen, on the contrary, when they are liberally paid by the piece, are very apt to overwork themselves, and to ruin their health and constitution in a few years. A carpenter in London, and in

High wages increase population.

The progressive state is the best for the labouring poor.

High wages encourage industry.

some other places, is not supposed to last in his utmost vigour above eight years. Something of the same kind happens in many other trades, in which the workmen are paid by the piece; as they generally are in manufactures, and even in country labour, wherever wages are higher than ordinary. Almost every class of artificers is subject to some peculiar infirmity occasioned by excessive application to their peculiar species of work. Ramazzini, an eminent Italian physician, has written a particular book concerning such diseases. We do not reckon our soldiers the most industrious set of people among us. Yet when soldiers have been employed in some particular sorts of work, and liberally paid by the piece, their officers have frequently been obliged to stipulate with the undertaker, that they should not be allowed to earn above a certain sum every day, according to the rate at which they were paid. Till this stipulation was made, mutual emulation and the desire of greater gain frequently prompted them to overwork themselves, and to hurt their health by excessive labour. Excessive application during four days of the week is frequently the real cause of the idleness of the other three, so much and so loudly complained of.

Great labour, either of mind or body, continued for several days together, is in most men naturally followed by a great desire of relaxation, which, if not restrained by force or by some strong necessity, is almost irresistible. It is the call of nature, which requires to be relieved by some indulgence, sometimes of ease only, but sometimes too of dissipation and diversion. If it is not complied with, the consequences are often dangerous, and sometimes fatal, and such as almost always, sooner or later, bring on the peculiar infirmity of the trade. If masters would always listen to the dictates of reason and humanity, they have frequently occasion rather to moderate, than to animate the application of many of their workmen. It will be found, I believe, in every sort of trade, that the man who works so moderately, as to be able to work constantly, not only preserves his health the longest, but, in the course of the year, executes the greatest quantity of work.

In cheap years, it is pretended, workmen are generally more idle, and in dear ones more industrious than ordinary. A plentiful subsistence, therefore, it has been concluded, relaxes, and a scanty one quickens their industry. That a little more plenty than ordinary may render some workmen idle, cannot well be doubted; but that it should have this effect upon the greater part, or that men in general should work better when they are ill fed than when they are well fed, when they are disheartened than when they are in good spirits, when they are frequently sick than when they are generally in good health, seems not very probable. Years of dearth, it is to be observed, are generally among the common people years of sickness and mortality, which cannot fail to diminish the produce of their industry.

The opinion that cheap years encourage idleness is erroneous.

In years of plenty, servants frequently leave their masters, and trust their subsistence to what they can make by their own industry.

Wages are high in cheap years, and low in dear years.

But the same cheapness of provisions, by increasing the fund which is destined for the maintenance of servants, encourages masters, farmers especially, to employ a greater number. Farmers upon such occasions expect more profit from their corn by maintaining a few more labouring servants, than by selling it at a low price in the market. The demand for servants increases, while the number of those who offer to supply that demand diminishes. The price of labour, therefore, frequently rises in cheap years.

In years of scarcity, the difficulty and uncertainty of subsistence make all such people eager to return to service. But the high price of provisions, by diminishing the funds destined for the maintenance of servants, disposes masters rather to diminish than to increase the number of those they have. In dear years too, poor independent workmen frequently consume the little stocks with which they had used to supply themselves with the materials of their work, and are obliged to become journeymen for subsistence. More people want employment than can easily get it; many are willing to take it upon lower terms than ordinary, and the wages of both servants and journeymen frequently sink in dear years. . . .

The scarcity of a dear year, by diminishing the demand for labour, tends to lower its price, as the high price of provisions tends to raise it.

The effect of variations in the price of provisions is thus counterbalanced.

The plenty of a cheap year, on the contrary, by increasing the demand, tends to raise the price of labour, as the cheapness of provisions tends to lower it. In the ordinary variations of the price of provisions, those two opposite causes seem to counterbalance one another; which is probably in part the reason why the wages of labour are everywhere so much more steady and permanent than the price of provisions.

The increase in the wages of labour necessarily increases the price of many commodities, by increasing that part of it which resolves itself into wages, and so far tends to diminish their consumption both at home and abroad.

Increase of wages increases prices, but the cause of increased wages tends to diminish prices.

The same cause, however, which raises the wages of labour, the increase of stock, tends to increase its productive powers, and to make a smaller quantity of labour produce a greater quantity of work. The owner of the stock which employs a great number of labourers, necessarily endeavours, for his own advantage, to make such a proper division and distribution of employment, that they may be enabled to produce the greatest quantity of work possible. For the same reason, he endeavours to supply them with the best machinery which either he or they can think of. What takes place among the labourers in a particular workhouse, takes place, for the same reason, among those of a great society. The greater their number, the more they naturally divide themselves into different classes and subdivisions of employment. More heads are occupied in inventing the most proper machinery for executing the work of each, and it is, therefore, more likely to be invented. There are many commodities, therefore, which, in consequence of these improvements, come to be produced by so much less labour than before, that the increase of its price is more than compensated by the diminution of its quantity.

CHAPTER IX
Of the Profits of Stock

The rise and fall in the profits of stock depend upon the same causes with the rise and fall in the wages of labour, the increasing or declining state of the wealth of the society; but those causes affect the one and the other very differently.

Profits depend on increase and decrease of wealth, falling with the increase of wealth.

The increase of stock, which raises wages, tends to lower profit. When the stocks of many rich merchants are turned into the same trade, their mutual competition naturally tends to lower its profit; and when there is a like increase of stock in all the different trades carried on in the same society, the same competition must produce the same effect in them all.

It is not easy, it has already been observed, to ascertain what are the average wages of labour even in a particular place, and at a particular time. We can, even in this case, seldom determine more than

The rate is difficult to ascertain, but may be inferred from the rate of interest.

what are the most usual wages. But even this can seldom be done with regard to the profits of stock. Profit is so very fluctuating, that the person who carries on a particular trade cannot always tell you himself what is the average of his annual profit. It is affected, not only by every variation of price in the commodities which he deals in, but by the good or bad fortune both of his rivals and of his customers, and by a thousand other accidents to which goods when carried either by sea or by land, or even when stored in a warehouse, are liable. It varies, therefore, not only from year to year, but from day to day, and almost from hour to hour. To ascertain what is the average profit of all the different trades carried on in a great kingdom, must be much more difficult; and to judge of what it may have been formerly, or in remote periods of time, with any degree of precision, must be altogether impossible.

But though it may be impossible to determine, with any degree of precision, what are or were the average profits of stock, either in the present, or in ancient times, some notion may be formed of them from the interest of money. It may be laid down as a maxim, that wherever a great deal can be made by the use of money, a great deal will commonly be given for the use of it; and that wherever little can be made by it, less will commonly be given for it. According, therefore, as the usual market rate of interest varies in any country, we may be assured that the ordinary profits of stock must vary with it, must sink as it sinks, and rise as it rises. The progress of interest, therefore, may lead us to form some notion of the progress of profit. . . .

In our North American and West Indian colonies, not only the wages of labour, but the interest of money, and consequently the profits of stock, are higher than in England. In the different colonies

In the peculiar case of new colonies high wages and high profits go together, but profits gradually diminish.

both the legal and the market rate of interest run from six to eight percent. High wages of labour and high profits of stock, however, are things, perhaps, which scarce ever go together, except in the peculiar circumstances of new colonies. A new colony must always for some time be more understocked in proportion to the extent of its territory, and more underpeopled in proportion to the extent of its stock, than the greater part of other countries. They have more land than they have stock to cultivate. What they have, therefore, is applied to the cultivation only of what is most fertile and most favourably situated, the lands near the seashore, and along the banks of navigable rivers. Such land too is frequently purchased at a price below the value even of its natural produce. Stock employed in the purchase and improvement of such lands must yield a very large profit, and consequently afford to pay a very large interest. Its rapid accumulation in so profitable an employment enables the planter to increase the number of his hands faster than he can find them in a new settlement. Those whom he can find, therefore, are very liberally rewarded. As the colony increases, the profits of stock gradually diminish. When the most fertile and best situated lands have been all occupied, less profit can be made by the cultivation of what is inferior both in soil and situation, and less interest can be afforded for the stock which is so employed. In the greater part of our colonies, accordingly, both the legal and the market rate of interest have been considerably reduced during the course of the present century. As riches, improvement, and population have increased, interest has declined. The wages of labour do not sink with the profits of stock. The demand for labour increases with the increase of stock whatever be its profits; and after these are diminished, stock may not only continue to increase, but to increase much faster than before. It is with industrious nations who are advancing in the acquisition of riches, as with industrious individuals.

A great stock, though with small profits, generally increases faster than a small stock with great profits. Money, says the proverb, makes money. When you have got a little, it is often easy to get more. The great difficulty is to get that little. The connection between the increase of stock and that of industry, or of the demand for useful labour, has partly been explained already, but will be explained more fully hereafter in treating of the accumulation of stock. . . .

In a country which had acquired that full complement of riches which the nature of its soil and
climate, and its situation with respect to other countries allowed it to acquire; which could, therefore,
advance no further, and which was not going back-

In a country as rich as it
possibly could be, prof-
its as well as wages
would be very low, but
there has never yet been
any such country.

wards, both the wages of labour and the profits of stock would probably
be very low. In a country fully peopled in proportion to what either its
territory could maintain or its stock employ, the competition for employment would necessarily be so great as to reduce the wages of labour to
what was barely sufficient to keep up the number of labourers, and, the
country being already fully peopled, that number could never be augmented. In a country fully stocked in proportion to all the business it
had to transact, as great a quantity of stock would be employed in every
particular branch as the nature and extent of the trade would admit. The
competition, therefore, would everywhere be as great, and consequently
the ordinary profit as low as possible.

But perhaps no country has ever yet arrived at this degree of opulence.
China seems to have been long stationary, and had probably long ago
acquired that full complement of riches which is consistent with the
nature of its laws and institutions. But this complement may be much
inferior to what, with other laws and institutions, the nature of its soil,
climate, and situation might admit of. A country which neglects or despises
foreign commerce, and which admits the vessels of foreign nations into
one or two of its ports only, cannot transact the same quantity of business
which it might do with different laws and institutions. In a country too,
where, though the rich or the owners of large capitals enjoy a good deal
of security, the poor or the owners of small capitals enjoy scarce any,
but are liable, under the pretence of justice, to be pillaged and plun-
dered at any time by the inferior mandarines, the quantity of stock
employed in all the different branches of business transacted within it,
can never be equal to what the nature and extent of that business might
admit. In every different branch, the oppression of the poor must establish the monopoly of the rich, who, by engrossing the whole trade to
themselves, will be able to make very large profits. Twelve percent
accordingly is said to be the common interest of money in China, and
the ordinary profits of stock must be sufficient to afford this large interest. . . .

CHAPTER X

Of Wages and Profit in the different Employments of Labour and Stock

The whole of the advantages and disadvantages of
the different employments of labour and stock must,

Advantages and disad-
vantages tend to equality

in the same neighbourhood, be either perfectly equal
or continually tending to equality. If in the same
neighbourhood, there was any employment evidently either more or less
advantageous than the rest, so many people would crowd into it in the
one case, and so many would desert it in the other, that its advantages
would soon return to the level of other employments. This at least would
be the case in a society where things were left to follow their natural
course, where there was perfect liberty, and where every man was perfectly free both to choose what occupation he thought proper, and to
change it as often as he thought proper. Every man's interest would
prompt him to seek the advantageous, and to shun the disadvantageous
employment.

Pecuniary wages and profit, indeed, are everywhere in Europe extremely different according to
the different employments of labour and stock. But
this difference arises partly from certain circumstances in the employments themselves, which, either
really, or at least in the imaginations of men, make
up for a small pecuniary gain in some, and counterbalance a great one
in others; and partly from the policy of Europe, which nowhere leaves
things at perfect liberty.

The particular consideration of those circumstances and of that policy
will divide this chapter into two parts.

where there is perfect liberty.

Actual differences of pecuniary wages and profits are due partly to counterbalancing circumstances and partly to want of perfect liberty.

Inequalities arising from the Nature of the Employments themselves

The five following are the principal circumstances which, so far as I have been able to observe,
make up for a small pecuniary gain in some
employments, and counterbalance a great one in others: first, the agreeableness or disagreeableness of the employments themselves; secondly,
the easiness and cheapness, or the difficulty and expence of learning
them; thirdly, the constancy or inconstancy of employment in them;
fourthly, the small or great trust which must be reposed in those who
exercise them; and, fifthly, the probability or improbability of success in
them.

First, the wages of labour vary with the ease or
hardship, the cleanliness or dirtiness, the honoura-
bleness or dishonourableness of the employment.
Thus in most places, take the year round, a journeyman tailor earns less
than a journeyman weaver. His work is much easier. A journeyman
weaver earns less than a journeyman smith. His work is not always easier, but it is much cleanlier. A journeyman blacksmith, though an artificer, seldom earns so much in twelve hours as a collier, who is only a

There are five counter-balancing circumstances:

(1) Wages vary with the agreeableness of the employment.

labourer, does in eight. His work is not quite so dirty, is less dangerous, and is carried on in daylight, and above ground. Honour makes a great part of the reward of all honourable professions. In point of pecuniary gain, all things considered, they are generally underrecompensed, as I shall endeavour to show by and by. Disgrace has the contrary effect. The trade of a butcher is a brutal and an odious business; but it is in most places more profitable than the greater part of common trades. The most detestable of all employments, that of public executioner, is in proportion to the quantity of work done, better paid than any common trade whatever.

Hunting and fishing, the most important employments of mankind in the rude state of society, become in its advanced state their most agreeable amusements, and they pursue for pleasure what they once followed from necessity. In the advanced state of society, therefore, they are all very poor people who follow as a trade, what other people pursue as a pastime. . . .

Some very agreeable employments are exceedingly ill paid.

Secondly, the wages of labour vary with the easiness and cheapness, or the difficulty and expence of learning the business.

(2) Wages vary with the cost of learning the business.

When any expensive machine is erected, the extraordinary work to be performed by it before it is worn out, it must be expected, will replace the capital laid out upon it, with at least the ordinary profits. A man educated at the expence of much labour and time to any of those employments which require extraordinary dexterity and skill, may be compared to one of those expensive machines. The work which he learns to perform, it must be expected, over and above the usual wages of common labour, will replace to him the whole expence of his education, with at least the ordinary profits of an equally valuable capital. It must do this too in a reasonable time, regard being had to the very uncertain duration of human life, in the same manner as to the more certain duration of the machine.

The difference between the wages of skilled labour and those of common labour, is founded upon this principle. . . .

Thirdly, the wages of labour in different occupations vary with the constancy or inconstancy of employment.

(3) Wages vary with constancy of employment.

Employment is much more constant in some trades than in others. In the greater part of manufactures, a journeyman may be pretty sure of employment almost every day in the year that he is able to work. A mason or bricklayer, on the contrary, can work neither in hard frost nor in foul weather, and his employment at all other times depends upon the occasional calls of his customers. He is liable, in consequence, to be frequently without any. What he earns, therefore, while he is employed, must not only maintain him while he is idle, but make him some compensation for those anxious and desponding moments which the thought of so precarious a situation must sometimes occasion. Where the computed earnings of the greater part of manufacturers, accordingly, are nearly upon a level with the day wages of common labourers, those of masons and bricklayers are generally from one half more to double those wages. Where common labourers earn four and five shillings a week, masons and bricklayers frequently earn seven and eight; where the former earn six, the latter often earn nine and ten; and where the former earn nine and ten, as in London, the latter commonly earn fifteen and eighteen. No species of skilled labour, however, seems more easy to learn than that of masons and bricklayers.

Chairmen in London, during the summer season, are said sometimes to be employed as bricklayers. The high wages of those workmen, therefore, are not so much the recompence of their skill, as the compensation for the inconstancy of their employment. . . .

Fourthly, the wages of labour vary according to the small or great trust which must be reposed in the workmen. (4) Wages vary with the trust to be reposed.

The wages of goldsmiths and jewellers are everywhere superior to those of many other workmen, not only of equal, but of much superior ingenuity; on account of the precious materials with which they are intrusted.

We trust our health to the physician; our fortune and sometimes our life and reputation to the lawyer and attorney. Such confidence could not safely be reposed in people of a very mean or low condition. Their reward must be such, therefore, as may give them that rank in the society which so important a trust requires. The long time and the great expence which must be laid out in their education, when combined with this circumstance, necessarily enhance still further the price of their labour. . . .

Fifthly, the wages of labour in different employments vary according to the probability or improbability of success in them. (5) Wages vary with the probability of success.

The probability that any particular person shall ever be qualified for the employment to which he is educated is very different in different occupations. In the greater part of mechanic trades, success is almost certain; but very uncertain in the liberal professions. Put your son apprentice to a shoemaker, there is little doubt of his learning to make a pair of shoes: But send him to study the law, it is at least twenty to one if ever he makes such proficiency as will enable him to live by the business. In a perfectly fair lottery, those who draw the prizes ought to gain all that is lost by those who draw the blanks. In a profession where twenty fail for one that succeeds, that one ought to gain all that should have been gained by the unsuccessful twenty. The counsellor at law who, perhaps, at near forty years of age, begins to make something by his profession, ought to receive the retribution, not only of his own so tedious and expensive education, but of that of more than twenty others who are never likely to make any thing by it. How extravagant soever the fees of counsellors at law may sometimes appear, their real retribution is never equal to this. Compute in any particular place, what is likely to be annually gained, and what is likely to be annually spent, by all the different workmen in any common trade, such as that of shoemakers or weavers, and you will find that the former sum will generally exceed the latter. But make the same computation with regard to all the counsellors and students of law, in all the different inns of court, and you will find that their annual gains bear but a very small proportion to their annual expence, even though you rate the former as high, and the latter as low, as can well be done. The lottery of the law, therefore, is very far from being a perfectly fair lottery; and that, as well as many other liberal and honourable professions, are, in point of pecuniary gain, evidently underrecompenced . . .

There are some very agreeable and beautiful talents of which the possession commands a certain sort of admiration; but of which the exercise for the sake of gain is considered, whether from reason or prejudice, as a sort of public prostitution. The pecuniary recompence, therefore, of those who exercise them in this manner, must be sufficient, not only to pay for the time, labour, and expence of acquiring the talents, but for the discredit which attends the employment of them as the means of subsistence. The exorbitant rewards of players, opera singers, opera dancers, etc., are founded upon those two principles; the rarity and beauty of the talents, and the discredit of employing them in this manner. It seems absurd at first sight that we should despise their persons, and yet reward their talents with the most profuse liberality. While we do the one, however, we must of necessity do the other. Should the public opinion or prejudice ever alter with regard to such occupations, their pecuniary recompence would quickly diminish. More people would apply to them, and the competition would quickly reduce the price of their labour. Such talents, though far from being common, are by no means so rare as is imagined. Many people possess them in great perfection, who disdain to make this use of them; and many more are capable of acquiring them, if anything could be made honourably by them. . . .

> Public admiration makes a part of the reward of superior abilities, except in the peculiar case of players, opera singers, etc.

The five circumstances above mentioned, though they occasion considerable inequalities in the wages of labour and profits of stock, occasion none in the whole of the advantages and disadvantages, real or imaginary, of the different employments of either. The nature of those circumstances is such, that they make up for a small pecuniary gain in some, and counterbalance a great one in others.

> The five circumstances thus counterbalance difference of pecuniary gains, but three things are necessary as well as perfect freedom:

In order, however, that this equality may take place in the whole of their advantages or disadvantages, three things are requisite even where there is the most perfect freedom. First, the employments must be well known and long established in the neighbourhood; secondly, they must be in their ordinary, or what may be called their natural state; and, thirdly, they must be the sole or principal employments of those who occupy them.

First, this equality can take place only in those employments which are well known, and have been long established in the neighbourhood.

(1) the employments must be well known and long established, since new trades yield higher wages, and higher profits:

Where all other circumstances are equal, wages are generally higher in new than in old trades. When a projector attempts to establish a new manufacture, he must at first entice his workmen from other employments by higher wages than they can either earn in their own trades, or than the nature of his work would otherwise require, and a considerable time must pass away before he can venture to reduce them to the common level. Manufactures for which the demand arises altogether from fashion and fancy, are continually changing, and seldom last long enough to be considered as old established manufactures. Those, on the contrary, for which the demand arises chiefly from use or necessity, are less liable to change, and the same form or fabric may continue in demand for whole centuries together. The wages of labour, therefore, are likely to be higher in manufactures of the former, than in those of the latter kind. Birmingham deals chiefly in manufactures of the former kind; Sheffield in those of the latter; and the wages of labour in those two different places, are said to be suitable to this difference in the nature of their manufactures.

The establishment of any new manufacture, of any new branch of commerce, or of any new practise in agriculture, is always a speculation, from which the projector promises himself extraordinary profits. These profits sometimes are very great, and sometimes, more frequently, perhaps, they are quite otherwise; but in general they bear no regular proportion to those of other old trades in the neighbourhood. If the project succeeds, they are commonly at first very high. When the trade or practise becomes thoroughly established and well known, the competition reduces them to the level of other trades.

Secondly, this equality in the whole of the advantages and disadvantages of the different employments of labour and stock, can take place only in the ordinary, or what may be called the natural state of those employments.

(2) the employments must be in their natural state, since the demand for labour in each employment varies from time to time and profits fluctuate with the price of the commodity produced:

The demand for almost every different species of labour, is sometimes greater and sometimes less than usual. In the one case the advantages of the employment rise above, in the other they fall below the common level. The demand for country labour is greater at hay time and harvest, than during the greater part of the year; and wages rise with the demand. In time of war, when forty or fifty thousand sailors are forced from the merchant service into that of the king, the demand for sailors to merchant ships necessarily rises with their scarcity, and their wages upon such occasions commonly rise from a guinea and seven-and-twenty-shillings, to forty shillings and three pounds a month. In a decaying manufacture, on the contrary, many workmen, rather than quit their old trade, are contented with smaller wages than would otherwise be suitable to the nature of their employment.

The profits of stock vary with the price of the commodities in which it is employed. As the price of any commodity rises above the ordinary or average rate, the profits of at least some part of the stock that is employed in bringing it to market, rise above their proper level, and as it falls they sink below it. All commodities are more or less liable to variations of price, but some are much more so than others. In all commodities which are produced by human industry, the quantity of industry annually employed is necessarily regulated by the annual demand, in such a manner that the average annual produce may, as nearly as possible, be equal to the average annual consumption. In some employments, it has already been observed, the same quantity of industry will always produce the same, or very nearly the same quantity of commodities. In the linen or woollen manufactures, for example, the same number of hands will annually work up very nearly the same quantity of linen and woollen cloth. The variations in the market price of such commodities, therefore, can arise only from some accidental variation in the demand. A public mourning raises the price of black cloth. But as the demand for most sorts of plain linen and woollen cloth is pretty uniform, so is likewise the price. But there are other employments in which the same quantity of industry will not always produce the same quantity of commodities. The same quantity of industry, for example, will, in different years, produce very different quantities of corn, wine, hops, sugar, tobacco, etc. The price of such commodities, therefore, varies not only with the variations of demand, but with the much greater and more frequent variations of quantity, and is consequently extremely fluctuating. But the profit of some of the dealers must necessarily fluctuate with the price of the commodities. The operations of the speculative merchant are principally employed about such commodities. He endeavours to buy them up when he foresees that their price is likely to rise, and to sell them when it is likely to fall.

Thirdly, this equality in the whole of the advantages and disadvantages of the different employments of labour and stock; can take place only in such as are the sole or principal employments of those who occupy them.

and (3) the employments must be the principal employment of those who occupy them, since people maintained by one employment will work cheap at another, like the Scotch cotters.

When a person derives his subsistence from one employment, which does not occupy the greater part of his time; in the intervals of his leisure he is often willing to work at another for less wages than would otherwise suit the nature of the employment.

There still subsists in many parts of Scotland a set of people called Cotters or Cottagers, though they were more frequent some years ago than they are now. They are a sort of out-servants of the landlords and farmers. The usual reward which they receive from their masters is a house, a small garden for pot-herbs, as much grass as will feed a cow, and, perhaps, an acre or two of bad arable land. When their master has occasion for their labour, he gives them, besides, two pecks of oatmeal a week, worth about sixteen-pence sterling. During a great part of the year he has little or no occasion for their labour, and the cultivation of their own little possession is not sufficient to occupy the time which is left at their own disposal. When such occupiers were more numerous than they are at present, they are said to have been willing to give their spare time for a very small recompence to any body, and to have wrought for less wages than other labourers. In ancient times they seem to have been common all over Europe. In countries ill cultivated and worse inhabited, the greater part of landlords and farmers could not otherwise provide themselves with the extraordinary number of hands, which country labour requires at certain seasons. The daily or weekly recompence which such labourers occasionally received from their masters was evidently not the whole price of their labour. Their small tenement made a considerable part of it. This daily or weekly recompence, however, seems to have been considered as the whole of it, by many writers who have collected the prices of labour and provisions in ancient times, and who have taken pleasure in representing both as wonderfully low. . . .

PART II

Inequalities occasioned by the Policy of Europe

Such are the inequalities in the whole of the advantages and disadvantages of the different employments of labour and stock, which the defect of any of the three requisites abovementioned must occasion, even where there is the most perfect liberty. But the policy of Europe, by not leaving things at perfect liberty, occasions other inequalities of much greater importance. *The policy of Europe occasions more important inequalities in three ways:*

It does this chiefly in the three following ways. First, by restraining the competition in some employments to a smaller number than would otherwise be disposed to enter into them; secondly, by increasing it in others beyond what it naturally would be; and, thirdly, by obstructing the free circulation of labour and stock, both from employment to employment and from place to place.

First, the policy of Europe occasions a very important inequality in the whole of the advantages and disadvantages of the different employments of labour and stock, by restraining the competition in some employments *(1) It restricts competition in some employments.*

to a smaller number than might otherwise be disposed to enter into them. . . .

The property which every man has in his own labour, as it is the original foundation of all other property, so it is the most sacred and inviolable. The patrimony of a poor man lies in the strength and dexterity of his hands; and to hinder him from employing this strength and dexterity in what manner he thinks proper without injury to his neighbour, is a plain violation of this most sacred property. It is a manifest encroachment upon the just liberty both of the workman, and of those who might be disposed to employ him. As it hinders the one from working at what he thinks proper, so it hinders the others from employing whom they think proper. To judge whether he is fit to be employed, may surely be trusted to the discretion of the employers whose interest it so much concerns. The affected anxiety of the lawgiver lest they should employ an improper person, is evidently as impertinent as it is oppressive. . . .

Secondly, the policy of Europe, by increasing the competition in some employments beyond what it naturally would be, occasions another inequality of an opposite kind in the whole of the advantages and disadvantages of the different employments of labour and stock.

(2) The policy of Europe increases competition in some trades.

It has been considered as of so much importance that a proper number of young people should be educated for certain professions, that, sometimes the public, and sometimes the piety of private founders have established many pensions, scholarships, exhibitions, bursaries, etc., for this purpose, which draw many more people into those trades than could otherwise pretend to follow them. . . .

Thirdly, the policy of Europe, by obstructing the free circulation of labour and stock both from employment to employment, and from place to place, occasions in some cases a very inconvenient inequality in the whole of the advantages and disadvantages of their different employments.

(3) The policy of Europe obstructs the free circulation of labour.

The statute of apprenticeship obstructs the free circulation of labour from one employment to another, even in the same place. The exclusive privileges of corporations obstruct it from one place to another, even in the same employment.

Apprenticeship and corporation privileges obstruct circulation from employment to employment and from place to place. Thus the changes of employment necessary to equalise wages are prevented.

It frequently happens that while high wages are given to the workmen in one manufacture, those in another are obliged to content themselves with bare subsistence. The one is in an advancing state, and has, therefore, a continual demand for new hands: The other is in a declining state, and the superabundance of hands is continually increasing. Those two manufactures many sometimes be in the same town, and sometimes in the same neighbourhood, without being able to lend the least assistance to one another. The statute of apprenticeship may oppose it in the one case, and both that and an exclusive corporation in the other. In many different manufactures, however, the operations are so much alike, that the workmen could easily change trades with one another, if those absurd laws did not hinder them. The arts of weaving plain linen and plain silk, for example, are almost entirely the same. That of weaving plain woollen is somewhat different; but the difference is so insignificant, that either a linen or a silk weaver might become a tolerable workman in a very few days. If any of those three capital manufactures, therefore, were decaying, the workmen might find a resource in one of the other two which was in a more prosperous condition; and their wages would neither rise too high in the thriving, nor sink too low in the decaying manufacture. The linen manufacture indeed is, in England, by a particular statute, open to every body; but, as it is not much cultivated through the greater part of the country, it can afford no general resource to the workmen of other decaying manufactures, who, wherever the statute of apprenticeship takes place, have no other choice but either to come upon the parish, or to work as common labourers, for which, by their habits, they are much worse qualified than for any sort of manufacture that bears any resemblance to their own. They generally, therefore, choose to come upon the parish. . . .

CHAPTER XI

Of the Rent of Land

Rent, considered as the price paid for the use of land, is naturally the highest which the tenant can afford to pay in the actual circumstances of the land. In adjusting the terms of the lease, the landlord endeavours to leave him no greater share of the produce than what is sufficient to keep up the stock from which he furnishes the seed, pays the labour, and purchases and maintains the cattle and other instruments of husbandry, together with the ordinary profits of farming stock in the neighbourhood. This is evidently the smallest share with which the tenant can content himself without being a loser, and the landlord seldom means to leave him any more. Whatever part of the produce, or, what is the same thing, whatever part of its price, is over and above this share, he naturally endeavours to reserve to himself as the rent of his land, which is evidently the highest the tenant can afford to pay in the actual circumstances of the land. Sometimes, indeed, the liberality, more frequently the ignorance, of the landlord, makes him accept of somewhat less than this portion; and sometimes too, though more rarely, the ignorance of the tenant makes him undertake to pay somewhat more,

Rent is the produce which is over what is necessary to pay the farmer ordinary profit.

or to content himself with somewhat less than the ordinary profits of farming stock in the neighbourhood. This portion, however, may still be considered as the natural rent of land, or the rent for which it is naturally meant that land should for the most part be let.

The rent of land, it may be thought, is frequently no more than a reasonable profit or interest for the stock laid out by the landlord upon its improvement. This, no doubt, may be partly the case upon some occasions; for it can scarce ever be more than partly the case. The landlord demands a rent even for unimproved land, and the supposed interest or profit upon the expence of improvement is generally an addition to this original rent. Those improvements, besides, are not always made by the stock of the landlord, but sometimes by that of the tenant. When the lease comes to be renewed, however, the landlord commonly demands the same augmentation of rent, as if they had been all made by his own.

It is not merely interest on stock laid out in improvements, and is sometimes obtained for land incapable of improvement, such as rocks where kelp grows; and for the opportunity to fish.

He sometimes demands rent for what is altogether incapable of human improvement. Kelp is a species of seaweed, which, when burnt, yields an alkaline salt, useful for making glass, soap, and for several other purposes. It grows in several parts of Great Britain, particularly in Scotland, upon such rocks only as lie within the high water mark, which are twice every day covered with the sea, and of which the produce, therefore, was never augmented by human industry. The landlord, however, whose estate is bounded by a kelp shore of this kind, demands a rent for it as much as for his corn fields.

The sea in the neighbourhood of the islands of Shetland is more than commonly abundant in fish, which make a great part of the subsistence of their inhabitants. But in order to profit by the produce of the water, they must have a habitation upon the neighbouring land. The rent of the landlord is in proportion, not to what the farmer can make by the land, but to what he can make both by the land and by the water. It is partly paid in seafish; and one of the very few instances in which rent makes a part of the price of that commodity, is to be found in that country.

The rent of land, therefore, considered as the price paid for the use of the land, is naturally a monopoly price. It is not at all proportioned to what the landlord may have laid out upon the improvement of the land, or to what he can afford to take; but to what the farmer can afford to give.

It is therefore a monopoly price. Whether particular parts of produce fetch a price sufficient to yield a rent depends on the demand.

Such parts only of the produce of land can commonly be brought to market of which the ordinary price is sufficient to replace the stock which must be employed in bringing them thither, together with its ordinary profits. If the ordinary price is more than this, the surplus part of it will naturally go to the rent of the land. If it is not more, though the commodity may be brought to market, it can afford no rent to the landlord. Whether the price is, or is not more, depends upon the demand. There are some parts of the produce of land for which the demand must always be such as to afford a greater price than what is sufficient to bring them to market; and there are others for which it either may or may not be such as to afford this greater price. The former must always afford a rent to the landlord. The latter sometimes may, and sometimes may not, according to different circumstances.

Rent, it is to be observed, therefore, enters into the composition of the price of commodities in a different way from wages and profit. High or low Wages and profit are causes of price; rent is an effect. wages and profit, are the causes of high or low price; high or low rent is the effect of it. It is because high or low wages and profit must be paid, in order to bring a particular commodity to market, that its price is high or low. But it is because its price is high or low; a great deal more, or very little more, or no more, than what is sufficient to pay those wages and profit, that it affords a high rent, or a low rent, or no rent at all. . . .

PART 1

Of the Produce of Land which always affords Rent

As men, like all other animals, naturally multiply in proportion to the means of their subsistence, food is always, more or less, in demand. It can always Food can always purchase as much labour as it can maintain. purchase or command a greater or smaller quantity of labour, and somebody can always be found who is willing to do something, in order to obtain it. The quantity of labour, indeed, which it can purchase, is not always equal to what it could maintain, if managed in the most economical manner, on account of the high wages which are sometimes given to labour. But it can always purchase such a quantity of labour as it can maintain, according to the rate at which that sort of labour is commonly maintained in the neighbourhood.

But land, in almost any situation, produces a greater quantity of food than what is sufficient to maintain all the labour necessary for bringing it to market, in the most liberal way in which that labour Almost all land produces more than enough food to maintain the labour and pay the profits, and therefore yields rent. is ever maintained. The surplus too is always more than sufficient to replace the stock which employed that labour, together with its profits. Something, therefore, always remains for a rent to the landlord.

The most desert moors in Norway and Scotland produce some sort of pasture for cattle, of which the milk and the increase are always more than sufficient, not only to maintain all the labour necessary for tending them, and to pay the ordinary profit to the farmer or owner of the herd or flock; but to afford some small rent to the landlord. The rent increases in proportion to the goodness of the pasture. The same extent of ground not only maintains a greater number of cattle, but as they are brought within a smaller compass, less labour becomes requisite to tend them, and to collect their produce. The landlord gains both ways; by the increase of the produce, and by the diminution of the labour which must be maintained out of it.

The rent of land not only varies with its fertility, whatever be its produce, but with its situation, whatever be its fertility. Land in the neighbourhood
The rent varies with situation as well as with fertility.
of a town, gives a greater rent than land equally fertile in a distant part of the country. Though it may cost no more labour to cultivate the one than the other, it must always cost more to bring the produce of the distant land to market. A greater quantity of labour, therefore, must be maintained out of it; and the surplus, from which are drawn both the profit of the farmer and the rent of the landlord, must be diminished. But in remote parts of the country the rate of profit, as has already been shown, is generally higher than in the neighbourhood of a large town. A smaller proportion of this diminished surplus, therefore, must belong to the landlord. . . .

Of the Produce of Land which sometimes does, and sometimes does not, afford Rent

Human food seems to be the only produce of land which always and necessarily affords some rent to the landlord. Other sorts of produce sometimes may and sometimes may not, according to different circumstances.

After food, clothing and lodging are the two great wants of mankind.
The materials of clothing and lodging, at first superabundant, come in time to afford a rent.

Land in its original rude state can afford the materials of clothing and lodging to a much greater number of people than it can feed. In its improved state it can sometimes feed a greater number of people than it can supply with those materials; at least in the way in which they require them, and are willing to pay for them. In the one state, therefore, there is always a superabundance of those materials, which are frequently, upon that account, of little or no value. In the other there is often a scarcity, which necessarily augments their value. In the one state a great part of them is thrown away as useless, and the price of what is used is considered as equal only to the labour and expence of fitting it for use, and can, therefore, afford no rent to the landlord. In the other they are all made use of, and there is frequently a demand for more than can be had. Somebody is always willing to give more for every part of them than what is sufficient to pay the expence of bringing them to market. Their price, therefore, can always afford some rent to the landlord.

The skins of the larger animals were the original   For example, hides and
materials of clothing. Among nations of hunters and   wool.
shepherds, therefore, whose food consists chiefly in
the flesh of those animals, every man, by providing himself with food,
provides himself with the materials of more clothing than he can wear.
If there was no foreign commerce, the greater part of them would be
thrown away as things of no value. This was probably the case among
the hunting nations of North America, before their country was discovered by the Europeans, with whom they now exchange their surplus
peltry, for blankets, firearms, and brandy, which gives it some value. In
the present commercial state of the known world, the most barbarous
nations, I believe, among whom land property is established, have some
foreign commerce of this kind, and find among their wealthier neighbours such a demand for all the materials of clothing, which their land
produces, and which can neither be wrought up nor consumed at home,
as raises their price above what it costs to send them to those wealthier
neighbours. It affords, therefore, some rent to the landlord. . . .

But when by the improvement and cultivation of   Population depends on
land the labour of one family can provide food for   food; so the demand for
the materials of clothing
two, the labour of half the society becomes suffi-   and lodging is increased
cient to provide food for the whole. The other half,   by greater ease of
obtaining food, which
therefore, or at least the greater part of them, can be   thus makes them afford
employed in providing other things, or in satisfying   rent.
the other wants and fancies of mankind. Clothing and lodging, household furniture, and what is called Equipage, are the principal objects of
the greater part of those wants and fancies. The rich man consumes no
more food than his poor neighbour. In quality it may be very different,
and to select and prepare it may require more labour and art; but in
quantity it is very nearly the same. But compare the spacious palace and
great wardrobe of the one, with the hovel and the few rags of the other,
and you will be sensible that the difference between their clothing, lodging and household furniture, is almost as great in quantity as it is in
quality. The desire of food is limited in every man by the narrow capacity of the human stomach; but the desire of the conveniences and ornaments of building, dress, equipage, and household furniture, seems to
have no limit or certain boundary. Those, therefore, who have the command of more food than they themselves can consume, are always willing to exchange the surplus, or, what is the same thing, the price of it,
for gratifications of this other kind. What is over and above satisfying the
limited desire, is given for the amusement of those desires which cannot
be satisfied, but seem to be altogether endless. The poor, in order to
obtain food, exert themselves to gratify those fancies of the rich, and to
obtain it more certainly, they vie with one another in the cheapness and
perfection of their work. The number of workmen increases with the
increasing quantity of food, or with the growing improvement and cul-

tivation of the lands; and as the nature of their business admits of the utmost subdivisions of labour, the quantity of materials which they can work up, increases in a much greater proportion than their numbers. Hence arises a demand for every sort of material which human invention can employ, either usefully or ornamentally, in building, dress, equipage, or household furniture; for the fossils and minerals contained in the bowels of the earth; the precious metals, and the precious stones.

Food is in this manner, not only the original source of rent, but every other part of the produce of land which afterwards affords rent, derives that part of its value from the improvement of the powers of labour in producing food by means of the improvement and cultivation of land.

Those other parts of the produce of land, however, which afterwards afford rent, do not afford it always. Even in improved and cultivated countries, the demand for them is not always such as to afford a greater price than what is sufficient to pay the labour, and replace, together with its ordinary profits, the stock which must be employed in bringing them to market. Whether it is or is not such, depends upon different circumstances.

They do not, however, even then always afford rent: for example, some coal mines are too barren to afford rent.

Whether a coal mine, for example, can afford any rent, depends partly upon its fertility, and partly upon its situation.

A mine of any kind may be said to be either fertile or barren, according as the quantity of mineral which can be brought from it by a certain quantity of labour, is greater or less than what can be brought by an equal quantity from the greater part of other mines of the same kind. . . .

[A brief discussion of the peculiar attributes of precious stones and metals has been excluded. The rent of these mines is determined according to the principle that "The demand for the precious stones arises altogether from their beauty. They are of no use, but as ornaments; and the merit of their beauty is greatly enhanced by their scarcity, or by the difficulty and expence of getting them from the mine. Wages and profits accordingly make up, upon most occasions, almost the whole of their high price. Rent comes in but for a very small share; frequently for no share; and the most fertile mines only afford any considerable rent"]

Of the Variations in the Proportion between the respective Values of that Sort of Produce which always affords Rent, and of that which sometimes does, and sometimes does not, afford Rent

The increasing abundance of food, in consequence of increasing improvement and cultivation, must necessarily increase the demand for every part of the produce of land which is not food, and which can be applied either to use or to ornament. In the whole progress of improvement, it might therefore be expected, there should be only one variation in the comparative values of those two different sorts of pro-

The general course of progress is for produce other than food to become dearer.

duce. The value of that sort which sometimes does and sometimes does not afford rent, should constantly rise in proportion to that which always affords some rent. As art and industry advance, the materials of clothing and lodging, the useful fossils and minerals of the earth, the precious metals and the precious stones should gradually come to be more and more in demand, should gradually exchange for a greater and a greater quantity of food, or in other words, should gradually become dearer and dearer. This accordingly has been the case with most of these things upon most occasions, and would have been the case with all of them upon all occasions, if particular accidents had not upon some occasions increased the supply of some of them in a still greater proportion than the demand. . . .

[The famous "Digression Concerning the Variations in the Value of Silver During the Course of the Last Four Centuries" has been omitted. Although it encompasses nearly one tenth of the text in the *Wealth of Nations*, the material is largely of interest to historians and scholars of the problem of value in Classical Political Economy.

In this "Digression" Smith utilizes a great deal of empirical evidence—the prices of various goods from 1350 to 1750—to support his claim that the prices of agricultural products tend to rise during the course of material progress, while those of manufactured articles tend to fall. This general observation has come to occupy a prominent place in economic analysis. Debates are still waged as to whether production in agriculture and industry is characterized by decreasing or increasing returns. But a wider, more controversial question pertains to the long-term consequences of this issue: Does the trajectory of economic society lead to hitchless growth or to eventual stagnation? Smith's own conclusions, as we know, envisage a long period of growth, terminating in decline. (See above, p. 210)]

Conclusion of the Chapter

. . . The whole annual produce of the land and labour of every country, or what comes to the same thing, the whole price of that annual produce, naturally divides itself, it has already been observed, into three parts; the rent of land, the wages of labour, and the profits of stock; and constitutes a revenue to three different orders of people; to those who live by rent, to those who live by wages, and to those who live by profit. These are the three great, original and constituent orders of every civilised society, from whose revenue that of every other order is ultimately derived.

There are three parts of produce and three original orders of society.

The interest of the first of those three great orders, it appears from what has been just now said, is strictly and inseparably connected with the general interest of the society. Whatever either promotes or obstructs the one, necessarily promotes or obstructs the other. When the public deliberates concerning any regulation of commerce or police, the pro-

The interest of the proprietors of land is inseparably connected with the general interest of the society.

prietors of land never can mislead it, with a view to promote the interest
of their own particular order; at least, if they have any tolerable knowledge of that interest. They are, indeed, too often defective in this tolerable knowledge. They are the only one of the three orders whose revenue
costs them neither labour nor care, but comes to them, as it were, of its
own accord, and independent of any plan or project of their own. That
indolence, which is the natural effect of the ease and security of their
situation, renders them too often, not only ignorant, but incapable of
that application of mind which is necessary in order to foresee and
understand the consequences of any public regulation.

The interest of the second order, that of those
who live by wages, is as strictly connected with the
interest of the society as that of the first. The wages
of the labourer, it has already been shown, are never
so high as when the demand for labour is continually rising, or when the quantity employed is every
year increasing considerably. When this real wealth of the society becomes
stationary, his wages are soon reduced to what is barely enough to enable
him to bring up a family, or to continue the race of labourers. When
the society declines, they fall even below this. The order of proprietors
may, perhaps, gain more by the prosperity of the society, than that of
labourers: but there is no order that suffers so cruelly from its decline.
But though the interest of the labourer is strictly connected with that of
the society, he is incapable either of comprehending that interest, or of
understanding its connexion with his own. His condition leaves him no
time to receive the necessary information, and his education and habits
are commonly such as to render him unfit to judge even though he was
fully informed. In the public deliberations, therefore, his voice is little
heard and less regarded, except upon some particular occasions, when
his clamour is animated, set on, and supported by his employers, not
for his, but their own particular purposes.

His employers constitute the third order, that of those who live by
profit. It is the stock that is employed for the sake of profit, which puts
into motion the greater part of the useful labour of every society. The
plans and projects of the employers of stock regulate and direct all the
most important operations of labour, and profit is the end proposed by
all those plans and projects.

But the rate of profit does not, like rent and wages, rise with the prosperity, and fall with the declension of the society. On the contrary, it is
naturally low in rich, and high in poor countries, and it is always highest
in the countries which are going fastest to ruin. The interest of this third
order, therefore, has not the same connexion with the general interest
of the society as that of the other two. Merchants and master manufacturers are, in this order, the two classes of people who commonly employ
the largest capitals, and who by their wealth draw to themselves the
greatest share of the public consideration. As during their whole lives

So also is that of those who live by wages, but the interest of those who live by profit has not the same connexion with the general interest of the society.

they are engaged in plans and projects, they have frequently more acuteness of understanding than the greater part of country gentlemen. As their thoughts, however, are commonly exercised rather about the interest of their own particular branch of business, than about that of the society, their judgment, even when given with the greatest candour (which it has not been upon every occasion) is much more to be depended upon with regard to the former of those two objects, than with regard to the latter. Their superiority over the country gentleman is, not so much in their knowledge of the public interest, as in their having a better knowledge of their own interest than he has of his.

It is by this superior knowledge of their own interest that they have frequently imposed upon his generosity, and persuaded him to give up both his own interest and that of the public, from a very simple but honest conviction, that their interest, and not his, was the interest of the public. The interest of the dealers, however, in any particular branch of trade or manufactures, is always in some respects different from, and even opposite to, that of the public. To widen the market and to narrow the competition, is always the interest of the dealers. To widen the market may frequently be agreeable enough to the interest of the public; but to narrow the competition must always be against it, and can serve only to enable the dealers, by raising their profits above what they naturally would be, to levy, for their own benefit, an absurd tax upon the rest of their fellow-citizens. The proposal of any new law or regulation of commerce which comes from this order, ought always to be listened to with great precaution, and ought never to be adopted till after having been long and carefully examined, not only with the most scrupulous, but with the most suspicious attention. It comes from an order of men, whose interest is never exactly the same with that of the public, who have generally an interest to deceive and even to oppress the public, and who accordingly have, upon many occasions, both deceived and oppressed it.

BOOK II

OF THE NATURE, ACCUMULATION, AND EMPLOYMENT OF STOCK

INTRODUCTION

In that rude state of society in which there is no division of labour, in which exchanges are seldom made, and in which every man provides every thing for himself, it is not necessary that any stock should be accumulated or

In the rude state of society stock is unnecessary.

stored up beforehand in order to carry on the business of the society. Every man endeavours to supply by his own industry his own occasional wants as they occur. When he is hungry, he goes to the forest to hunt; when his coat is worn out, he clothes himself with the skin of the first large animal he kills: and when his hut begins to go to ruin, he repairs it, as well as he can, with the trees and the turf that are nearest it.

But when the division of labour has once been thoroughly introduced, the produce of a man's own labour can supply but a very small part of his occasional wants. The far greater part of them are supplied by the produce of other mens labour, which he purchases with the produce, or, what is the same thing, with the price of the produce of his own. But this purchase cannot be made till such time as the produce of his own labour has not only been completed, but sold. A stock of goods of different kinds, therefore, must be stored up somewhere sufficient to maintain him, and to supply him with the materials and tools of his work till such time, at least, as both these events can be brought about. A weaver cannot apply himself entirely to his peculiar business, unless there is beforehand stored up somewhere, either in his own possession or in that of some other person, a stock sufficient to maintain him, and to supply him with the materials and tools of his work, till he has not only completed, but sold his web. This accumulation must, evidently, be previous to his applying his industry for so long a time to such a peculiar business.

Division of labour makes it necessary.

As the accumulation of stock must, in the nature of things, be previous to the division of labour, so labour can be more and more subdivided in proportion only as stock is previously more and more accumulated. The quantity of materials which the same number of people can work up, increases in a great proportion as labour comes to be more and more subdivided; and as the operations of each workman are gradually reduced to a greater degree of simplicity, a variety of new machines come to be invented for facilitating and abridging those operations. As the division of labour advances, therefore, in order to give constant employment to an equal number of workmen, an equal stock of provisions, and a greater stock of materials and tools than what would have been necessary in a ruder state of things, must be accumulated beforehand. But the number of workmen in every branch of business generally increases with the division of labour in that branch, or rather it is the increase of their number which enables them to class and subdivide themselves in this manner.

Accumulation of stock and division of labour advance together.

As the accumulation of stock is previously necessary for carrying on this great improvement in the productive powers of labour, so that accumulation naturally leads to this improvement. The person who employs his stock in maintaining labour, necessarily wishes to employ it in such a manner as to produce as great a quantity of work as possible.

Accumulation causes the same quantity of industry to produce more.

He endeavours, therefore, both to make among his workmen the most proper distribution of employment, and to furnish them with the best machines which he can either invent or afford to purchase. His abilities in both these respects are generally in proportion to the extent of his stock, or to the number of people whom it can employ. The quantity of industry, therefore, not only increases in every country with the increase of the stock which employs it, but, in consequence of that increase, the same quantity of industry produces a much greater quantity of work.

Such are in general the effects of the increase of stock upon industry and its productive powers.

In the following book I have endeavoured to explain the nature of stock, the effects of its accumulation into capitals of different kinds, and the effects of the different employments of those capitals. This book is divided into five chapters. In the first chapter, I have endeavoured to show what are the different parts or branches into which the stock, either of an individual, or of a great society, naturally divides itself. In the second, I have endeavoured to explain the nature and operation of money considered as a particular branch of the general stock of the society. The stock which is accumulated into a capital, may either be employed by the person to whom it belongs, or it may be lent to some other person. In the third and fourth chapters, I have endeavoured to examine the manner in which it operates in both these situations. The fifth and last chapter treats of the different effects which the different employments of capital immediately produce upon the quantity both of national industry, and of the annual produce of land and labour.

This book treats of the nature of stock, the effects of its accumulation, and its different employments.

CHAPTER I

Of the Division of Stock

When the stock which a man possesses is no more than sufficient to maintain him for a few days or a few weeks, he seldom thinks of deriving any revenue from it. He consumes it as sparingly as he can, and endeavours by his labour to acquire something which may supply its place before it be consumed altogether. His revenue is, in this case, derived from his labour only. This is the state of the greater part of the labouring poor in all countries.

A man does not think of obtaining revenue from a small stock, but when he has more than enough for immediate consumption, he endeavours to derive a revenue from the rest.

But when he possesses stock sufficient to maintain him for months or years, he naturally endeavours to derive a revenue from the greater part of it; reserving only so much for his immediate consumption as may maintain him till this revenue begins to come in. His whole stock, therefore, is distinguished into two parts. That part which, he expects, is to afford him this revenue, is called his capital. The other is that which supplies his immediate consumption; and which consists either, first, in that portion of his whole stock which was originally reserved for this purpose; or, secondly, in his revenue, from whatever source derived, as it gradually comes in; or, thirdly, in such things as had been purchased by either of these in former years, and which are not yet entirely consumed; such as a stock of clothes, household furniture, and the like. In one, or other, or all of these three articles, consists the stock which men commonly reserve for their own immediate consumption. . . .

In all countries where there is tolerable security, every man of common understanding will endeavour to employ whatever stock he can command in procuring either present enjoyment or future profit. If it is employed in procuring present enjoyment, it is a stock reserved for immediate consumption. If it is employed in procuring future profit, it must procure this profit either by staying with him, or by going from him. In the one case it is a fixed, in the other it is a circulating capital. A man must be perfectly crazy who, where there is tolerable security, does not employ all the stock which he commands, whether it be his own or borrowed of other people, in some one or other of those three ways. . . .

Where there is tolerable security all stock is employed in one or other of the three ways.

CHAPTER II

Of Money considered as a particular Branch of the general Stock of the Society, or of the Expence of maintaining the National Capital

It has been shown in the first book, that the price of the greater part of commodities resolves itself into three parts, of which one pays the wages of the labour, another the profits of the stock, and a third the rent of the land which had been employed in producing and bringing them to market: that there are, indeed, some commodities of which the price is made up of two of those parts only, the wages of labour, and the profits of stock: and a very few in which it consists altogether in one, the wages of labour: but that the price of every commodity necessarily resolves itself into some one, or other, or all of these three parts; every part of it which goes neither to rent nor to wages, being necessarily profit to somebody.

Since this is the case, it has been observed, with regard to every particular commodity, taken separately; it must be so with regard to all the commodities which compose the whole annual produce of the land and labour of every country, taken complexly. The whole price or exchangeable value of that annual produce, must resolve itself into the same three parts, and be parcelled out among the different inhabitants of the country, either as the wages of their labour, the profits of their stock, or the rent of their land.

Prices are divided into three parts, wages, profits, and rent, and the whole annual produce is divided into the same three parts; but we may distinguish between gross and net revenue.

But though the whole value of the annual produce of the land and labour of every country is thus divided among and constitutes a revenue to its different inhabitants, yet as in the rent of a private estate we distinguish between the gross rent and the net rent, so may we likewise in the revenue of all the inhabitants of a great country.

The gross rent of a private estate comprehends whatever is paid by the farmer; the net rent, what remains free to the landlord, after deducting the expence of management, of repairs, and all other *Gross rent is the whole sum paid by the farmer; net rent what is left free to the landlord.* necessary charges; or what, without hurting his estate, he can afford to place in his stock reserved for immediate consumption, or to spend upon his table, equipage, the ornaments of his house and furniture, his private enjoyments and amusements. His real wealth is in proportion, not to his gross, but to his net rent.

The gross revenue of all the inhabitants of a great country, comprehends the whole annual produce of their land and labour; the net revenue, what remains free to them after deducting the expence of maintaining; first, their fixed; and, secondly, their circu- *Gross revenue is the whole annual produce: net revenue what is left free after deducting the maintenance of fixed and circulating capital.* lating capital; or what, without encroaching upon their capital, they can place in their stock reserved for immediate consumption, or spend upon their subsistence, conveniences, and amusements. Their real wealth too is in proportion, not to their gross, but to their net revenue. . . .

Though the weekly, or yearly revenue of all the different inhabitants of any country, in the same manner, may be, and in reality frequently is paid to *The same is true of all the inhabitants of a country.* them in money, their real riches, however, the real weekly or yearly revenue of all of them taken together, must always be great or small in proportion to the quantity of consumable goods which they can all of them purchase with this money. The whole revenue of all of them taken together is evidently not equal to both the money and the consumable goods; but only to one or other of those two values, and to the latter more properly than to the former.

Though we frequently, therefore, express a person's revenue by the metal pieces which are annually paid to him, it is because the amount of those pieces regulates the extent of his power of purchasing, or the value of the goods which he can annually afford to consume. We still consider his revenue as consisting in this power of purchasing or consuming, and not in the pieces which convey it.

But if this is sufficiently evident even with regard to an individual, it is still more so with regard to a society. The amount of the metal pieces which are annually paid to an individual, is often precisely equal *The coins annually paid to an individual often equal his revenue, but the stock of coin in a society is never equal to its whole revenue.* to his revenue, and is upon that account the shortest and best expression of its value. But the amount of the metal pieces which circulate in a society, can never be equal to the revenue of all its members. As the same guinea which pays the weekly pension of one man today, may pay that of another tomorrow, and that of a third the day thereafter, the amount of the metal pieces which annually circulate in any country, must always be of much less value than the whole money pensions annually paid with them. But the power of purchasing, or the goods which can successively be bought with the whole of those money pensions as they are successively paid, must always be precisely of the same value with those pensions; as must likewise be the revenue of the different persons to whom they are paid. That revenue, therefore, cannot consist in those metal pieces, of which the amount is so much inferior to its value, but in the power of purchasing, in the goods which can successively be bought with them as they circulate from hand to hand.

Money, therefore, the great wheel of circulation, the great instrument of commerce, like all other instruments of trade, though it makes a part and a very valuable part of the capital, makes no part of the revenue of the society to which it belongs; and though the metal pieces of which it is composed, in the course of their annual circulation, distribute to every man the revenue which properly belongs to him, they make themselves no part of that revenue. . . .

Money is therefore no part of the revenue of the society.

[A lengthy account of banking practices in early eighteenth century Scotland and England has been omitted.]

It is not by augmenting the capital of the country, but by rendering a greater part of that capital active and productive than would otherwise be so, that the most judicious operations of banking can increase the industry of the country. That part of his capital which a dealer is obliged to keep by him unemployed, and in ready money for answering occasional demands, is so much dead stock, which, so long as it remains in this situation, produces nothing either to him or to his country. The judicious operations of banking enable him to convert this dead stock into active and productive stock; into materials to work upon, into tools to work with, and into provisions and subsistence to work for; into stock which produces something both to himself and to his country. The gold and silver money which circulates in any country, and by means of which, the produce of its land and labour is annually circulated and distributed to the proper consumers, is, in the same manner as the ready money of the dealer, all dead stock. It is a very valuable part of the capital of the country, which produces nothing to the country.

The operations of banking turn dead stock into productive capital, but make commerce and industry somewhat less secure.

The judicious operations of banking, by substituting paper in the room of a great part of this gold and silver, enables the country to convert a great part of this dead stock into active and productive stock; into stock

which produces something to the country. The gold and silver money
which circulates in any country may very properly be compared to a
highway, which, while it circulates and carries to market all the grass
and corn of the country, produces itself not a single pile of either. The
judicious operations of banking, by providing, if I may be allowed so
violent a metaphor, a sort of wagon-way through the air; enable the
country to convert, as it were, a great part of its highways into good
pastures and corn fields, and thereby to increase very considerably the
annual produce of its land and labour. The commerce and industry of
the country, however, it must be acknowledged, though they may be
somewhat augmented, cannot be altogether so secure, when they are
thus, as it were, suspended upon the Daedalian wings of paper money,
as when they travel about upon the solid ground of gold and silver. Over
and above the accidents to which they are exposed from the unskilful-
ness of the conductors of this paper money, they are liable to several
others, from which no prudence or skill of those conductors can guard
them. . . .

If bankers are restrained from issuing any circulating bank notes, or notes payable to the bearer, for
less than a certain sum; and if they are subjected to
the obligation of an immediate and unconditional
payment of such bank notes as soon as presented,
their trade may, with safety to the public, be ren-
dered in all other respects perfectly free. The late multiplication of banking companies in both parts of the united kingdom, an event by which
many people have been much alarmed, instead of diminishing, increases
the security of the public. It obliges all of them to be more circumspect
in their conduct, and, by not extending their currency beyond its due
proportion to their cash, to guard themselves against those malicious
runs, which the rivalship of so many competitors is always ready to bring
upon them. It restrains the circulation of each particular company within
a narrower circle, and reduces their circulating notes to a smaller number. By dividing the whole circulation into a greater number of parts,
the failure of any one company, an accident which, in the course of
things, must sometimes happen, becomes of less consequence to the
public. This free competition too obliges all bankers to be more liberal
in their dealings with their customers, lest their rivals should carry them
away. In general, if any branch of trade, or any division of labour, be
advantageous to the public, the freer and more general the competition,
it will always be the more so.

The only restrictions on banking which are necessary are the prohibition of small bank notes and the requirement that all notes shall be repaid on demand.

CHAPTER III

Of the Accumulation of Capital, or of productive and unproductive Labour

There is one sort of labour which adds to the value of the subject upon which it is bestowed: There is another which has no such effect. The former, as it

There are two sorts of labour, productive and unproductive.

produces a value, may be called productive; the latter, unproductive* labour. Thus the labour of a manufacturer adds, generally, to the value of the materials which he works upon, that of his own maintenance, and of his master's profit. The labour of a menial servant, on the contrary, adds to the value of nothing. Though the manufacturer has his wages advanced to him by his master, he, in reality, costs him no expence, the value of those wages being generally restored, together with a profit, in the improved value of the subject upon which his labour is bestowed. But the maintenance of a menial servant never is restored. A man grows rich by employing a multitude of manufacturers: He grows poor by maintaining a multitude of menial servants. The labour of the latter, however, has its value, and deserves its reward as well as that of the former. But the labour of the manufacturer fixes and realizes itself in some particular subject or vendible commodity, which lasts for some time at least after that labour is past. It is, as it were, a certain quantity of labour stocked and stored up to be employed, if necessary, upon some other occasion. That subject, or what is the same thing, the price of that subject, can afterwards, if necessary, put into motion a quantity of labour equal to that which had originally produced it. The labour of the menial servant, on the contrary, does not fix or realize itself in any particular subject or vendible commodity. His services generally perish in the very instant of their performance, and seldom leave any trace or value behind them, for which an equal quantity of service could afterwards be procured.

The labour of some of the most respectable orders in the society is, like that of menial servants, unproductive of any value, and does not fix or realize itself

Many kinds of labour besides menial service are unproductive.

in any permanent subject, or vendible commodity, which endures after that labour is past, and for which an equal quantity of labour could afterwards be procured. The sovereign, for example, with all the officers both of justice and war who serve under him, the whole army and navy, are unproductive labourers. They are the servants of the public, and are maintained by a part of the annual produce of the industry of other people. Their service, how honourable, how useful, or how necessary

---

*Some French authors of great learning and ingenuity have used those words in a different sense. In the last chapter of the fourth book, I shall endeavour to show that their sense is an improper one [Smith's note].

soever, produces nothing for which an equal quantity of service can afterwards be procured. The protection, security, and defence of the commonwealth, the effect of their labour this year, will not purchase its protection, security, and defence, for the year to come. In the same class must be ranked, some both of the gravest and most important, and some of the most frivolous professions: churchmen, lawyers, physicians, men of letters of all kinds; players, buffoons, musicians, opera singers, opera dancers, etc. The labour of the meanest of these has a certain value, regulated by the very same principles which regulate that of every sort of labour; and that of the noblest and most useful, produces nothing which could afterwards purchase or procure an equal quantity of labour. Like the declamation of the actor, the harangue of the orator, or the tune of the musician, the work of all of them perishes in the very instant of its production.

Both productive and unproductive labourers, and those who do not labour at all, are all equally maintained by the annual produce of the land and labour of the country. This produce, how great soever, can never be infinite, but must have certain limits. According, therefore, as a smaller or greater proportion of it is in any one year employed in maintaining unproductive hands, the more in the one case and the less in the other will remain for the productive, and the next year's produce will be greater or smaller accordingly; the whole annual produce, if we except the spontaneous productions of the earth, being the effect of productive labour.

The proportion of the produce employed in maintaining productive hands determines the next year's produce.

Though the whole annual produce of the land and labour of every country, is, no doubt, ultimately destined for supplying the consumption of its inhabitants, and for procuring a revenue to them; yet when it first comes either from the ground, or from the hands of the productive labourers, it naturally divides itself into two parts. One of them, and frequently the largest, is, in the first place, destined for replacing a capital, or for renewing the provisions, materials, and finished work, which had been withdrawn from a capital; the other for constituting a revenue either to the owner of this capital, as the profit of his stock; or to some other person, as the rent of his land. Thus, of the produce of land, one part replaces the capital of the farmer; the other pays his profit and the rent of the landlord; and thus constitutes a revenue both to the owner of this capital, as the profits of his stock; and to some other person, as the rent of his land. Of the produce of a great manufactory, in the same manner, one part, and that always the largest, replaces the capital of the undertaker of the work; the other pays his profit, and thus constitutes a revenue to the owner of this capital.

Part of the produce replaces capital, part constitutes profit and rent.

That part of the annual produce of the land and labour of any country which replaces a capital, never

That which replaces capital employs none

is immediately employed to maintain any but pro-   but productive hands,
ductive hands. It pays the wages of productive labour   while unproductive
                                                           hands and those who do
only. That which is immediately destined for con-   not labour are supported
stituting a revenue either as profit or as rent, may   by revenue.
maintain indifferently either productive or unproductive hands.

Whatever part of his stock a man employs as a capital, he always
expects is to be replaced to him with a profit. He employs it, therefore,
in maintaining productive hands only; and after having served in the
function of a capital to him, it constitutes a revenue to them. Whenever
he employs any part of it in maintaining unproductive hands of any
kind, that part is, from that moment, withdrawn from his capital, and
placed in his stock reserved for immediate consumption.

Unproductive labourers, and those who do not labour at all, are all
maintained by revenue; either, first, by that part of the annual produce
which is originally destined for constituting a revenue to some particular
persons, either as the rent of land or as the profits of stock; or, secondly,
by that part which, though originally destined for replacing a capital and
for maintaining productive labourers only, yet when it comes into their
hands, whatever part of it is over and above their necessary subsistence,
may be employed in maintaining indifferently either productive or
unproductive hands. Thus, not only the great landlord or the rich merchant, but even the common workman, if his wages are considerable,
may maintain a menial servant; or he may sometimes go to a play or a
puppet-show, and so contribute his share towards maintaining one set
of unproductive labourers; or he may pay some taxes, and thus help to
maintain another set, more honourable and useful, indeed, but equally
unproductive.

No part of the annual produce, however, which had been originally
destined to replace a capital, is ever directed towards maintaining unproductive hands, till after it has put into motion its full complement of
productive labour, or all that it could put into motion in the way in
which it was employed. The workman must have earned his wages by
work done, before he can employ any part of them in this manner. That
part too is generally but a small one. It is his spare revenue only, of
which productive labourers have seldom a great deal. They generally
have some, however; and in the payment of taxes the greatness of their
number may compensate, in some measure, the smallness of their contribution. The rent of land and the profits of stock are everywhere, therefore, the principal sources from which unproductive hands derive their
subsistence. These are the two sorts of revenue of which the owners have
generally most to spare. They might both maintain indifferently either
productive or unproductive hands. They seem, however, to have some
predilection for the latter. The expence of a great lord feeds generally
more idle than industrious people. The rich merchant, though with his
capital he maintains industrious people only, yet by his expence, that is,

by the employment of his revenue, he feeds commonly the very same sort as the great lord.

The proportion, therefore, between the productive and unproductive hands, depends very much in every country upon the proportion between that part of the annual produce, which, as soon as it comes either from the ground or from the hands of the productive labourers, is destined for replacing a capital, and that which is destined for constituting a revenue, either as rent, or as profit. This proportion is very different in rich from what it is in poor countries.

So the proportion of productive hands depends on the proportion between profit with rent and the part of produce which replaces capital.

Thus, at present, in the opulent countries of Europe, a very large, frequently the largest portion of the produce of the land, is destined for replacing the capital of the rich and independent farmer; the other for paying his profits, and the rent of the landlord. But anciently, during the prevalency of the feudal government, a very small portion of the produce was sufficient to replace the capital employed in cultivation. It consisted commonly in a few wretched cattle, maintained altogether by the spontaneous produce of uncultivated land, and which might, therefore, be considered as a part of that spontaneous produce. It generally too belonged to the landlord, and was by him advanced to the occupiers of the land. All the rest of the produce properly belonged to him too, either as rent for his land, or as profit upon this paltry capital. The occupiers of land were generally bondmen, whose persons and effects were equally his property. Those who were not bondmen were tenants at will, and though the rent which they paid was often nominally little more than a quit-rent, it really amounted to the whole produce of the land. Their lord could at all times command their labour in peace, and their service in war. Though they lived at a distance from his house, they were equally dependent upon him as his retainers who lived in it. But the whole produce of the land undoubtedly belongs to him, who can dispose of the labour and service of all those whom it maintains. In the present state of Europe, the share of the landlord seldom exceeds a third, sometimes not a fourth part of the whole produce of the land. The rent of land, however, in all the improved parts of the country, has been tripled and quadrupled since those ancient times; and this third or fourth part of the annual produce is, it seems, three or four times greater than the whole had been before. In the progress of improvement, rent, though it increases in proportion to the extent, diminishes in proportion to the produce of the land. . . .

Rent anciently formed a larger proportion of the produce of agriculture than now.

The proportion between capital and revenue, therefore, seems everywhere to regulate the proportion between industry and idleness. Wherever capital predominates, industry prevails: wherever

Increase or diminution of the capital of a country consequently increases or diminishes its annual produce.

revenue, idleness. Every increase or diminution of capital, therefore, naturally tends to increase or diminish the real quantity of industry, the number of productive hands, and consequently the exchangeable value of the annual produce of the land and labour of the country, the real wealth and revenue of all its inhabitants.

Capitals are increased by parsimony, and dimin-   Capitals are increased
ished by prodigality and misconduct.   by parsimony or saving.

Whatever a person saves from his revenue he adds to his capital, and either employs it himself in maintaining an additional number of productive hands, or enables some other person to do so, by lending it to him for an interest, that is, for a share of the profits. As the capital of an individual can be increased only by what he saves from his annual revenue or his annual gains, so the capital of a society, which is the same with that of all the individuals who compose it, can be increased only in the same manner.

Parsimony, and not industry, is the immediate cause of the increase of capital. Industry, indeed, provides the subject which parsimony accumulates. But whatever industry might acquire, if parsimony did not save and store up, the capital would never be the greater.

Parsimony, by increasing the fund which is destined for the maintenance of productive hands, tends to increase the number of those hands whose labour adds to the value of the subject upon which it is bestowed. It tends therefore to increase the exchangeable value of the annual produce of the land and labour of the country. It puts into motion an additional quantity of industry, which gives an additional value to the annual produce.

What is annually saved is as regularly consumed   What is saved is con-
as what is annually spent, and nearly in the same   sumed by productive
time too; but it is consumed by a different set of   hands.
people. That portion of his revenue which a rich man annually spends, is in most cases consumed by idle guests, and menial servants, who leave nothing behind them in return for their consumption. That portion which he annually saves, as for the sake of the profit it is immediately employed as a capital, is consumed in the same manner, and nearly in the same time too, but by a different set of people, by labourers, manufacturers, and artificers, who reproduce with a profit the value of their annual consumption. His revenue, we shall suppose, is paid him in money. Had he spent the whole, the food, clothing, and lodging which the whole could have purchased, would have been distributed among the former set of people. By saving a part of it, as that part is for the sake of the profit immediately employed as a capital either by himself or by some other person, the food, clothing, and lodging, which may be purchased with it, are necessarily reserved for the latter. The consumption is the same, but the consumers are different.

By what a frugal man annually saves, he not only   The frugal man estab-
affords maintenance to an additional number of   lishes a perpetual fund

productive hands, for that or the ensuing year, but, *for the employment of*
like the founder of a public workhouse, he estab- *productive hands.*
lishes as it were a perpetual fund for the maintenance of an equal number in all times to come. The perpetual allotment and destination of
this fund, indeed, is not always guarded by any positive law, by any
trust-right or deed of mortmain. It is always guarded, however, by
a very powerful principle, the plain and evident interest of every individual to whom any share of it shall ever belong. No part of it can ever
afterwards be employed to maintain any but productive hands, without
an evident loss to the person who thus perverts it from its proper destination.

The prodigal perverts it in this manner. By not *The prodigal perverts*
confining his expence within his income, he *such funds to other*
uses.
encroaches upon his capital. Like him who perverts
the revenues of some pious foundation to profane purposes, he pays the
wages of idleness with those funds which the frugality of his forefathers
had, as it were, consecrated to the maintenance of industry. By diminishing the funds destined for the employment of productive labour, he
necessarily diminishes, so far as it depends upon him, the quantity of
that labour which adds a value to the subject upon which it is bestowed,
and, consequently, the value of the annual produce of the land and
labour of the whole country, the real wealth and revenue of its inhabitants. If the prodigality of some was not compensated by the frugality of
others, the conduct of every prodigal, by feeding the idle with the bread
of the industrious, tends not only to beggar himself, but to impoverish
his country.

Though the expence of the prodigal should be *Whether he spends on*
altogether in homemade, and no part of it in foreign *home or foreign com-*
modities makes no dif-
commodities, its effect upon the productive funds *ference.*
of the society would still be the same. Every year
there would still be a certain quantity of food and clothing, which ought
to have maintained productive, employed in maintaining unproductive
hands. Every year, therefore, there would still be some diminution in
what would otherwise have been the value of the annual produce of the
land and labour of the country.

This expence, it may be said indeed, not being in *If he had not spent there*
foreign goods, and not occasioning any exportation *would have been just as*
much money in the
of gold and silver, the same quantity of money would *country and the goods*
remain in the country as before. But if the quantity *produced by productive*
hands as well.
of food and clothing, which were thus consumed by
unproductive, had been distributed among productive hands, they would
have reproduced, together with a profit, the full value of their consumption. The same quantity of money would in this case equally have
remained in the country, and there would besides have been a reproduction of an equal value of consumable goods. There would have been
two values instead of one. . . .

Whatever, therefore, we may imagine the real wealth and revenue of a country to consist in, whether in the value of the annual produce of its land and labour, as plain reason seems to dictate; or in the quantity of the precious metals which circulate within it, as vulgar prejudices suppose; in either view of the matter, every prodigal appears to be a public enemy, and every frugal man a public benefactor.

So even if the real wealth of a country consisted of its money, the prodigal would be a public enemy.

The effects of misconduct are often the same as those of prodigality. Every injudicious and unsuccessful project in agriculture, mines, fisheries, trade, or manufactures, tends in the same manner to diminish the funds destined for the maintenance of productive labour. In every such project, though the capital is consumed by productive hands only, yet, as by the injudicious manner in which they are employed, they do not reproduce the full value of their consumption, there must always be some diminution in what would otherwise have been the productive funds of the society.

Injudicious employment of capital has the same effect as prodigality.

It can seldom happen, indeed, that the circumstances of a great nation can be much affected either by the prodigality or misconduct of individuals; the profusion or imprudence of some being always more than compensated by the frugality and good conduct of others.

Frugality and prudence predominate.

With regard to profusion, the principle, which prompts to expence, is the passion for present enjoyment; which, though sometimes violent and very difficult to be restrained, is in general only momentary and occasional. But the principle which prompts to save is the desire of bettering our condition, a desire which, though generally calm and dispassionate, comes with us from the womb, and never leaves us till we go into the grave. In the whole interval which separates those two moments, there is scarce perhaps a single instant in which any man is so perfectly and completely satisfied with his situation, as to be without any wish of alteration or improvement, of any kind. An augmentation of fortune is the means by which the greater part of men propose and wish to better their condition. It is the means the most vulgar and the most obvious; and the most likely way of augmenting their fortune, is to save and accumulate some part of what they acquire, either regularly and annually, or upon some extraordinary occasions. Though the principle of expence, therefore, prevails in almost all men upon some occasions, and in some men upon almost all occasions, yet in the greater part of men, taking the whole course of their life at an average, the principle of frugality seems not only to predominate, but to predominate very greatly.

Prodigality is more intermittent than the desire to better our condition.

With regard to misconduct, the number of prudent and successful undertakings is everywhere much greater than that of injudicious and unsuccessful

Imprudent undertakings are small in number compared to prudent ones.

ones. After all our complaints of the frequency of bankruptcies, the unhappy men who fall into this misfortune make but a very small part of the whole number engaged in trade, and all other sorts of business; not much more perhaps than one in a thousand. Bankruptcy is perhaps the greatest and most humiliating calamity which can befall an innocent man. The greater part of men, therefore, are sufficiently careful to avoid it. Some, indeed, do not avoid it; as some do not avoid the gallows.

Great nations are never impoverished by private, though they sometimes are by public prodigality and misconduct. The whole, or almost the whole public revenue, is in most countries employed in maintaining unproductive hands. Such are the people who compose a numerous and splendid court, a great ecclesiastical establishment, great fleets and armies, who in time of peace produce nothing, and in time of war acquire nothing which can compensate the expence of maintaining them, even while the war lasts. Such people, as they themselves produce nothing, are all maintained by the produce of other men's labour. When multiplied, therefore, to an unnecessary number, they may in a particular year consume so great a share of this produce, as not to leave a sufficiency for maintaining the productive labourers, who should reproduce it next year. The next year's produce, therefore, will be less than that of the foregoing, and if the same disorder should continue, that of the third year will be still less than that of the second. Those unproductive hands, who should be maintained by a part only of the spare revenue of the people, may consume so great a share of their whole revenue, and thereby oblige so great a number to encroach upon their capitals, upon the funds destined for the maintenance of productive labour, that all the frugality and good conduct of individuals may not be able to compensate the waste and degradation of produce occasioned by this violent and forced encroachment.

Public prodigality and imprudence are more to be feared than private, but are counteracted by private frugality and prudence.

This frugality and good conduct, however, is upon most occasions, it appears from experience, sufficient to compensate, not only the private prodigality and misconduct of individuals, but the public extravagance of government. The uniform, constant, and uninterrupted effort of every man to better his condition, the principle from which public and national, as well as private opulence is originally derived, is frequently powerful enough to maintain the natural progress of things toward improvement, in spite both of the extravagance of government, and of the greatest errors of administration. Like the unknown principle of animal life, it frequently restores health and vigour to the constitution, in spite, not only of the disease, but of the absurd prescriptions of the doctor.

The annual produce of the land and labour of any nation can be increased in its value by no other means, but by increasing either the number of its productive labourers, or the productive powers of those labourers who had before been employed. The number of its productive labourers, it

To increase the produce of a nation an increase of capital is necessary.

is evident, can never be much increased, but in consequence of an increase of capital, or of the funds destined for maintaining them. The productive powers of the same number of labourers cannot be increased, but in consequence either of some addition and improvement to those machines and instruments which facilitate and abridge labour; or of a more proper division and distribution of employment. In either case an additional capital is almost always required. It is by means of an additional capital only that the undertaker of any work can either provide his workmen with better machinery, or make a more proper distribution of employment among them. When the work to be done consists of a number of parts, to keep every man constantly employed in one way, requires a much greater capital than where every man is occasionally employed in every different part of the work.

When we compare, therefore, the state of a nation at two different periods, and find, that the annual produce of its land and labour is evidently greater at the latter than at the former, that its lands are better cultivated, its manufactures more numerous and more flourishing, and its trade more extensive, we may be assured that its capital must have increased during the interval between those two periods, and that more must have been added to it by the good conduct of some, than had been taken from it either by the private misconduct of others, or by the public extravagance of government. But we shall find this to have been the case of almost all nations, in all tolerably quiet and peaceable times, even of those who have not enjoyed the most prudent and parsimonious governments. To form a right judgment of it, indeed, we must compare the state of the country at periods somewhat distant from one another. The progress is frequently so gradual, that, at near periods, the improvement is not only not sensible, but from the declension either of certain branches of industry, or of certain districts of the country, things which sometimes happen though the country in general be in great prosperity, there frequently arises a suspicion, that the riches and industry of the whole are decaying. . . .

If, therefore the produce has increased, we may be sure the capital has increased.

This has been the case of almost all nations in peaceable times.

But though the profusion of government must, undoubtedly, have retarded the natural progress of England towards wealth and improvement, it has not been able to stop it. The annual produce of its land and labour is, undoubtedly, much greater at present than it was either at the restoration or at the revolution. The capital, therefore, annually employed in cultivating this land, and in maintaining this labour, must likewise be much greater. In the midst of all the exactions of government, this capital has been silently and gradually accumulated by the private frugality and good conduct of individuals, by their universal, continual, and uninterrupted effort to better their own condition. It is this effort, protected by law and allowed by liberty to exert itself in the

Private frugality and prudence have silently counteracted these circumstances.

manner that is most advantageous, which has maintained the progress of England towards opulence and improvement in almost all former times, and which, it is to be hoped, will do so in all future times. England, however, as it has never been blessed with a very parsimonious government, so parsimony has at no time been the characteristical virtue of its inhabitants. It is the highest impertinence and presumption, therefore, in kings and ministers, to pretend to watch over the economy of private people, and to restrain their expence either by sumptuary laws, or by prohibiting the importation of foreign luxuries. They are themselves always, and without any exception, the greatest spendthrifts in the society. Let them look well after their own expence, and they may safely trust private people with theirs. If their own extravagance does not ruin the state, that of their subjects never will. . . .

[Chapter 4, "Of Stock Lent at Interest," has been omitted. The argument merely supports material already presented in the first three chapters of Book II. Smith's point in the chapter is that lending stock (capital) is no different than lending money. The reason is clear in the first two sentences: "The stock which is lent at interest is always considered as a capital by the lender. He expects that in due time the borrower is to pay him a certain annual rent for the use of it" p. 350, Glasgow ed.].

CHAPTER V

Of the different Employment of Capitals

Though all capitals are destined for the maintenance of productive labour only, yet the quantity of that labour, which equal capitals are capable of putting into motion, varies extremely according to the diversity of their employment; as does likewise the value which that employment adds to the annual produce of the land and labour of the country.

The quantity of labour put in motion and the value added to the annual produce by capitals vary with their employment.

There are four different ways of employing capital, all of which are necessary:

A capital may be employed in four different ways: either, first, in procuring the rude produce annually required for the use and consumption of the society; or, secondly, in manufacturing and preparing that rude produce for immediate use and consumption; or, thirdly, in transporting either the rude or manufactured produce from the places where they abound to those where they are wanted; or, lastly, in dividing particular portions of either into such small parcels as suit the occasional demands of those who want them. In the first way are employed the capitals of all those who undertake the improvement or cultivation of lands, mines, or fisheries; in the second, those of all master manufacturers; in the third, those of all wholesale merchants; and in the fourth, those of all retailers. It is difficult to conceive that a capital should be employed in any way which may not be classed under some one or other of those four.

Each of those four methods of employing a capital is essentially necessary either to the existence or extension of the other three, or to the general convenience of the society.

Unless a capital was employed in furnishing rude produce to a certain degree of abundance, neither manufactures nor trade of any kind could exist. (1) procuring rude produce,

Unless a capital was employed in manufacturing that part of the rude produce which requires a good deal of preparation before it can be fit for use and consumption, it either would never be produced, because there could be no demand for it; or if it was produced spontaneously, it would be of no value in exchange, and could add nothing to the wealth of the society. (2) manufacturing,

Unless a capital was employed in transporting, either the rude or manufactured produce, from the places where it abounds to those where it is wanted, no more of either could be produced than was necessary for the consumption of the neighbourhood. The capital of the merchant exchanges the surplus produce of one place for that of another, and thus encourages the industry and increases the enjoyments of both. (3) transportation,

Unless a capital was employed in breaking and dividing certain portions either of the rude or manufactured produce, into such small parcels as suit the occasional demands of those who want them, every man would be obliged to purchase a greater quantity of the goods he wanted, than his immediate occasions required. If there was no such trade as a butcher, for example, every man would be obliged to purchase a whole ox or a whole sheep at a time. This would generally be inconvenient to the rich, and much more so to the poor. If a poor workman was obliged to purchase a month's or six months provisions at a time, a great part of the stock which he employs as a capital in the instruments of his trade, or in the furniture of his shop, and which yields him a revenue, he would be forced to place in that part of his stock which is reserved for immediate consumption, and which yields him no revenue. Nothing can be more convenient for such a person than to be able to purchase his subsistence from day to day, or even from hour to hour as he wants it. He is thereby enabled to employ almost his whole stock as a capital. He is thus enabled to furnish work to a greater value, and the profit, which he makes by it in this way, much more than compensates the additional price which the profit of the retailer imposes upon the goods. and (4) distribution.

The prejudices of some political writers against shopkeepers and tradesmen are altogether without foundation. So far is it from being necessary, either to tax them, or to restrict their numbers, that they can never be multiplied so as to hurt the public, though they may so as to hurt one another. The quantity of grocery goods, for example, which can be sold in a particular town, is limited by the demand of that town and its neighbourhood. The capital, therefore, which can be employed in the grocery trade cannot exceed what is sufficient to purchase that quantity. If this capital is divided between two different grocers, their competition will tend to make both of them sell cheaper, than if it were in the hands of one only; and if it were divided among twenty, their competition would be just so much the greater, and the chance of their combining together, in order to raise the price, just so much the less. Their competition might perhaps ruin some of themselves; but to take care of this is the business of the parties concerned, and it may safely be trusted to their discretion. It can never hurt either the consumer, or the producer; on the contrary, it must tend to make the retailers both sell cheaper and buy dearer, than if the whole trade was monopolized by one or two persons. Some of them, perhaps, may sometimes decoy a weak customer to buy what he has no occasion for. This evil, however, is of too little importance to deserve the public attention, nor would it necessarily be prevented by restricting their numbers It is not the multitude of alehouses, to give the most suspicious example, that occasions a general disposition to drunkenness among the common people; but that disposition arising from other causes necessarily gives employment to a multitude of alehouses.

The persons whose capitals are employed in any of those four ways are themselves productive labourers. Their labour, when properly directed, fixes and realizes itself in the subject or vendible commodity upon which it is bestowed, and generally adds to its price the value at least of their own maintenance and consumption. The profits of the farmer, of the manufacturer, of the merchant, and retailer, are all drawn from the price of the goods which the two first produce, and the two last buy and sell. Equal capitals, however, employed in each of those four different ways, will immediately put into motion very different quantities of productive labour, and augment too in very different porportions the value of the annual produce of the land and labour of the society to which they belong. . . .

The employers of such capitals are productive labourers.

No equal capital puts into motion a greater quantity of productive labour than that of the farmer. Not only his labouring servants, but his labouring cattle, are productive labourers. In agriculture too nature labours along with man; and though her labour costs no expence, its produce has its value, as well as that of the most expensive workmen. The most important operations of agriculture seem intended, not so much to increase, though they do that too, as to direct the fertility of nature towards the production of the plants most profitable to man. A field overgrown with briars and brambles may fre-

The capital of the farmer employs his servants and his cattle, and adds a much greater value to the annual produce than other capital.

quently produce as great a quantity of vegetables as the best cultivated vineyard or corn field. Planting and tillage frequently regulate more than they animate the active fertility of nature; and after all their labour, a great part of the work always remains to be done by her.

The labourers and labouring cattle, therefore, employed in agriculture, not only occasion, like the workmen in manufactures, the reproduction of a value equal to their own consumption, or to the capital which employs them, together with its owner's profits; but of a much greater value. Over and above the capital of the farmer and all its profits, they regularly occasion the reproduction of the rent of the landlord. This rent may be considered as the produce of those powers of nature, the use of which the landlord lends to the farmer. It is greater or smaller according to the supposed extent of those powers, or in other words, according to the supposed natural or improved fertility of the land. It is the work of nature which remains after deducting or compensating every thing which can be regarded as the work of man. It is seldom less than a fourth, and frequently more than a third of the whole produce. No equal quantity of productive labour employed in manufactures can ever occasion so great a reproduction. In them nature does nothing; man does all; and the reproduction must always be in proportion to the strength of the agents that occasion it. The capital employed in agriculture, therefore, not only puts into motion a greater quantity of productive labour than any equal capital employed in manufactures, but in proportion too to the quantity of productive labour which it employs, it adds a much greater value to the annual produce of the land and labour of the country, to the real wealth and revenue of its inhabitants. Of all the ways in which a capital can be employed, it is by far the most advantageous to the society. . . .

. . . After agriculture, the capital employed in manufactures puts into motion the greatest quantity of productive labour, and adds the greatest value to the annual produce. That which is employed in the trade of exportation, has the least effect of any of the three.

The larger the proportion employed in agriculture, the larger will be the annual produce.

The quickest way to make the capital sufficient for all these purposes is to begin with the most profitable.

The country, indeed, which has not capital sufficient for all those three purposes, has not arrived at that degree of opulence for which it seems naturally destined. To attempt, however, prematurely and with an insufficient capital, to do all the three, is certainly not the shortest way for a society, no more than it would be for an individual, to acquire a sufficient one. The capital of all the individuals of a nation, has its limits in the same manner as that of a single individual, and is capable of executing only certain purposes. The capital of all the individuals of a nation is increased in the same manner as that of a single individual, by their continually accumulating and adding to it whatever they save out of their revenue. It is likely to increase the fastest, therefore, when it is employed in the way that affords the greatest revenue to all the inhabitants of the country, as they will thus be enabled to make the greatest savings. But the revenue of all the inhabitants of the country is necessarily in proportion to the value of the annual produce of their land and labour.

It has been the principal cause of the rapid progress of our American colonies towards wealth and
greatness, that almost their whole capitals have
hitherto been employed in agriculture. They have *That they have done so is the principal cause of the progress of the American colonies.*
no manufactures, those household and coarser manufactures excepted which necessarily accompany the progress of agriculture, and which are the work of the women and children in every private family. The greater part both of the exportation and coasting trade of America, is carried on by the capitals of merchants who reside in Great Britain. Even the stores and warehouses from which goods are retailed in some provinces, particularly in Virginia and Maryland, belong many of them to merchants who reside in the mother country, and afford one of the few instances of the retail trade of a society being carried on by the capitals of those who are not resident members of it. Were the Americans, either by combination or by any other sort of violence, to stop the importation of European manufactures, and, by thus giving a monopoly to such of their own countrymen as could manufacture the like goods, divert any considerable part of their capital into this employment, they would retard instead of accelerating the further increase in the value of their annual produce, and would obstruct instead of promoting the progress of their country towards real wealth and greatness. This would be still more the case, were they to attempt, in the same manner, to monopolize to themselves their whole exportation trade. . . .

When the produce of any particular branch of
industry exceeds what the demand of the country
requires, the surplus must be sent abroad, and
exchanged for something for which there is a demand *The surplus of the produce of particular branches of industry must be sent abroad.*
at home. Without such exportation, a part of the productive labour of the country must cease, and the value of its annual produce diminish. The land and labour of Great Britain produce generally more corn, woollens, and hardware, than the demand of the home market requires. The surplus part of them, therefore, must be sent abroad, and exchanged for something for which there is a demand at home. It is only by means of such exportation, that this surplus can acquire a value sufficient to compensate the labour and expence of producing it. The neighbourhood of the seacoast, and the banks of all navigable rivers, are advantageous situations for industry, only because they facilitate the exportation and exchange of such surplus produce for something else which is more in demand there. . . .

BOOK III

OF THE DIFFERENT PROGRESS OF OPULENCE IN DIFFERENT NATIONS

CHAPTER I

Of the natural Progress of Opulence

The great commerce of every civilised society is
that carried on between the inhabitants of the town
and those of the country. It consists in the exchange
of rude for manufactured produce, either immedi-

The great commerce is that between town and country, which is obviously advantageous to both.

ately, or by the intervention of money, or of some sort of paper which
represents money. The country supplies the town with the means of
subsistence, and the materials of manufacture. The town repays this
supply by sending back a part of the manufactured produce to the inhabitants of the country. The town, in which there neither is nor can be
any reproduction of substances, may very properly be said to gain its
whole wealth and subsistence from the country. We must not, however,
upon this account, imagine that the gain of the town is the loss of the
country. The gains of both are mutual and reciprocal, and the division
of labour is in this, as in all other cases, advantageous to all the different persons employed in the various occupations into which it is subdivided.

The inhabitants of the country purchase of the town a greater quantity
of manufactured goods, with the produce of a much smaller quantity of
their own labour, than they must have employed had they attempted to
prepare them themselves. The town affords a market for the surplus
produce of the country, or what is over and above the maintenance of
the cultivators, and it is there that the inhabitants of the country exchange
it for something else which is in demand among them. The greater the
number and revenue of the inhabitants of the town, the more extensive
is the market which it affords to those of the country; and the more
extensive that market, it is always the more advantageous to a great number. The corn which grows within a mile of the town, sells there for the
same price with that which comes from twenty miles distance. But the
price of the latter must generally, not only pay the expence of raising
and bringing it to market, but afford too the ordinary profits of agriculture to the farmer. The proprietors and cultivators of the country, therefore, which lies in the neighbourhood of the town, over and above the
ordinary profits of agriculture, gain, in the price of what they sell, the
whole value of the carriage of the like produce that is brought from more
distant parts, and they save, besides, the whole value of this carriage in

the price of what they buy. Compare the cultivation of the lands in the
neighbourhood of any considerable town, with that of those which lie at
some distance from it, and you will easily satisfy yourself how much the
country is benefited by the commerce of the town. Among all the absurd
speculations that have been propagated concerning the balance of trade,
it has never pretended that either the country loses by its commerce with
the town, or the town by that with the country which maintains it.

As subsistence is, in the nature of things, prior to
convenience and luxury, so the industry which procures the former, must necessarily be prior to that
which ministers to the latter. The cultivation and
improvement of the country, therefore, which affords
subsistence, must, necessarily, be prior to the increase

The cultivation of the country must be prior to the increase of the town, though the town may sometimes be distant from the country from which it derives its subsistence.

of the town, which furnishes only the means of convenience and luxury.
It is the surplus produce of the country only, or what is over and above
the maintenance of the cultivators, that constitutes the subsistence of
the town, which can therefore increase only with the increase of this
surplus produce. The town, indeed, may not always derive its whole
subsistence from the country in its neighbourhood, or even from the
territory to which it belongs, but from very distant countries; and this,
though it forms no exception from the general rule, has occasioned considerable variations in the progress of opulence in different ages and
nations.

That order of things which necessity imposes in
general, though not in every particular country, is,
in every particular country, promoted by the natural
inclinations of man. If human institutions had never

This order of things is favoured by the natural preference of man for agriculture.

thwarted those natural inclinations, the towns could nowhere have
increased beyond what the improvement and cultivation of the territory
in which they were situated could support; till such time, at least, as the
whole of that territory was completely cultivated and improved. Upon
equal, or nearly equal profits, most men will choose to employ their
capitals rather in the improvement and cultivation of land, than either
in manufactures or in foreign trade. The man who employs his capital
in land, has it more under his view and command, and his fortune is
much less liable to accidents than that of the trader, who is obliged
frequently to commit it, not only to the winds and the waves, but to the
more uncertain elements of human folly and injustice, by giving great
credits in distant countries to men, with whose character and situation
he can seldom be thoroughly acquainted. The capital of the landlord,
on the contrary, which is fixed in the improvement of his land, seems
to be as well secured as the nature of human affairs can admit of. The
beauty of the country besides, the pleasures of a country life, the tran-
quility of mind which it promises, and wherever the injustice of human
laws does not disturb it, the independence which it really affords, have

charms that more or less attract every body; and as to cultivate the ground was the original destination of man, so in every stage of his existence he seems to retain a predilection for this primitive employment.

Without the assistance of some artificers, indeed, the cultivation of land cannot be carried on, but with great inconvenience and continual interruption. Smiths, carpenters, wheelwrights, and ploughwrights, masons, and bricklayers, tanners, shoemakers, and tailors, are people, whose service *Cultivators require the assistance of artificers, who settle together and form a village, and their employment augments with the improvement of the country.* the farmer has frequent occasion for. Such artificers too stand, occasionally, in need of the assistance of one another; and as their residence is not, like that of the farmer, necessarily tied down to a precise spot, they naturally settle in the neighbourhood of one another, and thus form a small town or village. The butcher, the brewer, and the baker, soon join them, together with many other artificers and retailers, necessary or useful for supplying their occasional wants, and who contribute still further to augment the town.

The inhabitants of the town and those of the country are mutually the servants of one another. The town is a continual fair or market, to which the inhabitants of the country resort, in order to exchange their rude for manufactured produce. It is this commerce which supplies the inhabitants of the town both with the materials of their work, and the means of their subsistence. The quantity of the finished work which they sell to the inhabitants of the country, necessarily regulates the quantity of the materials and provisions which they buy. Neither their employment nor subsistence, therefore, can augment, but in proportion to the augmentation of the demand from the country for finished work; and this demand can augment only in proportion to the extension of improvement and cultivation. Had human institutions, therefore, never disturbed the natural course of things, the progressive wealth and increase of the towns would, in every political society, be consequential, and in proportion to the improvement and cultivation of the territory or country.

In our North American colonies, where uncultivated land is still to be had upon easy terms, no manufactures for distant sale have ever yet been established in any of their towns. When an artificer has acquired a little more stock than is necessary for carrying on his own business in supplying the neighbouring country, he does not, in North America, attempt to establish with it a manufacture for more distant sale, but employs it in the purchase and improvement of uncultivated land. From artificer he becomes planter, and neither the large wages nor the easy subsistence which that country affords to artificers, can bribe him rather to work for other people than for himself. He feels that an artificer is the *In the American colonies an artificer who has acquired sufficient stock becomes a planter instead of manufacturing for distant sale, as in countries where no uncultivated land can be procured.*

servant of his customers, from whom he derives his subsistence; but that a planter who cultivates his own land, and derives his necessary subsistence from the labour of his own family, is really a master, and independent of all the world.

In countries, on the contrary, where there is either no uncultivated land, or none that can be had upon easy terms, every artificer who has acquired more stock than he can employ in the occasional jobs of the neighbourhood, endeavours to prepare work for more distant sale. The smith erects some sort of iron, the weaver some sort of linen or woollen manufactory. Those different manufactures come, in process of time, to be gradually subdivided, and thereby improved and refined in a great variety of ways, which may easily be conceived, and which it is therefore unnecessary to explain any further.

In seeking for employment to a capital, manufactures are, upon equal or nearly equal profits, naturally preferred to foreign commerce, for the same reason that agriculture is naturally preferred to manufactures. As the capital of the landlord or farmer is more secure than that of the manufacturer, so the capital of the manufacturer, being at all times more within his view and command, is more secure than that of the foreign merchant. In every period, indeed, of every society, the surplus part both of the rude and manufactured produce, or that for which there is no demand at home, must be sent abroad in order to be exchanged for something for which there is some demand at home. But whether the capital, which carries this surplus produce abroad, be a foreign or a domestic one, is of very little importance. If the society has not acquired sufficient capital both to cultivate all its lands, and to manufacture in the completest manner the whole of its rude produce, there is even a considerable advantage that that rude produce should be exported by a foreign capital, in order that the whole stock of the society may be employed in more useful purposes. The wealth of ancient Egypt, that of China and Indostan, sufficiently demonstrate that a nation may attain a very high degree of opulence, though the greater part of its exportation trade be carried on by foreigners. The progress of our North American and West Indian colonies would have been much less rapid, had no capital but what belonged to themselves been employed in exporting their surplus produce.

Manufactures are naturally preferred to foreign commerce.

According to the natural course of things, therefore, the greater part of the capital of every growing society is, first, directed to agriculture, afterwards to manufactures, and last of all to foreign commerce.

So the natural course of things is first agriculture, then manufactures, and finally foreign commerce.

This order of things is so very natural, that in every society that had any territory, it has always, I believe, been in some degree observed. Some of their lands must have been cultivated before any considerable towns could be established, and some sort of coarse industry of the manufacturing kind must have been carried on in those towns, before they could well think of employing themselves in foreign commerce.

But though this natural order of things must have taken place in some degree in every such society, it has, in all the modern states of Europe, been, in many respects, entirely inverted. The foreign commerce of some of their cities has introduced all their finer manufactures, or such as were fit for distant sale; and manufactures and foreign commerce together, have given birth to the principal improvements of agriculture. The manners and customs which the nature of their original government introduced, and which remained after that government was greatly altered, necessarily forced them into this unnatural and retrograde order. . . .

But this order has been in many respects inverted.

[Chapter 2, "Of the Discouragement of Agriculture in the Ancient State of Europe After the Fall of the Roman Empire," and chapter 3, "Of the Rise and Progress of Cities and Towns After the Fall of the Roman Empire," have been excluded. Both chapters draw heavily on the *Lectures on Juris-prudence*, historically elaborating the breakdown of feudal order in a manner similar to many figures in the Scottish Enlightenment—especially David Hume, Adam Ferguson, and James Millar. Chapter 4 nicely illustrates Smith's contribution to this mode of stylized history, the predecessor of the "materialist" conception found in Marx.]

CHAPTER IV

How the Commerce of the Towns contributed to the Improvement of the Country

The increase and riches of commercial and man-ufacturing towns, contributed to the improvement and cultivation of the countries to which they belonged, in three different ways.

First, by affording a great and ready market for the rude produce of the country, they gave encour-agement to its cultivation and further improvement. This benefit was not even confined to the countries in which they were situated, but extended more or less to all those with which they had any dealings. To all of them they afforded a market for some part either of their rude or manufactured produce, and conse-quently gave some encouragement to the industry and improvement of all. Their own country, however, on account of its neighbourhood, nec-essarily derived the greatest benefit from this market. Its rude produce being charged with less carriage, the traders could pay the growers a better price for it, and yet afford it as cheap to the consumers as that of more distant countries.

The rise of towns bene-fited the country, because they afforded (1) a ready market for its produce, (2) because merchants bought land in the country and improved it, and (3) because order and good government were intro-duced.

Secondly, the wealth acquired by the inhabitants of cities was frequently employed in purchasing such lands as were to be sold, of which a great part would frequently be uncultivated. Merchants are commonly ambitious of becoming country gentlemen, and when they do, they are generally the best of all improvers. A merchant is accustomed to employ his money chiefly in profitable projects; whereas a mere country gentleman is accustomed to employ it chiefly in expence. The one often sees his money go from him and return to him again with a profit: the other, when once he parts with it, very seldom expects to see any more of it. Those different habits naturally affect their temper and disposition in every sort of business. A merchant is commonly a bold; a country gentleman, a timid undertaker. The one is not afraid to lay out at once a large capital upon the improvement of his land, when he has a probable prospect of raising the value of it in proportion to the expence. The other, if he has any capital, which is not always the case, seldom ventures to employ it in this manner. If he improves at all, it is commonly not with a capital, but with what he can save out of his annual revenue. Whoever has had the fortune to live in a mercantile town situated in an unimproved country, must have frequently observed how much more spirited the operations of merchants were in this way, than those of mere country gentlemen. The habits, besides, of order, economy, and attention, to which mercantile business naturally forms a merchant, render him much fitter to execute, with profit and success, any project of improvement.

Thirdly, and lastly, commerce and manufactures gradually introduced order and good government, and with them, the liberty and security of individuals, among the inhabitants of the country, who had before lived almost in a continual state of war with their neighbours, and of servile dependency upon their superiors. This, though it has been the least observed, is by far the most important of all their effects. Mr. Hume is the only writer who, so far as I know, has hitherto taken notice of it.

In a country which has neither foreign commerce, nor any of the finer manufactures, a great proprietor, having nothing for which he can exchange the greater part of the produce of his lands which is over and above the maintenance of the cultivators, *Before foreign commerce and fine manufactures are introduced great proprietors are surrounded by bands of retainers.* consumes the whole in rustic hospitality at home. If this surplus produce is sufficient to maintain a hundred or a thousand men, he can make use of it in no other way than by maintaining a hundred or a thousand men. He is at all times, therefore, surrounded with a multitude of retainers and dependants, who having no equivalent to give in return for their maintenance, but being fed entirely by his bounty, must obey him, for the same reason that soldiers must obey the prince who pays them. Therefore the extension of commerce and manufactures in Europe, the hospitality of the rich and the great, from the sovereign down to the smallest baron, exceeded every thing which in the present times we can easily form a notion of. . . .

Upon the authority which the great proprietors necessarily had in such a state of things over their tenants and retainers, was founded the power of the ancient barons.

The power of the ancient barons was founded on this.

They necessarily became the judges in peace, and the leaders in war, of all who dwelt upon their estates. They could maintain order and execute the law within their respective demesnes, because each of them could there turn the whole force of all the inhabitants against the injustice of any one. No other person had sufficient authority to do this. The king in particular had not. In those ancient times he was little more than the greatest proprietor in his dominions, to whom, for the sake of common defence against their common enemies, the other great proprietors paid certain respects. To have enforced payment of a small debt within the lands of a great proprietor, where all the inhabitants were armed and accustomed to stand by one another, would have cost the king, had he attempted it by his own authority, almost the same effort as to extinguish a civil war. He was, therefore, obliged to abandon the administration of justice through the greater part of the country, to those who were capable of administering it; and for the same reason to leave the command of the country militia to those whom that militia would obey.

It is a mistake to imagine that those territorial jurisdictions took their origin from the feudal law. Not only the highest jurisdictions both civil and

It was anterior to and independent of the feudal law.

criminal, but the power of levying troops, of coining money, and even that of making bylaws for the government of their own people, were all rights possessed allodially by the great proprietors of land several centuries before even the name of the feudal law was known in Europe. The authority and jurisdiction of the Saxon lords in England, appear to have been as great before the conquest, as that of any of the Norman lords after it. But the feudal law is not supposed to have become the common law of England till after the conquest. That the most extensive authority and jurisdictions were possessed by the great lords in France allodially, long before the feudal law was introduced into that country, is a matter of fact that admits of no doubt. That authority and those jurisdictions all necessarily flowed from the state of property and manners just now described. . . .

The introduction of the feudal law, so far from extending, may be regarded as an attempt to moderate the authority of the great allodial lords. It established a regular subordination, accompanied

It was moderated by the feudal law, and undermined by foreign commerce.

with a long train of services and duties, from the king down to the smallest proprietor. During the minority of the proprietor, the rent, together with the management of his lands, fell into the hands of his immediate superior, and, consequently, those of all great proprietors into the hands of the king, who was charged with the maintenance and education of the pupil, and who, from his authority as guardian, was supposed to have a right of disposing of him in marriage, provided it was in a manner not unsuitable to his rank. But though this institution necessarily tended to strengthen the authority of the king, and to weaken that of the great proprietors, it could not do either sufficiently for establishing order and good government among the inhabitants of the country; because it could not alter sufficiently that state of property and manners from which the disorders arose. The authority of government still continued to be, as before, too weak in the head and too strong in the inferior members, and the excessive strength of the inferior members was the cause of the weakness of the head. After the institution of feudal subordination, the king was as incapable of restraining the violence of the great lords as before. They still continued to make war according to their own discretion, almost continually upon one another, and very frequently upon the king; and the open country still continued to be a scene of violence, rapine, and disorder.

But what all the violence of the feudal institutions could never have effected, the silent and insensible operation of foreign commerce and manufactures gradually brought about. These gradually furnished the great proprietors with something for which they could exchange the whole surplus produce of their lands, and which they could consume themselves without sharing it either with tenants or retainers. All for ourselves, and nothing for other people, seems, in every age of the world, to have been the vile maxim of the masters of mankind. As soon, therefore, as they could find a method of consuming the whole value of their rents themselves, they had no disposition to share them with any other persons. For a pair of diamond buckles perhaps, or for something as frivolous and useless, they exchanged the maintenance, or what is the same thing, the price of the maintenance of a thousand men for a year, and with it the whole weight and authority which it could give them. The buckles, however, were to be all their own, and no other human creature was to have any share of them; whereas in the more ancient method of expence they must have shared with at least a thousand people. With the judges that were to determine the preference, this difference was perfectly decisive; and thus, for the gratification of the most childish, the meanest and the most sordid of all vanities, they gradually bartered their whole power and authority. . . .

When the great proprietors of land spend their rents in maintaining their tenants and retainers, each of them maintains entirely all his own tenants and all his own retainers. But when they spend them in maintaining tradesmen and artificers, they may, all of them taken together, perhaps, maintain as great, or, on account of the waste which attends rustic hospitality, a greater number of people than before. Each of them, however, taken singly, contributes often but a very small share to the maintenance of any individual of this greater number. Each tradesman or artificer derives his subsistence from the employment, not of one, but of a hundred or a thousand different customers. Though in some measure obliged to them all, therefore, he is not absolutely dependent upon any one of them.

The personal expence of the great proprietors having in this manner gradually increased, it was impossible that the number of their retainers should not as gradually diminish, till they were at last dismissed altogether. The same cause gradually led them to dismiss the unnecessary part of their tenants. Farms were enlarged, and the occupiers of land, notwithstanding the complaints of depopulation, reduced to the number necessary for cultivating it, according to the imperfect state of cultivation and improvement in those times. By the removal of the unnecessary mouths, and by exacting from the farmer the full value of the farm, a greater surplus, or what is the same thing, the price of a greater surplus, was obtained for the proprietor, which the merchants and manufacturers soon furnished him with a method of spending upon his own person in the same manner as he had done the rest. The same cause continuing to operate, he was desirous to raise his rents above what his lands, in the actual state of their improvement, could afford. His tenants could agree to this upon one condition only, that they should be secured in their possession, for such a term of years as might give them time to recover with profit whatever they should lay out in the further improvement of the land. The expensive vanity of the landlord made him willing to accept of this condition; and hence the origin of long leases. . . .

> To meet their new expences the great proprietors dismissed their retainers and their unnecessary tenants, and gave the remaining tenants long leases, thus making them independent.

The tenants having in this manner become independent, and the retainers being dismissed, the great proprietors were no longer capable of interrupting the regular execution of justice, or of disturbing the peace of the country. Having sold their birthright, not like Esau for a mess of pottage in time of hunger and necessity, but in the wantonness of plenty, for trinkets and baubles, fitter to be the playthings of children than the serious pursuits of men, they became as insignificant as any substantial burgher or tradesman in a city. A regular government was established in the country as well as in the city, nobody having sufficient power to disturb its operations in the one, any more than in the other. . . .

> The great proprietors thus became insignificant.

A revolution of the greatest importance to the public happiness, was in this manner brought about by two different orders of people, who had not the least intention to serve the public. To gratify the most childish vanity was the sole motive of the great proprietors. The merchants and artificers, much less ridiculous, acted merely from a view to their own interest, and in pursuit of their own pedlar principle of turning a penny wherever a penny was

> A revolution was thus insensibly brought about, and commerce and manufactures became the cause of the improvement of the country.

to be got. Neither of them had either knowledge or foresight of that great revolution which the folly of the one, and the industry of the other, was gradually bringing about.

It is thus that through the greater part of Europe the commerce and manufactures of cities, instead of being the effect, have been the cause and occasion of the improvement and cultivation of the country.

This order, however, being contrary to the natural course of things, is necessarily both slow and uncertain. Compare the slow progress of those European countries of which the wealth depends very much upon their commerce and manufactures, with the rapid advances of our North American colonies, of which the wealth is founded altogether in agriculture. Through the greater part of Europe, the number of inhabitants is not supposed to double in less than five hundred years. In several of our North American colonies, it is found to double in twenty or five-and-twenty years. In Europe, the law of primogeniture, and perpetuities of different kinds, prevent the division of great estates, and thereby hinder the multiplication of small proprietors. A small proprietor, however, who knows every part of his little territory, who views it with all the affection which property, especially small property, naturally inspires, and who upon that account takes pleasure not only in cultivating but in adorning it, is generally of all improvers the most industrious, the most intelligent, and the most successful. The same regulations, besides, keep so much land out of the market, that there are always more capitals to buy than there is land to sell, so that what is sold always sells at a monopoly price. The rent never pays the interest of the purchase money, and is besides burdened with repairs and other occasional charges, to which the interest of money is not liable.

This order of things is both slow and uncertain compared with the natural order, as may be shown by the rapid progress of the North American colonies.

To purchase land is everywhere in Europe a most unprofitable employment of a small capital. For the sake of the superior security, indeed, a man of moderate circumstances, when he retires from business, will sometimes choose to lay out his little capital in land. A man of profession too, whose revenue is derived from another source, often loves to secure his savings in the same way. But a young man, who, instead of applying to trade or to some profession, should employ a capital of two or three thousand pounds in the purchase and cultivation of a small piece of land, might indeed expect to live very happily, and very independently, but must bid adieu, forever, to all hope of either great fortune or great illustration, which by a different employment of his stock he might have had the same chance of acquiring with other people. Such a person too, though he cannot aspire at being a proprietor, will often disdain to be a farmer.

The small quantity of land, therefore, which is brought to market, and the high price of what is brought thither, prevents a great number of capitals from being employed in its cultivation and improvement which would otherwise have taken that direction. In North America, on the contrary, fifty or sixty pounds is often found a sufficient stock to begin a plantation with. The purchase and improvement of uncultivated land, is there the most profitable employment of the smallest as well as of the greatest capitals, and the most direct road to all the fortune and illustration which can be acquired in that country. Such land, indeed, is in North America to be had almost for nothing, or at a price much below the value of the natural produce; a thing impossible in Europe, or, indeed, in any country where all lands have long been private property. If landed estates, however, were divided equally among all the children, upon the death of any proprietor who left a numerous family, the estate would generally be sold. So much land would come to market, that it could no longer sell at a monopoly price. The free rent of the land would go nearer to pay the interest of the purchase money, and a small capital might be employed in purchasing land as profitably as in any other way. . . .

BOOK IV
OF SYSTEMS OF POLITICAL ECONOMY

INTRODUCTION

Political economy, considered as a branch of the science of a statesman or legislator, proposes two distinct objects; first, to provide a plentiful revenue or subsistence for the people, or more properly to enable them to provide such a revenue or subsistence for themselves; and secondly, to supply the state or commonwealth with a revenue sufficient for the public services. It proposes to enrich both the people and the sovereign.

The first object of political economy is to provide subsistence for the people.

Two different systems proposed for this end will be explained.

The different progress of opulence in different ages and nations, has given occasion to two different systems of political economy, with regard to enriching the people. The one may be called the system of commerce, the other that of agriculture. I shall endeavour to explain both as fully and distinctly as I can, and shall begin with the system of commerce. It is the modern system, and is best understood in our own country and in our own times.

CHAPTER I

Of the Principle of the commercial, or mercantile System

That wealth consists in money, or in gold and silver, is a popular notion which naturally arises from the double function of money, as the instrument of commerce, and as the measure of value. In consequence of its being the instrument of commerce, when we have money we can more readily obtain whatever else we have occasion for, than by means of any other commodity. The great affair, we always find, is to get money. When that is obtained, there is no difficulty in making any subsequent purchase. In consequence of its being the measure of value, we estimate that of all other commodities by the quantity of money which they will exchange for. We say of a rich man that he is worth a great deal, and of a poor man that he is worth very little money. A frugal man, or a man eager to be rich, is said to love money; and a careless, a generous, or a profuse man, is said to be indifferent about it. To grow rich is to get money; and wealth and money, in short, are, in common language, considered as in every respect synonymous.

Wealth and money in common language are considered synonymous.

A rich country, in the same manner as a rich man, is supposed to be a country abounding in money; and to heap up gold and silver in any country is supposed to be the readiest way to enrich it. For some time after the discovery of America, the first enquiry of the Spaniards, when they arrived upon any unknown coast, used to be, if there was any gold or silver to be found in the neighbourhood? By the information which they received, they judged whether it was worthwhile to make a settlement there, or if the country was worth the conquering. Plano Carpino, a monk sent ambassador from the king of France to one of the sons of the famous Genghis Khan, says that the Tartars used frequently to ask him, if there was plenty of sheep and oxen in the kingdom of France? Their enquiry had the same object with that of the Spaniards. They wanted to know if the country was rich enough to be worth the conquering. Among the Tartars, as among all other nations of shepherds, who are generally ignorant of the use of money, cattle are the instruments of commerce and the measures of value. Wealth, therefore, according to them, consisted in cattle, as according to the Spaniards it consisted in gold and silver. Of the two, the Tartar notion, perhaps, was the nearest to the truth.

Similarly the Tartars thought wealth consisted of cattle.

Mr. Locke remarks a distinction between money and other moveable goods. All other moveable goods, he says, are of so consumable a nature that the wealth which consists in them cannot be much depended on, and a nation which abounds in them one year may, without any

Locke thought gold and silver the most substantial part of the wealth of a nation.

exportation, but merely by their own waste and extravagance, be in great want of them the next. Money, on the contrary, is a steady friend, which, though it may travel about from hand to hand, yet if it can be kept from going out of the country, is not very liable to be wasted and consumed. Gold and silver, therefore, are, according to him, the most solid and substantial part of the moveable wealth of a nation, and to multiply those metals ought, he thinks, upon that account, to be the great object of its political economy. . . .

In consequence of these popular notions, all the different nations of Europe have studied, though to little purpose, every possible means of accumulating gold and silver in their respective countries. Spain and Portugal, the proprietors of the principal mines which supply Europe with those metals, have either prohibited their exportation under the severest penalties, or subjected it to a considerable duty. The

So all European nations have tried to accumulate gold and silver.

At first by a prohibition of exportation, but merchants found this inconvenient, and therefore argued that exportation did not always diminish the stock in the country.

like prohibition seems anciently to have made a part of the policy of most other European nations. It is even to be found, where we should least of all expect to find it, in some old Scotch acts of parliament, which forbid under heavy penalties the carrying gold or silver *forth of the kingdom.* The like policy anciently took place both in France and England.

When those countries became commercial, the merchants found this prohibition, upon many occasions, extremely inconvenient. They could frequently buy more advantageously with gold and silver than with any other commodity, the foreign goods which they wanted, either to import into their own, or to carry to some other foreign country. They remonstrated, therefore, against this prohibition as hurtful to trade.

They represented, first, that the exportation of gold and silver in order to purchase foreign goods did not always diminish the quantity of those metals in the kingdom. That, on the contrary, it might frequently increase that quantity; because, if the consumption of foreign goods was not thereby increased in the country, those goods might be re-exported to foreign countries, and being there sold for a large profit, might bring back much more treasure than was originally sent out to purchase them. Mr. Mun compares this operation of foreign trade to the seed-time and harvest of agriculture. "If we only behold," says he, "the actions of the husbandman in the seed-time, when he casteth away much good corn into the ground, we shall account him rather a madman than a husbandman. But when we consider his labours in the harvest, which is the end of his endeavours, we shall find the worth and plentiful increase of his actions." . . .

Such as they were, however, those arguments convinced the people to whom they were addressed. They were addressed by merchants to parliaments, and to the councils of princes, to nobles and to

Their arguments were partly sophistical, but they convinced parliaments and councils.

country gentlemen; by those who were supposed to
understand trade, to those who were conscious to
themselves that they knew nothing about the matter. That foreign trade enriched the country, experience demonstrated to the nobles and country
gentlemen, as well as to the merchants; but how, or
in what manner, none of them well knew. The
merchants knew perfectly in what manner it enriched

The exportation of for-
eign coin and bullion
was permitted by France
and England, and the
exportation of Dutch
coin by Holland.

That treasure was
obtained by foreign
trade became a received
maxim.

themselves. It was their business to know it. But to know in what manner
it enriched the country, was no part of their business. This subject never
came into their consideration, but when they had occasion to apply to
their country for some change in the laws relating to foreign trade. It
then became necessary to say something about the beneficial effects of
foreign trade, and the manner in which those effects were obstructed by
the laws as they then stood. To the judges who were to decide the business, it appeared a most satisfactory account of the matter, when they
were told that foreign trade brought money into the country, but that
the laws in question hindered it from bringing so much as it otherwise
would do. Those arguments therefore produced the wished-for effect.
The prohibition of exporting gold and silver was in France and England
confined to the coin of those respective countries. The exportation of
foreign coin and of bullion was made free. In Holland, and in some
other places, this liberty was extended even to the coin of the country.
The attention of government was turned away from guarding against the
exportation of gold and silver, to watch over the balance of trade, as the
only cause which could occasion any augmentation or diminution of
those metals.

From one fruitless care it was turned away to another care much more
intricate, much more embarrassing, and just equally fruitless. The title
of Mun's book, England's Treasure in Foreign Trade, became a funda-
mental maxim in the political economy, not of England only, but of all
other commercial countries. The inland or home trade, the most important of all, the trade in which an equal capital affords the greatest revenue, and creates the greatest employment to the people of the country,
was considered as subsidiary only to foreign trade. It neither brought
money into the country, it was said, nor carried any out of it. The country therefore could never become either richer or poorer by means of it,
except so far as its prosperity or decay might indirectly influence the state
of foreign trade. . . .

It is not because wealth consists more essentially
in money than in goods, that the merchant finds it
generally more easy to buy goods with money, than
to buy money with goods; but because money is the

It is easier to buy than
to sell simply because
money is the instrument
of commerce.

known and established instrument of commerce, for which every thing
is readily given in exchange, but which is not always with equal readi-

ness to be got in exchange for every thing. The greater part of goods besides are more perishable than money, and he may frequently sustain a much greater loss by keeping them. When his goods are upon hand too, he is more liable to such demands for money as he may not be able to answer, than when he has got their price in his coffers. Over and above all this, his profit arises more directly from selling than from buying, and he is upon all these accounts generally much more anxious to exchange his goods for money, than his money for goods.

But though a particular merchant, with abundance of goods in his warehouse, may sometimes be ruined by not being able to sell them in time, a nation or country is not liable to the same accident. The whole capital of a merchant frequently consists in perishable goods destined for purchasing money. But it is but a very small part of the annual produce of the land and labour of a country which can ever be destined for purchasing gold and silver from their neighbours. The far greater part is circulated and consumed among themselves; and even of the surplus which is sent abroad, the greater part is generally destined for the purchase of other foreign goods. Though gold and silver, therefore, could not be had in exchange for the goods destined to purchase them, the nation would not be ruined. It might, indeed, suffer some loss and inconvenience, and be forced upon some of those expedients which are necessary for supplying the place of money. The annual produce of its land and labour, however, would be the same, or very nearly the same, as usual, because the same, or very nearly the same consumable capital would be employed in maintaining it. And though goods do not always draw money so readily as money draws goods, in the long run they draw it more necessarily than even it draws them. Goods can serve many other purposes besides purchasing money, but money can serve no other purpose besides purchasing goods.

Money, therefore, necessarily runs after goods, but goods do not always or necessarily run after money. The man who buys, does not always mean to sell again, but frequently to use or to consume; whereas he who sells, always means to buy again. The one may frequently have done the whole, but the other can never have done more than the one half of his business. It is not for its own sake that men desire money, but for the sake of what they can purchase with it.

Consumable commodities, it is said, are soon destroyed; whereas gold and silver are of a more durable nature, and, were it not for this continual exportation, might be accumulated for ages together, to the incredible augmentation of the real wealth of the country. Nothing, therefore, it is pretended, can be more disadvantageous to any country, than the trade which consists in the exchange of such lasting for such perishable commodities. We do not, however, reckon that trade disadvantageous which consists in the exchange of the hardware of England

The durability of a
commodity is no reason
for accumulating more
of it than is wanted.

for the wines of France; and yet hardware is a very durable commodity, and were it not for this continual exportation, might too be accumulated for ages together, to the incredible augmentation of the pots and pans of the country. But it readily occurs that the number of such utensils is in every country necessarily limited by the use which there is for them; that it would be absurd to have more pots and pans than were necessary for cooking the victuals usually consumed there; and that if the quantity of victuals were to increase, the number of pots and pans would readily increase along with it, a part of the increased quantity of victuals being employed in purchasing them, or in maintaining an additional number of workmen whose business it was to make them.

It should as readily occur that the quantity of gold and silver is in every country limited by the use which there is for those metals; that their use consists in circulating commodities as coin, and in affording a species of household furniture as plate; that the quantity of coin in every country is regulated by the value of the commodities which are to be circulated by it: increase that value, and immediately a part of it will be sent abroad to purchase, wherever it is to be had, the additional quantity of coin requisite for circulating them: that the quantity of plate is regulated by the number and wealth of those private families who choose to indulge themselves in that sort of magnificence: increase the number and wealth of such families, and a part of this increased wealth will most probably be employed in purchasing, wherever it is to be found, an additional quantity of plate: that to attempt to increase the wealth of any country, either by introducing or by detaining in it an unnecessary quantity of gold and silver, is as absurd as it would be to attempt to increase the good cheer of private families, by obliging them to keep an unnecessary number of kitchen utensils.

As the expence of purchasing those unnecessary utensils would diminish instead of increasing either the quantity or goodness of the family provisions; so the expence of purchasing an unnecessary quantity of gold and silver must, in every country, as necessarily diminish the wealth which feeds, clothes, and lodges, which maintains and employs the people. Gold and silver, whether in the shape of coin or of plate, are utensils, it must be remembered, as much as the furniture of the kitchen. Increase the use for them, increase the consumable commodities which are to be circulated, managed, and prepared by means of them, and you will infallibly increase the quantity; but if you attempt, by extraordinary means, to increase the quantity, you will as infallibly diminish the use and even the quantity too, which in those metals can never be greater than what the use requires. Were they ever to be accumulated beyond this quantity, their transportation is so easy, and the loss which attends their lying idle and unemployed so great, that no law could prevent their being immediately sent out of the country. . . .

monopoly against countries (handwritten margin note)

CHAPTER II

Of Restraints upon the Importation from foreign Countries of such Goods as can be produced at Home

By restraining, either by high duties, or by absolute prohibitions, the importation of such goods from foreign countries as can be produced at home, the monopoly of the home market is more or less secured to the domestic industry employed in producing them. Thus the prohibition of importing either live cattle or salt provisions from foreign countries secures to the graziers of Great Britain the monopoly of the home market for butchers-meat. The high duties upon the importation of corn, which in times of moderate plenty amount to a prohibition, give a like advantage to the growers of that commodity. The prohibition of the importation of foreign woollens is equally favourable to the woollen manufacturers. The silk manufacture, though altogether employed upon foreign materials, has lately obtained the same advantage. The linen manufacture has not yet obtained it, but is making great strides towards it. Many other sorts of manufacturers have, in the same manner, obtained in Great Britain, either altogether, or very nearly a monopoly against their countrymen. The variety of goods of which the importation into Great Britain is prohibited, either absolutely, or under certain circumstances, greatly exceeds what can easily be suspected by those who are not well acquainted with the laws of the customs.

> High duties and prohibitions giving a monopoly to a particular home industry are very common.

That this monopoly of the home market frequently gives great encouragement to that particular species of industry which enjoys it, and frequently turns towards that employment a greater share of both the labour and stock of the society than would otherwise have gone to it, cannot be doubted. But whether it tends either to increase the general industry of the society, or to give it the most advantageous direction, is not, perhaps, altogether so evident.

> They encourage the particular industry, but neither increase general industry nor give it the best direction.

The general industry of the society never can exceed what the capital of the society can employ. As the number of workmen that can be kept in employment by any particular person must bear a certain proportion to his capital, so the number of those that can be continually employed by all the members of a great society, must bear a certain proportion to the whole capital of that society, and never can exceed that proportion. No regulation of commerce can increase the quantity of industry in any society beyond what its capital can maintain. It can only divert a part of it into a direction into which it might not otherwise have gone; and it is by no means certain that this artificial direction is likely to be more advantageous to the society than that into which it would have gone of its own accord. . . .

> The number of persons employed cannot exceed a certain proportion to the capital of the society.

[Smith's argument against the mercantile system continues with a direct appeal to the Invisible Hand. This is the only place where it is mentioned by name in the *Wealth of Nations*.]

But the annual revenue of every society is always precisely equal to the exchangeable value of the whole annual produce of its industry, or rather is precisely the same thing with that exchangeable value. As every individual, therefore, endeavours as much as he can both to employ his capital in the support of domestic industry, and so to direct that industry that its produce may be of the greatest value; every individual necessarily labours to render the annual revenue of the society as great as he can. He generally, indeed, neither intends to promote the public interest, nor knows how much he is promoting it. By preferring the support of domestic to that of foreign industry, he intends only his own security; and by directing that industry in such a manner as its produce may be of the greatest value, he intends only his own gain, and he is in this, as in many other cases, led by an invisible hand to promote an end which was no part of his intention. Nor is it always the worse for the society that it was no part of it. By pursuing his own interest he frequently promotes that of the society more effectually than when he really intends to promote it. I have never known much good done by those who affected to trade for the public good. It is an affectation, indeed, not very common among merchants, and very few words need be employed in dissuading them from it.

What is the species of domestic industry which his capital can employ, and of which the produce is likely to be of the greatest value, every individual, it is evident, can, in his local situation, judge much better than any statesman or lawgiver can do for him. The statesman, who should attempt to direct private people in what manner they ought to employ their capitals, would not only load himself with a most unnecessary attention, but assume an authority which could safely be trusted, not only to no single person, but to no council or senate whatever, and which would nowhere be so dangerous as in the hands of a man who had folly and presumption enough to fancy himself fit to exercise it.

> The individual can judge of this much better than the statesman.

To give the monopoly of the home market to the produce of domestic industry, in any particular art or manufacture, is in some measure to direct private people in what manner they ought to employ their capitals, and must, in almost all cases, be either a useless or a hurtful regulation. If the produce of domestic can be brought there as cheap as that of foreign industry, the regulation is evidently useless. If it cannot, it must generally be hurtful. It is the maxim of every prudent master of a family, never to attempt to make at home what it will cost him more to make than to buy. The tailor does not attempt to make his own shoes, but buys them of the shoemaker. The shoemaker

> High duties and prohibitions direct people to employ capital in producing at home what they could buy cheaper from abroad.

Strategies

I. Free trading

does not attempt to make his own clothes, but employs a tailor. The farmer attempts to make neither the one nor the other, but employs those different artificers. All of them find it for their interest to employ their whole industry in a way in which they have some advantage over their neighbours, and to purchase with a part of its produce, or what is the same thing, with the price of a part of it, whatever else they have occasion for.

What is prudence in the conduct of every private family, can scarce be folly in that of a great kingdom. If a foreign country can supply us with a commodity cheaper than we ourselves can make it, better buy it of them with some part of the produce of our own industry, employed in a way in which we have some advantage. . . .

> It is as foolish for a nation as for an individual to make what can be bought cheaper.
>
> Retaliation may be good policy where it is likely to secure the abolition of foreign restraints.

The case in which it may sometimes be a matter of deliberation how far it is proper to continue the free importation of certain foreign goods, is, when some foreign nation restrains by high duties or prohibitions the importation of some of our manufactures into their country. Revenge in this case naturally dictates retaliation, and that we should impose the like duties and prohibitions upon the importation of some or all of their manufactures into ours. Nations, accordingly seldom fail to retaliate in this manner. . . .

There may be good policy in retaliations of this kind, when there is a probability that they will procure the repeal of the high duties or prohibitions complained of. The recovery of a great foreign market will generally more than compensate the transitory inconvenience of paying dearer during a short time for some sorts of goods. To judge whether such retaliations are likely to produce such an effect, does not, perhaps, belong so much to the science of a legislator, whose deliberations ought to be governed by general principles which are always the same, as to the skill of that insidious and crafty animal, vulgarly called a statesman or politician, whose councils are directed by the momentary fluctuations of affairs. When there is no probability that any such repeal can be procured, it seems a bad method of compensating the injury done to certain classes of our people, to do another injury ourselves, not only to those classes, but to almost all the other classes of them. When our neighbours prohibit some manufacture of ours, we generally prohibit, not only the same, for that alone would seldom affect them considerably, but some other manufacture of theirs. This may no doubt give encouragement to some particular class of workmen among ourselves, and by excluding some of their rivals, may enable them to raise their price in the home market. Those workmen, however, who suffered by our neighbour's prohibition will not be benefited by ours. On the contrary, they and almost all the other classes of our citizens will thereby be obliged to pay dearer than before for certain goods. Every such law, therefore, imposes a real tax upon the whole country, not in favour of that particular class of workmen who were injured by our neighbour's prohibition, but of some other class. . . .

[The next four chapters in Book IV, listed as follows, have been omitted:

Chapter 3 Of the extraordinary Restraints upon the Importation of Goods of almost all Kinds, From those Countries with which the Balance is supposed to be disadvantageous.

Part I Of the Unreasonableness of those Restraints even upon the Principles of the Commercial System.

Digression concerning Banks of Deposit, particularly concerning that of Amsterdam.

Part II Of the Unreasonableness of those extraordinary Restraints upon other Principles.

Chapter 4 Of Drawbacks

Chapter 5 Of Bounties

Digression concerning the Corn Trade and Corn Laws.

Chapter 6 Of Treaties of Commerce.

In these chapters Smith counters arguments for the policies of the mercantile system by detailed reference to comtemporary examples. These are mainly of interest to scholars of the period.

Below, however, are two interesting passages from chapter 3. The first gives an indication of Smith's humour, the second considers the question of the growth or decline of national wealth.]

It is a losing trade, it is said, which a workman carries on with the ale-house; and the trade which a manufacturing nation would naturally carry on with a wine country, may be considered as a trade of the same nature. I answer, that the trade with the alehouse is not necessarily a losing trade. In its own nature it is just as advantageous as any other, though, perhaps, somewhat more liable to be abused. The employment of a brewer, and even that of a retailer of fermented liquors, are as necessary divisions of labour as any other. It will generally be more advantegeous for a workman to buy of the brewer the quantity he has occasion for, than to brew it himself, and if he is a poor workman, it will generally be more advantageous for him to buy it, by little and little of the retailer, than a large quantity of the brewer. He may no doubt buy too much of either, as he may of any other dealers in his neighbourhood, of the butcher, if he is a glutton, or of the draper, if he affects to be a beau among his companions.

> The arguments against the French wine trade are fallacious.

It is advantageous to the great body of workmen, notwithstanding, that all these trades should be free, though this freedom may be abused in all of them, and is more likely to be so, perhaps, in some than in others. Though individuals, besides, may sometimes ruin their fortunes by an excessive consumption of fermented liquors, there seems to be no risk that a nation should do so. Though in every country there are many people who spend upon such liquors more than they can afford, there are always many more who spend less. . . .

Were the duties upon foreign wines, and the excises upon malt, beer, and ale, to be taken away all at once, it might, in the same manner, occasion in Great Britain a pretty general and temporary drunkenness among the middling and inferior ranks of people, which would probably be soon followed by a permanent and almost universal sobriety. At present drunkenness is by no means the vice of people of fashion, or of those who can easily afford the most expensive liquors. A gentleman drunk with ale has scarce ever been seen among us. The restraints upon the wine trade in Great Britain, besides, do not so much seem calculated to hinder the people from going, if I may say so, to the alehouse, as from going where they can buy the best and cheapest liquor. They favour the wine trade of Portugal, and discourage that of France. The Portuguese, it is said, indeed, are better customers for our manufactures than the French, and should therefore be encouraged in preference to them. As they give us their custom, it is pretended, we should give them ours. The sneaking arts of underling tradesmen are thus erected into political maxims for the conduct of a great empire: for it is the most underling tradesmen only who make it a rule to employ chiefly their own customers. A great trader purchases his goods always where they are cheapest and best, without regard to any little interest of this kind. . . .

There is another balance, indeed, which has already been explained, very different from the balance of trade, and which, according as it happens to be either favourable or unfavourable, necessarily occasions the prosperity or decay of every nation. This is the balance of the annual produce and consumption. If the exchangeable value of the annual produce, it has already been observed, exceeds that of the annual consumption, the capital of the society must annually increase in proportion to this excess. The society in this case lives within its revenue, and what is annually saved out of its revenue, is naturally added to its capital, and employed so as to increase still further the annual produce. If the exchangeable value of the annual produce, on the contrary, fall short of the annual consumption, the capital of the society must annually decay in proportion to this deficiency. The expence of the society in this case exceeds its revenue, and necessarily encroaches upon its capital. Its capital, therefore, must necessarily decay, and, together with it, the exchangeable value of the annual produce of its industry.

Prosperity and decay depend on the balance of produce and consumption, which is quite different from the balance of trade, and may be constantly in favour of a nation when the balance of trade is against it.

This balance of produce and consumption is entirely different from what is called the balance of trade. It might take place in a nation which had no foreign trade, but which was entirely separated from all the world.

It may take place in the whole globe of the earth, of which the wealth, population, and improvement may be either gradually increasing or gradually decaying.

The balance of produce and consumption may be constantly in favour of a nation, though what is called the balance of trade be generally against it. A nation may import to a greater value than it exports for half a century, perhaps, together; the gold and silver which comes into it during all this time may be all immediately sent out of it; its circulating coin may gradually decay, different sorts of paper money being substituted in its place, and even the debts too which it contracts in the principal nations with whom it deals, may be gradually increasing; and yet its real wealth, the exchangeable value of the annual produce of its lands and labour, may, during the same period, have been increasing in a much greater proportion. The state of our North American colonies, and of the trade which they carried on with Great Britain, before the commencement of the present disturbances,* may serve as a proof that this is by no means an impossible supposition.

CHAPTER VII

Of Colonies

PART I

Of the Motives for establishing new Colonies

. . . The establishment of the European colonies in America and the West Indies arose from no necessity: and though the utility which has resulted from them has been very great, it is not altogether so clear and evident. It was not understood at their first establishment, and was not the motive either of that establishment or of the discoveries which gave occasion to it, and the nature, extent, and limits of that utility are not, perhaps, well understood at this day. . . .

The utility of the American colonies is not so evident.

Some years before this, while the expectations of Europe were in suspence about the projects of the Portuguese, of which the success appeared yet to be doubtful, a Genoese pilot formed the yet more daring project of sailing to the East Indies by the West. The situation of those countries was at that time very imperfectly known in Europe. The few European travellers who had been there had magnified the distance; perhaps through simplicity and ignorance, what was really very great, appearing almost infinite to those who could not measure it; or, perhaps, in order to increase somewhat more the marvellous of their own adventures in visiting regions

Columbus endeavoured to reach the East Indies by sailing westwards.

_____
*This paragraph was written in the year 1775.

so immensely remote from Europe. The longer the way was by the East, Columbus very justly concluded, the shorter it would be by the West. He proposed, therefore, to take that way, as both the shortest and the surest, and he had the good fortune to convince Isabella of Castile of the probability of his project. He sailed from the port of Palos in August 1492, near five years before the expedition of Vasco de Gama set out from Portugal, and, after a voyage of between two and three months, discovered first some of the small Bahama or Lucayan islands, and afterwards the great island of St. Domingo.

But the countries which Columbus discovered, either in this or in any of his subsequent voyages, had no resemblance to those which he had gone in quest of. Instead of the wealth, cultivation, and populousness of China and Indostan, he found, in St. Domingo, and in all the other parts of the new world which he ever visited, nothing but a country quite covered with wood, uncultivated, and inhabited only by some tribes of naked and miserable savages. He was not very willing, however, to believe that they were not the same with some of the countries described by Marco Polo, the first European who had visited, or at least had left behind him, any description of China or the East Indies; and a very slight resemblance, such as that which he found between the name of Cibao, a mountain in St. Domingo, and that of Cipango, mentioned by Marco Polo, was frequently sufficient to make him return to this favourite prepossession, though contrary to the clearest evidence. In his letters to Ferdinand and Isabella he called the countries which he had discovered the Indies. He entertained no doubt but that they were the extremity of those which had been described by Marco Polo, and that they were not very distant from the Ganges, or from the countries which had been conquered by Alexander. Even when at last convinced that they were different, he still flattered himself that those rich countries were at no great distance, and, in a subsequent voyage, accordingly, went in quest of them along the coast of Terra Firma, and towards the isthmus of Darien.

Columbus mistook the countries he found for the Indies.

In consequence of this mistake of Columbus, the name of the Indies has stuck to those unfortunate countries ever since; and when it was at last clearly discovered that the new were altogether different from the old Indies, the former were called the West, in contradistinction to the latter, which were called the East Indies. . . .

Hence the names East and West Indies.

Finding nothing either in the animals or vegetables of the newly discovered countries, which could justify a very advantageous representation of them, Columbus turned his view towards their minerals; and in the richness of the productions of this third kingdom, he flattered himself, he had found a full compensation for the insignificance of those of the other two. The

So Columbus relied on the minerals.

little bits of gold with which the inhabitants ornamented their dress, and which, he was informed, they frequently found in the rivulets and torrents that fell from the mountains, were sufficient to satisfy him that those mountains abounded with the richest gold mines. St. Domingo, therefore, was represented as a country abounding with gold, and, upon that account (according to the prejudices not only of the present times, but of those times), an inexhaustible source of real wealth to the crown and kingdom of Spain. When Columbus, upon his return from his first voyage, was introduced with a sort of triumphal honours to the sovereigns of Castile and Arragon, the principal productions of the countries which he had discovered were carried in solemn procession before him. The only valuable part of them consisted in some little fillets, bracelets, and other ornaments of gold, and in some bales of cotton. The rest were mere objects of vulgar wonder and curiosity; some reeds of an extraordinary size, some birds of a very beautiful plumage, and some stuffed skins of the huge alligator and manati; all of which were preceded by six or seven of the wretched natives, whose singular colour and appearance added greatly to the novelty of the show.

In consequence of the representations of Columbus, the council of Castile determined to take possession of countries of which the inhabitants were plainly incapable of defending themselves. The pious purpose of converting them to Christianity sanctified the injustice of the project. But the hope of finding treasures of gold there was the sole motive which prompted to undertake it; and to give this motive the greater weight, it was proposed by Columbus that the half of all the gold and silver that should be found there should belong to the crown. This proposal was approved of by the council. . . .

> The Council of Castile was attracted by the gold, Columbus proposing that the government should have half the gold and silver discovered.

All the other enterprises of the Spaniards in the new world, subsequent to those of Columbus, seem to have been prompted by the same motive. It was the sacred thirst of gold that carried Oieda, Nicuessa, and Vasco Nugnes de Balboa, to the isthmus of Darien, that carried Cortez to Mexico, and Almagro and Pizzarro to Chili and Peru. When those adventurers arrived upon any unknown coast, their first enquiry was always if there was any gold to be found there; and according to the information which they received concerning this particular, they determined either to quit the country or to settle in it.

> The subsequent Spanish enterprises were all prompted by the same motive.

Of all those expensive and uncertain projects, however, which bring bankruptcy upon the greater part of the people who engage in them, there is none perhaps more perfectly ruinous that the search after new silver and gold mines. It is perhaps the most disadvantageous lottery in the world, or the one in which the gain of those who draw the prizes

> A prudent lawgiver would not wish to encourage gold and silver mining.

bears the least proportion to the loss of those who draw the blanks: for though the prizes are few and the blanks many, the common price of a ticket is the whole fortune of a very rich man. Projects of mining, instead of replacing the capital employed in them, together with the ordinary profits of stock, commonly absorb both capital and profit. They are the projects, therefore, to which of all others a prudent lawgiver, who desired to increase the capital of his nation, would least choose to give any extraordinary encouragement, or to turn towards them a greater share of that capital than what would go to them of its own accord. Such in reality is the absurd confidence which almost all men have in their own good fortune, that wherever there is the least probability of success, too great a share of it is apt to go to them of its own accord. . . .

The first adventurers of all the other nations of Europe, who attempted to make settlements in America, were animated by the like chimerical views; but they were not equally successful. It was more than a hundred years after the first settlement of the Brazils, before any silver, gold, or diamond mines were discovered there. In the English, French, Dutch, and Danish colonies, none have ever yet been discovered; at least none that are at present supposed to be worth the working. The first English settlers in North America, however, offered a fifth of all the gold and silver which should be found there to the king, as a motive for granting them their patents. In the patents to Sir Walter Raleigh, to the London and Plymouth companies, to the council of Plymouth, etc., this fifth was accordingly reserved to the crown. To the expectation of finding gold and silver mines, those first settlers too joined that of discovering a northwest passage to the East Indies. They have hitherto been disappointed in both.

Other nations were not so successful.

PART II

Causes of the Prosperity of new Colonies

The colony of a civilised nation which takes possession, either of a waste country, or of one so thinly inhabited, that the natives easily give place to the new settlers, advances more rapidly to wealth and greatness than any other human society.

The colonists carry out with them a knowledge of agriculture and of other useful arts, superior to what can grow up of its own accord in the course of many centuries among savage and barbarous nations. They carry out with them too the habit of subordination, some notion of the regular government which takes place in their own country, of the system of laws which support it, and of a regular administration of justice; and they naturally establish something of the same kind in the new settlement. But among savage and barbarous nations, the natural progress of law and government is still slower than the natural progress of arts, after law and government have

Colonists take out knowledge and regular government, land is plentiful and cheap, wages are high, and children are taken care of and are profitable.

been so far established, as is necessary for their protection. Every colonist gets more land than he can possibly cultivate. He has no rent, and scarce any taxes to pay. No landlord shares with him in its produce, and the share of the sovereign is commonly but a trifle. He has every motive to render as great as possible a produce, which is thus to be almost entirely his own. But his land is commonly so extensive, that with all his own industry, and with all the industry of other people whom he can get to employ, he can seldom make it produce the tenth part of what it is capable of producing. He is eager, therefore, to collect labourers from all quarters, and to reward them with the most liberal wages. But those liberal wages, joined to the plenty and cheapness of land, soon make those labourers leave him in order to become landlords themselves, and to reward, with equal liberality, other labourers, who soon leave them for the same reason that they left their first master. The liberal reward of labour encourages marriage. The children, during the tender years of infancy, are well fed and properly taken care of, and when they are grown up, the value of their labour greatly overpays their maintenance. When arrived at maturity, the high price of labour, and the low price of land, enable them to establish themselves in the same manner as their fathers did before them.

In other countries, rent and profit eat up wages, and the two superior orders of people oppress the inferior one. But in new colonies, the interest of the two superior orders obliges them to treat the inferior one with more generosity and humanity; at least, where that inferior one is not in a state of slavery. Waste lands, of the greatest natural fertility, are to be had for a trifle. The increase of revenue which the proprietor, who is always the undertaker, expects from their improvement, constitutes his profit; which in these circumstances is commonly very great. But this great profit cannot be made without employing the labour of other people in clearing and cultivating the land; and the disproportion between the great extent of the land and the small number of the people, which commonly takes place in new colonies, makes it difficult for him to get this labour. He does not, therefore, dispute about wages, but is willing to employ labour at any price. The high wages of labour encourage population. The cheapness and plenty of good land encourage improvement, and enable the proprietor to pay those high wages. In those wages consists almost the whole price of the land; and though they are high, considered as the wages of labour, they are low, considered as the price of what is so very valuable. What encourages the progress of population and improvement, encourages that of real wealth and greatness. . . .

Population and improvement, which mean wealth and greatness, are encouraged.

Towards the end of the fifteenth, and during the greater part of the sixteenth century, Spain and Portugal were the two great naval powers upon the ocean; for though the commerce of Venice extended to every

When Spain declined, various countries obtained a footing in America.

part of Europe, its fleets had scarce ever sailed beyond the Mediterranean. The Spaniards, in virtue of the first discovery, claimed all America as their own; and though they could not hinder so great a naval power as that of Portugal from settling in Brazil, such was, at that time, the terror of their name, that the greater part of the other nations of Europe were afraid to establish themselves in any other part of that great continent. The French, who attempted to settle in Florida, were all murdered by the Spaniards. But the declension of the naval power of this latter nation, in consequence of the defeat or miscarriage of, what they called, their Invincible Armada, which happened towards the end of the sixteenth century, put it out of their power to obstruct any longer the settlements of the other European nations. In the course of the seventeenth century, therefore, the English, French, Dutch, Danes, and Swedes, all the great nations who had any ports upon the ocean, attempted to make some settlements in the new world. . . .

But there are no colonies of which the progress has been more rapid than that of the English in North America.

But the progress of the English colonies has been the most rapid.

Plenty of good land, and liberty to manage their own affairs their own way, seem to be the two great causes of the prosperity of all new colonies. . . .

To prohibit a great people, however, from making all that they can of every part of their own produce, or from employing their stock and industry in the way that they judge most advantageous to themselves, is a manifest violation of the most sacred rights of mankind. Unjust, however, as such prohibitions may be, they have not hitherto been very hurtful to the colonies. Land is still so cheap, and, consequently, labour so dear among them, that they can import from the mother country, almost all the more refined or more advanced manufactures cheaper than they could make them for themselves. Though they had not, therefore, been prohibited from establishing such manufactures, yet in their present state of improvement, a regard to their own interest would, probably, have prevented them from doing so. In their present state of improvement, those prohibitions, perhaps, without cramping their industry, or restraining it from any employment to which it would have gone of its own accord, are only impertinent badges of slavery imposed upon them, without any sufficient reason, by the groundless jealousy of the merchants and manufacturers of the mother country. In a more advanced state they might be really oppressive and insupportable. . . .

Prohibitions, though a violation of sacred rights, have not as yet been very hurtful.

In all European colonies the culture of the sugarcane is carried on by negro slaves. The constitution of those who have been born in the temperate climate of Europe could not, it is supposed, support the labour of digging the ground under the burning sun of the West Indies; and the culture of the sugarcane, as it is managed at present, is all hand labour, though, in the opinion of many, the drill plough might be introduced into it with great advantage. But, as the profit and success of the cultivation which is carried on by means of cattle, depend very much upon the good management of those cattle; so the profit and success of that which is carried on by slaves, must depend equally upon the good management of those slaves; and in the good management of their slaves the French planters, I think it is generally allowed, are superior to the English. The law, so far as it gives some weak protection to the slave against the violence of his master, is likely to be better executed in a colony where the government is in a great measure arbitrary, than in one where it is altogether free. In every country where the unfortunate law of slavery is established, the magistrate, when he protects the slave, intermeddles in some measure in the management of the private property of the master; and, in a free country, where the master is perhaps either a member of the colony assembly, or an elector of such a member, he dare not do this but with the greatest caution and circumspection. The respect which he is obliged to pay to the master renders it more difficult for him to protect the slave. But in a country where the government is in a great measure arbitrary, where it is usual for the magistrate to intermeddle even in the management of the private property of individuals, and to send them, perhaps, a lettre de cachet if they do not manage it according to his liking, it is much easier for him to give some protection to the slave; and common humanity naturally disposes him to do so. The protection of the magistrate renders the slave less contemptible in the eyes of his master, who is thereby induced to consider him with more regard, and to treat him with more gentleness. Gentle usage renders the slave not only more faithful, but more intelligent, and therefore, upon a double account, more useful. He approaches more to the condition of a free servant, and may possess some degree of integrity and attachment to his master's interest, virtues which frequently belong to free servants, but which never can belong to a slave, who is treated as slaves commonly are in countries where the master is perfectly free and secure. . . .

PART III

Of the Advantages which Europe has derived from the Discovery of America, and from that of a Passage to the East Indies by the Cape of Good Hope.

. . . The monopoly of the colony trade besides, by forcing towards it a much greater proportion of the capital of Great Britain than what would naturally have gone to it, seems to have broken altogether that natural balance which would otherwise have taken place among all the different branches of British industry. The industry of Great Britain, instead of being accommodated to a great

A monopoly of the colony trade makes industry and commerce less secure owing to its being driven into one channel.

number of small markets, has been principally suited to one great market. Her commerce, instead of running in a great number of small channels, has been taught to run principally in one great channel. But the whole system of her industry and commerce has thereby been rendered less secure; the whole state of her body politic less healthful, than it otherwise would have been. In her present condition, Great Britain resembles one of those unwholesome bodies in which some of the vital parts are overgrown, and which, upon that account, are liable to many dangerous disorders scarce incident to those in which all the parts are more properly proportioned. A small stop in that great blood vessel, which has been artificially swelled beyond its natural dimensions, and through which an unnatural proportion of the industry and commerce of the country has been forced to circulate, is very likely to bring on the most dangerous disorders upon the whole body politic.

The expectation of a rupture with the colonies, accordingly, has struck the people of Great Britain with more terror than they ever felt for a Spanish armada, or a French invasion. It was this terror, whether well or ill grounded, which rendered the repeal of the stamp act, among the merchants at least, a popular measure. In the total exclusion from the colony market, was it to last only for a few years, the greater part of our merchants used to fancy that they foresaw an entire stop to their trade; the greater part of our master manufacturers, the entire ruin of their business; and the greater part of our workmen, an end of their employment. A rupture with any of our neighbours upon the continent, though likely too to occasion some stop or interruption in the employments of some of all these different orders of people, is foreseen, however, without any such general emotion. The blood, of which the circulation is stopped in some of the smaller vessels, easily disgorges itself into the greater, without occasioning any dangerous disorder; but, when it is stopped in any of the greater vessels, convulsions, apoplexy, or death, are the immediate and unavoidable consequences. If but one of those overgrown manufactures, which by means either of bounties, or of the monopoly of the home and colony markets, have been artificially raised up to an unnatural height, finds some small stop or interruption in its employment, it frequently occasions a mutiny and disorder alarming to government, and embarrassing even to the deliberations of the legislature. How great, therefore, would be the disorder and confusion, it was thought, which must necessarily be occasioned by a sudden and entire stop in the employment of so great a proportion of our principal manufacturers?

Some moderate and gradual relaxation of the laws which give to Great Britain the exclusive trade to the colonies, till it is rendered in a great measure free, seems to be the only expedient which can, in all future times, deliver her from this danger, which can enable her or even force her to

The gradual relaxation of the monopoly is desirable.

withdraw some part of her capital from this overgrown employment, and to turn it, though with less profit, towards other employments; and which, by gradually diminishing one branch of her industry and gradually increasing all the rest, can by degrees restore all the different branches of it to that natural, healthful, and proper proportion which perfect liberty necessarily establishes, and which perfect liberty can alone preserve. To open the colony trade all at once to all nations, might not only occasion some transitory inconvenience, but a great permanent loss to the greater part of those whose industry or capital is at present engaged in it. The sudden loss of the employment even of the ships which import the eighty-two thousand hogsheads of tobacco, which are over and above the consumption of Great Britain, might alone be felt very sensibly.

Such are the unfortunate effects of all the regulations of the mercantile system! They not only introduce very dangerous disorders into the state of the body politic, but disorders which it is often difficult to remedy, without occasioning, for a time at least, still greater disorders. In what manner, therefore, the colony trade ought gradually to be opened; what are the restraints which ought first, and what are those which ought last to be taken away; or in what manner the natural system of perfect liberty and justice ought gradually to be restored, we must leave to the wisdom of future statesmen and legislators to determine. . . .

If the manufactures of Great Britain, however, have been advanced, as they certainly have, by the colony trade, it has not been by means of the monopoly of that trade, but in spite of the monopoly. The effect of the monopoly has been, not to augment the quantity, but to alter the quality and shape of a part of the manufactures of Great Britain, and to accommodate to a market, from which the returns are slow and distant, what would otherwise have been accommodated to one from which the returns are frequent and near. Its effect has consequently been to turn a part of the capital of Great Britain from an employment in which it would have maintained a greater quantity of manufacturing industry, to one in which it maintains a much smaller, and thereby to diminish, instead of increasing, the whole quantity of manufacturing industry maintained in Great Britain.

The colony trade has benefited British manufactures in spite of the monopoly, not in consequence of it.

The monopoly of the colony trade, therefore, like all the other mean and malignant expedients of the mercantile system, depresses the industry of all other countries, but chiefly that of the colonies, without in the least increasing, but on the contrary diminishing, that of the country in whose favour it is established.

The monopoly hinders the capital of that country, whatever may at any particular time be the extent of that capital, from maintaining so great a quantity of productive labour as it would otherwise maintain, and from affording so great a revenue to the

The monopoly reduces wages in the mother country, raises profits, and thereby tends to lower rents and the price of land.

278 THE ESSENTIAL ADAM SMITH

industrious inhabitants as it would otherwise afford. But as capital can be increased only by savings from revenue, the monopoly, by hindering it from affording so great a revenue as it would otherwise afford, necessarily hinders it from increasing so fast as it would otherwise increase, and consequently from maintaing a still greater quantity of productive labour, and affording a still greater revenue to the industrious inhabitants of that country. One great original source of revenue, therefore, the wages of labour, the monopoly must necessarily have rendered at all times less abundant than it otherwise would have been.

By raising the rate of mercantile profit, the monopoly discourages the improvement of land. The profit of improvement depends upon the difference between what the land actually produces, and what, by the application of a certain capital, it can be made to produce. If this difference affords a greater profit than what can be drawn from an equal capital in any mercantile employment, the improvement of land will draw capital from all mercantile employments. If the profit is less, mercantile employments will draw capital from the improvement of land. Whatever therefore raises the rate of mercantile profit, either lessens the superiority or increases the inferiority of the profit of improvement; and in the one case hinders capital from going to improvement, and in the other draws capital from it. But by discouraging improvement, the monopoly necessarily retards the natural increase of another great original source of revenue, the rent of land. By raising the rate of profit too the monopoly necessarily keeps up the market rate of interest higher than it otherwise would be. But the price of land in proportion to the rent which it affords, the number of years purchase which is commonly paid for it, necessarily falls as the rate of interest rises, and rises as the rate of interest falls. The monopoly, therefore, hurts the interest of the landlord two different ways, by retarding the natural increase, first, of his rent, and secondly, of the price which he would get for his land in proportion to the rent which it affords.

The monopoly indeed, raises the rate of mercantile profit, and thereby augments somewhat the gain of our merchants. But as it obstructs the natural increase of capital, it tends rather to diminish than to increase the sum total of the revenue which the inhabitants of the country derive from the profits of stock; a small profit upon a great capital generally affording a greater revenue than a great profit upon a small one. The monopoly raises the rate of profit, but it hinders the sum of profit from rising so high as it otherwise would do.

It reduces the absolute amount of profit, thus rendering all the original sources of revenue less abundant. More fatal still, it destroys parsimony.

All the original sources of revenue, the wages of labour, the rent of land, and the profits of stock, the monopoly renders much less abundant than they otherwise would be. To promote the little interest of one little order of men in one country, it hurts the interest of all other orders of men in that country, and of all men in all other countries.

It is solely by raising the ordinary rate of profit that the monopoly either has proved or could prove advantageous to any one particular order of men. But besides all the bad effects to the country in general, which have already been mentioned as necessarily resulting from a high rate of profit; there is one more fatal, perhaps, than all these put together, but which, if we may judge from experience, is inseparably connected with it. The high rate of profit seems everywhere to destroy that parsimony which in other circumstances is natural to the character of the merchant. When profits are high, that sober virtue seems to be superfluous, and expensive luxury to suit better the affluence of his situation.

But the owners of the great mercantile capitals are necessarily the leaders and conductors of the whole industry of every nation, and their example has a much greater influence upon the manners of the whole industrious part of it than that of any other order of men. If his employer is attentive and parsimonious, the workman is very likely to be so too; but if the master is dissolute and disorderly, the servant who shapes his work according to the pattern which his master prescribes to him, will shape his life too according to the example which he sets him. Accumulation is thus prevented in the hands of all those who are naturally the most disposed to accumulate; and the funds destined for the maintenance of productive labour receive no augmentation from the revenue of those who ought naturally to augment them the most. The capital of the country, instead of increasing, gradually dwindles away, and the quantity of productive labour maintained in it grows every day less and less. Have the exorbitant profits of the merchants of Cadiz and Lisbon augmented the capital of Spain and Portugal? Have they alleviated the poverty, have they promoted the industry of those two beggarly countries? Such has been the tone of mercantile expence in those two trading cities, that those exorbitant profits, far from augmenting the general capital of the country, seem scarce to have been sufficient to keep up the capitals upon which they were made. Foreign capitals are every day intruding themselves, if I may say so, more and more into the trade of Cadiz and Lisbon. It is to expel those foreign capitals from a trade which their own grows every day more and more insufficient for carrying on, that the Spaniards and Portuguese endeavour every day to straiten more and more the galling bands of their absurd monopoly.

Compare the mercantile manners of Cadiz and Lisbon with those of Amsterdam, and you will be sensible how differently the conduct and character of merchants are affected by the high and by the low profits of stock. The merchants of London, indeed, have not yet generally become such magnificent lords as those of Cadiz and Lisbon; but neither are they in general such attentive and parsimonious burghers as those of Amsterdam. They are supposed, however, many of them, to be a good deal richer than the greater part of the former, and not quite so rich as many of the latter. But the rate of their profit is commonly much lower than that of the former, and a good deal higher than that of the latter.

Light come light go, says the proverb; and the ordinary tone of expence seems everywhere to be regulated, not so much according to the real ability of spending, as to the supposed facility of getting money to spend. . . .

Towards the declension of the Roman republic, the allies of Rome, who had borne the principal burden of defending the state and extending the empire, demanded to be admitted to all the privi- leges of Roman citizens. Upon being refused, the social war broke out. During the course of that war Rome granted those privileges to the greater part of the them, one by one, and in proportion as they detached them- selves from the general confederacy. The parliament of Great Britain insists upon taxing the colonies; and they refuse to be taxed by a parlia- ment in which they are not represented. If to each colony, which should detach itself from the general confederacy, Great Britain should allow such a number of representatives as suited the proportion of what it contributed to the public revenue of the empire, in consequence of its being subjected to the same taxes, and in compensation admitted to the same freedom of trade with its fellow-subjects at home; the number of its representatives to be augmented as the proportion of its contribution might afterwards augment; a new method of acquiring importance, a new and more dazzling object of ambition would be presented to the leading men of each colony. Instead of piddling for the little prizes which are to found in what may be called the paltry raffle of colony faction; they might then hope, from the presumption which men naturally have in their own ability and good fortune, to draw some of the great prizes which sometimes come from the wheel of the great state lottery of British politics.

Unless this or some other method is fallen upon, and there seems to be none more obvious than this, of preserving the importance and of gratifying the ambition of the leading men of America, it is not very probable that they will ever voluntarily submit to us; and we ought to consider that the blood which must be shed in forcing them to do so, is, every drop of it, the blood either of those who are, or of those whom we wish to have for our fellow-citizens. They are very weak who flatter themselves that, in the state to which things have come, our colonies will be easily con- quered by force alone. The persons who now govern the resolutions of that they call their continental congress, feel in themselves at this moment a degree of importance which, perhaps, the greatest subjects in Europe scarce feel. From shopkeepers, tradesmen, and attorneys, they are become statesmen and legislators, and are employed in contriving a new form of government for an extensive empire, which, they flatter themselves, will become, and which, indeed, seems very likely to become, one of the greatest and most formidable that ever was in the world. Five hundred

Representation in par- liament in proportion to taxation should be offered.

Otherwise it seems hopeless to expect sub- mission.

different people, perhaps, who in different ways act immediately under the continental congress; and five hundred thousand, perhaps, who act under those five hundred, all feel in the same manner a proportionable rise in their own importance. Almost every individual of the governing party in America, fills, at present in his own fancy, a station superior, not only to what he had ever filled before, but to what he had ever expected to fill; and unless some new object of ambition is present either to him or to his leaders, if he has the ordinary spirit of a man, he will die in defence of that station. . . .

The discovery of America, and that of a passage to the East Indies by the Cape of Good Hope, are the two greatest and most important events recorded in the history of mankind. Their consequences have already been very great: but, in the short period of between two and three centuries which has elapsed since these discoveries were made, it is impossible that the whole extent of their consequences can have been seen. What benefits, or what misfortunes to mankind may hereafter result from those great events no human wisdom can foresee. By uniting, in some measure, the most distant parts of the world, by enabling them to relieve one another's wants, to increase one another's enjoyments, and to encourage one another's industry, their general tendency would seem to be beneficial. To the natives, however, both of the East and West Indies, all the commercial benefits which can have resulted from those events have been sunk and lost in the dreadful misfortunes which they have occasioned. These misfortunes, however, seem to have arisen rather from accident than from any thing in the nature of those events themselves. At the particular time when these discoveries were made, the superiority of force happened to be so great on the side of the Europeans, that they were enabled to commit with impunity every sort of injustice in those remote countries. Hereafter, perhaps, the natives of those countries may grow stronger, or those of Europe may grow weaker, and the inhabitants of all the different quarters of the world may arrive at that equality of courage and force which, by inspiring mutual fear, can alone overawe the injustice of independent nations into some sort of respect for the rights of one another. But nothing seems more likely to establish this equality of force than that mutual communication of knowledge and of all sorts of improvements which an extensive commerce from all countries to all countries naturally, or rather necessarily, carries along with it. . . .

After all the unjust attempts, therefore, of every country in Europe to engross to itself the whole advantage of the trade of its own colonies, no country has yet been able to engross to itself any thing but the expence of supporting in time of peace and of defending in time

The discovery of America and the Cape passage are the greatest events in history: the misfortunes of the natives of the East and West Indies may be temporary, so the results may be beneficial to all.

The mother countries have engrossed only the expence and inconveniences of possessing colonies.

of war the oppressive authority which it assumes over them. The inconveniences resulting from the possession of its colonies, every country has engrossed to itself completely. The advantages resulting from their trade it has been obliged to share with many other countries.

At first sight, no doubt, the monopoly of the great commerce of America, naturally seems to be an acquisition of the highest value. To the undiscerning eye of giddy ambition, it naturally presents itself amidst the confused scramble of politics and war, as a very dazzling object to fight for. The dazzling splendour of the object, however, the immense greatness of the commerce, is the very quality which renders the monopoly of it hurtful, or which makes one employment, in its own nature necessarily less advantageous to the country than the greater part of other employments, absorb a much greater proportion of the capital of the country than what would otherwise have gone to it.

The monopoly of American trade is a dazzling object.

The mercantile stock of every country, it has been shown in the second book, naturally seeks, if one may say so, the employment most advantageous to that country. If it is employed in the carrying trade, the country to which it belongs becomes the emporium of the goods of all the countries whose trade that stock carries on. But the owner of that stock necessarily wishes to dispose of as great a part of those goods as he can at home. He thereby saves himself the trouble, risk, and expence, of exportation, and he will upon that account be glad to sell them at home, not only for a much smaller price, but with somewhat a smaller profit than he might expect to make by sending them abroad. He naturally, therefore, endeavours as much as he can to turn his carrying trade into a foreign trade of consumption. If his stock again is employed in a foreign trade of consumption, he will, for the same reason, be glad to dispose of at home as great a part as he can of the home goods, which he collects in order to export to some foreign market, and he will thus endeavour, as much as he can, to turn his foreign trade of consumption into a home trade. The mercantile stock of every country naturally courts in this manner the near, and shuns the distant employment; naturally courts the employment in which the returns are frequent, and shuns that in which they are distant and slow; naturally courts the employment in which it can maintain the greatest quantity of productive labour in the country to which it belongs, or in which its owner resides, and shuns that in which it can maintain there the smallest quantity. It naturally courts the employment which in ordinary cases is most advantageous, and shuns that which in ordinary cases is least advantageous to that country.

The stock of a country naturally seeks the employment most advantageous to the country, preferring the near to the more distant employments, unless profits are higher in the more distant, which indicates that the more distant employment is necessary.

But if any of those distant employments, which in ordinary cases are less advantageous to the country, the profit should happen to rise some-

what higher than what is sufficient to balance the natural preference
which is given to nearer employments, this superiority of profit will draw
stock from those nearer employments, till the profits of all return to their
proper level. This superiority of profit, however, is a proof that in the
actual circumstances of the society, those distant employments are
somewhat understocked in proportion to other employments, and that
the stock of the society is not distributed in the properest manner among
all the different employments carried on in it. It is a proof that something is either bought cheaper or sold dearer than it ought to be, and
that some particular class of citizens is more or less oppressed either by
paying more or by getting less than what is suitable to that equality,
which ought to take place, and which naturally does take place among
all the different classes of them.

Though the same capital never will maintain the same quantity of
productive labour in a distant as in a near employment, yet a distant
employment may be as necessary for the welfare of the society as a near
one; the goods which the distant employment deals in being necessary,
perhaps, for carrying on many of the nearer employments. But if the
profits of those who deal in such goods are above their proper level, those
goods will be sold dearer than they ought to be, or somewhat above their
natural price, and all those engaged in the nearer employments will be
more or less oppressed by this high price. Their interest, therefore, in
this case requires that some stock should be withdrawn from those nearer
employments, and turned towards that distant one, in order to reduce
its profits to their proper level, and the price of the goods which it deals
in to their natural price. In this extraordinary case, the public interest
requires that some stock should be withdrawn from those employments
which in ordinary cases are more advantageous, and turned towards one
which in ordinary cases is less advantageous to the public: and in this
extraordinary case, the natural interests and inclinations of men coincide as exactly with the public interest as in all other ordinary cases, and
lead them to withdraw stock from the near, and to turn it towards the
distant employment.

It is thus that the private interests and passions of
individuals naturally dispose them to turn their stock
towards the employments which in ordinary cases
are most advantageous to the society. But if from

If too much goes to any
employment, profit falls
in that employment and
the proper distribution is
soon restored.

this natural preference they should turn too much of it towards those
employments, the fall of profit in them and the rise of it in all others
immediately dispose them to alter this faulty distribution. Without any
intervention of law, therefore, the private interests and passions of men
naturally lead them to divide and distribute the stock of every society,
among all the different employments carried on in it, as nearly as possible in the proportion which is most agreeable to the interest of the
whole society . . .

[Chapter 8, "Conclusion of the Mercantile System," has been omitted. There is however no more succinct statement of Smith's argument against mercantilism than the following excerpt from that chapter.]

Consumption is the sole end and purpose of all production; and the interest of the producer ought to be attended to, only so far as it may be necessary for promoting that of the consumer. The maxim is so perfectly self-evident that it would be absurd to attempt to prove it.

> The mercantile system absurdly considers production and not consumption to be the end of industry and commerce.

But in the mercantile system, the interest of the consumer is almost constantly sacrificed to that of the producer; and it seems to consider production, and not consumption, as the ultimate end and object of all industry and commerce. . . .

CHAPTER IX

Of the agricultural Systems, or of those Systems of political Economy, which represent the Produce of Land as either the sole or the principal Source of the Revenue and Wealth of every Country

The agricultural systems of political economy will not require so long an explanation as that which I have thought it necessary to bestow upon the mercantile or commercial system.

> The agricultural systems will require less lengthy explanation than the mercantile system.

That system which represents the produce of land as the sole source of the revenue and wealth of every country, has, so far as I know, never been adopted by any nation, and it at present exists only in the

> There are three classes in their system: (1) proprietors, (2) cultivators, and (3) artificers, manufacturers, and merchants.

speculations of a few men of great learning and ingenuity in France. It would not, surely, be worthwhile to examine at great length the errors of a system which never has done, and probably never will do any harm in any part of the world. I shall endeavour to explain, however, as distinctly as I can, the great outlines of this very ingenious system. . . .

The different orders of people who have ever been supposed to contribute in any respect towards the annual produce of the land and labour of the country, they divide into three classes. The first is the class of the proprietors of land. The second is the

> Proprietors contribute to production by expences on improvement of land, cultivators, by original and annual expences of cultivation.

class of the cultivators, of farmers and country labourers, whom they honour with the peculiar appellation of the productive class. The third is the class of artificers, manufacturers and merchants, whom they endeavour to degrade by the humiliating appellation of the barren or unproductive class.

The class of proprietors contributes to the annual produce by the expence which they may occasionally lay out upon the improvement of the land, upon the buildings, drains, enclosures and other ameliorations, which they may either make or maintain upon it, and by means of which the cultivators are enabled, with the same capital, to raise a greater produce, and consequently to pay a greater rent. This advanced rent may be considered as the interest of profit due to the proprietor upon the expence or capital which he thus employs in the improvement of his land. Such expences are in this system called ground expences (*depenses foncières*).

The cultivators or farmers contribute to the annual produce by what are in this system called the original and annual expences (*depenses primitives et depenses annuelles*) which they lay out upon the cultivation of the land. The original expences consist in the instruments of husbandry, in the stock of cattle, in the seed, and in the maintenance of the farmer's family, servants and cattle, during at least a great part of the first year of his occupancy, or till he can receive some return from the land. The annual expences consist in the seed, in the wear and tear of the instruments of husbandry, and in the annual maintenance of the farmer's servants and cattle, and of his family too, so far as any part of them can be considered as servants employed in cultivation. . . .

Artificers and manufacturers, in particular whose industry, in the common apprehensions of men, increases so much the value of the rude produce of land, are in this system represented as a class of people altogether barren and unproductive. Their labour, it is said, replaces only the stock which employs them, together with its ordinary profits. That stock consists in the materials, tools, and wages, advanced to them by their employer; and is the fund destined for their employment and maintenance. Its profits are the fund destined for the maintenance of their employer. Their employer, as he advances to them the stock of materials, tools and wages necessary for their employment, so he advances to himself what is necessary for his own maintenance, and this maintenance he generally proportions to the profit which he expects to make by the price of their work. . . .

All other expences and orders of people are unproductive.

The labour of artificers and manufacturers never adds anything to the value of the whole annual amount of the rude produce of the land. It adds indeed greatly to the value of some particular parts of it. But the consumption which in the meantime it occasions of other parts, is precisely equal to the value which it adds to those parts; so that the value of the whole amount is not, at any one moment of time, in the least augmented by it. . . .

The labour of artificers and manufacturers adds nothing to the value of the annual produce.

The unproductive class, that of merchants, artificers, and manufacturers, is maintained and

The unproductive class is maintained at the

employed altogether at the expence of the two other
classes, of that of proprietors, and of that of cultivators. They furnish it both with the materials of its
work and with the fund of its subsistence, with the
corn and cattle which it consumes while it is
employed about that work. The proprietors and cultivators finally pay both the wages of all the workmen of the unproductive class, and the profits of all their employers. Those workmen and
their employers are properly the servants of the proprietors and cultivators. They are only servants who work without doors, as menial servants
work within. Both the one and the other, however, are equally maintained at the expence of the same masters. The labour of both is equally
unproductive. It adds nothing to the value of the sum total of the rude
produce of the land. Instead of increasing the value of that sum total, it
is a charge and expence which must be paid out of it.

expence of the other two, but is useful to them, and it is not their interest to discourage its industry; nor is it ever the interest of the unproductive class to oppress the others.

The unproductive class, however, is not only useful, but greatly useful to the other two classes. By means of the industry of merchants,
artificers and manufacturers, the proprietors and cultivators can purchase both the foreign goods and the manufactured produce of their own
country which they have occasion for, with the produce of a much smaller
quantity of their own labour, than what they would be obliged to employ,
if they were to attempt, in an awkward and unskilful manner, either to
import the one, or to make the other for their own use. By means of the
unproductive class, the cultivators are delivered from many cares which
would otherwise distract their attention from the cultivation of land. . . .

It can never be the interest of the proprietors and cultivators to restrain
or to discourage in any respect the industry of merchants, artificers and
manufacturers. The greater the liberty which this unproductive class
enjoys, the greater will be the competition in all the different trades
which compose it, and the cheaper will the other two classes be supplied, both with foreign goods and with the manufactured produce of
their own country.

It can never be the interest of the unproductive class to oppress the
other two classes. It is the surplus produce of the land, or what remains
after deducting the maintenance, first, of the cultivators, and afterwards,
of the proprietors, that maintains and employs the unproductive class.
The greater this surplus, the greater must likewise be the maintenance
and employment of that class. The establishment of perfect justice, of
perfect liberty, and of perfect equality, is the very simple secret which
most effectually secures the highest degree of prosperity to all the three
classes. . . .

According to this liberal and generous system,
therefore, the most advantageous method in which
a landed nation can raise up artificers, manufacturers, and merchants of its own, is to grant the most
perfect freedom of trade to the artificers, manufacturers, and merchants

Freedom of trade therefore is best for introducing manufactures and foreign trade.

of all other nations. It thereby raises the value of the surplus produce of its own land, of which the continual increase gradually establishes a fund which in due time necessarily raises up all the artificers, manufacturers and merchants whom it has occasion for. . . .

Some speculative physicians seem to have imag- Nations can prosper in ined that the health of the human body could be spite of hurtful regula- preserved only by a certain precise regimen of diet tions. and exercise, of which every, the smallest, violation necessarily occasioned some degree of disease or disorder proportioned to the degree of the violation. Experience, however, would seem to show that the human body frequently preserves, to all appearance at least, the most perfect state of health under a vast variety of different regimens; even under some which are generally believed to be very far from being perfectly wholesome. But the healthful state of the human body, it would seem, contains in itself some unknown principle of preservation, capable either of preventing or of correcting, in many respects, the bad effects even of a very faulty regimen.

Mr. Quesnay,* who was himself a physician, and a very speculative physician, seems to have entertained a notion of the same kind concerning the political body, and to have imagined that it would thrive and prosper only under a certain precise regimen, the exact regimen of perfect liberty and perfect justice. He seems not to have considered that in the political body, the natural effort which every man is continually making to better his own condition, is a principle of preservation capable of preventing and correcting, in many respects, the bad effects of a political economy, in some degree, both partial and oppressive. Such a political economy, though it no doubt retards more or less, is not always capable of stopping altogether the natural progress of a nation towards wealth and prosperity, and still less of making it go backwards. If a nation could not prosper without the enjoyment of perfect liberty and perfect justice, there is not in the world a nation which could ever have prospered. In the political body, however, the wisdom of nature has fortunately made ample provision for remedying many of the bad effects of the folly and injustice of man; in the same manner as it has done in the natural body, for remedying those of his sloth and intemperance.

The capital error of this system, however, seems The system is wrong in to lie in its representing the class of artificers, man- representing artificers, ufacturers, and merchants, as altogether barren and etc., as unproductive, unproductive. The following observations may serve since, to show the impropriety of this representation. (1) they reproduce at least their annual con-

First, this class, it is acknowledged, reproduces sumption and continue annually the value of its own annual consumption, the capital which and continues, at least, the existence of the stock or employs them, capital which maintains and employs it. But upon this account alone

* François Quesnay (1694–1774), the founder of Physiocracy.

the denomination of barren or unproductive should seem to be very improperly applied to it. We should not call a marriage barren or unproductive, though it produced only a son and a daughter, to replace the father and mother, and though it did not increase the number of the human species, but only continued it as it was before. Farmers and country labourers, indeed, over and above the stock which maintains and employs them, reproduce annually a net produce, a free rent to the landlord. As a marriage which affords three children is certainly more productive than one which affords only two; so the labour of farmers and country labourers is certainly more productive than that of merchants, artificers, and manufacturers. The superior produce of the one class, however, does not render the other barren or unproductive.

Secondly, it seems, upon this account, altogether improper to consider artificers, manufacturers, and merchants in the same light as menial servants. The labour of menial servants does not continue the existence of the fund which maintains and employs them. Their maintenance and employment is altogether at the expence of their masters, and the work which they perform is not of a nature to repay that expence. That work consists in services which perish generally in the very instant of their performance, and does not fix or realize itself in any vendible commodity which can replace the value of their wages and maintenance. The labour, on the contrary, of artificers, manufacturers, and merchants, naturally does fix and realize itself in some such vendible commodity. It is upon this account that, in the chapter in which I treat of productive and unproductive labour, I have classed artificers, manufacturers, and merchants, among the productive labourers, and menial servants among the barren or unproductive. . . . *(2) they are not like menial servants.*

This system, however, with all its imperfections is, perhaps, the nearest approximation to the truth that has yet been published upon the subject of political economy, and is upon that account well worth the consideration of every man who wishes to examine with attention the principles of that very important science. Though in representing the labour which is employed upon land as the only productive labour, the notions which it inculcates are perhaps too narrow and confined; yet in representing the wealth of nations as consisting, not in the unconsumable riches of money, but in the consumable goods annually reproduced by the labour of the society; and in representing perfect liberty as the only effectual expedient for rendering this annual reproduction the greatest possible, its doctrine seems to be in every respect as just as it is generous and liberal. Its followers are very numerous; and as men are fond of paradoxes, and of appearing to understand what surpasses the comprehension of ordinary people, the paradox which it maintains, concerning the unproductive nature of manufacturing labour, has not perhaps contributed a little to increase the number of its admirers. They have for *In spite of its errors the system has been valuable.*

some years past made a pretty considerable sect, distinguished in the French republic of letters by the name of The Economists. Their works have certainly been of some service to their country; not only by bringing into general discussion, many subjects which had never been well examined before, but by influencing in some measure the public administration in favour of agriculture. It has been in consequence of their representations, accordingly, that the agriculture of France has been delivered from several of the oppressions which it before laboured under. . . .

All systems either of preference or of restraint, therefore, being thus completely taken away, the obvious and simple system of natural liberty establishes itself of its own accord. Every man, as long as he does not violate the laws of justice, is left perfectly free to pursue his own interest his own way,

The system of natural liberty leaves the sovereign only three duties: (1) the defence of the country; (2) the administration of justice, and (3) the maintenance of certain public works.

and to bring both his industry and capital into competition with those of any other man, or order of men. The sovereign is completely discharged from a duty, in the attempting to perform which he must always be exposed to innumerable delusions, and for the proper performance of which no human wisdom or knowledge could ever be sufficient; the duty of superintending the industry of private people, and of directing it towards the employments most suitable to the interest of the society. According to the system of natural liberty, the sovereign has only three duties to attend to; three duties of great importance, indeed, but plain and intelligible to common understandings: first, the duty of protecting the society from the violence and invasion of other independent societies; secondly, the duty of protecting, as far as possible, every member of the society from the injustice or oppression of every other member of it, or the duty of establishing an exact administration of justice; and, thirdly, the duty of erecting and maintaining certain public works and certain public institutions, which it can never be for the interest of any individual, or small number of individuals to erect and maintain; because the profit could never repay the expence to any individual or small number of individuals, though it may frequently do much more than repay it to a great society.

The proper performance of those several duties of the sovereign necessarily supposes a certain expence; and this expence again necessarily requires a certain revenue to support it. In the following book, therefore, I shall endeavour to explain; first, what are the necessary expences of the sovereign or commonwealth; and which of those expences ought to be defrayed by the general contribution of the whole society; and which of them, by that of some particular part only, or of some particular members of the society: secondly, what are the different methods in which the whole society may be made to contribute towards defraying the expences incumbent on the whole society, and what are the principal advantages and inconveniences of each of those methods: and, thirdly, what are the reasons and causes which have induced almost all modern governments to mortgage some part of this revenue, or to contract debts, and what have been the effects of those debts upon the real wealth, the annual produce of the land and labour of the society. The following book, therefore, will naturally be divided into three chapters.

BOOK V

OF THE REVENUE OF THE SOVEREIGN OR COMMONWEALTH

CHAPTER I

Of the Expences of the Sovereign or Commonwealth

PART I

Of the Expence of Defence

The first duty of the sovereign, that of protecting the society from the violence and invasion of other independent societies, can be performed only by means of a military force. But the expence both of preparing this military force in time of peace, and of employing it in time of war, is very different in the different states of society, in the different periods of improvement.

The expence of a military force is different at different periods. Among hunters it costs nothing.

Among nations of hunters, the lowest and rudest state of society, such as we find it among the native tribes of North America, every man is a warrior as well as a hunter. When he goes to war, either to defend his society, or to revenge the injuries which have been done to it by other societies, he maintains himself by his own labour, in the same manner as when he lives at home. His society, for in this state of things there is properly neither sovereign nor commonwealth, is at no sort of expence, either to prepare him for the field, or to maintain him while he is in it.

Among nations of shepherds, a more advanced state of society, such as we find it among the Tartars and Arabs, every man is, in the same manner, a warrior. Such nations have commonly no fixed habitation, but live, either in tents, or in a sort of covered wagons which are easily transported from place to place. The whole tribe or nation changes its situation according to the different seasons of the year, as well as according to other accidents. When its herds and flocks have consumed the forage of one part of the country, it removes to another, and from that to a third. In the dry season, it comes down to the banks of the rivers; in the wet season it retires to the upper country. When such a nation goes to

When shepherds go to war the whole nation moves with its property.

war, the warriors will not trust their herds and flocks to the feeble defence of their old men, their women and children; and their old men, their women and children, will not be left behind without defence and without subsistence. The whole nation, besides, being accustomed to a wandering life, even in time of peace, easily takes the field in time of war. . . .

Agriculture, even in its rudest and lowest state, supposes a settlement; some sort of fixed habitation which cannot be abandoned without great loss. When a nation of mere husbandmen, therefore, goes to war, the whole people cannot take the field together. The old men, the women and children, at least, must remain at home to take care of the habitation. All the men of the military age, however, may take the field, and, in small nations of this kind, have frequently done so. . . .

In a more advanced state of society, two different causes contribute to render it altogether impossible that they, who take the field, should maintain themselves at their own expence. Those two causes are, the progress of manufactures, and the improvement in the art of war.

Later it becomes necessary to pay those who take the field, since artificers and manufacturers must be maintained by the public when away from their work, and the greater length of campaigns makes service without pay too heavy a burden even for husbandmen.

Though a husbandman should be employed in an expedition, provided it begins after seed-time and ends before harvest, the interruption of his business will not always occasion any considerable diminution of his revenue. Without the intervention of his labour, nature does herself the greater part of the work which remains to be done. But the moment that an artificer, a smith, a carpenter, or a weaver, for example, quits his workhouse, the sole source of his revenue is completely dried up. Nature does nothing for him, he does all for himself. When he takes the field, therefore, in defence of the public, as he has no revenue to maintain himself, he must necessarily be maintained by the public. But in a country of which a great part of the inhabitants are artificers and manufacturers, a great part of the people who go to war must be drawn from those classes, and must therefore be maintained by the public as long as they are employed in its service.

When the art of war too has gradually grown up to be a very intricate and complicated science, when the event of war ceases to be determined, as in the first ages of society, by a single irregular skirmish or battle, but when the contest is generally spun out through several different campaigns, each of which lasts during the greater part of the year; it becomes universally necessary that the public should maintain those who serve the public in war, at least while they are employed in that service. . . .

The art of war, however, as it is certainly the noblest of all arts, so in the progress of improvement it necessarily becomes one of the most complicated among them. The state of the mechanical, as well

But as war becomes more complicated, division of labour becomes necessary to carry the art to perfection.

as of some other arts, with which it is necessarily connected, determines the degree of perfection to which it is capable of being carried at any particular time. But in order to carry it to this degree of perfection, it is necessary that it should become the sole or principal occupation of a particular class of citizens, and the division of labour is as necessary for the improvement of this, as of ever other art. Into other arts the division of labour is naturally introduced by the prudence of individuals, who find that they promote their private interest better by confining themselves to a particular trade, than by exercising a great number. But it is the wisdom of the state only which can render the trade of a soldier a particular trade separate and distinct from all others. A private citizen who, in time of profound peace, and without any particular encouragement from the public, should spend the greater part of his time in military exercises, might, no doubt, both improve himself very much in them, and amuse himself very well; but he certainly would not promote his own interest. It is the wisdom of the state only which can render it for his interest to give up the greater part of his time to this peculiar occupation: and states have not always had this wisdom, even when their circumstances had become such, that the preservation of their existence required that they should have it. . . .

Before the invention of firearms, that army was superior in which the soldiers had, each individually, the greatest skill and dexterity in the use of their arms. Strength and agility of body were of the highest consequence, and commonly determined the fate of battles. But this skill and dexterity in the use of their arms, could be acquired only, in the same manner as fencing is at present, by practising, not in great bodies, but each man separately, in a particular school, under a particular master, or with his own particular equals and companions. Since the invention of firearms, strength and agility of body, or even extraordinary dexterity and skill in the use of arms, though they are far from being of no consequence, are, however, of less consequence. The nature of the weapon, though it by no means puts the awkward upon a level with the skilful, puts him more nearly so than he ever was before. All the dexterity and skill, it is supposed, which are necessary for using it, can be well enough acquired by practising in great bodies.

Firearms brought about the change by making dexterity less important, and discipline much more so.

Regularity, order, and prompt obedience to command, are qualities which, in modern armies, are of more importance towards determining the fate of battles, than the dexterity and skill of the soldiers in the use of their arms. But the noise of firearms, the smoke, and the invisible death to which every man feels himself every moment exposed, as soon as he comes within cannon-shot, and frequently a long time before the battle can be well said to be engaged, must render it very difficult to maintain any considerable degree of this regularity, order, and prompt obedience, even in the beginning of a modern battle. In an ancient battle there was no noise but what arose from the human voice; there was no smoke, there was no invisible cause of wounds or death. Every man, till some mortal weapon actually did approach him, saw clearly that no such weapon was near him. In these circumstances, and among troops who had some confidence in their own skill and dexterity in the use of their arms, it must have been a good deal less difficult to preserve some degree of regularity and order, not only in the beginning, but through the whole progress of an ancient battle, and till one of the two armies was fairly defeated. But the habits of regularity, order, and prompt obedience to command, can be acquired only by troops which are exercised in great bodies. . . .

The first duty of the sovereign, therefore, that of defending the society from the violence and injustice of other independent societies, grows gradually more and more expensive, as the society advances in civilisation. The military force of the society, which originally cost the sovereign no expence either in time of peace or in time of war, must, in the progress of improvement, first be maintained by him in time of war, and afterwards even in time of peace. . . .

Defence thus grows more expensive.

PART II

Of the Expence of Justice

The second duty of the sovereign, that of protecting, as far as possible, every member of the society from the injustice or oppression of every other member of it, or the duty of establishing an exact administration of justice, requires too very different degrees of expence in the different periods of society.

The expence of justice is different at different periods.

Civil government was first rendered necessary by the introduction of property.

Among nations of hunters, as there is scarce any property, or at least none that exceeds the value of two or three days labour; so there is seldom any established magistrate or any regular administration of justice. Men who have no property can injure one another only in their persons or reputations. But when one man kills, wounds, beats, or defames another, though he to whom the injury is done suffers, he who does it receives no benefit. It is otherwise with the injuries to property. The benefit of the person who does the injury is often equal to the loss of him who suffers it. Envy, malice, or resentment, are the only passions which can prompt one man to injure another in his person or reputation. But the greater part of men are not very frequently under the influence of those passions; and the very worst men are so only occasionally. As their gratification too, how agreeable soever it may be to certain characters, is not attended with any real or permanent advantage, it is in the greater part of men commonly restrained by prudential considerations.

Men may live together in society with some tolerable degree of security, though there is no civil magistrate to protect them from the injustice of those passions. But avarice and ambition in the rich, in the poor the hatred of labour and the love of present ease and enjoyment, are the passions which prompt to invade property, passions much more steady in their operation, and much more universal in their influence.

Wherever there is great property, there is great inequality. For one very rich man, there must be at least five hundred poor, and the affluence of the few supposes the indigence of the many. The affluence of the rich excites the indignation of the poor, who are often both driven by want, and prompted by envy, to invade his possessions. It is only under the shelter of the civil magistrate that the owner of that valuable property, which is acquired by the labour of many years, or perhaps of many successive generations, can sleep a single night in security. He is at all times surrounded by unknown enemies, whom, though he never provoked, he can never appease, and from whose injustice he can be protected only by the powerful arm of the civil magistrate continually held up to chastise it. The acquisition of valuable and extensive property, therefore, necessarily requires the establishment of civil government. Where there is no property, or at least none that exceeds the value of two or three days labour, civil government is not so necessary.

Civil government supposes a certain subordination. But as the necessity of civil government gradually grows up with the acquisition of valuable property, so the principal causes which naturally introduce subordination gradually grow up with the growth of that valuable property. *Property strengthens the causes of subordination.*

The causes or circumstances which naturally introduce subordination, or which naturally, and antecedent to any civil institution, give some men some superiority over the greater part of their brethren, seem to be four in number. *There are four causes of subordination,*

The first of those causes or circumstances is the superiority of personal qualifications, of strength, beauty, and agility of body; of wisdom, and virtue, of prudence, justice, fortitude, and moderation of mind. The qualifications of the body, unless supported by those of the mind, can give little authority in any period of society. He is a very strong man who, by mere strength of body, can force two weak ones to obey him. The qualifications of the mind can alone give very great authority. They are, however, invisible qualities; always disputable, and generally disputed. No society, whether barbarous or civilised, has ever found it convenient to settle the rules of precedency, of rank and subordination, according to those invisible qualities; but according to something that is more plain and palpable. *(1) superiority of personal qualifications,*

The second of those causes or circumstances is the superiority of age. An old man, provided his age *(2) superiority of age,* is not so far advanced as to give suspicion of dotage, is everywhere more respected than a young man of equal rank, fortune, and abilities. Among nations of hunters, such as the native tribes of North America, age is the sole foundation of rank and precedency. Among them, father is the appellation of a superior; brother, of an equal; and son, of an inferior. In the most opulent and civilised nations, age regulates rank among those who are in every other respect equal, and among whom, therefore, there is nothing else to regulate it. Among brothers and among sisters, the eldest always take place; and in the succession of the paternal estate every thing which cannot be divided, but must go entire to one person, such as a title of honour, is in most cases given to the eldest. Age is a plain and palpable quality which admits of no dispute.

The third of those causes or circumstances is the superiority of fortune. The authority of riches, how- (3) superiority of fortune, ever, though great in every age of society, is perhaps greatest in the rudest age of society which admits of any considerable inequality of fortune. A Tartar chief, the increase of whose herds and flocks is sufficient to maintain a thousand men, cannot well employ that increase in any other way than in maintaining a thousand men. The rude state of his society does not afford him any manufactured produce, any trinkets or baubles of any kind, for which he can exchange that part of his rude produce which is over and above his own consumption. The thousand men whom he thus maintains, depending entirely upon him for their subsistence, must both obey his orders in war, and submit to his jurisdiction in peace. He is necessarily both their general and their judge, and his chieftainship is the necessary effect of the superiority of his fortune.

In an opulent and civilised society, a man may possess a much greater fortune, and yet not be able to command a dozen of people. Though the produce of his estate may be sufficient to maintain, and may perhaps actually maintain, more than a thousand people, yet as those people pay for every thing which they get from him, as he gives scarce any thing to any body but in exchange for an equivalent, there is scarce any body who considers himself as entirely dependent upon him, and his authority extends only over a few menial servants. The authority of fortune, however, is very great even in an opulent and civilised society. That it is much greater than that, either of age, or of personal qualities, has been the constant complaint of every period of society which admitted of any considerable inequality of fortune. The first period of society, that of hunters, admits of no such inequality. Universal poverty establishes there universal equality, and the superiority, either of age, or of personal qualities, are the feeble, but the sole foundations of authority and subordination. There is therefore little or no authority or subordination in this period of society. The second period of society, that of shepherds, admits of very great inequalities of fortune, and there is no period in which the superiority of fortune gives so great authority to those who possess it. There is no period accordingly in which authority and subordination are more perfectly established. The authority of an Arabian sharif is very great; that of a Tartar khan altogether despotical.

The fourth of those causes or circumstances is the superiority of birth. Superiority of birth supposes an ancient superiority of fortune in the family of the person who claims it. All families are equally ancient; and the ancestors of the prince, though they may be better known, cannot well be more numerous than those of the beggar. Antiquity of family means everywhere the antiquity either of wealth, or of that greatness which is commonly either founded upon wealth, or accompanied with it. Upstart greatness is everywhere less respected than ancient greatness. The hatred of usurpers, the love of the family of an ancient monarch, are, in a great measure, founded upon the contempt which men naturally have for the former, and upon their veneration for the latter. As a military officer submits without reluctance to the authority of a superior by whom he has always been commanded, but cannot bear that his inferior should be set over his head; so men easily submit to a family to whom they and their ancestors have always submitted; but are fired with indignation when another family, in whom they had never acknowledged any such superiority, assumes a dominion over them.

and (4) superiority of birth.

The distinction of birth, being subsequent to the inequality of fortune, can have no place in nations of hunters, among whom all men, being equal in fortune, must likewise be very nearly equal in birth. The son of a wise and brave man may, indeed, even among them, be somewhat more respected than a man of equal merit who has the misfortune to be the son of a fool or a coward. The difference, however, will not be very great; and there never was, I believe, a great family in the world whose illustration was entirely derived from the inheritance of wisdom and virtue.

The distinction of birth is not present among hunters, but always among shepherds.

The distinction of birth not only may, but always does take place among nations of shepherds. Such nations are always strangers to every sort of luxury, and great wealth can scarce ever be dissipated among them by improvident profusion. There are no nations accordingly who abound more in families revered and honoured on account of their descent from a long race of great and illustrious ancestors; because there are no nations among whom wealth is likely to continue longer in the same families.

Birth and fortune are evidently the two circumstances which principally set one man above another. They are the two great sources of personal distinction, and are therefore the principal causes which naturally establish authority and subordination among men. Among nations of shepherds both those causes operate with their full force. The

Distinctions of birth and fortune are both most powerful among shepherds.

great shepherd or herdsman, respected on account of his great wealth, and of the great number of those who depend upon him for subsistence, and revered on account of the nobleness of his birth, and of the immemorial antiquity of his illustrious family, has a natural authority over all the inferior shepherds or herdsmen of his horde or clan. He can command the united force of a greater number of people than any of them. His military power is greater than that of any of them. In time of war they are all of them naturally disposed to muster themselves under his banner, rather than under that of any other person, and his birth and fortune thus naturally procure to him some sort of executive power. By commanding too the united force of a greater number of people than any of them, he is best able to compel any one of them who may have injured another to compensate the wrong. He is the person, therefore, to whom all those who are too weak to defend themselves naturally look up for protection. It is to him that they naturally complain of the injuries which they imagine have been done to them, and his interposition in such cases is more easily submitted to, even by the person complained of, than that of any other person would be. His birth and fortune thus naturally procure him some sort of judicial authority.

It is in the age of shepherds, in the second period of society, that the inequality of fortune first begins to take place, and introduces among men a degree of authority and subordination which could not possibly exist before. It thereby introduces some degree of that civil government which is indispensably necessary for its own preservation: and it seems to do this naturally, and even independent of the consideration of that necessity. The consideration of that necessity comes no doubt afterwards to contribute very much to maintain and secure that authority and subordination. The rich, in particular, are necessarily interested to support that order of things, which can alone secure them in the possession of their own advantages. Men of inferior wealth combine to defend those of superior wealth in the possession of their property, in order that men of superior wealth may combine to defend them in the possession of theirs. All the inferior shepherds and herdsmen feel that the security of their own herds and flocks depends upon the security of those of the great shepherd or herdsman; that the maintenance of their lesser authority depends upon that of his greater authority, and that upon their subordination to him depends his power of keeping their inferiors in subordination to them. They constitute a sort of little nobility, who feel themselves interested to defend the property and to support the authority of their own little sovereign, in order that he may be able to defend their property and to support their authority. Civil government, so far as it is instituted for the security of property, is in reality instituted for the defence of the rich against the poor, or of those who have some property against those who have none at all. . . .

Among shepherds inequality of fortune arises and introduces civil government.

Of the Expence of public Works and public Institutions

The third and last duty of the sovereign or commonwealth is that of erecting and maintaining those public institutions and those public works, which, though they may be in the highest degree advantageous to a great society, are, however, of such a nature, that the profit could never repay the

The third duty of the sovereign is the erection and maintenance of those public works and institutions which are useful but not capable of bringing in a profit to individuals.

expence to any individual or small number of individuals, and which it, therefore, cannot be expected that any individual or small number of individuals should erect or maintain. The performance of this duty requires too very different degrees of expence in the different periods of society.

After the public institutions and public works necessary for the defence of the society, and for the administration of justice, both of which have already been mentioned, the other works and institutions of this kind are chiefly those for facilitating the commerce of the society, and those for promoting the instruction of the people. The institutions for instruction are of two kinds; those for the education of the youth, and those for the instruction of people of all ages. The consideration of the manner in which the expence of those different sorts of public works and institutions may be most properly defrayed, will divide this third part of the present chapter into three different articles.

Of the public Works and Institutions for facilitating the Commerce of the Society
And, first, of those which are necessary for facilitating Commerce in general

That the erection and maintenance of the public works which facilitate the commerce of any country, such as good roads, bridges, navigable canals,

The expence of institutions increases.

harbours, etc., must require very different degrees of expence in the different periods of society, is evident without any proof. The expence of making and maintaining the public roads of any country must evidently increase with the annual produce of the land and labour of that country, or with the quantity and weight of the goods which it becomes necessary to fetch and carry upon those roads. The strength of a bridge must be suited to the number and weight of the carriages, which are likely to pass over it. The depth and the supply of water for a navigable canal must be proportioned to the number of tonnage of the lighters, which are likely to carry goods upon it; the extent of a harbour to the number of the shipping which are likely to take shelter in it.

It does not seem necessary that the expence of those public works should be defrayed from that

The expence need not be defrayed from the

public revenue, as it is commonly called, of which the collection and application is in most countries assigned to the executive power. The greater part of such public works may easily be so managed, as to afford a particular revenue sufficient for defraying their own expence, without bringing any burden upon the general revenue of the society.

general public revenue, but may be raised by tolls and other particular charges.

A highway, a bridge, a navigable canal, for example, may in most cases be both made and maintained by a small toll upon the carriages which make use of them: a harbour, by a moderate port-duty upon the tonnage of the shipping which load or unload in it. The coinage, another institution for facilitating commerce, in many countries, not only defrays its own expence, but affords a small revenue or seignorage to the sovereign. The post-office, another institution for the same purpose, over and above defraying its own expence, affords in almost all countries a very considerable revenue to the sovereign. . . .

Even those public works which are of such a nature that they cannot afford any revenue for maintaining themselves, but of which the convenience is nearly confined to some particular place or district, are always better maintained by a local or provincial revenue, under the management of a local and provincial administration, than by the general revenue of the state, of which the executive power must always have the management. Were the streets of London to be lighted and paved at the expence of the treasury, is there any probability that they would be so well lighted and paved as they are at present, or even at so small an expence? The expence, besides, instead of being raised by a local tax upon the inhabitants of each particular street, parish, or district in London, would, in this case, be defrayed out of the general revenue of the state, and would consequently be raised by a tax upon all the inhabitants of the kingdom, of whom the greater part derive no sort of benefit from the lighting and paving of the streets of London. . . .

Public works of a local nature should be maintained by local revenue.

Of the Public Works and Institutions which are necessary for facilitating particular Branches of Commerce

The object of the public works and institutions above mentioned is to facilitate commerce in general. But in order to facilitate some particular branches of it, particular institutions are necessary, which again require a particular and extraordinary expence.

Some particular institutions are required to facilitate particular branches of commerce, as trade with barbarous nations requires forts, and trade with other nations requires ambassadors.

Some particular branches of commerce, which are carried on with barbarous and uncivilised nations, require extraordinary protection. An ordinary store or counting-house could give little security to the goods of the merchants who trade to the western coast of

Africa. To defend them from the barbarous natives, it is necessary that the place where they are deposited, should be, in some measure, fortified. The disorders in the government of Indostan have been supposed to render a like precaution necessary even among that mild and gentle people; and it was under pretence of securing their persons and property from violence, that both the English and French East India Companies were allowed to erect the first forts which they possessed in that country. Among other nations, whose vigorous government will suffer no strangers to possess any fortified place within their territory, it may be necessary to maintain some ambassador, minister, or consul, who may both decide, according to their own customs, the differences arising among his own countrymen; and, in their disputes with the natives, may, by means of his public character, interfere with more authority, and afford them a more powerful protection, than they could expect from any private man. The interests of commerce have frequently made it necessary to maintain ministers in foreign countries, where the purposes, either of war or alliance, would not have required any. The commerce of the Turkey Company first occasioned the establishment of an ordinary ambassador at Constantinople. The first English embassies to Russia arose altogether from commercial interests. The constant interference which those interests necessarily occasioned between the subjects of the different states of Europe, has probably introduced the custom of keeping, in all neighbouring countries, ambassadors, or ministers constantly resident even in the time of peace. This custom, unknown to ancient times, seems not to be older than the end of the fifteenth or beginning of the sixteenth century; that is, than the time when commerce first began to extend itself to the greater part of the nations of Europe, and when they first began to attend to its interests.

It seems not unreasonable, that the extraordinary expence, which the protection of any particular branch of commerce may occasion, should be defrayed by a moderate tax upon that particular branch; by a moderate fine, for example, to be paid by the traders when they first enter into it, or, what is more equal, by a particular duty of so much percent upon the goods which they either import into, or export out of, the particular countries with which it is carried on. The protection of trade in general, from pirates and freebooters, is said to have given occasion to the first institution of the duties of customs. But, if it was thought reasonable to lay a general tax upon trade, in order to defray the expence of protecting trade in general, it should seem equally reasonable to lay a particular tax upon a particular branch of trade, in order to defray the extraordinary expence of protecting that branch. . . .

Branches of commerce which require extraordinary expence for their protection may reasonably bear a particular tax.

With the right of possessing forts and garrisons, in distant and barbarous countries, is necessarily connected the right of making peace and war in those

Companies misuse the right of making peace and war.

countries. The joint stock companies which have had the one right, have constantly exercised the other, and have frequently had it expressly conferred upon them. How unjustly, how capriciously, how cruelly they have commonly exercised it, is too well known from recent experience.

When a company of merchants undertake, at their own risk and expence, to establish a new trade with some remote and barbarous nation, it may not be unreasonable to incorporate them into a joint stock company, and to grant them, in case of their success, a monopoly of the trade for a certain number of years. It is the easiest and most natural way in which the state can recompense them for hazarding a dangerous and expensive experiment, of which the public is afterwards to reap the benefit. A temporary monopoly of this kind may be vindicated upon the same principles upon which a like monopoly of a new machine is granted to its inventor, and that of a new book to its author. But upon the expiration of the term, the monopoly ought certainly to determine; the forts and garrisons, if it was found necessary to establish any, to be taken into the hands of government, their value to be paid to the company, and the trade to be laid open to all the subjects of the state.

The grant of a temporary monopoly to a joint stock company may sometimes be reasonable, but a perpetual monopoly creates an absurd tax.

By a perpetual monopoly, all the other subjects of the state are taxed very absurdly in two different ways; first, by the high price of goods, which, in the case of a free trade, they could buy much cheaper; and, secondly, by their total exclusion from a branch of business, which it might be both convenient and profitable for many of them to carry on. It is for the most worthless of all purposes too that they are taxed in this manner. It is merely to enable the company to support the negligence, profusion, and malversation of their own servants, whose disorderly conduct seldom allows the dividend of the company to exceed the ordinary rate of profit in trades which are altogether free, and very frequently makes it fall even a good deal short of that rate.

Without a monopoly, however, a joint stock company, it would appear from experience, cannot long carry on any branch of foreign trade. To buy in one market, in order to sell, with profit, in another, when there are many competitors in both; to watch over, not only the occasional variations in the demand, but the much greater and more frequent variations in the competition, or in the supply which that demand is likely to get from other people, and to suit with dexterity and judgment both the quantity and quality of each assortment of goods to all these circumstances, is a species of warfare of which the operations are continually changing, and which can scarce ever be conducted successfully, without such an unremitting exertion of vigilance and attention, as cannot long be expected from the directors of a joint stock company. . . .

Of the Expence of the Institutions for the Education of Youth

. . . In the progress of the division of labour, the employment of the far greater part of those who live by labour, that is, of the great body of the people, comes to be confined to a few very simple operations; frequently to one or two. But the understandings of the greater part of men are necessarily formed by their ordinary employments. The man whose whole life is spent in performing a few simple operations, of which the effects too are, perhaps, always the same, or very nearly the same, has no occasion to exert his understanding, or to exercise his invention in finding out expedients for removing difficulties which never occur. He naturally loses, therefore, the habit of such exertion, and generally becomes as stupid and ignorant as it is possible for a human creature to become. The torpor of his mind renders him, not only incapable of relishing or bearing a part in any rational conversation, but of conceiving any generous, noble, or tender sentiment, and consequently of forming any just judgment concerning many even of the ordinary duties of private life. Of the great and extensive interests of his country, he is altogether incapable of judging; and unless very particular pains have been taken to render him otherwise, he is equally incapable of defending his country in war. The uniformity of his stationary life naturally corrupts the courage of his mind, and makes him regard with abhorrence the irregular, uncertain, and adventurous life of a soldier. It corrupts even the activity of his body, and renders him incapable of exerting his strength with vigour and perseverance, in any other employment than that to which he has been bred. His dexterity at his own particular trade seems, in this manner, to be acquired at the expence of his intellectual, social, and martial virtues. But in every improved and civilised society this is the state into which the labouring poor, that is, the great body of the people, must necessarily fall, unless government takes some pains to prevent it.

Division of labour destroys intellectual, social, and martial virtues unless government takes pains to prevent it, whereas in barbarous societies those virtues are kept alive by constant necessity.

It is otherwise in the barbarous societies, as they are commonly called, of hunters, of shepherds, and even of husbandmen in that rude state of husbandry which precedes the improvement of manufactures, and the extension of foreign commerce. In such societies the varied occupations of every man oblige every man to exert his capacity, and to invent expedients for removing difficulties which are continually occurring. Invention is kept alive, and the mind is not suffered to fall into that drowsy stupidity, which, in a civilised society, seems to benumb the understanding of almost all the inferior ranks of people. In those barbarous societies, as they are called, every man, it has already been observed, is a warrior. Every man too is in some measure a statesman, and can form a tolerable judgment concerning the interest of the society, and the conduct of those who govern it. How far their chiefs are good judges in peace, or good leaders in war, is obvious to the observation of almost every single man among them. In such a society indeed, no man can well acquire that improved and refined understanding, which a few men sometimes possess in a more civilised state.

Though in a rude society there is a good deal of variety in the occupations of every individual, there is not a great deal in those of the whole society. Every man does, or is capable of doing, almost every thing which any other man does, or is capable of doing. Every man has a considerable degree of knowledge, ingenuity, and invention; but scarce any man has a great degree. The degree, however, which is commonly possessed, is generally sufficient for conducting the whole simple business of the society.

In a civilised state, on the contrary, though there is little variety in the occupations of the greater part of individuals, there is an almost infinite variety in those of the whole society. These varied occupations present an almost infinite variety of objects to the contemplation of those few, who, being attached to no particular occupation themselves, have leisure and inclination to examine the occupations of other people. The contemplation of so great a variety of objects necessarily exercises their minds in endless comparisons and combinations, and renders their understandings, in an extraordinary degree, both acute and comprehensive. Unless those few, however, happen to be placed in some very particular situations, their great abilities, though honourable to themselves, may contribute very little to the good government or happiness of their society. Notwithstanding the great abilities of those few, all the nobler parts of the human character may be, in a great measure, obliterated and extinguished in the great body of the people.

The education of the common people requires, perhaps, in a civilized and commercial society, the attention of the public more than that of people of some rank and fortune. People of some rank and fortune are generally eighteen or nineteen years of age before they enter upon that particular business, profession, or trade, by which they propose to distinguish themselves in the world. They have before that full time to acquire, or at least to fit themselves for afterwards acquiring, every accomplishment which can recommend them to the public esteem, or render them worthy of it. Their parents or guardians are generally sufficiently anxious that they should be so accomplished, and are, in most cases, willing enough to lay out the expence which is necessary for that purpose. If they are not always properly educated, it is seldom from the want of expence laid out upon their education; but from the improper application of that expence. It is sel-

The education of the common people requires attention from the state more than that of people of rank and fortune, whose parents can look after their interests, and who spend their lives in varied occupations chiefly intellectual, unlike the children of the poor.

dom from the want of masters; but from the negligence and incapacity of the masters who are to be had, and from the difficulty, or rather from the impossibility which there is, in the present state of things, of finding any better.

The employments too in which people of some rank or fortune spend the greater part of their lives, are not, like those of the common people, simple and uniform. They are almost all of them extremely complicated, and such as exercise the head more than the hands. The understandings of those who are engaged in such employments can seldom grow torpid for want of exercise. The employments of people of some rank and fortune, besides, are seldom such as harass them from morning to night. They generally have a good deal of leisure, during which they may perfect themselves in every branch either of useful or ornamental knowledge of which they may have laid the foundation, or for which they may have acquired some taste in the earlier part of life.

It is otherwise with the common people. They have little time to spare for education. Their parents can scarce afford to maintain them even in infancy. As soon as they are able to work, they must apply to some trade by which they can earn their subsistence. That trade too is generally so simple and uniform as to give little exercise to the understanding; while, at the same time, their labour is both so constant and so severe, that it leaves them little leisure and less inclination to apply to, or even to think of any thing else.

But though the common people cannot, in any civilised society, be so well instructed as people of some rank and fortune, the most essential parts of education, however, to read, write, and account, can be acquired at so early a period of life, that the greater part even of those who are to be bred to the lowest occupations, have time to acquire them before they can be employed in those occupations. For a very small expence the public can facilitate, can encourage, and can even impose upon almost the whole body of the people, the necessity of acquiring those most essential parts of education.

The state can encourage or insist on the general acquirement of reading, writing, and arithmetic, by establishing parish schools, giving prizes, and requiring men to pass an examination before setting up in trade.

The public can facilitate this acquisition by establishing in every parish or district a little school where children may be taught for a reward so moderate, that even a common labourer may afford it; the master being partly, but not wholly paid by the public; because if he was wholly, or even principally paid by it, he would soon learn to neglect his business. In Scotland the establishment of such parish schools has taught almost the whole common people to read, and a very great proportion of them to write and account. In England the establishment of charity schools has had an effect of the same kind, though not so universally, because the establishment is not so universal. If in those little schools the books, by which the children are taught to read, were a little more instructive than they commonly are: and if, instead of a little smattering of Latin; which the children of the common people are sometimes taught here, and which can scarce ever be of any use to them: they were instructed in the elementary parts of geometry and mechanics, the literary education of this rank of people would perhaps be as complete as it can be. There is scarce a common trade which does not afford some opportunities of applying to it the principles of geometry and mechanics, and which would not therefore gradually exercise and improve the common people in those principles, the necessary introduction to the most sublime as well as to the most useful sciences.

The public can encourage the acquisition of those most essential parts of education by giving small premiums, and little badges of distinction, to the children of the common people who excel in them.

The public can impose upon almost the whole body of the people the necessity of acquiring those most essential parts of education, by obliging every man to undergo an examination or probation in them before he can obtain the freedom in any corporation, or be allowed to set up any trade either in a village or town corporate.

It was in this manner, by facilitating the acquisition of their military and gymnastic exercises, by encouraging it, and even by imposing upon the whole body of the people the necessity of learning those exercises, that the Greek and Roman republics maintained the martial spirit of their respective citizens. They facilitated the acquisition of those exercises by appointing a certain place for learning and practising them, and by granting to certain masters the privilege of teaching in that place. Those masters do not appear to have had either salaries or exclusive privileges of any kind. Their reward consisted altogether in what they got from their scholars; and a citizen who had learned his exercises in the public Gymnasia, had no sort of legal advantage over one who had learned them privately, provided the latter had learned them equally well. Those republics encouraged the acquisition of those exercises, by bestowing little premiums and badges of distinction upon those who excelled in them. To have gained a prize in the Olympic, Isthmian, or Nemaean games, gave illustration, not only to the person who gained it, but to his whole family and kindred. The obligation which every citizen was under to serve a certain number of years, if called upon, in the armies of the republic, sufficiently imposed the necessity of learning those exercises without which he could not be fit for that service. *In this way the Greeks and Romans maintained a martial spirit.*

That in the progress of improvement the practice of military exercises, unless government takes proper pains to support it, goes gradually to decay, and, together with it, the martial spirit of the great body of the people, the example of modern Europe sufficiently demonstrates. But the security of every society must always depend, more or less, upon *Martial spirit in the people would diminish both the necessary size and the danger of a standing army.*

the martial spirit of the great body of the people. In the present times, indeed, that martial spirit alone, and unsupported by a well-disciplined standing army, would not, perhaps, be sufficient for the defence and security of any society. But where every citizen had the spirit of a soldier, a smaller standing army would surely be requisite. That spirit, besides, would necessarily diminish very much the dangers to liberty, whether real or imaginary, which are commonly apprehended from a standing army. As it would very much facilitate the operations of that army against a foreign invader, so it would obstruct them as much if unfortunately they should ever be directed against the constitution of the state.

The ancient institutions of Greece and Rome seem to have been much more effectual, for maintaining the martial spirit of the great body of the people, than the establishment of what are called the militias of modern times. They were much more simple. *The Greek and Roman institutions were more effectual than modern militias, which only include a small portion of the people.* When they were once established, they executed themselves, and it required little or no attention from government to maintain them in the most perfect vigour. Whereas to maintain even in tolerable execution the complex regulations of any modern militia, requires the continual and painful attention of government, without which they are constantly falling into total neglect and disuse. The influence, besides, of the ancient institutions was much more universal. By means of them the whole body of the people was completely instructed in the use of arms. Whereas it is but a very small part of them who can ever be so instructed by the regulations of any modern militia; except, perhaps, that of Switzerland.

But a coward, a man incapable either of defending or of revenging himself, evidently wants one of the most essential parts of the character of a man. He is as much mutilated and deformed in his mind, *It is the duty of government to prevent the growth of cowardice, gross ignorance, and stupidity.* as another is in his body, who is either deprived of some of its most essential members, or has lost the use of them. He is evidently the more wretched and miserable of the two; because happiness and misery, which reside altogether in the mind, must necessarily depend more upon the healthful or unhealthful, the mutilated or entire state of the mind, than upon that of the body. Even though the martial spirit of the people were of no use towards the defence of the society, yet to prevent that sort of mental mutilation, deformity and wretchedness, which cowardice necessarily involves in it, from spreading themselves through the great body of the people, would still deserve the most serious attention of government; in the same manner as it would deserve its most serious attention to prevent a leprosy or any other loathsome and offensive disease, though neither mortal nor dangerous, from spreading itself among them; though, perhaps, no other public good might result from such attention besides the prevention of so great a public evil.

The same thing may be said of the gross ignorance and stupidity which, in a civilised society, seem so frequently to benumb the understandings of all the inferior ranks of people. A man, without the proper use of the intellectual faculties of a man, is, if possible, more contemptible than even a coward, and seems to be mutilated and deformed in a still more essential part of the character of human nature. Though the state was to derive no advantage from the instruction of the inferior ranks of people, it would still deserve its attention that they should not be altogether uninstructed. The state, however, derives no inconsiderable advantage from their instruction. The more they are instructed, the less liable they are to the delusions of enthusiasm and superstition, which, among ignorant nations, frequently occasion the most dreadful disorders. An instructed and intelligent people besides are always more decent and orderly than an ignorant and stupid one. They feel themselves, each individually, more respectable, and more likely to obtain the respect of their lawful superiors, and they are therefore more disposed to respect those superiors. They are more disposed to examine, and more capable of seeing through, the interested complaints of faction and sedition, and they are, upon that account, less apt to be misled into any wanton or unnecessary opposition to the measures of government. In free countries, where the safety of government depends very much upon the favourable judgment which the people may form of its conduct, it must surely be of the highest importance that they should not be disposed to judge rashly or capriciously concerning it.

ARTICLE III

Of the Expence of the Institutions for the Instruction of People of all Ages

The institutions for the instruction of people of all ages are chiefly those for religious instruction. This is a species of instruction of which the object is not so much to render the people good citizens in this world, as to prepare them for another and a better world in a life to come. The teachers of the doctrine which contains this instruction, in the same manner as other teachers, may either depend altogether for their subsistence upon the voluntary contributions of their hearers; or they may derive it from some other fund to which the law of their country may entitle them; such as a landed estate, a tithe or land tax, an established salary or stipend. Their exertion, their zeal and industry, are likely to be much greater in the former situation than in the latter. In this respect the teachers of new religions have always had a considerable advantage in attacking those ancient and established systems of which the clergy, reposing themselves upon their benefices, had neglected to keep up the fervour of faith and devotion in the great body of the people; and having given themselves up to indolence, were become altogether incapable of making any vig-

These institutions are chiefly for religious instruction. Religious like other teachers are more vigorous if unestablished and unendowed.

orous exertion in defence even of their own establishment. The clergy
of an established and well-endowed religion frequently become men of
learning and elegance, who possess all the virtues of gentlemen, or which
can recommend them to the esteem of gentlemen; but they are apt gradually to lose the qualities, both good and bad, which gave them authority and influence with the inferior ranks of people, and which had perhaps
been the original causes of the success and establishment of their religion. Such a clergy, when attacked by a set of popular and bold, though
perhaps stupid and ignorant enthusiasts, feel themselves as perfectly
defenceless as the indolent, effeminate, and full fed nations of the south-
ern parts of Asia, when they were invaded by the active, hardy, and
hungry Tartars of the North.

Such a clergy, upon such an emergency, have commonly no other
resource than to call upon the civil magistrate to persecute, destroy, or
drive out their adversaries, as disturbers of the public peace. It was thus
that the Roman catholic clergy called upon the civil magistrate to persecute the protestants; and the church of England, to persecute the dis-
senters; and that in general every religious sect, when it has once enjoyed
for a century or two the security of a legal establishment, has found itself
incapable of making any vigorous defence against any new sect which
chose to attack its doctrine of discipline. . . .

In every civilised society, in every society where
the distinction of ranks has once been completely
established, there have been always two different
schemes or systems of morality current at the same
time; of which the one may be called the strict or
austere; the other the liberal, or, if you will, the
loose system. The former is generally admired and revered by the common people: The latter is commonly more esteemed and adopted by
what are called people of fashion. The degree of disapprobation with
which we ought to mark the vices of levity, the vices which are apt to
arise from great prosperity, and from the excess of gaiety and good
humour, seems to constitute the principal distinction between those two
opposite schemes or systems.

In the liberal or loose system, luxury, wanton and even disorderly
mirth, the pursuit of pleasure to some degree of intemperance, the breach
of chastity, at least in one of the two sexes, etc., provided they are not
accompanied with gross indecency, and do not lead to falsehood or
injustice, are generally treated with a good deal of indulgence, and are
easily either excused or pardoned altogether. In the austere system, on
the contrary, those excesses are regarded with the utmost abhorrence and
detestation. The vices of levity are always ruinous to the common people, and a single week's thoughtlessness and dissipation is often sufficient
to undo a poor workman forever, and to drive him through despair upon
committing the most enormous crimes. The wiser and better sort of the

Of the two systems of morality, the strict or austere and the liberal or loose, the first is favoured by the common people, the second by people of fashion.

common people, therefore, have always the utmost abhorrence and
detestation of such excesses, which their experience tells them are so
immediately fatal to people of their condition. The disorder and extravagance of several years, on the contrary, will not always ruin a man of
fashion, and people of that rank are very apt to consider the power of
indulging in some degree of excess as one of the advantages of their
fortune, and the liberty of doing so without censure or reproach, as one
of the privileges which belong to their station. In people of their own
station, therefore, they regard such excesses with but a small degree of
disapprobation, and censure them either very slightly or not at all.

Almost all religious sects have begun among the common people, from whom they have generally drawn their earliest, as well as their most numerous proselytes. The austere system of morality has, accordingly, been adopted by those sects almost constantly, or with very few exceptions; for there have

Religious sects usually
begin with the austere
system, and in small
religious sects morals
are regular and orderly
and even disagreeably
rigorous and unsocial.

been some. It was the system by which they could best recommend
themselves to that order of people to whom they first proposed their plan
of reformation upon what had been before established. Many of them,
perhaps the greater part of them, have even endeavoured to gain credit
by refining upon this austere system, and by carrying it to some degree
of folly and extravagance; and this excessive rigour has frequently recommended them more than any thing else to the respect and veneration
of the common people.

A man of rank and fortune is by his station the distinguished member
of a great society, who attend to every part of his conduct, and who
thereby oblige him to attend to every part of it himself. His authority
and consideration depend very much upon the respect which this society
bears to him. He dare not do any thing which would disgrace or discredit
him in it, and he is obliged to a very strict observation of that species of
morals, whether liberal or austere, which the general consent of this
society prescribes to persons of his rank and fortune.

A man of low condition, on the contrary, is far from being a distinguished member of any great society. While he remains in a country
village his conduct may be attended to, and he may be obliged to attend
to it himself. In this situation, and in this situation only, he may have
what is called a character to lose. But as soon as he comes into a great
city, he is sunk in obscurity and darkness. His conduct is observed and
attended to by nobody, and he is therefore very likely to neglect it himself, and to abandon himself to every sort of low profligacy and vice. He
never emerges so effectually from this obscurity, his conduct never excites
so much the attention of any respectable society, as by his becoming the
member of a small religious sect. He from that moment acquires a degree
of consideration which he never had before. All his brother sectaries are,
for the credit of the sect, interested to observe his conduct, and if he

gives occasion to any scandel, if he deviates very much from those austere morals which they almost always require of one another, to punish
him by what is always a very severe punishment, even where no civil
effects attend it, expulsion or excommunication from the sect. In little
religious sects, accordingly, the morals of the common people have been
almost always remarkably regular and orderly; generally much more so
than in the established church. The morals of those little sects, indeed,
have frequently been rather disagreeably rigorous and unsocial.

There are two very easy and effectual remedies,
however, by whose joint operation the state might,
without violence, correct whatever was unsocial or
disagreeably rigorous in the morals of all the little
sects into which the country was divided.

The first of those remedies is the study of science
and philosophy, which the state might render almost

> There are two possible
> remedies, (1) the
> requirement of a knowl-
> edge of science and phi-
> losophy from candidates
> for professions and
> offices; and (2) un...
> encouragement of pub-
> lic diversions.

universal among all people of middling or more than middling rank and
fortune; not by giving salaries to teachers in order to make them negligent and idle, but by instituting some sort of probation, even in the
higher and more difficult sciences, to be undergone by every person
before he was permitted to exercise any liberal profession, or before he
could be received as a candidate for any honourable office of trust or
profit. If the state imposed upon this order of men the necessity of learning, it would have no occasion to give itself any trouble about providing
them with proper teachers. They would soon find better teachers for
themselves than any whom the state could provide for them. Science is
the great antidote to the poison of enthusiasm and superstition; and where
all the superior ranks of people were secured from it, the inferior ranks
could not be much exposed to it.

The second of those remedies is the frequency and gaiety of public
diversions. The state, by encouraging, that is by giving entire liberty to
all those who for their own interest would attempt, without scandel or
indecency, to amuse and divert the people by painting, poetry, music,
dancing; by all sorts of dramatic representations and exhibitions, would
easily dissipate, in the greater part of them, that melancholy and gloomy
humour which is almost always the nurse of popular superstition and
enthusiasm. Public diversions have always been the objects of dread and
hatred to all the fanatical promoters of those popular frenzies. The gaiety
and good humour which those diversions inspire were altogether inconsistent with that temper of mind, which was fittest for their purpose, or
which they could best work upon. Dramatic representations besides, frequently exposing their artifices to public ridicule, and sometimes even
to public execration, were upon that account, more than all other diversions, the objects of their peculiar abhorrence. . . .

PART IV

Of the Expence of supporting the Dignity of the Sovereign

Over and above the expence necessary for enabling the sovereign to perform his several duties, a
certain expence is requisite for the support of his
dignity. This expence varies both with the different
periods of improvement, and with the different forms
of government.

*The expence of support-
ing the dignity of the
sovereign increases as
the expenditure of the
people increases, and is
greater in a monarchy
than in a republic.*

In an opulent and improved society, where all the different orders of
people are growing every day more expensive in their houses, in their
furniture, in their tables, in their dress, and in their equipage; it cannot
well be expected that the sovereign should alone hold out against the
fashion. He naturally, therefore, or rather necessarily becomes more
expensive in all those different articles too. His dignity even seems to
require that he should become so.

As in point of dignity, a monarch is more raised above his subjects
than the chief magistrate of any republic is ever supposed to be above
his fellow-citizens; so a greater expence is necessary for supporting that
higher dignity. We naturally expect more splendour in the court of a
king than in the mansion-house of a doge or burgomaster.

Conclusion of the Chapter

The expence of defending the society, and that of
supporting the dignity of the chief magistrate, are
both laid out for the general benefit of the whole
society. It is reasonable, therefore, that they should

*The expence of defence
and of maintaining the
dignity of the sovereign
should be paid by gen-
eral contribution.*

be defrayed by the general contribution of the whole society, all the
different members contributing, as nearly as possible, in proportion to
their respective abilities.

The expence of the administration of justice too,
may, no doubt, be considered as laid out for the
benefit of the whole society. There is no impropriety, therefore, in its being defrayed by the general
contribution of the whole society. The persons,

*But the expence of jus-
tice may be defrayed by
fees of court, and exp-
ences of local benefit
ought to be defrayed by
local revenue.*

however, who give occasion to this expence are those who, by their
injustice in one way or another, make it necessary to seek redress or
protection from the courts of justice. The persons again most immediately benefited by this expence, are those whom the courts of justice
either restore to their rights, or maintain in their rights. The expence of
the administration of justice, therefore, may very properly be defrayed
by the particular contribution of one or other, or both of those two different sets of persons, according as different occasions may require, that
is, by the fees of court. It cannot be necessary to have recourse to the

general contribution of the whole society, except for the conviction of those criminals who have not themselves any estate or fund sufficient for paying those fees.

Those local or provincial expences of which the benefit is local or provincial (what is laid out, for example, upon the police of a particular town or district) ought to be defrayed by a local or provincial revenue, and ought to be no burden upon the general revenue of the society. It is unjust that the whole society should contribute towards an expence of which the benefit is confined to a part of the society.

The expence of maintaining good roads and communications is, no doubt, beneficial to the whole society, and may, therefore, without any injustice, be defrayed by the general contribution of the whole society. *The expence of roads may not unjustly be defrayed by general contribution, but better by tolls.* This expence, however, is most immediately and directly beneficial to those who travel or carry goods from one place to another, and to those who consume such goods. The turnpike tolls in England, and the duties called peages in other countries, lay it altogether upon those two different sets of people, and thereby discharge the general revenue of the society from a very considerable burden.

The expence of the institutions for education and religious instruction, is likewise, no doubt, beneficial to the whole society, and may, therefore, without injustice, be defrayed by the general contribution of the whole society. *The expence of education and religious instruction may also be defrayed by general contribution, but better by fees and voluntary contribution.* This expence, however, might perhaps with equal propriety, and even with some advantage, be defrayed altogether by those who receive the immediate benefit of such education and instruction, or by the voluntary contribution of those who think they have occasion for either the one or the other.

When the institutions or public works which are beneficial to the whole society, either cannot be maintained altogether, or are not maintained altogether by the contribution of such particular members of the society as are most immediately benefited by them, the deficiency must in most cases be made up by the general contribution of the whole society. *Any deficiencies in the revenue of institutions beneficial to the whole society must be made up by general contribution.*

The general revenue of the society, over and above defraying the expence of defending the society, and of supporting the dignity of the chief magistrate, must make up for the deficiency of many particular branches of revenue. The sources of this general or public revenue, I shall endeavour to explain in the following chapter.

CHAPTER II

Of the Sources of the general or public Revenue of the Society

The revenue which must defray, not only the expence of defending the society and of supporting the dignity of the chief magistrate, but all the other necessary expences of government, for which the constitution of the state has not provided any particular revenue, may be drawn, either, first, from some fund which peculiarly belongs to the sovereign or commonwealth, and which is independent of the revenue of the people; or, secondly, from the revenue of the people.

All revenue comes from one of two sources: (1) property belonging to the sovereign; (2) the revenue of the people.

[The remainder of chapter 2, an account of different forms of taxation, has been omitted. The following four maxims from Part II, "Of Taxes," outline Smith's general guide to effective and equitable taxation.]

I. The subjects of every state ought to contribute towards the support of the government, as nearly as possible, in proportion to their respective abilities; that is, in proportion to the revenue which they respectively enjoy under the protection of the state. The expence of government to the individuals of a great nation, is like the expence of management to the joint tenants of a great estate, who are all obliged to contribute in proportion to their respective interests in the estate. In the observation or neglect of this maxim consists, what is called the equality or inequality of taxation. Every tax, it must be observed once for all, which falls finally upon one only of the three sorts of revenue abovementioned, is necessarily unequal, in so far as it does not affect the other two. In the following examination of different taxes I shall seldom take much further notice of this sort of inequality, but shall, in most cases, confine my observations to that inequality which is occasioned by a particular tax falling unequally even upon that particular sort of private revenue which is affected by it.

There are four maxims with regard to taxes in general, (1) equality,

II. The tax which each individual is bound to pay ought to be certain, and not arbitrary. The time of payment, the manner of payment, the quantity to be paid ought all to be clear and plain to the contributor, and to every other person. Where it is otherwise, every person subject to the tax is put more or less in the power of the tax-gatherer, who can either aggravate the tax upon any obnoxious contributor, or extort, by the terror of such aggravation, some present or perquisite to himself. The uncertainty of taxation encourages the insolence and favours the corruption of an order of men who are naturally unpopular, even where they are neither insolent nor corrupt. The certainty of what each individual ought to pay is, in taxation, a

(2) certainty,

matter of so great importance, that a very considerable degree of inequality, it appears, I believe, from the experience of all nations, is not near so great an evil as a very small degree of uncertainty.

III. Every tax ought to be levied at the time, or (3) convenience of payin the manner in which it is most likely to be con-   ment,
venient for the contributor to pay it. A tax upon the
rent of land or of houses, payable at the same term at which such rents are usually paid, is levied at the time when it is most likely to be convenient for the contributor to pay; or, when he is most likely to have wherewithal to pay. Taxes upon such consumable goods as are articles of luxury are all finally paid by the consumer, and generally in a manner that is very convenient for him. He pays them by little and little, as he has occasion to buy the goods. As he is at liberty too, either to buy, or not to buy as he pleases, it must be his own fault if he ever suffers any considerable inconvenience from such taxes.

IV. Every tax ought to be so contrived as both to   and (4) economy in col-
take out and to keep out of the pockets of the people   lection.
as little as possible, over and above what it brings
into the public treasury of the state. A tax may either take out or keep out of the pockets of the people a great deal more than it brings into the public treasury, in the four following ways. First, the levying of it may require a great number of officers, whose salaries may eat up the greater part of the produce of the tax, and whose perquisites may impose another additional tax upon the people. Secondly, it may obstruct the industry of the people, and discourage them from applying to certain branches of business which might give maintenance and employment to great multitudes. While it obliges the people to pay, it may thus diminish, or perhaps destroy some of the funds, which might enable them more easily to do so. Thirdly, by the forfeitures and other penalties which those unfortunate individuals incur who attempt unsuccessfully to evade the tax, it may frequently ruin them, and thereby put an end to the benefit which the community might have received from the employment of their capitals. An injudicious tax offers a great temptation to smuggling. But the penalties of smuggling must rise in proportion to the temptation. The law, contrary to all the ordinary principles of justice, first creates the temptation, and then punishes those who yield to it; and it commonly enhances the punishment too in proportion to the very circumstance which ought certainly to alleviate it, the temptation to commit the crime. Fourthly, by subjecting the people to the frequent visits, and the odious examination of the tax-gatherers, it may expose them to much unnecessary trouble, vexation, and oppression; and though vexation is not, strictly speaking, expence, it is certainly equivalent to the expence at which every man would be willing to redeem himself from it. It is in some one or other of these four different ways that taxes are frequently so much more burdensome to the people than they are beneficial to the sovereign. . . .

CHAPTER III
Of public Debts

. . . When the public expence is defrayed by funding, it is defrayed by the annual destruction of some capital which had before existed in the country; by the perversion of some portion of the annual produce which had before been destined for the maintenance of productive labour, towards that of unproductive labour. As in this case, however, the taxes are lighter than they would have been, had a

When it is met by borrowing, it diverts labour from productive to unproductive employment, and the only advantage is that people can continue to save more during the war, which advantage disappears immediately peace is concluded.

revenue sufficient for defraying the same expence been raised within the year; the private revenue of individuals is necessarily less burdened, and consequently their ability to save and accumulate some part of that revenue into capital is a good deal less impaired. If the method of funding destroys more old capital, it at the same time hinders less the accumulation or acquisition of new capital, than that of defraying the public expence by a revenue raised within the year. Under the system of funding, the frugality and industry of private people can more easily repair the breaches which the waste and extravagance of government may occasionally make in the general capital of the society.

It is only during the continuance of war, however, that the system of funding has this advantage over the other system. Were the expence of war to be defrayed always by a revenue raised within the year, the taxes from which that extraordinary revenue was drawn would last no longer than the war. The ability of private people to accumulate, though less during the war, would have been greater during the peace than under the system of funding. War would not necessarily have occasioned the destruction of any old capitals, and peace would have occasioned the accumulation of many more new. Wars would in general be more speedily concluded, and less wantonly undertaken. The people feeling, during the continuance of the war, the complete burden of it, would soon grow weary of it, and government, in order to humour them, would not be under the necessity of carrying it on longer than it was necessary to do so. The foresight of the heavy and unavoidable burdens of war would hinder the people from wantonly calling for it when there was no real or solid interest to fight for. The seasons during which the ability of private people to accumulate was somewhat impaired, would occur more rarely, and be of shorter continuance. Those on the contrary, during which that ability was in the highest vigour, would be of much longer duration than they can well be under the system of funding.

When funding, besides, has made a certain progress, the multiplication of taxes which it brings along with it sometimes impairs as much the ability of private people to accumulate even in time of peace,

Moreover funding at length burdens the revenue so greatly that the ordinary peace expenditure exceeds that which would under the other

as the other system would in time of war. The peace revenue of Great Britain amounts at present to more than ten millions a year. *system have been sufficient in war.* If free and unmortgaged, it might be sufficient, with proper management and without contracting a shilling of new debt, to carry on the most vigorous war. The private revenue of the inhabitants of Great Britain is at present as much encumbered in time of peace, their ability to accumulate is as much impaired as it would have been in the time of the most expensive war, had the pernicious system of funding never been adopted.

In the payment of the interest of the public debt, it has been said, it is the right hand which pays the left. The money does not go out of the country. It *The fact of part or the whole of the debt being held at home makes no difference.* is only a part of the revenue of one set of the inhabitants which is transferred to another; and the nation is not a farthing the poorer. This apology is founded altogether in the sophistry of the mercantile system, and after the long examination which I have already bestowed upon that system, it may perhaps be unnecessary to say any thing further about it. It supposes, besides, that the whole public debt is owing to the inhabitants of the country, which happens not to be true; the Dutch, as well as several other foreign nations, having a very considerable share in our public funds. But though the whole debt were owing to the inhabitants of the country, it would not upon that account be less pernicious.

Land and capital stock are the two original sources of all revenue both private and public. Capital stock pays the wages of productive labour, whether employed in agriculture, manufacturers, or com- *Land and capital, the two original sources of all revenue, are managed by landlords and owners of capital.* merce. The management of those two original sources of revenue belongs to two different sets of people; the proprietors of land, and the owners or employers of capital stock.

The proprietor of land is interested for the sake of his own revenue to keep his estate in as good con- dition as he can, by building and repairing his ten- ants' houses, by making and maintaining the *Taxation may diminish or destroy the landlord's ability to improve his land, and induce the capital to remove it from the country.* necessary drains and enclosures, and all those other expensive improvements which it properly belongs to the landlord to make and maintain. But by different land taxes the revenue of the land- lord may be so much diminished; and by different duties upon the necessaries and conveniences of life, that diminished revenue may be rendered of so little real value, that he may find himself altogether unable to make or maintain those expensive improvements. When the land- lord, however, ceases to do his part, it is altogether impossible that the tenant should continue to do his. As the distress of the landlord increases, the agriculture of the country must necessarily decline.

When, by different taxes upon the necessaries and conveniences of life, the owners and employers of capital stock find, that whatever revenue they derive from it, will not, in a particular country, purchase the same quantity of those necessaries and conveniences, which an equal revenue would in almost any other; they will be disposed to remove to some other. And when, in order to raise those taxes, all or the greater part of merchants and manufacturers; that is, all or the greater part of the employers of great capitals, come to be continually exposed to the mortifying and vexatious visits of the tax-gatherers; this disposition to remove will soon be changed into an actual removal. The industry of the country will necessarily fall with the removal of the capital which supported it, and the ruin of trade and manufactures will follow the declension of agriculture.

To transfer from the owners of those two great sources of revenue, land and capital stock, from the persons immediately interested in the good condition of every particular portion of land, and in the good management of every particular portion of capital stock, to another set of persons (the creditors *The transference of the sources of revenue from the owners of particular portions of them to the creditors of the public must occasion neglect of land and waste or removal of capital.*
of the public, who have no such particular interest) the greater part of the revenue arising from either, must, in the long run, occasion both the neglect of land, and the waste or removal of capital stock. A creditor of the public has no doubt a general interest in the prosperity of the agriculture, manufactures, and commerce of the country; and consequently in the good condition of its lands, and in the good management of its capital stock. Should there be any general failure or declension in any of these things, the produce of the different taxes might no longer be sufficient to pay him the annuity or interest which is due to him. But a creditor of the public, considered merely as such, has no interest in the good condition of any particular portion of land, or in the good management of any particular portion of capital stock. As a creditor of the public he has no knowledge of any such particular portion. He has no inspection of it. He can have no care about it. Its ruin may in some cases be unknown to him, and cannot directly affect him.

The practise of funding has gradually enfeebled every state which has adopted it. The Italian repub- *The practise of funding has always enfeebled states.*
lics seem to have begun it. Genoa and Venice, the only two remaining which can pretend to an independent existence, have both been enfeebled by it. Spain seems to have learned the practise from the Italian republics, and (its taxes being probably less judicious than theirs) it has, in proportion to its natural strength, been still more enfeebled. The debts of Spain are of very old standing. It was deeply in debt before the end of the sixteenth century, about a hundred years before England owed a shilling. France, notwithstanding all its natural resources, languishes under an oppressive load of the same kind. The republic of the United Provinces is as much enfeebled by its debts as

either Genoa or Venice. Is it likely that in Great Britain alone a practise, which has brought either weakness or desolation into every other country, should prove altogether innocent?

The system of taxation established in those different countries, it may be said, is inferior to that of England. I believe it is so. But it ought to be remembered, that when the wisest government has exhausted all the proper subjects of taxation, it must, in cases of urgent necessity, have recourse to improper ones. The wise republic of Holland has upon some occasions been obliged to have recourse to taxes as inconvenient as the greater part of those of Spain. Another war begun before any considerable liberation of the public revenue had been brought about, and growing in its progress as expensive as the last war, may, from irresistible necessity, render the British system of taxation as oppressive as that of Holland, or even as that of Spain. To the honour of our present system of taxation, indeed, it has hitherto given so little embarrassment to industry, that, during the course even of the most expensive wars, the frugality and good conduct of individuals seem to have been able, by saving and accumulation, to repair all the breaches which the waste and extravagance of government had made in the general capital of the society.

At the conclusion of the late war, the most expensive that Great Britain ever waged, her agriculture was as flourishing, her manufacturers as numerous and as fully employed, and her commerce as extensive, as they had ever been before. The capital, therefore, which supported all those different branches of industry, must have been equal to what it had ever been before. Since the peace, agriculture has been still further improved, the rents of houses have risen in every town and village of the country, a proof of the increasing wealth and revenue of the people; and the annual amount of the greater part of the old taxes, of the principal branches of the excise and customs in particular, has been continually increasing, an equally clear proof of an increasing consumption, and consequently of an increasing produce, which could alone support that consumption. Great Britain seems to support with ease, a burden which, half a century ago, nobody believed her capable of supporting. Let us not, however, upon this account rashly conclude that she is capable of supporting any burden; nor even be too confident that she could support, without great distress, a burden a little greater than what has already been laid upon her.

When national debts have once been accumu-   Bankruptcy is always the
lated to a certain degree, there is scarce, I believe, a   end of great accumula-
single instance of their having been fairly and com-   tion of debt.
pletely paid. The liberation of the public revenue, if it has ever been brought about at all, has always been brought about by a bankruptcy; sometimes by an avowed one, but always by a real one, though frequently by a pretended payment. . . .

[The *Wealth of Nations* concludes with this prescient passage.]

If it should be found impracticable for Great Brit- If no such augmentation
ain to draw any considerable augmentation of reve- of revenue can be
obtained Great Britain
nue from any of the resources above mentioned; the should reduce her ex-
only resource which can remain to her is a dimi- pences by ridding herself
of the cost of the colo-
nution of her expence. In the mode of collecting, nies in peace and war.
and in that of expending the public revenue; though
in both there may be still room for improvement; Great Britain seems to
be at least as economical as any of her neighbours. The military establishment which she maintains for her own defence in time of peace is
more moderate than that of any European state which can pretend to
rival her either in wealth or in power. None of those articles, therefore,
seem to admit of any considerable reduction of expence. The expence
of the peace establishment of the colonies was, before the commencement of the present disturbances, very considerable, and is an expence
which may, and if no revenue can be drawn from them, ought certainly
to be saved altogether. This constant expence in time of peace, though
very great, is insignificant in comparison with what the defence of the
colonies has cost us in time of war. The last war, which was undertaken
altogether on account of the colonies, cost Great Britain, it has already
been observed, upwards of ninety millions. The Spanish war of 1739
was principally undertaken on their account; in which, and in the French
war that was the consequence of it, Great Britain spent upwards of forty
millions, a great part of which ought justly to be charged to the colonies.
In those two wars the colonies cost Great Britain much more than double the sum which the national debt amounted to before the commencement of the first of them. Had it not been for those wars that debt might,
and probably would by this time, have been completely paid; and had it
not been for the colonies, the former of those wars might not, and the
latter certainly would not have been undertaken.

It was because the colonies were supposed to be provinces of the British empire, that this expence was laid out upon them. But countries
which contribute neither revenue nor military force towards the support
of the empire, cannot be considered as provinces. They may perhaps be
considered as appendages, as a sort of splendid and showy equipage of
the empire. But if the empire can no longer support the expence of
keeping up this equipage, it ought certainly to lay it down; and if it
cannot raise its revenue in proportion to its expence, it ought, at least,
to accommodate its expence to its revenue. If the colonies, notwithstanding their refusal to submit to British taxes, are still to be considered
as provinces of the British empire, their defence in some future war may
cost Great Britain as great an expence as it ever has done in any former
war. The rulers of Great Britain have, for more than a century past,
amused the people with the imagination that they possessed a great empire

on the west side of the Atlantic. This empire, however, has hitherto existed in imagination only. It has hitherto been, not an empire, but the project of an empire; not a gold mine, but the project of a gold mine; a project which has cost, which continues to cost, and which, if pursued in the same way as it has been hitherto, is likely to cost immense expence, without being likely to bring any profit: for the effects of the monopoly of the colony trade, it has been shown, are, to the great body of the people, mere loss instead of profit. It is surely now time that our rulers should either realize this golden dream, in which they have been indulging themselves, perhaps, as well as the people; or, that they should awake from it themselves and endeavour to awaken the people. If the project cannot be completed, it ought to be given up. If any of the provinces of the British empire cannot be made to contribute towards the support of the whole empire, it is surely time that Great Britain should free herself from the expence of defending those provinces in time of war, and of supporting any part of their civil or military establishments in time of peace, and endeavour to accommodate her future views and designs to the real mediocrity of her circumstances.

Aphorisms and Famous Passages from the *Wealth of Nations*

This brief and necessarily arbitrary collection of Smith's better-known pronouncements is presented as a guide to readers—for quotation or reference, or simply for enjoyment. The page number following the passage is in all cases from the Glasgow edition. Where the quotation has already appeared in the readings, the page reference is given in brackets.

The division of labour . . . is the necessary, though very slow and gradual, consequence of a certain propensity in human nature . . . to truck, barter, and exchange one thing for another. 25 [168]

Nobody ever saw a dog make a fair and deliberate exchange of one bone for another with another dog. 26 [168]

It is not from the benevolence of the butcher, the brewer, or the baker that we expect our dinner, but from their regard to their own interest. We address ourselves, not to their humanity but to their self-love, and never talk to them of our own necessities but of their advantages. 26–27 [169]

By nature a philosopher is not in genius and disposition half so different from a street porter, as is a mastiff from a greyhound. 30 [170]

If among a nation of hunters . . . it usually costs twice the labour to kill a beaver which it does to kill a deer, one beaver should naturally exchange for or be worth two deer. 65 [181]

As soon as the land of any country has all become private property, the landlords, like all other men, love to reap where they never sowed, and demand a rent even for its natural produce. 67 [182]

A public mourning raises the price of black cloth. 76 [190]

We rarely hear, it has been said, of the combinations of the masters; though frequently of those of workmen. But whoever imagines, upon this account, that masters rarely combine, is as ignorant of the world as of the subject. Masters are always and everywhere in a sort of tacit, but constant and uniform combination, not to raise the wages of labour above its natural rate. 84 [196]

[A] man is of all sorts of luggage the most difficult to be transported. 93 [201]

It is not because one man keeps a coach while his neighbor walks a-foot, that the one is rich and the other poor; but because the one is rich he keeps a coach, and because the other is poor he walks a-foot. 93 [202]

No society can surely be flourishing and happy, of which the far greater part of the members are poor and miserable. 96 [203]

The chance of gain is by every man more or less overvalued, and the chance of loss is by most men undervalued. 125

The property which every man has in his own labour, as it is the original foundation of all other property, so it is the most sacred and inviolable. 138

People of the same trade seldom meet together, even for merriment and diversion, but the conversation ends in a conspiracy against the public, or in some contrivance to raise prices. 145

The desire for food is limited in every man by the narrow capacity of the human stomach; but the desire for the conveniences and ornaments of building, dress, equipage, and household furniture, seem to have no limit or certain boundary. 181 [223]

With the greater part of rich people, the chief enjoyment of riches consists in the parade of riches, which in their eyes is never so complete as when they appear to possess those decisive marks of opulence which nobody can possess but themselves. 190

To widen the market and to narrow the competition is always the interest of the dealers. . . . The proposal of any new law or regulation of commerce which comes from this order, ought always to be listened to with great precaution, and ought never to be adopted, till after having been long and carefully examined, not only with the most scrupulous, but with the most suspicious attention. It comes from an order of men, whose interest is never exactly the same with that of the public, who have generally an interest to deceive and even to oppress the public, and who accordingly have, upon many occasions, both deceived and oppressed it. 267

Capitals are increased by parsimony, and diminished by prodigality and misconduct. 337 [238]

Parsimony, and not industry, is the immediate cause of the increase of capital. 337 [238]

What is annually saved is as regularly consumed as what is annually spent, and nearly in the same time, too; but it is consumed by a different set of people. 337–338 [238]

By what a frugal man annually saves, he not only affords maintenance to an additional number of productive hands, for that or the ensuing year, but like the founder of a public workhouse, he establishes as it were a perpetual fund for the maintenance of an equal number in all times to come. 338 [238]

The prodigal perverts it in this manner. By not confining his expence within his income, he encroaches upon his capital. Like him who perverts the revenues of some pious foundation to profane purposes, he pays the wages of idleness with those funds which the frugality of his forefathers has, as it were, consecrated for to the maintenance of industry. 338 [239]

[T]he principle which prompts [us] to save is the desire of bettering our condition, a desire which, though generally calm and dispassionate, comes with us from the womb, and never leaves us till we go into the grave. In the whole interval which separates those two moments, there is scarce perhaps a single instant in which any man is so perfectly and completely satisfied with his situation, as to be without any wish of alteration or improvement of any kind. An augmentation of fortune is the means by which the greater part of men propose and wish to better their condition. 341 [240]

Bankruptcy is perhaps the greatest and most humiliating calamity which can befall an innocent man. 342 [241]

The uniform, constant, and uninterrupted effort of every man to better his condition, the principle from which public and national, as well as private opulence is originally derived, is frequently powerful enough to maintain the natural progress of things toward improvement, in spite of both the extravagance of government, and of the greatest errors of administration. 343 [241]

It is the highest impertinence and presumption . . . in kings and ministers, to pretend to watch over the economy of private people, and to restrain their expence, either by sumptuary laws, or by prohibiting the importation of foreign luxuries. They are themselves always, and without exception, the greatest spendthrifts in society. . . . If their own extravagance does not ruin the state, that of their subjects never will. 346 [243]

It is not the multitude of ale-houses . . . that occasions a general disposition to drunkenness among the common people; but that disposition arising from other causes necessarily gives employment to a multitude of ale-houses. 362 [245]

Money . . . necessarily runs after goods, but goods do not always or necessarily run after money. The man who buys, does not always mean to sell again, but frequently to use or consume; whereas he who sells, always means to buy again. 439 [262]

[Every individual generally] neither intends to promote the public interest, nor knows how much he is promoting it. . . . [H]e is in this case, as in many cases, led by an invisible hand to promote an end which was no part of his intention. Nor is it always the worse for society that it was no part of it. By pursuing his own interest he frequently promotes that of society more effectually than when he really intends to promote it. I have never known much good done by those who affected to trade for the public good. It is an affectation, indeed, not very common among merchants, and very few words need be employed in dissuading them from it. 456 [265]

What is prudence in the conduct of every private family, can scarce be folly in that of a great kingdom. 457 [266]

The sneaking arts of underling tradesmen are thus erected into political maxims for the conduct of a great empire. 493 [268]

Commerce, which ought naturally to be, among nations, as among individuals, a bond of union and friendship, has become the most fertile source of discord and animosity. The capricious ambition of kings and ministers has not, during the present and preceding century, been more fatal to the repose of Europe, than the impertinent jealousy of merchants and manufacturers. The violence and injustice of the rulers of mankind is an ancient evil, for which, I am afraid, the nature of human affairs can scarce admit of a remedy. But the mean rapacity, the monopolizing spirit of merchants and manufacturers, who neither are, nor ought to be the rulers of mankind, though it cannot perhaps be corrected, may very easily be prevented from disturbing the tranquillity of anybody but themselves. 493

The natural effort of every individual to better his own condition, when suffered to exert itself with freedom and security, is so powerful, that it is alone, and without any assistance, not only capable of carrying on the society to wealth and prosperity, but of surmounting a hundred impertinent obstructions with which the folly of human laws too often encumbers its operations. 540

To found a great empire for the sole purpose of raising up a people of customers may at first appear a project fit only for a nation of shopkeepers. 613

It is a very singular government in which every member of the administration wishes to get out of the country, . . . and to whose interest, the day after he has left it and carried his whole fortune with him, it is perfectly indifferent though the whole country was swallowed up by an earthquake. 640

Consumption is the sole end and purpose of all production; and the interest of the producer ought to be attended to, only so far as it may be necessary for promoting that of the consumer. 660 [284]

According to the system of natural liberty, the sovereign has only three duties to attend to; three duties of great importance, indeed, but plain and intelligible to common understandings: first, the duty of protecting the society from the violence and invasion of other independent societies; secondly, the duty of protecting, so far as possible, every member of the society from the injustice or oppression of every other member of it, or the duty of establishing an exact administration of justice, and, thirdly, the duty of erecting and maintaining certain public works and certain public institutions, which it can never be for the interest of any individual, or small number of individuals, to erect and maintain; because the profit could never repay the expence to any individual or small number of individuals, though it may frequently do more than repay it to a great society. 687–688 [289]

Wherever there is great property, there is great inequality. For one very rich man, there must be at least five hundred poor, and the affluence of the few supposes the indigence of the many. 709–710 [294]

Civil government, so far as it is instituted for the security of property, is in reality instituted for the defence of the rich against the poor, or of those who have some property against those who have none at all. 715 [297]

The man whose whole life is spent in performing a few simple operations, of which the effects too are, perhaps, always the same, or very nearly the same, has no occasion to exert his understanding, or to exercise his invention in finding out expedients for removing difficulties which never occur. He naturally loses, therefore, the habit of such exertion, and generally becomes as stupid and ignorant as it is possible for a human creature to become . . . [I]n every improved and civilised society this is the state into which the labouring poor, that is, the great body of the people, must necessarily fall, unless government takes some pains to prevent it. 782 [302]

Envoi

No "last words" can sum up the works of this remarkable man. Instead I wish to round out the essential Adam Smith by presenting him, in our farewell view, in as personal a manner as his reticent and retiring person permits. I have done so by printing a few letters from his correspondence with and about David Hume, his dearest friend.

The first is Hume's warm, teasing account of the reception accorded the *Theory of Moral Sentiments*.

Lisle Street, Leicester Fields, 12 Apr. 1759

Dear Smith

I give you thanks for the agreeable Present of your Theory Wedderburn and I made Presents of our Copies to such of our Acquaintance as we thought good Judges, and proper to spread the Reputation of the Book. I sent one to the Duke of Argyle, to Lord Lyttleton, Horace Walpole, Soames Jennyns, and Burke, an Irish Gentleman, who wrote lately a very pretty Treatise on the Sublime. Millar desird my Permission to send one in your Name to Dr. Warburton. I have delayd writing to you till I cou'd tell you something of the Success of the Book, and coud prognosticate with some Probability whether it should be finally damnd to Oblivion, or should be registerd in the Temple of Immortality. Tho' it has been publishd only a few Weeks, I think there appear already such strong Symptoms, that I can almost venture to fortell its Fate. It is in short this——But I have been interrupted in my Letter by a foolish impertinent Visit of one who has lately come from Scotland. He tells me, that the University of Glasgow intend to declare Rouets Office Vacant upon his going abroad with Lord Hope. I question not but you will have our Friend, Ferguson, in your Eye, in case another Project for procuring him a Place in the University of Edinburgh shou'd fail. Ferguson has very much polishd and improved his Treatise on Refinement, and with some Amendments it will make an admirable Book, and discovers an elegant and a singular Genius. The Epigoniad, I hope, will do; but it is somewhat up-hill Work. As I doubt not but you consult the Reviews sometimes at present, you will see in the critical Review a Letter upon that Poem; and I desire you to employ your Conjectures in finding out the Author. Let me see a Sample of your Skill in knowing hands by your guessing at the Person. I am afraid of Lord Kaims's Law Tracts. A man might as well think of making a fine Sauce by a Mixture of Wormwood and Aloes as an agreeable Composition by joining Metaphysics and Scotch Law. However, the Book, I believe, has Merit; tho' few People will take the Pains of diving into it. But to return to your Book, and its Success in this Town, I must tell you——A Plague of Interruptions! I orderd myself to be deny'd; and yet here is one that has broke in upon me again. He is a man of Letters, and we have had a good deal of literary Conversation. You told me, that you was curious of literary Anecdotes, and therefore I shall inform you of a few, that have come to my Knowledge. I believe I have mentiond to you already Helvetius's Book de l'Esprit. It is worth your Reading, not for its Philosophy, which I do not highly value, but for its agreeable Composition. I had a Letter from him a few days ago, wherein he tells me that my Name was much oftener in the Manuscript, but that the Censor of Books at Paris oblig'd him to strike it out. Voltaire has lately publishd a small Work called *Candide, ou L'optimisme*. It is full of Sprightliness and Impiety, and is indeed a Satyre upon Providence, under Pretext of criticizing the Leibnitian System. I shall give you a Detail of it——But what is all this to my Book? say you.——My Dear Mr Smith, have Patience: Compose yourself to Tranquillity: Show yourself a Philosopher in Practice as well as Profession: Think on the Emptiness, and Rashness, and Futility of the common Judgements of Men: How little they are regulated by Reason in any Subject, much more in philosophical Subjects, which so far exceed the Comprehension of the Vulgar. *Non si quid improba Roma, Elevet, accedas examenque improbum in illa, Perpendas trutina, nec te quaesiveris extra.* A wise man's Kingdom is his own Breast: Or, if he ever looks farther, it will only be to the Judgement of a select few, who are free from Prejudices, and capable of examining his Work. Nothing indeed can be a stronger Presumption of Falsehood than the Approbation of the Multitude; and Phocion, you know, always suspected himself of some Blunder, when he was attended with the Applauses of the Populace.

Supposing, therefore, that you have duely prepard yourself for the worst by all these Reflections; I proceed to tell you the melancholy News, that your Book has been very unfortunate: For the Public seem disposed to applaud it extremely. It was lookd for by the foolish People with some Impatience; and the Mob of Literati are beginning already to be very loud in its Praises. Three Bishops calld yesterday at Millar's Shop in order to buy Copies, and to ask Questions about the Author: The Bishop of Peterborough said he had passd the Evening in a Company, where he heard it extolld above all Books in the World. You may conclude what Opinion true Philosophers will entertain of it, when these Retainers to Superstition praise it so highly. The Duke of Argyle is more decisive than he uses to be in its Favour: I suppose he either considers it as an Exotic, or thinks the Author will be serviceable to him in the Glasgow Elections. Lord Lyttleton says, that Robertson and Smith and Bower are the Glories of English Literature. Oswald protests he does not know whether he has reap'd more Instruction or Entertainment from it: But you may easily judge what Reliance can be put on his Judgement, who has been engagd all his Life in public Business and who never sees any Faults in his Friends. Millar exults and brags that two thirds of the Edition are already sold, and that he is now sure of Success. You see what a Son of the Earth that is, to value Books only by the Profit they bring him. In that View, I believe it may prove a very good Book.

Charles Townshend, who passes for the cleverest Fellow in England, is so taken with the Performance, that he said to Oswald he wou'd put the Duke of Buccleugh under the Authors Care, and woud endeavour to make it worth his while to accept of that Charge. As soon as I heard this, I calld on him twice with a View of talking with him about the Matter, and of convincing him of the Propriety of sending that young Nobleman to Glasgow: For I coud not hope, that he coud offer you any Terms, which woud tempt you to renounce your Professorship: But I missd him. Mr. Townsend passes for being a little uncertain in his Resolutions; so perhaps you need not build much on this Sally.

In recompense for so many mortifying things, which nothing but Truth could have extorted from me, and which I could easily have multiply'd to a greater Number; I doubt not but you are so good a Christian as to return good for evil and to flatter my Vanity, by telling me, that all the Godly in Scotland abuse me for my Account of John Knox and the Reformation etc. I suppose you are glad to see my Paper end, and that I am obligd to conclude with

Your humble Servant
David Hume

The second—typically short, for Smith was a wretched correspondent, tells of the dissipations of Toulouse and speaks of beginning "a book."

Toulouse, 5 July 1764
My Dearest Friend
The Duke of Buccleugh proposes soon to set out for Bordeaux where he intends to stay a fortnight or more. I should be much obliged to you if you could send us recommendations to the Duke of Richelieu, the Marquis de Lorges and Intendant of the Province. Mr Townshend assured me that the Duke de Choiseul was to recommend us to all the people of fashion here and everywhere else in France. We have heard nothing, however, of these recommendations and have had our way to make as well as we could by the help of the Abbé who is a Stranger here almost as much as we. The Progress, indeed, we have made is not very great. The Duke is acquainted with no french man whatever. I cannot cultivate the acquaintance of the few with whom I am acquainted, as I cannot bring them to our house and am not always at liberty to go to theirs. The Life which I led at Glasgow was a pleasurable, dissipated life in comparison of that which I lead here at Present. I have begun to write a book in order to pass away the time. You may believe I have very little to do. If Sir James would come and spend a month with us in his travels it would not only be a great Satisfaction to me but he might by his influence and example be of great service to the Duke. Mention these matters, however, to nobody but to him. Remember me in the most respectful manner to Lord Beauchamp and to Dr Trail and believe me my Dear Friend

Ever yours,
Adam Smith

The third are Smith's instructions to Hume—seventeen years before Smith's death—regarding the disposition of his papers.

Edinburgh, 16 Apr. 1773

My Dear Friend

As I have left the care of all my literary papers to you, I must tell you that except those which I carry along with me there are none worth the publishing, but a fragment of a great work which contains a history of the Astronomical Systems that were successively in fashion down to the time of Des Cartes. Whether that might not be published as a fragment of an intended juvenile work, I leave entirely to your judgement; tho I begin to suspect myself that there is more refinement than solidity in some parts of it. This little work you will find in a thin folio paper book in my writing desk in my bedroom. All the other loose papers which you will find either in that desk or within the glass folding doors of a bureau which stands in My bed room together with about eighteen thin paper folio books which you will likewise find within the same glass folding doors I desire may be destroyed without any examination. Unless I die very suddenly I shall take care that the Papers I carry with me shall be carefully sent to you. I ever am

My Dear Friend, Most faithfully yours

Adam Smith

Last is the beautiful letter that Smith wrote to his (and Hume's) publisher, William Strahan, on Hume's death. I do not know a better way to present the truly essential Smith than in the tone and humanity of this account.

Kirkaldy, Fifeshire, 9 Nov. 1776

Dear Sir,

It is with a real, though a very melancholy pleasure, that I sit down to give you some account of the behaviour of our late excellent friend, Mr. Hume, during his last illness.

Though, in his own judgement, his disease was mortal and incurable, yet he allowed himself to be prevailed upon, by the entreaty of his friends, to try what might be the effects of a long journey. A few days before he set out, he wrote that account of his own life, which, together with his other papers, he has left to your care. My account, therefore, shall begin where his ends.

He set out for London towards the end of April, and at Morpeth met with Mr. John Home and myself, who had both come down from London on purpose to see him, expecting to have found him at Edinburgh. Mr. Home returned with him, and attended him during the whole of his stay in England, with that care and attention which might be expected from a temper so perfectly friendly and affectionate. As I had written to my mother that she might expect me in Scotland, I was under the necessity of continuing my journey. His disease seemed to yield to exercise and change of air, and when he arrived in London, he was apparently in much better health than when he left Edinburgh. He was advised to go to Bath to drink the waters, which appeared for some time to have so good an effect upon him, that even he himself began to entertain, what he was not apt to do, a better opinion of his own health. His symptoms, however, soon returned with their usual violence, and from that moment he gave up all thoughts of recovery, but submitted with the utmost cheerfulness, and the most perfect complacency and resignation. Upon his return to Edinburgh, though he found himself much weaker, yet his cheerfulness never abated, and he continued to divert himself, as usual, with correcting his own works for a new edition, with reading books of amusement, with the conversation of his friends; and, sometimes in the evening, with a party at his favourite game of whist. His cheerfulness was so great, and his conversation and amusements run so much in their usual strain, that, notwithstanding all bad symptoms, many people could not believe he was dying. "I shall tell your friend, Colonel Edmondstone," said Doctor Dundas to him one day, "that I left you much better, and in a fair way of recovery." "Doctor," said he, "as I believe you would not chuse to tell any thing but the truth, you had better tell him, that I am dying as fast as my enemies, if I have any, could wish, and as easily and cheerfully as my best friends could desire." Colonel Edmondstone soon afterwards came to see him, and take leave of him; and on his way home, he could not forbear writing him a letter bidding him once more an eternal adieu, and applying to him, as to a dying man, the beautiful French verses in which the Abbé Chaulieu, in expectation of his own death, laments his approaching separation from his friend, the Marquis de la Fare. Mr. Hume's magnanimity and firmness were such, that his most affectionate friends knew, that they hazarded nothing in talking or writing to him as to a dying man, and that so far from being hurt by this frankness, he was rather pleased and flattered by it. I happened to come into his room while he was reading this letter, which he had just received, and which he immediately showed me. I told him, that though I was sensible how very much he was weakened, and that appearances were in many respects very bad, yet his cheerfulness was still so great, the spirit of life seemed still to be so very strong in him, that I could not help entertaining some faint hopes. He answered, "Your hopes are groundless. An habitual diarrhoea of more than a year's standing, would be a very bad disease at any age: at my age it is a mortal one. When I lie down in the evening, I feel myself weaker than when I rose in the morning; and when I rise in the morning, weaker than when I lay down in the evening. I am sensible, besides, that some of my vital parts are affected, so that I must soon die." "Well," said I, "if it must be so, you have at least the satisfaction of leaving all your friends, your brother's family in particular, in great prosperity." He said that he felt that satisfaction so sensibly, that when he was reading a few days before, Lucian's Dialogues of the Dead, among all the excuses which are alleged to Charon for not entering readily into his boat, he could not find one that fitted him; he had no house to finish, he had no daughter to provide for, he had no enemies upon whom he wished to revenge himself. "I could not well imagine," said he, "what excuse I could make to Charon in order to obtain a little delay. I have done every thing of consequence which I ever meant to do, and I could at no time expect to leave my relations and friends in a better situation than that in which I am now likely to leave them; I, therefore, have all reason to die contented." He then diverted himself with inventing several jocular excuses, which he supposed he might make to Charon, and with imagining the very surly answers which it might suit the character of Charon to return to them. "Upon further consideration," said he, "I thought I might say to him, Good Charon, I have been correcting my works for a new edition. Allow me a little time, that I may see how the Public receives the alterations." But Charon would answer, "When you have seen the effect of these, you will be for making other alterations. There will be no end of such excuses; so, honest friend, please step into the boat." But I might still urge, "Have a little patience, good Charon, I have been endeavouring to open the eyes of the Public. If I live a few years longer, I may have the satisfaction of seeing the downfal of some of the prevailing systems of superstition." But Charon would then lose all temper and decency. "You loitering rogue, that will not happen these many hundred years. Do you fancy I will grant you a lease for so long a term? Get into the boat this instant, you lazy loitering rogue."

But, though Mr. Hume always talked of his approaching dissolution with great cheerfulness, he never affected to make any parade of his magnanimity. He never mentioned the subject but when the conversation naturally led to it, and never dwelt longer upon it than the course of the conversation happened to require: it was a subject indeed which occurred pretty frequently, in consequence of the inquiries which his friends, who came to see him, naturally made concerning the state of his health. The conversation which I mentioned above, and which passed on Thursday the 8th of August, was the last, except one, that I ever had with him. He had now become so very weak, that the company of his most intimate friends fatigued him; for his cheerfulness was still so great, his complaisance and social disposition were still so entire, that when any friend was with him, he could not help talking more, and with greater exertion, than suited the weakness of his body. At his own desire, therefore, I agreed to leave Edinburgh, where I was staying partly upon his account, and returned to my mother's house here, at Kirkaldy, upon condition that he would send for me whenever he wished to see me; the physician who saw him most frequently, Doctor Black, undertaking, in the mean time, to write me occasionally an account of the state of his health.

On the 22d of August, the Doctor wrote me the following letter:

"Since my last, Mr. Hume has passed his time pretty easily, but is much weaker. He sits up, goes down stairs once a day, and amuses himself with reading, but seldom sees any body. He finds that even the conversation of his most intimate friends fatigues and oppresses him; and it is happy that he does not need it, for he is quite free from anxiety, impatience, or low spirits, and passes his time very well with the assistance of amusing books."

I received the day after a letter from Mr. Hume himself, of which the following is an extract

Edinburgh, 23d August, 1776.

"My Dearest Friend,

I am obliged to make use of my nephew's hand in writing to you, as I do not rise today . . . I go very fast to decline, and last night had a small fever, which I hoped might put a quicker period to this tedious illness, but unluckily it has, in a great measure, gone off. I cannot submit to your coming over here on my account, as it is possible for me to see you so small a part of the day, but Doctor Black can better inform you concerning the degree of strength which may from time to time remain with me. Adieu, etc."

Three days after I received the following letter from Doctor Black.

Edinburgh, Monday, 26th August, 1776.

"Dear Sir,

Yesterday about four o'clock afternoon, Mr. Hume expired. The near approach of his death became evident in the night between Thursday and Friday, when his disease became excessive, and soon weakened him so much, that he could no longer rise out of his bed. He continued to the last perfectly sensible, and free from much pain or feelings of distress. He never dropped the smallest expression of impatience; but when he had occasion to speak to the people about him, always did it with affection and tenderness. I thought it improper to write to bring you over, especially as I heard that he had dictated a letter to you desiring you not to come. When he became very weak, it cost him an effort to speak, and he died in such a happy composure of mind, that nothing could exceed it."

Thus died our most excellent, and never to be forgotten friend; concerning whose philosophical opinions men will, no doubt, judge variously, every one approving or condemning them, according as they happen to coincide or disagree with his own; but concerning whose character and conduct there can scarce be a difference of opinion. His temper, indeed, seemed to be more happily balanced, if I may be allowed such an expression, than that perhaps of any other man I have ever known. Even in the lowest state of his fortune, his great and necessary frugality never hindered him from exercising, upon proper occasions, acts both of charity and generosity. It was a frugality founded, not upon avarice, but upon the love of independency. The extreme gentleness of his nature never weakened either the firmness of his mind, or the steadiness of his resolutions. His constant pleasantry was the genuine effusion of good-nature and good-humour, tempered with delicacy and modesty, and without even the slightest tincture of malignity, so frequently the disagreeable source of what is called wit in other men. It never was the meaning of his raillery to mortify; and therefore, far from offending, it seldom failed to please and delight, even those who were the objects of it. To his friends, who were frequently the objects of it, there was not perhaps any one of all his great and amiable qualities, which contributed more to endear his conversation. And that gaiety of temper, so agreeable in society, but which is so often accompanied with frivolous and superficial qualities, was in him certainly attended with the most severe application, the most extensive learning, the greatest depth of thought, and a capacity in every respect the most comprehensive. Upon the whole, I have always considered him, both in his lifetime and since his death, as approaching as nearly to the idea of a perfectly wise and virtuous man, as perhaps the nature of human frailty will permit.

I ever am, dear Sir,
Most affectionately your's,
Adam Smith.

Index

accumulation of stock, 227–30
acquisitive drive, as means to betterment,
    120, 153, 240, 322–23, 324
admiration:
    desire for, 103
    of the great, 80–83, 121
    of heroes, 137, 144, 145
    of patriots, 137
    of performers, 214
    of restraint of passions, 143
    of rich and great, 3, 39, 61, 62, 86, 119–
    20, 121, 150–51
    sympathy principle and, 73
advanced society, *see* nation of commerce
aesthetics, 118, 123–27
age, as source of authority, 38–39, 294–95
agricultural products:
    price of:
        component parts of, 183, 185–86, 191–
        92
        fluctuations in, 216
        and rent, 221–22
    see also food
agriculture:
    division of labor in, 163–64
    predominates in American colonies, 247,
    250–51, 257
    preference for, 249–50, 251
    productivity in, 245–47
alehouses, 245, 267, 323
altruism, *vs.* self-love, 59–63, 105–9
ambition, social utility of, 76–86
America, *see* colonies, American; North
    America
anger:
    difficulty of sympathizing with, 67
    restraint of, 143, 146–47
    righteous, 77
apprenticeship, statutes of, 193, 218–19
approval:
    of conduct, 109–10, 147
        conscience and, 105–9
        custom and fashion and, 128–32
        vs. motivation, 98–99
        by self *vs.* others, 100–104
    desire for, and morality, 109–10, 115
    of opinions, 70
    of passions, 69–75
    of the rich and great, 86–88
architecture, custom and fashion in, 125–26
Aristotle, 29, 33, 132
army, *see* military forces
artificers:
    in American colonies, 250–51
    and farmers, 250

under Physiocracy, 284, 285–86, 287–88
    supported by great proprietors, 255–56
astronomy, Newton's, 32–36
atheism, 141
authority:
    of government, feudal, 254–55
    in nations of hunters and shepherds, 39–
    41
    sources of, 38–39, 294–96
    support of, in peace and turmoil, 138–40
    weakness of, in early societies, 56

baker, *see* butcher and brewer and baker
bankruptcy, 241, 271, 318, 323
banks and banking, 232–33
barons, feudal (power of), 254
barter:
    and division of labor, 49–50, 168–71, 321
    lacking in animals, 49, 50, 168–69, 171
    and rise of money, 172–73
beaver, value of, *vs.* deer, 181, 321
beggar(s), 49, 169
beneficence, 91–92, 145
    gratitude for, 89
    Invisible Hand and, 96–98
    motive for, 89, 96–97
    order of persons commended to, 135–36
benevolence, universal, 140–43
bettering our condition, 240
birth, advantages of, 39, 41, 136, 296–97
Brahe, Tycho, 33
bread, price of, 183
bricklayers and masons, 212–13
butcher and brewer and baker:
    difficulty of barter among, 172–73, 177
    farmers and, 171, 250
    not by benevolence of, do we expect din-
    ner, 169, 321

Caesar, Augustus, 43
Cantillon, Richard, 197
Cape of Good Hope, 281
capital, 229–30
    employed in four ways, 243–44
    fixed and circulating, 230, 231
    increased:
        causes increase of produce, 241–42
        by parsimony, 238–39, 322
    proportionate to revenue, 237–38
    relative efficiency of investment in agricul-
    ture and manufactures, 245–47
    replaced by portion of annual labor, 235–
    36, 237
    see also stock, capital